MR. EMERSON'S
REVOLUTION

Mr. Emerson's Revolution

Edited by
Jean McClure Mudge

OpenBook Publishers

http://www.openbookpublishers.com

External links were active on 11 September 2015 and archived at the Internet Archive WayBack Machine at https://archive.org/web/

ISBN Paperback: 978-1-78374-097-0
ISBN Hardback: 978-1-78374-098-7
ISBN Digital (PDF): 978-1-78374-099-4
ISBN Digital ebook (epub): 978-1-78374-100-7
ISBN Digital ebook (mobi): 978-1-78374-101-4
DOI: 10.11647/OBP.0065

Cover image: oil painting of Emerson at 45 in typical lecturing pose by David Scott (1848). Courtesy Concord Free Public Library, all rights reserved.

All paper used by Open Book Publishers is SFI (Sustainable Forestry Initiative) and PEFC (Programme for the Endorsement of Forest Certification Schemes) Certified.

Printed in the United Kingdom, United States and Australia by Lightning Source for Open Book Publishers

Contents

Contributors

Steven Brown writes on nineteenth century environmental aesthetics in American literature and history. Brown is also a widely-published poet and photography critic. He is currently co-editor for Edition Galerie Vevais, Germany and a PhD candidate in Harvard's American Studies program.

Phyllis Cole, Professor of English, Women's Studies and American Studies at Penn State Brandywine, is a past President of the Ralph Waldo Emerson Society (2004-2005) and winner of the Society's Distinguished Achievement Award (2011). Her work on Emerson and the Transcendentalist movement includes many articles and the book, *Mary Moody Emerson and The Origins of Transcendentalism: A Family History* (Oxford University Press, 1998), runner-up for the MLA's James Russell Lowell Prize. Her recent work has focused on the legacy of Margaret Fuller. She is co-editor of the essay collection, *Toward a Female Genealogy of Transcendentalism* (University of Georgia Press, 2014). E-mail: pbc2@psu.edu

Len Gougeon, Professor of American Literature and Distinguished University Fellow at the University of Scranton, is the author of *Virtue's Hero: Emerson, Antislavery, and Reform* (University of Georgia Press, 1990), *Emerson's Truth, Emerson's Wisdom* (American Transcendental Press, 2010), *Emerson & Eros: The Making of a Cultural Hero* (SUNY Press, 2011), and coeditor of *Emerson's Antislavery Writings* (Yale University Press, 2002). In 2008, he received the Distinguished Achievement Award from the Emerson Society. His most recent work is "Militant Abolitionism: Douglass, Emerson, and the Rise of the Anti-Slave," in *The New England Quarterly*. Currently, he is at work on a book dealing with the cultural warfare that occurred between America and Great Britain as a result of tensions and conflicts arising from the Civil War and the struggle to end slavery. E-mail: GougeonL1@uofs.edu

Alan Hodder, Rosamond Stewardson Taylor Professor of the Comparative Study of Religion at Hampshire College, teaches a wide array of courses in early American literature and religious history, and world religions. He is the author of *Thoreau's Ecstatic Witness* (Yale University Press, 2001) and *Emerson's Rhetoric of Revelation: Nature, the Reader, and the Apocalypse Within* (Penn State University Press, 1989). Together with Robert Meagher, he is also the co-editor of *The Epic Voice* (Praeger, 2002). In addition, he is the author of numerous articles and review essays on such topics as Puritan pulpit rhetoric, Transcendentalist spirituality, early American orientalism, Whitman's poetry and poetics, and American nature writing. E-mail: adhHA@hampshire.edu

Wesley T. Mott, Professor of English at Worcester Polytechnic Institute, is author of *"The Strains of Eloquence": Emerson and His Sermons* (Penn State University Press, 1989). He has edited several reference books on New England Transcendentalism and antebellum literature. He has also edited volumes of the writings of both Emerson (vol. 4 of *The Complete Sermons*) and Thoreau (vol. 9 of *The Journal: 1854-1855* [forthcoming]). In 1989, he organized the Ralph Waldo Emerson Society, which he has served as secretary/treasurer, president, and, for twenty years, publisher of its newsletter, *Emerson Society Papers*; he is also a recipient of the Society's Distinguished Achievement Award. He is editor of *Ralph Waldo Emerson in Context* (Cambridge University Press, 2014). E-mail: wmott@wpi.edu

Jean McClure Mudge, Yale Ph.D. (American Studies), and independent scholar/documentary filmmaker, is the editor of *Mr. Emerson's Revolution*. Mudge has written four books and several articles, among them *Emily Dickinson and the Image of Home* (University of Massachusetts Press, 1975; 2nd ed., 1976), which discussed Emerson's influence on Dickinson. Her award-winning documentary series on early American writers, *Emily Dickinson, Herman Melville and Edgar Allan Poe* has been shown on PBS, in leading festivals, and in U.S. embassies. Funded by several grants, including one from the Emerson Society, she began this collaborative book project in 2002. She has also written a documentary script about Emerson. At the American Literature Association in 2012, she presented a paper on "The Emerson-Lincoln Relationship." Mudge has recently edited the posthumous work of her husband, ecumenical ethicist Lewis Mudge, *We Can Make the World Economy a Sustainable Global Home* (Eerdmans, 2014). See http://www.jeanmudgemedia.org. E-mail: mudge.jean@gmail.com

David M. Robinson is Distinguished Professor of American Literature and Director of the Center for the Humanities at Oregon State University. He is author of *Emerson and the Conduct of Life* (Cambridge University Press, 2009) and *Natural Life: Thoreau's Worldly Transcendentalism* (Cornell University Press, 2004). From 1988 through 2008, he was author of the chapter "Emerson, Thoreau, Fuller and Transcendentalism" for the annual publication *American Literary Scholarship* (Duke University Press). He has served as Fulbright Guest Professor at the University of Heidelberg, Germany, and held fellowships from the National Endowment for the Humanities and the American Council of Learned Societies. In 2010, he was elected a Fellow of the Massachusetts Historical Society. E-mail: drobinson@orst.edu

Beniamino Soressi holds a B.A./M.A., *summa cum laude* in philosophy from the University of Parma, where he also received his doctorate and currently serves as a teaching assistant of Theoretical Philosophy. He has translated into Italian, written introductions for, and edited several collections of Emerson's essays, including *The Conduct of Life*. He has published the monograph *Ralph Waldo Emerson: il pensiero e la solitudine*, with a foreword by Alessandro Ferrara (Armando, 2004). This book is a systematic analysis, along interpretive lines suggested by Stanley Cavell, of Emerson as a thinker who stands at the intersection of modern Continental philosophy, American Idealism, American Pragmatism, and Nietzschean philosophy. Soressi will publish another monograph about Emerson with Edwin Mellen Press. E-mail: bensore@yahoo.it

John Stauffer is a Harvard University professor of English and American Literature, American Studies and African American Studies. He is a leading authority on antislavery, the Civil War era, social protest movements and photography. Stauffer's eight books include *The Black Hearts of Men: Radical Abolitionists and the Transformation of Race* (Harvard University Press, 2002) and *Giants: The Parallel Lives of Frederick Douglass and Abraham Lincoln* (Twelve, 2008), which both won numerous awards.

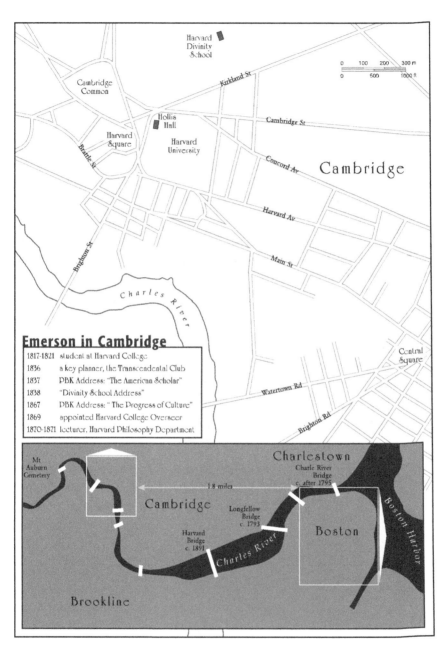

Emerson in Cambridge

1817-1821	student at Harvard College
1836	a key planner, the Transcendental Club
1837	PBK Address: "The American Scholar"
1838	"Divinity School Address"
1867	PBK Address: " The Progress of Culture"
1869	appointed Harvard College Overseer
1870-1871	lecturer, Harvard Philosophy Department

Emerson in Cambridge, 1817-1871.

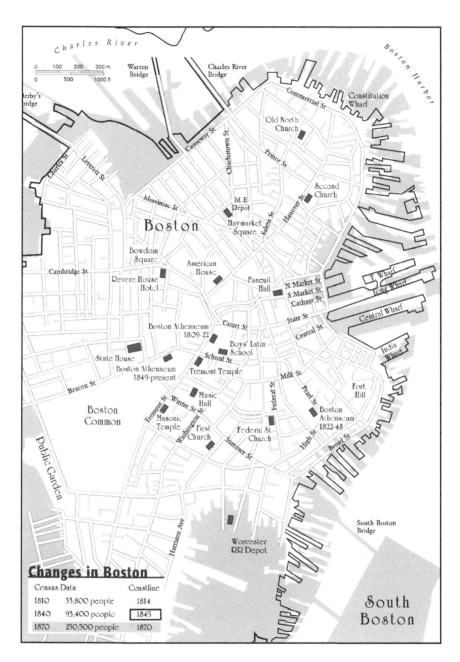

Changes in Boston, 1810-1870.

Foreword: Emerson's Renewing Power

John Stauffer and Steven Brown

The Mr. Emerson to which this volume pays tribute is a figure so ensconced in America's intellectual framework that we sometimes forget how iconoclastic he actually was. In his essays, Emerson fought intolerance, extolled imagination over doctrine, indicted fundamentalism, and demystified American exceptionalism. Simply put, Emerson was a Disturber of the Peace—an anti-honorific to which history has attached a gold star.

When closely examined alongside his radical peers, his prominence seems just as odd. Take, for instance, Frederick Douglass, Harriett Beecher Stowe, or Abraham Lincoln, each of whom exhibited a focus and clarity of vision not commonly attributed to Emerson's writing. These representative men and women told their stories with beginnings, middles, and oracular ends.

An ex-slave masters his master. An author popularizes the black hero. A president decimates an institution of injustice.

Emerson, on the other hand, wondered. He puzzled over the nation like a Sphinx, writing aphoristically about the enigmas of nature, mind, spirit, and heart. "The world," he said, "is emblematic. Parts of speech are metaphors, because the whole of nature is a metaphor of the human mind."[1]

But these metaphysical conceits mattered little to Emerson when detached from their function in the real world. The necessity of a useable

---

1 *The Collected Works of Ralph Waldo Emerson,* 10 vols., eds. Robert E. Spiller, et al. (Cambridge, Mass.: Belknap Press, 1971-2013), 1: 21. Hereafter *CW.*

http://dx.doi.org/10.11647/OBP.0065.10

past, a useable spirituality, and a useable independence underscored his existential dilemmas. "More than any other writer," argues Lawrence Buell, "Emerson invites you to kill him off, if you don't find him useful."[2] Never mind art, philosophy, religion or history for their own sake. If they didn't answer the question "How should I live?," then they were no more than sounding brass and tinkling cymbals.[3]

It is the "I" of "How should I live?" that often loses its contextual significance when examined against the abstractions of Transcendentalism. Certainly there is an "I," or an "eye," altogether Emerson's alone. But there is also *Mr.* Emerson, for whom self-reliance prioritizes the well-being and justice of the larger public sphere. Emerson, while still young, learned the lesson from the French philosopher, Joseph Gerando: "We cannot fully enter into the conceptions of what is just, without putting ourselves, in imagination, completely into the situation of another, so as to perceive how he would see and feel, and thus understand what should be done for him, as if it were done for ourselves."[4]

There could be no ethics, no justice, no revolution without empathy. At the "crucial moments," Emerson freed himself from cloistered study and joined in the mutual-reliance of his neighbors.

Emerson's career, however, might suggest that he was a selective participant in the public realm. After all, he planted no bean rows near Walden. He did not spend time in jail for protesting the poll tax. Although he shared the educational and reform goals of his close friend Bronson Alcott and his relative George Ripley, he declined to participate in either Fruitlands or Brook Farm, their respective Utopian communes. And during the 1830s and 40s, he maintained a cautious distance between himself and the abolitionist struggle.

But in a sense, the whole of Emerson's life (1803-1882) spanned an extended crucial moment.

Fate nested him in a hotbed of political activism. Boston, like no other city in America, bred utopians, suffragists, religious and educational dissenters, abolitionists, perfectionists, vegetarians. The residual fervor of a revolution not three decades old at the time of Emerson's birth, coupled with the

---

2   Lawrence Buell, *Emerson* (Cambridge, Mass.: Belknap Press, 2003), 292.
3   Richard D. Richardson Jr., *Emerson: The Mind on Fire* (Berkeley, CA: University of California Press, 1995), 16.
4   Joseph-Marie, baron de Gerando, *Self-Education, or the Means and Art of Moral Progress* (Boston, Mass.: Carter and Hendee, 1830), 98.

enthusiasms of the second Great Awakening, doubtlessly contributed to this surplus of nonconformity.

Overseas, revolutions and merciless retaliations in Italy and Greece set Europe on edge. In the States, President Jackson broke treaty and enforced the Indian Removal Act. Nat Turner's Rebellion panicked the masses. Garrison's *Liberator* encouraged abolitionist resolve. Polk invaded Mexico. The Compromise of 1850 catalyzed the indignation of John Brown. And the Civil War, to borrow from Yeats, slouched toward Sumter to be born.

Like Lincoln, Emerson resented slavery even in his youth but, like him as well, fell prey to prevailing assumptions regarding racial hierarchy. To Emerson's advantage, a cohort of fiercely intelligent abolitionist women—his Aunt Mary Moody Emerson, his second wife Lydia Jackson, and Margaret Fuller (to name only three)—constantly challenged his conscience and complacency. His transition to full-blown abolitionism needed only a nudge.

But what he got was a blow to the head. Provoked by the barbarity of events, from the enactment of the Fugitive Slave Law to Bleeding Kansas and the brutal caning of Charles Sumner, Emerson's outrage—unlike Lincoln's—transcended his desire for union. He had been a devotee of civilization, culture, and refinement. If there was one thing he could not stomach, it was barbarity: "I do not see how a barbarous community and a civilized community can constitute one state. I think we must get rid of slavery, or we must get rid of freedom."[5] And if that meant bloodshed, so be it. He incited efforts to arm the champions of freedom in Kansas. He first urged, and then strenuously stood behind, Lincoln's Emancipation Proclamation, and campaigned for his re-election. He evangelized the Declaration of Independence over the Constitution. He openly supported reparations for slaves and aided in efforts to recruit black men to fight the South. Freedom and equality dictated the moral center of his lectures on American civilization throughout the war.

So what makes Emerson's voice stand out among those of equal conviction and perhaps clearer motivation? There is no single answer, but one in particular deserves consideration. Emerson was drawn to symbols, but during the war he too became a living symbol: a bridge between the virtuosity of Awakening thinkers and the common sense of Revolutionary

---

5   *Emerson's Antislavery Writings*, eds. Len Gougeon and Joel Myerson (New Haven and London: Yale University Press, 1995), 107; see also Len Gougeon, *Virtue's Hero: Emerson, Antislavery, and Reform* (Athens, GA: University of Georgia Press, 1990), 7.

activists. "Long hereafter," he said, "amidst agitation and terror in national councils,—in the hour of *revolution*,—these solemn images shall reappear in their morning lustre as fit symbols and words of the thoughts which the passing events shall *awaken*" (emphasis added).[6] Just as principle revealed itself in action, action awoke the mind to new symbols of reason and justice.

The cultural anthropologist Anthony Wallace's characterization of Awakenings puts Emerson in proper context. The first thing that precedes a communal or national revitalization movement is a general feeling of alienation among the citizenry. Time passes and the individual begins to redirect her antipathies toward the governing bodies. Consequently (or serendipitously), a revivalist prophet or visionary appears. Younger generations are drawn to the visionary, who finally convinces enough of the undecided to alter the status quo.[7] Emerson meets all five of these conditions. Disaffected by his Unitarian upbringing, he became critical of religious and political tradition. Having searched his books, his schools, and his peers for a prophet, he discovered one—not from without, but from within. And with the publication of *Nature* (1836) and deliverance of "The American Scholar" (1837), Emerson found his following.

It is Wallace's final step—"convincing the undecided"—that really bridges Emerson the Idealist with Mr. Emerson the Activist (or, in different terms, the Transcendentalist and the Revolutionary). To inspire radical reform, he took advantage of shared experience. According to Len Gougeon, Emerson "appealed to the nation's youth to commit itself to renew the country's founding ideals" under a "Second Declaration of Independence." The move was strategic. Few documents of justice would have been so widely and intimately familiar to the people. "A great revolution" was at hand: the "promise" of an "ideal Republic."[8]

Jean McClure Mudge calls Emerson's transformation from idealist to activist his "metamorphosis," a word he would have approved. He alludes to that idea at the end of "Compensation" (1841), championing "incessant" change within the individual.[9] By concentrating, enriching, and

---

6   CW 1: 21.

7   Anthony Wallace, "Revitalization Movements," *American Anthropologist*, New Series, 58: 2 (April 1956), 269-70; William McLoughlin, *Revivals, Awakenings, and Reform* (Chicago, IL: University of Chicago Press, 1980), 12-17.

8   See Ch. 3 of this volume by Len Gougeon, "Emerson the Reformer: A Pragmatic Idealist in Action, 1850-1865," 155; Gougeon, *Virtue's Hero*, 243; Emerson compares Harper's Ferry with the Boston Massacre.

9   CW 2: 72.

strengthening the mind, the individual self widens its circle of experience to contain multitudes. For Emerson that circle exceeded the circumference of the present and encompassed the future. It embraced North and South, black and white, male and female. Unlike other revolutions that defined injustices endemic to their moments in history, Mr. Emerson's revolution is an orbit in which we continue to exist.

Introduction: Emerson as Spiritual and Social Revolutionary

Jean McClure Mudge

In the 1830s, when the Puritan-Romantic Ralph Waldo Emerson (1803-1882) first proposed transforming every citizen's heart and soul, he was extending America's political revolution of 1776 into the country's core consciousness. From the mid-1840s on, by applying the "new thinking" of his American Transcendentalism to abolition and to a nascent women's rights movement, that inner revolution penetrated incalculable numbers of disenfranchised blacks and women in numbers far beyond his imaginings. By the mid-nineteenth century, he had become a leading American modernist with vast influence in this country and abroad. Yet early and late, Emerson's public democratic principles were waging a battle for his soul against his private social prejudices. This interior civil war and its nuances kept him perpetually struggling toward a final resolution. The contest not only helps explain his delay in speaking out for reform. It also exposes Emerson's most closely-guarded secret self. All the while, this central paradox in his psyche has its stylistic parallel among his often arresting, still-quoted aphorisms, as in: "God builds his temple in the heart on the ruins of churches and religions."[1]

---

1   *The Collected Works of Ralph Waldo Emerson*, 10 vols., eds. Robert E. Spiller, et al. (Cambridge, Mass.: Belknap Press, 1971-2013), 6: 108. Hereafter *CW*.

http://dx.doi.org/10.11647/OBP.0065.11

This book follows two interrelated themes along the arc of Emerson's whole career. The dominant one examines his dramatic metamorphosis from idealist philosopher to idealist-turned-activist for fundamental social change while simultaneously fighting his biases against blacks and women. This shift, with its hidden debates, affected him personally and philosophically. It also enlarged him politically and socially, empowering him to help alter the nation's psyche, its values, and eventually, its laws. Emerson's growth into a reformer also arguably defined the climax of his career, as his activism surely made tangible the power of applied American Transcendentalism.

Lengthy biographies of Emerson, such as those of John McAleer, Gay Wilson Allen and Robert D. Richardson, Jr., have touched on this change, but their comprehensive purpose tends to bury its centrality as well as its high drama. The opposite effect arises in dedicated studies of Emerson as a reformer, notably the works of Len Gougeon and T. Gregory Garvey. They rightly draw attention to Emerson's previously minimized activism, but their dedicated focus sacrifices a wider angle on the man. This book takes a step back from details that are proper to both strict biography and specific reform studies to see Emerson's shift as integral to the whole spectrum of his life and interests, from youth to the Civil War years and beyond, while also examining the deeper complexity of that turn.

The second, supplementary theme of this book traces Emerson's debt to world letters and, in turn, the reverberation of his revolutionary message abroad. In some cases, his contributions arrived on soil fertile for change; in others, they re-enforced traditional views about nature, strengthened ideas about the self, or suggested concrete reforms. Either way, his legacy of revolution was literally heard "round the world." Emerson's international legacy is increasingly appreciated, as in the recent multi-authored works, *Emerson for the Twenty-First Century: Global Perspectives on an American Icon* (2010) and *Ralph Waldo Emerson in Context* (2014). But such studies with their particular slants, like the biographies and reform-focused works mentioned above, also obscure the change stressed by this book. *Mr. Emerson's Revolution* frames a pointed and succinct, yet nuanced, view of Emerson's private and public development from philosopher to philosopher-in-action. Today, as part of a burgeoning global interest in American Studies in general, scholars in Great Britain, on the Continent—especially in Germany, Italy, and France—and in India and Japan are focusing on Emerson. In these pages, a chapter on Emerson's relationships with the West is paralleled by a similar treatment of his influence in the

East. The former is longer than the latter, but only because, until now, more Emerson followers have existed in South America, Great Britain, and on the Continent than in the Middle and Far East.

A book about Emerson's life advancing toward a fulcrum moment in the 1840s, when he took up the abolitionist and women's rights causes while still conflicted over his attitudes to race and gender, is important right now. Today, he faces an articulate spectrum of critics. With few exceptions, for example, Nell Irvin Painter's *The History of White People* (2010), for example, portrays him as a consistent racist. If generally accepted, this misinterpretation would lead readers to dismiss his lasting positive effect on the freedoms of both blacks and women. Other writers have faulted him for being too slow to take up reform. But such criticism largely rests on Emerson quotes that Painter has arbitrarily selected with little regard to time or place, thus missing his ongoing inner debate about these matters. In contrast, by closely following the course and context of his opinions, mainly expressed in his journals, this book tracks Emerson's constant questioning and sometime self-chastisement, leading to the gradual amendment and dissolution of his prejudices. Doing so, it may encourage twenty-first-century readers who quietly share such biases to escape them, perhaps more swiftly than he did.[2]

Since youth, family and faith had so nurtured Emerson's abhorrence of slavery that once he became a pastor in his late twenties, he readily made that position clear on his own. But slavery was a subject in only eight of his eighty sermons from 1830 to 1837, and then he listed it only in passing among other social problems.[31] As for women, Emerson's lifelong indebtedness to his mother, his aunt, and other women, including both his first and second wives, made him naturally value female talents and directly led to his endorsement of women's rights. But for some time, he held to the conditioned belief that the proper place of even gifted women was not in public, but in the home, and that women, prone to sentimentalism, were "weaker" than men. Furthermore, from childhood on, he struggled—now painfully, now proudly—with a temperamental aloofness from anyone, no

---

2   Such prejudices apparently pervade academe as well as society at large. See "Professors Are Prejudiced, too," *New York Times*, 9 May 2014, http://nyti.ms/1ghpQ8F For America's persistent racism, see "The Case for Reparations" by senior editor Ta-Nehisi Coates in the June 2014 issue of the *Atlantic*, http://www.theatlantic.com/features/archive/2014/05/the-case-for-reparations/361631/

3   *The Complete Sermons of Ralph Waldo Emerson*, vol. 3, ed. Ronald A. Bosco (Columbia, MO: University of Missouri Press, 1991). Ibid., vol. 4, ed. Wesley T. Mott (1992).

matter race or gender. That cool defensiveness covered his passionate and sensitive nature. It also led him to repeatedly state that using his mind as a dedicated scholar was his best service to society, a sense confirmed by his success as a lecturer. (He welcomed regular, quality conversationalists, but wanted no disciples.) This distancing from others indirectly sustained his recurring doubts about blacks' abilities and women's suitable public roles. Such doubts also fed his disdain for self-righteous abolitionists, temperance advocates and philanthropists, impractical communitarians, and, in general, one-note do-gooders. This nexus of reasons complicated and delayed his entry into the public world of reform.

In 1837, as he approached the final year of his preaching, Emerson's distance from the plight of blacks, reformers and women revealed its complexity in a private complaint he made in his journal about his second wife Lidian, a member of Concord's Female Anti-Slavery Society. Weary of hearing her grieve over the Middle Passage and "the wretched negro," he chides her for being totally removed from "the obtuse & barbarous [black]," whom, he claims, found the "stinking hold" of ships "only a little worse" than "cannibal war." In his view, Lidian suffers nothing of what he calls their "crucifixions," implying that her protest is much too easy, cheap, perhaps even hypocritical. He quickly reminds himself of his basic position: the "horrors of the middle passage" are a "violation of nature." Yet, because he would not put himself in Lidian's false position, he was not ready, nor would he be for seven years, to join her and others in the public antislavery cause.[42] By 1841, his estimate of blacks as "obtuse" and

---

4   *The Journals and Miscellaneous Notebooks of Ralph Waldo Emerson*, 16 vols., eds. William H. Gilman, et al. (Cambridge, Mass.: Harvard University Press, 1960-1982), 5: 382. Hereafter *JMN*. A month later, his anger over slavery makes him passionately eloquent: "The fury with which the slaveholder & the slavetrader defend every inch of their plunder [,] of their bloody deck, & howling Auction, only serves as Trump of Doom to alarum the ear of Mankind . . . to take sides & listen to the argument & to the Verdict which Justice shall finally pronounce" (ibid., 440). This fierce principle vs. slaveholders ironically lies at the heart of what has made him annoyed with Lidian. By spring 1838, his annoyance has become disgust in denouncing "dog-cheap" reformers, who've invaded Concord ("where every third man lectures on Slavery"). "The martyrs," he mockingly dubs them, are come "to turn the world upside down." But without any suffering comparable to blacks, they've won no martyrdom: their "skin was never scratched" (ibid., 505). Emerson would not be one of these semi-frauds, as he makes clear a month later, "I hate goodies . . . . Goodies make us very bad . . . . We will almost sin to spite them." Yet Lidian and others were affecting him. In the same passage, Emerson allows, "A little electricity of virtue lurks here & there in kitchens & among the obscure — chiefly women, that flashes out occasional light & makes the existence of the thing [preaching reform] still credible" (ibid., 7: 31).

"barbaric" had seemingly faded. As an amateur anthropologist, he did not agree with extreme theories asserting that blacks and whites are of different species. Yet he did assume that blacks' "degradation" had come from a long-ago "sin," from which, however, he considered them able to "redeem" themselves. Yet, without a black "saint engaged in that cause" (Frederick Douglass had not yet come to his notice), Emerson concluded that abolitionists' efforts added up to nothing.[53]

Nevertheless, by the mid-1840s, Emerson the Transcendentalist and Emerson the Reformer began to meld. His ideas and actions were noticeably affecting each other, even though the tension between his private views about race and gender and his platform declarations only slowly abated in the years immediately before and after the Civil War.[64] Early in this transition came a softening of his reserve that even he realized increased the passion and energy he poured into his lectures. In short, in making his revolutionary ideas concrete, by degrees Emerson was revolutionizing himself.

Besides highlighting Emerson's inner debates about social issues and exploring his impact in America and the world, this book enriches Emerson studies in other ways. First, it breaks open his marble bust to reveal a man whose cool aloofness was actually a self-described "mask," a check to any embarrassing emotion and a protection against possible hurt. This double veil, which he himself thought "churlish," went unperceived even by his keenly observant close friend and "best critic," Margaret Fuller. The closest she came was to charge him with being an emotionally "incomplete man." Other longstanding close friends, notably Thoreau and Alcott, complained of his distance in their journals. Yet Emerson—when cantankerous, downright ornery or especially when righteously enraged—could so slip his mask as to entirely lose emotional control. In print, critics labeled him a "dangerous" revolutionary, reflecting the degree he put his passions into lecturing. By becoming a virtual performance artist on "stage," as he put it, he wanted to stir audiences to maximum emotion. That aim helped him

---

5   Even as he puts the responsibility of "redemption" from slavery on blacks themselves, Emerson still wonders about their capability to do the job: "As far as they can emancipate the North from Slavery, well" (*JMN* 8: 119).

6   Three of these four issues—race, blacks, and abolitionists—could overlap in Emerson's journal jottings, which were explorations, rather than finished arguments, as proven by degrees of change in his entries. Also, they might depend upon his mood. Cf. his varying forays into race matters, in *JMN* 13: 54, 286, 466; 14: 387. Women's issues were normally treated independently.

endure his tightly scheduled annual tours through challenging winters across a wide swath of America and Great Britain. (Such far-flung activity, illustrated by maps in these pages, belies his reputation as the isolated "Sage of Concord.") Emerson's emotional purpose also helps explain his increasing followers. At the outset, he had drawn both the young elite and culture-hungry workmen. By mid-career, he had begun to attract previously marginalized whites and blacks of both genders.

Second, this book offers a set of different points of view while presenting a unified argument. From its inception, seven Emerson scholars including the editor have collaborated in writing this study, often referring forward or backward to one another's chapters. Unity comes, too, from editing for a common easy-to-read style, while all along distinct voices are preserved. The result is the sort of informed "conversation" familiar to Emerson, and on which he leaned. Those scholars who have previously written on similar themes have here blended their own work with the best past literature and latest research to produce new and previously unpublished work.

Third, the book's many illustrations include several that have not been widely republished since their first appearance in print, such as a detailed engraving of the King's Garden (the *Jardin du Roi* or, later, *Jardin des Plantes* in Paris), much as Emerson saw it on his visit in 1833. Its classified plants and animals led to his epiphany about the unity of creation, a key aspect of his philosophy. A second, twenty-first-century view of the garden, now the National Museum of Natural History, shows that despite its expanded and updated galleries, its general plan is much the same. Other new photographs include a set of color transparencies of major rooms in Emerson's house in Concord, Massachusetts, furnished much as he left them. They include selected personal items of Emerson's, among them his preaching gown and house robe, a terrestrial/celestial globe, a penknife inscribed with his name, and an Italian print of Endymion that, by his own testimony, objectified a major aspect of his emotional life. Of special usefulness are novel custom maps based on historic ones, which for the first time show details of Emerson's surroundings in Boston, Cambridge and Concord in ways that small-print archival ones cannot, or never attempted. Other custom maps trace Emerson's three trips abroad and the demanding itineraries he followed at the height of his lecturing career. (The most detailed of his biographies have no maps.) Finally, for the first time in Emerson chronologies, his life is seen in the widest possible context of national and international events. Milestone moments in his life appear side by side with notable national and international events as well as inventions, visually linking him with nineteenth-century America and in relation to both East and West.

Finally, the book is interdisciplinary, drawing upon period and current biographical, literary, historical, philosophical, religious, artistic, social, economic, gender and racial data of a wide sort: reinterpreted, newly discovered or as yet unpublished. It also makes connections between pivotal events in Emerson's life and the political, cultural and social contexts of his times. The confluence of all these sources gives dimension to philosopher Stanley Cavell's observation that, as Emerson's inheritors, Americans are still a "half-Transcendental, half-pragmatic people."

Structurally, chapters 1 through 3 move chronologically, interweaving Emerson's public and private lives as they progress up to and through his last productive years. Chapters 1 and 2 are divided into two related parts. Chapters 3 through 5 are solo chapters, focusing respectively on Emerson's apogee as a social reformer, his post-Civil War years, and his legacy in America. The return to a two-part format in Chapter 6 measures Emerson's influence abroad. The first part explores mutual influences between Emerson and Europe. The second does the same for Emerson and Asia.

Chapter 1, "The Making of a Protester," covers Emerson's boyhood, youth and young manhood as he moves toward becoming his own man. In the first part, "A Legacy of Revolt, 1803-1821," Phyllis Cole traces Emerson growing up in Boston, living only a stone's throw from the city's black district, the "West End," and in a historically distinguished family that becomes increasingly impoverished after his father's death. His mother and his father's sister, Mary Moody Emerson, nurture high ambitions in the young Ralph. At Harvard College, he adopts his middle name "Waldo," an individualistic young person's fresh start as a solo Romantic artist who was also standing apart from the theological controversies that swirled about him on campus. Within the framework of the Missouri Compromise of 1820, he begins to explore his own attitudes toward race. In the second part, "Becoming an American 'Adam,' 1822-1835," Wesley Mott reveals Emerson's post-Harvard emotional and intellectual growth, including his extended inner debate about slavery at nineteen. Mott continues to track his changes through ongoing family relationships, a first marriage to Ellen Tucker ending in her early death, his resignation from the ministry, his continuing spiritual search, an early interest in science, a seminal 1832-1833 trip to Europe, his early lectures, a move to Concord and his second marriage to Lydia (Lidian) Jackson, a woman who fast becomes an ardent abolitionist.

In Part 2, "Public and Private Revolutions," David Robinson devotes Chapter 1, "The 'New Thinking,' 1836-1850" to the description of Emerson's reshaping of central neo-idealist ideas from England and the Continent. Within the national and personal contexts of the Jacksonian Era, he discusses Emerson's pioneering first book *Nature* and his early essays, and describes their magnetic role in the formation of the "Transcendental Club" and *The Dial*. He then highlights the major turning point in Emerson's personal life, the death of his son Waldo, and its role in the central shift of his thought and career from pure Transcendentalism to a Romantic pragmatism. In the second part, "Dialogues with the Self and Society, 1836-1850," Jean McClure Mudge follows Emerson's attempts to align his idealism with the reality of personal relationships. First focusing on his sensitivity to the nature of words and dialogue, basic to his philosophy, social reform, and self-understanding, she then shows how key friends—Bronson Alcott, Henry David Thoreau, Margaret Fuller, and his second wife Lidian—lead Emerson to unveil his "hidden" self. This discovery directs his emotional energies into lecturing, which vaults him to prominence as a leading intellectual at home and abroad.

In Chapter 3, "Emerson the Reformer: Pragmatic Idealist in Action, 1850-1865," Len Gougeon first frames Emerson's stress on individual spiritual change and the Constitution's acceptance of slavery, then showcases the melding of his philosophy with social movements as he becomes a leader among the abolitionists. All along, Emerson is shown to support women's rights, at first conditionally, then wholeheartedly. For the first time in book form, Gougeon evaluates old and new critics of Emerson's supposed racism.

Chapter 4, "Emerson's Evolving Emphases: Actively Entering Old Age, 1865-1882," reveals Emerson's remarkable post-Civil War career, testifying to his considerable remaining intellectual vigor despite a physical decline. Jean McClure Mudge freshly measures the permanent mark that his emphasis on reform had made upon his thinking, which now emphasizes ethics over metaphysics. She analyzes ideas from three essays, "Fate," "Worship" and "Character," first delivered in the 1850s and published in *The Conduct of Life* (1860)—the effective basis of his postwar platform. Emerson's reactions to the Reconstruction Era reflect this final ethical focus as does his full support for women in their desire to serve in public life.

Now a celebrated hero of the women's movement, he supports the career of the young poet Emma Lazarus. A trip to California rejuvenates him, and his third and last tour of Europe helps cement his international reputation. In its last version, Emerson's poem "Terminus" (1867), in progress over decades, becomes a retrospective self-judgment of his entire career.

In Chapter 5, "Emerson's Legacy in America: Spawning a Wide New Consciousness," Jean McClure Mudge examines the different ways in which Emerson left a wide and deep mark upon American politics, poetry, philosophy, and the arts. She traces his influence on Abraham Lincoln, Walt Whitman, Emily Dickinson, William James, and Frank Lloyd Wright, while also discussing other figures, past and present, who caught Emerson's fire.

Chapter 6, "Emerson in the West and East," returns again to the two-part format of the first two chapters. In "Europe in Emerson and Emerson in Europe," Beniamino Soressi traces the influence of Old World ideas on Emerson as prelude to a more extensive study of Emerson's export of American Transcendentalism and his reform ideas. So influenced, leading minds in England and on the Continent helped define the birth of modernism, while tragically, in Germany and Italy, intellectuals subverted Emerson's ideas into the all-too-real nightmares of Hitler's national socialism and Mussolini's fascism. In "Asia in Emerson and Emerson in Asia," Alan Hodder examines Emerson's exposure to, and his close focus on, the cultures of Persia, India, China and Japan, framing this fascination within the context of the West's religious, political and cultural forays into the Middle and Far East. Hodder then traces Emerson's reception and influence, from ideas to action, in the East, with his impact on Gandhi a notable example.

In the end, even as Emerson disrupted the establishment of his day, his revolution was basically conservative. Change, he believed, was fated—an inevitable good following nature's model and the self-evident truths of the Declaration. But he wished his revolution of heart and mind to have the same high aim as our War for Independence: to establish a new order of well-being, not endless warfare, unrest and anarchy. (Above his bureau, Fitz Hugh Lane's framed lithograph "View of the Battle Ground at Concord, Mass," featuring the field above the town's Old North Bridge, reminded him of that struggle every day.) Though imperfect, the Constitution had brought about that new order. In 1863, he wrote, "If we continued in Boston to throw tea into the bay at pleasure, that were revolutionary. But our *revolution* was in the interest of the moral or anti-revolutionary." In the midst of civil war, he saw slavery as "a violent conservatism" that was "more revolutionary than abolition or freedom of speech & of [the] press," a "perpetual revolution" of the most dangerous sort: "Society upside down, head over heels, & man eating his breakfast with pistols by his plate. It is man degraded to cat & dog. & Society has come to an end, and all gentlemen die out." A consummate gentlemen himself and first advocate of America's civilizing role, Emerson looked to another gentleman, George Washington, for his leading model of "a moral policy."[75] It is for this sort of calm and structured change that Emerson's revolution, which spread without a formal body of followers, has so many diverse adherents and innumerable beneficiaries today.

My debts to people who helped bring this book to birth are many. Along with Emerson's nineteenth- and twentieth-century biographers, editors of his works and other Emerson scholars who are individually credited in the Selected Bibliography, our contributors head the list: Phyllis Cole, Len Gougeon, Alan Hodder, Wesley Mott, David Robinson and Beniamino Soressi. They warmly accepted my invitation to participate in this group conversation, willingly adjusted their chapters as they developed through many editing sessions, and stayed loyal to this project over several years (see List of Contributors for more detail about each). My gratitude also goes out to the joint authors of the foreword to this volume, John Stauffer, professor of English and of African and African American Studies, Harvard University, and to Steven Brown, Ph.D. candidate, American Studies, Harvard University.

Equally generous and dedicated was Margaret "Bay" Bancroft, president of the Ralph Waldo Emerson Memorial Association, which is responsible for Emerson's house in Concord, Mass. From the start, she swiftly supported every request for photography and information about objects with unfailing patience and interest. Leslie Perrin Wilson of the Concord Free Public Library early and enthusiastically expedited my research about Emerson and facilitated, with Conni Manoli-Skocay, my selection of numerous images from the library's special collections. Carol L. Haines of the Concord Museum helped in producing several custom photographs of Emerson and Emerson-related objects. For sheet music included in a photograph of Thoreau's desk, I also wish to thank Jan Turnquist, executive director of Louisa May Alcott's Old Orchard House.

---

7   *JMN* 16: 391.

In Cambridge, Leslie Morris, Tom Ford and other staff at the Houghton Library gave me every assistance in research and custom photography. Also in that town, I am indebted to the Harvard University Library, the Cambridge Historical Society, and the Radcliffe Institute for Advanced Studies. In Boston, I wish to thank Catharina Slautterback and Patricia Boulos of the Boston Athenaeum for assistance in image research, the Boston Public Library Prints and Photographs Division and the Massachusetts Historical Society. Further afield, often by e-mail, I benefitted from help given by Michael Kelly, Special Collections Librarian, Amherst College; the New York Public Library; and the Library of Congress. Other miscellaneous institutions are credited in the List of Illustrations.

Beyond archival prints from these collections, I wish to thank photographer J. David Bohl for his aesthetic eye in producing a number of excellent custom transparencies of period rooms, paintings and prints from Emerson's house in Concord. At Emerson's house, too, my late husband Lew Mudge, an experienced amateur photographer, took several views of specific objects. In addition, I am greatly indebted to cartographer Darin Jensen whose custom maps for the first time vividly portray important contextual information about Emerson: his Boston, Cambridge and Concord settings as well as his lecturing and travel itineraries in the U.S. and abroad. I am indebted to Jenkins, too, for making image-scanning arrangements. His colleague Sasha Helton carefully, sometimes painstakingly, scanned over a third of the book's illustrations. For miscellaneous matters in the book's development, I wish to thank Peter Balaam, Susan Dunston and my son Bill Mudge.

Above all, as this book was being prepared for digital publication, I benefited from the intelligent, tireless work of OBP's Managing Director, Alessandra Tosi, and her associate and designer, Bianca Gualandi. They helped with innumerable details of final manuscript preparation, formatting, illustrations, permissions, and, in general, introduced me to the novelty of digital publishing. I am indebted, too, to Ben Fried for his careful editing of the whole manuscript, questioning important matters of expression, meaning, and format. Corin Throsby has not only carefully executed the index, but also valuably caught a number of errors throughout the manuscript. For both jobs, I warmly thank her. The computer expertise and patience of Malcolm Lowe in a final formatting of the book's text and intricate list of illustrations was invaluable. Reliable technical service was provided, too, by Bryan Woodhams in his careful formatting of the Chronology and in the electronic transmission of key images. In addition, Laura Robinson Hanlan, Research Librarian at Worcester Polytechnic Institute, expertly assisted Wes Mott with the mechanics of his chapter. Finally, I appreciate the generous subvention support for this book by the Ralph Waldo Emerson Society and by an anonymous Emerson scholar. If I have inadvertently missed mentioning anyone who is due thanks, I hope that their knowledge of participation and pleasure in this book will be some compensation.

THE MAKING OF A PROTESTER

1.1 A Legacy of Revolt, 1803-1821

Phyllis Cole

I find myself often idle, vagrant, stupid, & hollow. This is somewhat appalling & if I do not discipline myself with diligent care I shall suffer severely from remorse & the sense of inferiority hereafter. All around me are industrious & will be great, I am indolent & shall be insignificant. Avert it heaven! avert it virtue! I need excitement.

Emerson, Journal, 25 October 1820

At sixteen, while a junior at Harvard College, Ralph Waldo Emerson wrote his first entry in a new journal. It would become the personal record of his trajectory toward vision and revolution. Many students kept journals, commonplace books, or diaries, but Emerson's title for this one—"The Wide World"—measured his unusually ambitious compass. Since the year before, he had been accumulating notebooks for college themes, lists of books read, course notes, and commonplace books with quotations from his reading. But now in January 1820, he wrote of uniting his "new thoughts" with the "old ideas" of other writers. Imagination would be their ordering principal, the "generalissimo" of "all the luckless ragamuffin Ideas" gathered here, he announced. Only that faculty, he felt, gave form to the "thousand pursuits & passions & objects of the world."[1]

Emerson's wealth of growing entries richly displayed this power in romantic fantasies, vivid and often critical self-portraits, poems, watercolors

---

1   *The Journals and Miscellaneous Notebooks of Ralph Waldo Emerson*, 16 vols., eds. William H. Gilman, et al. (Cambridge, Mass.: Harvard University Press, 1960-1982), 1: 3-4. Hereafter *JMN*. For Emerson's journal as literary expression, see Lawrence Rosenwald, *Emerson and the Art of the Diary* (New York: Oxford University Press, 1988).

http://dx.doi.org/10.11647/OBP.0065.01

and drawings, ironic asides, and philosophical musings. Though the particulars would change, this journal and its allegiance to imagination would ground his career as a writer and reformer for the next five decades. Of course, he had been prepared for such a boldly active philosophical beginning. Emerson's boyhood had allowed him to find resources within himself, required him to muster strength against loss and difficulty, and embedded a strong habit of questioning the status quo. Furthermore, he had started life in a time and place that made a wide, and ever wider, world available to his curious mind. His immediate surroundings beckoned with incentives to create, out of his forefathers' protesting past and participation in the Revolution, his own call to citizens of the nation and world.

At a Leading Center of American Culture and Change

When Emerson was born in Boston on May 25, 1803, American horizons were rapidly expanding at home and abroad. The United States, fourteen years after the enactment of its Constitution, was newly enlarged and confident. Less than a month before, President Thomas Jefferson had seized the unexpected opportunity of purchasing the Louisiana territory from France. That act extended the nation, and its constitutionally legal shadow of slavery, to the western reaches of the plains, the Rockies, and the Spanish Southwest. Yet Boston remained arguably the most cultured city in all of the seventeen states. Nearby in Cambridge, Harvard College continued to lead the region's two hundred year old tradition of close intellectual ties to England and Europe. Boston itself, though long a major East Coast port, was rapidly enlarging from the size of a town, growing from 25,000 in 1800 to more than 90,000 forty years later.[2]

Among its residents at the turn of the nineteenth century was a small community of blacks, free since Massachusetts outlawed slavery in 1790. By 1830, they numbered 1,875, or three percent of the city's total population, the majority living in the West End, just over the hill from Boston's State House and Emerson's boyhood home. In the three decades that Emerson would call Boston home, the people in its streets always included black seamen, barbers, waiters, and even rising shop-owners.[3]

---

2   Statistics in Lawrence W. Kennedy, *Planning the City Upon a Hill: Boston Since 1630* (Amherst, Mass.: University of Massachusetts Press, 1992). See also http://www.iboston.org

3   Adelaide M. Cromwell, "The Black Presence in the West End of Boston, 1800-1864:

1.1 View of Boston, 1810.

Like its population, Boston's contacts abroad were growing exponentially. Just a few minutes' walk from the Emerson home on Chauncy Place, wharves and ships ringed the city, displaying New England's role in the country's newly independent trade with China. Since the mid-1780s, Boston and Salem's venture capitalists, veteran leaders in colonial coastwise shipping, had been among the first Americans in China. They led the United States in the Far East, a trade forced by Britain's post-Revolutionary embargo of the West Indies and England. The adventure to China meant sending ships around the world with the high-risk goal of safely reaching Canton, the single port of exchange. En route, like all Westerners for the two previous centuries, sea-going Americans touched multiple ports in both the Atlantic and Pacific; the round trip often took a matter of years. Like their predecessors as well, New Englanders braved the long and dangerous voyage for the promise of 100 to 300 per cent profit on their cargoes. The most successful of them were among the nation's first millionaires.[4]

A Demographic Map," in *Courage and Conscience: Black & White Abolitionists in Boston* (Bloomington, IN: Indiana University Press, 1993), 156-57.

4   Jean McClure Mudge, *Chinese Export Porcelain for the American Trade, 1785-1835*, 2nd ed., revised (East Brunswick, NJ: Associated University Presses, 1981), ch. 2; and *Chinese Export Porcelain in North America* (New York: Clarkson N. Potter, 1986; 2nd ed. (New York: Riverside Book Company, Inc., 2000), ch. 6.

Emerson's parents, William and Ruth Haskins Emerson, were connected with this global enterprise through Ruth's brother, Ralph Haskins, a business agent or supercargo in the trade, for whom they named their third son in 1803. Haskins returned that June from a voyage to China of nearly three years on the ship *Atahualpa*. Sailing by way of Cape Horn to the northwest coast of Canada, his company had exchanged muskets and West India goods for otter skins with the Indians, then proceeded across the Pacific to Canton for a second trade that brought the ship home, after circling the globe, laden with Asian imports.[5] Boston households like the Emersons' grew elegant with mahogany furniture, silks, spices, teas, and blue-and-white Canton and Nanking porcelain. This far-flung trade exposed Boston's intellectual circles to new foreign literatures as well as exotic objects. Privileged at the outset, Ralph grew up keenly aware of his expanding nation and fascinated by distant lands. No wonder he titled his first journals "The Wide World."

Two Different Parental Influences

If Boston's trade lay not far from the Emerson house, the family's essential mission in these changing times was the city's religion.

FIRST CONGREGATIONAL CHURCH.

1.2 First Congregational Church, 1843.

---

5   David Greene Haskins, *Ralph Waldo Emerson: His Maternal Ancestors* (Boston, Mass.: Cupples, Upham & Co., 1887), 83-84; David Greene Haskins, "Ralph Haskins," in *Memorial Biographies of the New England Historic Genealogical Society* (Boston, Mass: New England Historic Genealogical Society, 1880), 1: 467-70.

William Emerson served as minister of First Church, Boston's most prominent assembly in a Congregational order that had direct theological roots in seventeenth-century Puritanism. Through ministerial and civic leadership, he aspired to create an intellectual culture out of the raw materials of a new prosperity. Four years before, William and Ruth had arrived from the country parish of Harvard, twenty-five miles to the west. Six generations of his ancestors had ministered to New England towns, but none before had claimed the liberal theology that would soon be called Unitarian, and none had achieved the leadership of a Boston church. Now William aimed for influence even beyond his prominent congregation, which included former President John Adams and his son, John Quincy Adams. On the cultural and social front, William helped to found several Boston institutions: the city's first library (the Boston Athenaeum), its first literary magazine (the *Monthly Anthology*), and the Massachusetts Historical Society (publishing Ralph Haskins' travel journal in its proceedings). He also observed the stars with a Society for the Study of Natural Philosophy. In the realm of social action, he supported the Female Asylum and the new school for black children in Smith Court.

1.3 Ruth Haskins and William Emerson, Emerson's parents.

William's liberal religious doctrines emphasized reason and active virtue in improving society. But, along with the ruling class of Federalist Massachusetts, he was politically conservative, opposing the extreme democracy of President Jefferson and what he considered worse, the possible contagion of French anarchy. On Independence Day in 1802, William's official oration at Boston's Faneuil Hall had asked citizens to preserve the American Revolution by recalling the recent eras of Washington and Adams, with their greater social order and deference to authority.[6] Elegant in dress and gregarious in style, William lived for the public. The day Ralph was born—Election Day in Massachusetts, a holiday—William dined with the governor, listened to the day's official sermon, and spent the evening at his club. But he was far from indifferent to his growing brood of children, with Ralph the fourth of eventually eight siblings. Instead, he took on childrearing as if it were another project for public improvement, with the fervor of something personal to prove. Yet for all his prominence and dedication, William was undisciplined, especially in money matters. And insecurity led to his habit of putting on courtly airs and an elevated speech that encouraged some parishioners, first in Harvard and then in Boston, to hold him in contempt. He privately blamed his inadequacies on a lack of guidance from his father, who had died in the Revolution when he was five. This felt deprivation motivated his insistence that his children become "intelligent as well as moral beings . . . to take rank with professional characters and the upper classes of society."[7]

William's discipline, enforced primarily by verbal injunction rather than physical punishment, sought to imbue his offspring with these values. "It will grieve me exceedingly to have you a blockhead," he wrote to eldest son John at six. "I hope you will be as bright as silver." By Ralph's second birthday, his father was offering rewards and imposing conditions: "Papa will bring home cake for little boys who behave well at the dinner table," he reminded the toddler. When Ralph's instruction in a dame school began not many months later, William confided to John that his little brother was "rather a dull scholar"; and as the child neared three, his father wrote a friend, "[He] does not read very well yet." William's negative attention took aim at Ralph's behavior as well as his pace of learning. Away on a trip in April

---

6   Phyllis Cole, *Mary Moody Emerson and the Origins of Transcendentalism: A Family History* (New York: Oxford University Press, 1998), 103, 121, 127. Hereafter *MME*. D. G. Haskins, "Ralph Haskins," 470; William Emerson, *An Oration Pronounced July 5, 1802... in Commemoration of the Anniversary of American Independence* (Boston, Mass: Manning and Loring, 1802), 23.

7   William Emerson, Journal and Commonplace Book No. 1, May 25, 1803, Sept. 6, 1803, Houghton Library bMS Am 1280H (150); John McAleer, *Ralph Waldo Emerson: Days of Encounter* (Boston, Mass.: Little, Brown & Co., 1984), 17; William Emerson to Phebe Bliss Emerson Ripley, Jan. 11, 1810, Houghton bMS Am 1280.226 (2925).

1810, William wrote his wife that he hoped his third son "regards his words, does not eat his dinner too fast, and is gradually resigning his impetuosity to younger boys."[8] At almost seven, Ralph showed a certain headstrong, impulsive nature that would later blossom into full revolt.

Emerson's adult career as one of America's first public intellectuals owed a considerable debt to his father, but he rarely acknowledged it. Instead, he disparaged William's era, represented by his *Monthly Anthology*, as an "early ignorant & transitional Month-of-March" in American culture. In general, he recalled childhood as "unpleasing," beginning with his fear of this godlike parent. "Twice or thrice he put me in mortal terror by forcing me into the salt water off some wharf or bathing house," Emerson later wrote, "and I still recall the fright with which, after some of this salt experience, I heard his voice one day (as Adam that of the Lord God in the garden), summoning us to a new bath, and I vainly endeavouring to hide myself."[9] William believed in cold-water bathing as a strategy for health. But to Ralph—who recalled the day with grim humor—his father's words were divine thunder.

William's regimen, however, strengthened the bonds among these bright young Emerson children. Sadly, their group soon narrowed to four boys. John, receiver of his father's strongest guidance, died of tuberculosis at the age of eight, and two girls fell victim to illness in infancy. Meanwhile, younger brother Bulkeley proved to be mentally disabled, part of the family circle but not up to its ambition. Ralph's chief partners and competitors would be elder brother William and younger brothers Edward and Charles. When small, they were restricted to the yellow, gambrel-roofed parsonage on Chauncy Place and its enclosed half-acre yard, three blocks from the gold-domed State House. From an early age Ralph was looking beyond its bounds. When father William had traveled to Waterford, Maine to visit family members, Ruth reported the make-believe play of two-year-old Ralph and his brother, "riding to Waterford to carry and bring intelligence to you." Emerson later described himself as a small boy sitting on the brick wall around his yard, coveting the pears in his neighbor's orchard. His school friend William Henry Furness once claimed that Emerson's childhood had been without play, but personal recollections

---

8   William Emerson to John Clarke Emerson, May 17, 1806; William Emerson to Ruth Haskins Emerson, May 25, 1805; William Emerson to John Clarke Emerson, Dec. 13, 1805; William Emerson to Ruth Haskins Emerson, April 14, 1810, Houghton bMS Am 1280.226 (2839, 2864, 2837, 2877). James Elliot Cabot, *A Memoir of Ralph Waldo Emerson* (Cambridge, Mass.: Riverside Press, 1887), 1: 41.

9   *JMN* 2: 309; *The Letters of Ralph Waldo Emerson*, 6 vols., ed. Ralph L. Rusk (New York: Columbia University Press, 1939), 4: 179. Hereafter *L*.

tell a different story. As an adult Emerson remembered "trundling a hoop in Chauncy Place" and could call before his mind's eye "the old school-entry where . . . we spun tops and snapped marbles."[10]

Ruth's maternal affection was the rock supporting young Ralph's childhood, but her native reserve and pressing household duties left little time to show it. Though the daughter of a prosperous brewer and businessman, Ruth rather than William modeled the life of prayer in their family. Each morning she dedicated an hour to solitary devotions, following the traditional ways of the Bible and the Anglican Book of Common Prayer. Not brought up a Congregationalist, she nevertheless dutifully supported her husband's ministerial position, serving dinner to his Boston colleagues every Thursday as well as wine to the deacons on Sunday evenings. The Emerson parsonage was a perpetual open house: Ruth's surviving recipe book tells how to make a "plumb cake" with twenty-eight pounds of flour, sixteen of currents, and seven dozen eggs. As a young woman who lived in the household later recalled, Ruth raised her children with firm discipline and gentle restraint. But one of Emerson's memories suggests he wished for more. When Ralph and his brother William spent an entire Election Day holiday enjoying the town's festivities, they were surprised that Ruth met their return with relief: "My sons, I have been in an agony for you!" "I went to bed," Emerson remembered, "in bliss at the interest she showed."[11]

Still, Ruth and her son Ralph shared unspoken bonds, as well as physical, temperamental, and spiritual traits. Many saw the strong physical likeness of son to mother, and her calm exterior became his own. Most of all, Emerson's alienation from his father did not extend to his mother; in fact, he willingly provided her with a home throughout her elder years. Near the end of her life, having fallen out of bed and broken her hip, Ruth remained silent until morning so as not to disturb others. Her son reproved such extreme self-discipline but could be equally stoical himself. It was another sign of the intense emotional reserve, the "native frost" he once noted as common to New Englanders.[12]

---

10   Ruth Haskins Emerson to William Emerson, Oct. 3 and 5, 1805, Houghton bMS Am 1280.226 (2764); Franklin B. Sanborn, *Transcendental and Literary New England*, ed. Kenneth W. Camerson (Hartford: Transcendental Books, 1975), 198; *Records of a Lifelong Friendship: Ralph Waldo Emerson and William Henry Furness*, ed. Horace H. Furness (Boston, Mass.: Houghton Mifflin, 1910), 88, 159; *JMN* 8: 258; *L* 2: 255.

11   Gay Wilson Allen, *Waldo Emerson* (New York: Viking Press, 1981), 7; D. G. Haskins, *Emerson*, 53-54, 59-60; William and Ruth Haskins Emerson, "Receipts," 27, Houghton bMS Am 1280.235 (445); Cabot, *Memoir of Ralph Waldo Emerson*, 1: 35.

12   McAleer, 21, 23, 27; *JMN* 7: 395.

The Rebellious Example of Mary Moody Emerson

The influence of a more headstrong blend of love and piety than Ruth's, with the addition of considerable barbed wit, came from William's sister Mary Moody Emerson.

1.4 Mary Moody Emerson, silhouette, [n.d].

So did she model the value of reading and intelligence in a different manner from William. This strong-willed aunt, contemptuous of many social conventions, joined Ralph's more conservative mother as a primary first mentor. Thus Emerson came early to appreciate female mental capabilities and emotional sensibilities. In their separate ways, these two women set Emerson on a path toward eventual adoption of social causes that female friends as well as family held dear: abolition and their own legal rights. Though less than five feet in height, Mary carved out larger space for herself as a self-taught spiritual seeker and a feisty, even rudely memorable debater. From the start, she served as a vital catalytic figure for the whole family. It had been Mary who proposed her exemplary friend Ruth as a wife for William. He and Mary had been born shortly before the American Revolution in the Concord parsonage later made famous by Nathaniel Hawthorne as the "Old Manse." Their father, also named William, had served as chaplain to Concord's Minutemen; and their mother, Phebe, was daughter of the zealous pastor Daniel Bliss, who had led Concord during the disruptive, spirit-filled revivals of the First Great Awakening. Later,

Mary would celebrate these spiritual heroes to her nephews, urging them to make an equal mark. However, after her father's death when Mary was two, she had grown up under different circumstances from her siblings. She was "exiled" (as she later recounted) to the household of kinswomen in nearby Malden and formed by their Calvinist piety rather than by the religion of reason and social order that her ministerial step-father, Ezra Ripley, brought to Concord.[13]

In Mary's lifelong search for religious power, however, she became a self-educated reader of both new and traditional books. After reuniting as young adults, William and Mary, only three years apart, often supported each other. His *Monthly Anthology* in 1804 and 1805 carried her essays on nature and imagination as avenues to God. But they agreed about almost nothing, including the subjects of Mary's essays. He charged that her "imagination, all fascinating and balloon-like as it is," had carried her away from correct judgment. In turn, she criticized his worldliness and urged him to retire from Boston, "commune with nature sublime and tranquil . . . and take leave of the earth."[14]

1.5 Old Manse, Concord, c. 1890-1895.

---

13   For this family history in detail, see Cole, *MME*, ch. 1-4.
14   *Monthly Anthology* 1 (July 1804), 456-57; 1 (December 1804), 646. William Emerson to Mary Moody Emerson, April 10, 1806, Houghton bMS Am 1280.226 (2841); *Selected Letters of Mary Moody Emerson*, ed. Nancy Craig Simmons (Athens, GA: University of Georgia Press, 1993), 55. Hereafter *Letters of MME*.

In a generation still energized by the Revolution's spirit of change, William and Mary, each an innovator of sorts, argued for fundamentally different worldviews. William believed that his position at First Church would begin to fulfill his father's goal of a new American order. Earlier, he had even dreamed of founding a national, nondenominational church in Washington, D.C.; human reason was reliable enough to make it succeed. Mary, raised by Calvinists, doubted his faith in reason. She believed that humanity was born in sin and needed Christ's salvation. However, she had experienced that salvation on her own, not through the agency of church ritual or authority. Thus she valued "enthusiasm"—the direct influence of divine spirit—as shown in both her father's Revolutionary heroism and in her own solitary devotion. Going further, she was even able to forget Christ as "mediator," perceiving God's truth directly in natural landscapes and in lines of poetry. Though all her life she would reflect a Calvinist upbringing and sense of human depravity, the adult Mary began reading books popular with the most daring liberals—becoming familiar with a wide variety of thinkers across time and space, from England and France to ancient Greece and even India. Her endorsement of imagination and nature in 1804, when Ralph was still an infant, shows that she was absorbing the leading ideas of European Romanticism into her own individualistic faith.[15]

Mary passed on a revolution of the spirit to all her nephews, especially Ralph. Though she influenced him through long and intimate involvement, at first she did not focus on him as a special charge. A single woman, Mary lived at the beck and call of relatives, stretching herself across the distances between Concord, Malden, Boston and her new and preferred home, "Elm Vale," near the White Mountains in the frontier town of Waterford, Maine, where two sisters and their families had settled. From adolescence, she had cared for relatives' children; the Emerson boys in Boston were not her sole focus. But their potential stimulated her best efforts and opinions. More than either of their parents, Mary could both play with children and exhort them to religious devotion. When little John was sent to Maine in an attempt to cure his tuberculosis, she coaxed him into trying to swing. To Ruth, she wrote about the value of music in harmonizing the minds of children, and to nine-year-old William, appreciation for his letter and advice to "reflect on your condition." "Give my love to R. Waldo," she added. "I shall write to him very soon."[16] Already Mary was emphasizing seven-year-old Ralph's

---

15   Cole, *MME*, 103, 120-29.
16   *Letters of MME*, 36; Mary Moody Emerson to Ruth Haskins Emerson, Dec. 30, [1805],

ancestral middle name (from her great-grandmother) that recalled to her the family's devout origins. Giving him that name in 1810 was an early signal of their nascent special relationship.[17]

William especially asked for Mary's assistance with the family because of his fragile health. The tuberculosis that cut short little John's life also plagued the father. In 1799, William had taken up the call to preach at First Church despite feeling "alarmed about my health" and "sore at my lungs." A few years later, following medical advice of the day to ride rough roads in order to clear the lungs, he rode several times to Waterford, Maine, both to see young John and to regain his strength. His journal, along with self-accusations for failing to achieve more, often included the terse note, "quite unwell." But William kept his illness private until 1808, when he was felled by a massive hemorrhage of the lungs, a sure sign of the disease in its acute phase. Through his months of recuperation, Mary stayed in Boston to help Ruth in sickroom and nursery.[18]

That July, William rose from bed to preach in the splendid neoclassical church that First Church had built at Summer Street and Chauncy Place, along with a spacious new parsonage nearby. Since the country was enduring an economic depression brought on by Jefferson's anti-British shipping embargo, many in the congregation thought these new structures extravagant. Simultaneously, William's excessive spending put him permanently in debt. When Mary returned to Maine a year later, William pleaded with her to "come home . . . and help to alleviate the burdens of a minister of religion weighed down to the earth by a consciousness of incompetence to his awful function . . . The boys' minds and hearts afford a fine field for the display of talents such as their aunt possesses."[19]

William died in May 1811 not from tuberculosis but, surprisingly, from stomach cancer. Mary was present and afterward stayed with the family for months at a time. Witnessing the pomp and ceremony of his father's funeral, Ralph, almost eight, felt more awe than sorrow. He and William

---

Houghton bMS Am 1280.226 (974); *Letters of MME*, 57.

17   Rebecca Waldo, daughter of Deacon Cornelius Waldo of Chelmsford, Massachusetts, married Deacon Edward Emerson in 1697. Her epitaph in the Malden cemetery, which Mary would have grown up knowing, declares in devoutly Puritan terms, "Prudent and pious, meek and kind/Virtue and Grace Adorned her Mind./ This stone may crumble into Dust;/ But her Dear Name continue must." Benjamin Kendall Emerson, *The Ipswich Emersons* (Boston, Mass.: D. Clapp, 1900), 50-51.

18   William Emerson, Journal and Commonplace Book No. 1, Sept. 22 and 23, 1799, March 2, 1802 etc., Houghton bMS Am 1280H (150); Cole, *MME*, 130.

19   Cole, *MME*, 130-31; William Emerson to Mary Moody Emerson, Oct. 23, 1809, Houghton bMS Am 1280.226 (2847).

walked behind the hearse in a parade to King's Chapel Burial Ground led by the Ancient and Honorable Artillery Company. "As we went up School Street and saw them sweep round the corner into Tremont Street," he later told his daughter, "it seemed to me a grand sight." Other than that, he could remember little of William except certain moments of discipline. This largely negative feeling about his father reflected the trauma of pain, stress, and death buried within his terse description of his childhood as "unpleasing."[20]

Furthermore, William's name was not often mentioned afterward. "I have never heard sentence or sentiment of his repeated by Mother or Aunt," the adult Emerson asserted. As these two women worked to keep the family together—a goal they had shared with William before his death— silence rather than fond recollection led them forward. Although Ruth was bent with grief at her loss, she might also have felt shame and resentment at William's failure to leave an estate for his young family. Mary would always recall the anniversary of William's death, but her differences with him on fundamental theological and philosophical matters now led her to assert her own voice. She would raise the boys her way and fulfill a potential greatness lost to two successive male generations in the Emerson family. As Ralph once joked, Mary now became "Father Mum" to the boys.[21]

Hard Times and High Objectives

The family's reduced means following William's death cut short all expectation of ease for the growing sons. William left behind only the mahogany furniture, China tea sets, a telescope, and 452 books that supported his stylish urban ministry. He also left debts of $2,458, or $42,100 today, well above his entire assets and nearly twice his annual salary. For the first three years after William's death, the family stayed in the First Church parsonage, taking boarders and selling the books to pay debts. Afterward, they shared the Haskins' house on Rainsford Lane and moved on to a succession of rented quarters, where Ruth continued boarding guests to supplement her widow's stipend. The family's position among Boston's elite became fragile. Living on Beacon Street among the

---

20   Ellen Emerson, "What I Can Remember about Father," 7, Houghton bMS Am 1280.227. For Emerson's childhood grief and its impact on his development, see Evelyn Barish, *Emerson: The Roots of Prophecy* (Princeton, NJ: Princeton University Press, 1989), chs. 1 and 4.

21   *L* 4: 179, 1: 197.

highest class, they rarely saw their affluent neighbors, as Mary wrote to a friend: "Ladies do not like to visit where [there] are boarders." From this humiliation and loss of face, Ralph learned an early lesson in compensation: the value of family solidarity. In his later essay "Domestic Life," Emerson pictured boys collaborating in chores and, as Ruth and Mary had taught them, entertaining each other with the treasure of their day's reading. "What is the hoop that holds them staunch? It is the iron band of poverty, of necessity, of austerity, which, excluding them from the sensual enjoyments which make other boys too early old, has directed their activity into safe and right channels."[22] His father had provided a model of elite generosity to the poor by supporting the Female Asylum and school for black children, but Emerson's later sympathy for the marginalized grew also from direct experience of poverty's "iron band."

In 1812, at age nine, Ralph entered Boston Public Latin School, although the cost of tuition and suitable clothing added to the family's financial burden.

1.6 Boston Public Boys' Latin School, 1812-1844.

---

22   William Emerson Inventory, List of Debts (Suffolk Probate No. 23771); http://www. measuringworth.com/ppowerus/; Ralph L. Rusk, *The Life of Ralph Waldo Emerson* (New York: Charles Scribner's Sons, 1949), 30; *Letters of MME*, 93; *The Complete Works of Ralph Waldo Emerson*, Centenary Edition, 12 vols., ed. Edward Waldo Emerson (Boston, Mass.: Houghton Mifflin, 1903-1904), 2: 133. Hereafter *W*.

He never forgot the anxiety of searching for the dollar he had lost while on his way to buy shoes. One winter, he and Edward had to share an overcoat on alternate days, enduring schoolmates' taunts about whose turn it was to wear it. Nonetheless, Boston Latin gave Ralph a strong social and intellectual foundation over the next five years. Here he grew in the company of boys such as William Henry Furness and Samuel Bradford, who would become lifelong friends. Here, too, after one reputedly drunken master was dismissed, the kind and invigorating young Benjamin Gould replaced him. Gould taught geography not only from the textbook, but with a globe, atlas, and stories of Napoleon's recent campaigns in the African desert. Gould's Greek lessons came alive with enough clarity and force that for life Emerson could repeat the lines he learned. Most of all, this teacher passed on his love of writing and oratory. Ralph responded by composing his first serious essays, reciting passages from literature each week, and presenting his poem "Eloquence" to a visiting expert on the subject.[23]

He later recalled, however, that his best education had come from "some idle books under the bench at Latin School." His own choice of reading always led to his most important learning. Ruth had kept the family's membership in the Boston Athenaeum, so that mother, aunt, and sons could all borrow volumes freely. Whether or not he read these on the sly at Latin School, he enjoyed bookish conversations at home. Mary provided constant challenges out of her own knowledge of poetry and philosophy, seeking to "unfold . . . powers" that, in her view, each child already possessed. Ralph believed that his aunt had read every known book, and he afterwards remembered the sentences of Milton, Shakespeare, and Antoninus as she had quoted them. Mary's faith that the boys were "born to be educated" anticipated their achieving greatness from within, a goal far different from the academic rank and social station to which her brother might have driven them.[24]

Each evening, she led the family in hymns and prayers, after which they took turns reading Rollin's *Ancient History*. Rollin's Athenian heroes affected Ralph so deeply that he wrote verses extolling their bravery. He showed his lines to Mary's intellectually gifted friend, Sarah Alden Bradford, who often visited in the evenings and, as Mary put it, "animate[d] the boys to study."

---

23   Rusk, *Life of Ralph Waldo Emerson*, 55, 57-59.
24   W 2: 133. Rusk, *Life of Ralph Waldo Emerson*, 60; Cole, *MME*, 146-49.

1.7 Sarah Alden Bradford Ripley.

Sarah's conversations with Ralph continued after she became his aunt by marrying his half-uncle Samuel Ripley, and along with Samuel taught school in Waltham to prepare boys for Harvard. "As to her knowledge," Ralph later wrote to brother William, "talk on what you will, she can always give you a new idea."[25]

An early Emerson biographer noted his unusual, female-influenced education, referring to Ruth, Mary, and Sarah Ripley as the "three Fates" who had set the direction of young Ralph's life. His adult friend Bronson Alcott more boldly declared the result: "The best of Emerson's intellect comes out of its feminine traits." Neither observer was disparaging the grown man as effeminate, but instead was praising Emerson's intuition and receptivity, traits that their culture associated with women. Free of father-son struggles for control, the impressionable Ralph readily made this collective female mind part of his own psyche. Later, in a journal entry of 1842, Emerson realized the value of a bisexual sensibility in the

---

25   *Letters of MME*, 82; *L* 1: 4-6, 75.

revolutionary consciousness he was proposing: "The finest people marry the two sexes in their own person. Hermaphrodite is then the symbol of the finished soul."[26] This later openness to women and to the womanly side of himself grew naturally from his early formation. The encouragement of his kinswomen directly affected Ralph's reading and creativity, his love of language and composing poetry. Ruth asked the boys every Sunday to learn a hymn. At nine, Ralph wrote one instead, which Edward read for Ruth's approval before triumphantly revealing the author. His poem "The Sabbath" also survives from that same age. Two years later, during idle moments at Rufus Webb's noontime writing school, he collaborated as writer with his friend William Furness, who drew the pictures, for the bloody and adventurous "History of Fortus." Whether or not he had formal drawing lessons, Ralph also liked to sketch, as his elaborate rebus-letter to brother William in November 1814 and later watercolors show.[27]

1.8 Rebus letter, 1814, p. 1.

26 Moncure Daniel Conway, *Emerson at Home and Abroad* (Boston, Mass.: James Osgood, 1882), 41; *The Journals of Bronson Alcott*, ed. Odell Shepard (Boston, Mass.: Little, Brown & Co., 1938), 221; *JMN* 8: 380.

27 Albert J. von Frank, "Emerson's Boyhood and Collegiate Verse: Unpublished and New Texts Edited from Manuscript," *Studies in the American Renaissance*, 1983, ed. Joel Myerson (Boston, Mass.: Twayne, 1983), 2-3, 5; *L* 1: frontispiece.

1.9 Rebus letter, 1814, p. 2.

Since his mother was preoccupied with boarders and Aunt Mary often away in Concord or Waterford, Ralph now felt both the loneliness and the advantage of independence. This freedom allowed him to explore Boston neighborhoods of both the rich and the poor. On the Election Day, when he and William were reprimanded for being gone so long, they must have taken full advantage of the festivities for this major state holiday. After school and even while truant from it, they skated and played ball on the nearby Boston Common, explored the city's docks and ropewalks on Charles Street, and soaked up the sights and sounds of street-criers and fire engines. The Common, a large public space in the city's center, was a playground he shared with its black community from the nearby West End. Down by the docks, Ralph first encountered even more races and classes. Sailors disembarking from ships were black as well as white, and they also included the natives of far-flung ports. Once he and Edward ventured over the bridge to Charlestown and were bullied by street boys — their race unmentioned — on the way back; later he declared he could have used more such education. From these wanderings, along with observing all types of humanity, Emerson's intellectual curiosity grew: "When a boy I used to go to the wharves," he later wrote, "and pick up shells out of the sand which vessels had brought as ballast, and also plenty of stones, gypsum, which I discovered would be luminous when I rubbed two bits together in a dark closet, to my great wonder."[28] Such wonder fed both his poetic mind and his lifelong interest in science.

The War of 1812 brought new excitements to Boston, martial music in the streets and warships in the harbor. Ralph was especially proud of Uncle Ralph Haskins' "manly beauty" as a member of the Boston Hussars, a troop of fifty leading citizens who paraded in showy green uniforms trimmed with red, ready to defend the city if the British attacked.[29] Though the die-hard Federalists of New England still opposed war with the British, by the end of 1812 new national pride rallied, especially after the Boston-built *Constitution* summarily destroyed the *Guerrière* not far off-shore. Two years later, after Oliver Hazard Perry defeated the British on Lake Erie, eleven-year-old Ralph's verses on "Perry's Victory" both celebrated America's military might and displayed a naive love of rhyming: "When late Columbia's patriot brave/ Sail'd forth on Erie[']s tranquil wave/ No hero yet had found a grave—/ Within her watery cemetery./ But soon that wave was stained with gore/ And soon on every concave shore/ Reechoed with the dreadful roar/ Of thundering artillery." Ralph had his own moment of patriotic service the same year, when the students of Boston Latin were enlisted to help build fortifications against British attack on Noddle's Island at the harbor's mouth. Later, he fondly mocked their boyish efforts, noting that Great Britain had probably made peace as a direct result.[30] But now, on the cusp of his impressionable teens, Ralph's enthusiasm for his revolutionary heritage and the promise of extending independence in America was only strengthened by the war.

Such proud rebellious stirrings were also encouraged by a temporary move to Concord. Inflation and a serious threat of invasion to Boston during the war led Ruth and Mary temporarily to evacuate the boys to that ancestral home. Eleven-year-old Ralph had often visited his grandmother and step-grandfather Ezra Ripley's manse on the Concord River. Now, from November 1814 through the spring of 1815, he actually lived in the house built by his blood grandfather, William Emerson. Just behind it in 1775, as Mary loved to tell her nephews, William had invoked divine

---

28 Cabot, *Memoir of Ralph Waldo Emerson*, 1: 35; Rusk, *Life of Ralph Waldo Emerson*, 33-34; *JMN* 16: 263.

29 D. G. Haskins, *Emerson*, 84; Haskins, "Ralph Haskins," 471-72.

30 Von Frank, "Emerson's Boyhood and Collegiate Verse," 4-5, 24-25; Edward Waldo Emerson, *Emerson in Concord: A Memoir* (Boston, Mass.: Houghton Mifflin, 1888), 17.

blessing on the Minutemen as they fought the British at Old North Bridge. When grandfather Ripley took him on ministerial rounds, Ralph heard stories about parishioners that also helped make Concord's rich pre-Revolutionary and wartime history his own. Meanwhile, to add to his positive memories of the place, the village schoolmaster frequently invited him to recite his poems in class. Once he even spoke his lines for a larger public while standing on top of a sugar barrel at the village store, a future performing orator enjoying his first public audience.[31]

Equally delightful to Ralph was the town's natural landscape. As he recalled, "this place was . . . all 'the Country' which we knew." It was a far different playing field from Boston's streets, Common, and shore. William had already gone to college, so Ralph spent his after-school hours with Edward and Charles, now nine and six, in the woods and hills. As his memorial to these brothers later recalled, "They took this valley for their toy,/ They played with it in every mood;/ A cell for prayer, a hall for joy,—/ They treated nature as they would." At the time, Ralph expressed no hint of interest in Concord as a one-day home. But Emerson's son Edward later remarked that its fields "bound him unconsciously with ties which drew him back before many years to live and dream and prophesy and die in them."[32]

Once peace was declared in 1815, Ruth brought the family back to Boston, where Ralph continued to grow under Mary's influence. Throughout the war years she had told and retold her nephews stories of ancestors, not only recent family heroes but a long line of Protestant pastors whose charity and power rose from the Holy Spirit at work in them. Ralph heard these "with awe." Every day he also read aloud her prayers for family devotions, their "prophetic & apocalyptic ejaculations" still sounding in his ear years later. Now, as he reached his teens, his direct give and take of ideas and jokes with Mary also intensified. In 1813, at age ten, he had written her about his daily schedule in stiff, schoolboy prose. Three years later, he shared his learning while also revealing a new ability to mimic his aunt's satirical style, poking fun at her insistence that morning should make one "feel inspired." The same year, Ralph parodied Mary's literary advice in substance and style when he advised Edward that a letter "fill'd by 'sentiment' and taste/ On common stuff should, no black fluid waste." Such slight sarcasm was allowable, because by now he knew that he and Charles had become Mary's favorites among the Emerson brothers. While she hoped that Charles, whom

31 Rusk, *Life of Ralph Waldo Emerson*, 50-53; W 10: 385; Allen, 33.
32 Furness, *Records of a Lifelong Friendship*, 31; E. W. Emerson, *Emerson in Concord*, 18-19.

she had taken to Maine for a time to care for alone, would eventually rise to political power, she hailed Ralph as the most creative of the brothers with language and ideas. When he was about fourteen, she both complimented his growing talent and added a characteristic barb: "I remember no hour of our solitude so pleasantly as the last sab.[bath] eve. The Justice of your theological views was noticeable for your age and non-application—that is there are some books you have not read. But some serious questions were inferred which I did not put. You will. To know one's duty is a great step."[33]

Independence at Harvard with Mary Emerson as Continuing Mentor

Both aunt and nephew took major life steps in the fall of 1817. Ralph followed family tradition and entered Harvard College in nearby Cambridge.

1.10 Harvard College, Old Quad, North Side, 1828.

In contrast, Mary left Boston to live at her farm, Elm Vale, in western Maine, doing what she had once advised her brother William: to retire from society and commune with nature. Though in 1817 Ralph had not yet visited Mary's farm, he already idealized this sublime natural landscape, a place he later described as "within sight of the White Mountains," with a lake, neighboring

---

33   *JMN* 5: 323; *L* 7: 102-04; *L* 1: 42; postscript to Ralph in Mary Moody Emerson to Ruth Haskins Emerson, Aug. 7, [1817?], Houghton bMS Am 1280.226 (1015) (dated by Nancy Craig Simmons, "A Calendar of the Letters of Mary Moody Emerson," *Studies in the American Renaissance 1993*, 15). For fuller discussion of Mary's different hopes for Charles and Ralph, see Cole, *MME*, especially 139-43, 147-50, and 184-86.

mountain, a brook running over granite, "and noble forests all around." At college, he began receiving Mary's letters reflecting on such scenes—as well as on the new, defining texts of European Romanticism that she associated with them. Having affirmed French novelist and essayist Germaine de Staël's dictum, "Enthusiasm is God within us," and William Wordsworth's admission that a humble flower creates thoughts that "lie too deep for tears," she was now urging a life of similar natural inspiration upon her nephew. [34]

In their exchange of learned, playful letters, both Mary and Ralph benefited. As a woman in her forties, lacking formal education or means to publish her ideas, Mary was attempting to make this promising nephew her literary surrogate by transferring her wealth of insights and hopes. In mock humility, she pictured the supposed cultural divide between them: "What dull Prosaic Muse would venture from the humble dell of an unlettered district to address a son of Harvard?" she asked that November. But Mary's serious vision for Ralph as a poet went well beyond Harvard. Her incomplete phrases left open an unlimited future: "Son of — — — of poetry — — of genius — ah were it so — and I destined to stand in near consanguinity to this magical possession."[35] If her nephew had the "genius" to write original works, it would be enough that she had served as his mentor.

Mary's compliments offered the gangly, six-foot, fourteen-year-old Ralph—superior by heritage and education but shy by nature and poverty— an invaluable sense of self-worth. He needed confidence as the youngest in his class.

1.11 Emerson at 14 (painted 1845).

34   *W* 10: 401; Cole, *MME*, 151.
35   *Letters of MME*, 104.

Also, as President John T. Kirkland's freshman messenger in exchange for room and board, he was living alone at the rear of the president's house, while fellow students were readily making new friends in the dormitories. Kirkland's nephew Samuel Lothrop, whom Ralph helped prepare for college, recalled that his tutor had "a wall of reserve around him which he would not let anybody penetrate." Yet at times he relaxed enough to share his poems with Lothrop and give "comic views of persons" at Harvard. Classmate John Gardner also noted that Ralph, though rarely speaking, had "a certain flash when he uttered anything." When brother William began college three years before, Mary had advised him to avoid the look of "dependance [sic]." Instead he should act "generous and great" so as to begin giving society benefit rather than receiving it.[36] For Ralph, satirical skills and verbal "flash" were his form of pride and gift to society at this moment. Later, he would use them as a bridge from literature and philosophy to the world of reform.

A seemingly slight incident at college was already a harbinger of social action to come. By his second year, Ralph, now living in Hollis Hall with other classmates, worked in the college commons to help his mother and brother put him through college. This employment gave him a catbird seat to witness a small class rebellion there, a food fight on All Hallows Eve in 1818. When President Kirkland suspended its ring-leaders, the sophomores arose in collective protest at Harvard's Rebellion Tree, revered since the Revolution. Ralph had not participated in the riot, whether from personal reserve or desire to keep his job at the commons, but he joined his peers at the tree.

HOLLIS HALL AND REBELLION TREE.

1.12 Hollis Hall with Rebellion Tree, 1875.

36   Rusk, *Life of Ralph Waldo Emerson*, 62, 65-67, 69; McAleer, 53; *Letters of MME*, 85.

Afterward, he wrote what brother William in amusement called a "history of your very praiseworthy resistance to lawful authority." In similar spirit and around the same time, Ralph joined several student societies fostering reading and debate. Sometimes he composed drinking songs for them and sampled "a great deal of wine (for me)," though instead of loosening up, he grew "graver with every glass."[37]

A deeper and longer-lasting conflict near the end of Ralph's sophomore year was the mounting battle between conservative and liberal clergy, centered at Harvard and long brewing within New England's dominant Congregationalism. It would both win his commitments and prompt his acts of resistance.

1.13 Room 15, Hollis Hall, 1822, Emerson watercolor.

The controversy had begun in 1805, when Henry Ware, Sr. was elected Hollis Professor of Divinity at Harvard over objections from the orthodox clergy. Ralph's father William had sided with Ware and the liberals: that year he devoted pages of the *Monthly Anthology* to defending Ware. His sister Mary, though raised orthodox, showed her liberal bent by contributing a letter portraying Christ as a divinely human "hero," rather than part of the three-person God. Even more at issue for the opposing heirs of New England Puritanism than a single or tri-part God was the

---

37   Rusk, *Life of Ralph Waldo Emerson*, 71-74.

question of how redemption would occur: by humanity's own will to goodness or through the undeserved gift of God's grace? The stakes were high. A host of new spiritual competitors caught up in the fervor of the Second Great Awakening—Baptists, Methodists, Shakers—were offering the populace emotional conversion in a way that undermined all the old churches. William Ellery Channing of Boston's Federal Street Church emerged as chief leader of the liberals, and soon thereafter the energetic, far-sighted Kirkland began reforming Harvard in this light. By 1816, the year before Ralph arrived, Ware had begun a new Divinity School to train liberal clergy.[38]

In May of 1819, Channing preached a sermon in Baltimore that named and defined a new denomination, "Unitarian Christianity." For Ralph, family history placed his initial allegiance to Unitarianism beyond doubt. His father had been Channing's Boston colleague and Kirkland's close friend. Mary had followed Channing's career closely over the years, mixing her occasional dissents from his views with wishes for "the youth . . . to imbibe his spirit." Her ideas of Christ as God's "mediator," but not himself divine, paralleled Channing's theology as it had developed to this point. Two years earlier, Ralph had won Mary's praise for his theological questions, indicating his ability to follow these debates. By 1821, when Channing gave his definitions of natural and revealed religion in the Dudleian lecture at Harvard, young Emerson praised him for showing the highest form of "moral imagination."[39] But sectarian distinctions never deeply mattered to him. Less than a decade later, he quoted Augustine, "'Let others wrangle, I will wonder,'" adding, "It shall be my speech to the Calvinist & the Unitarian." Such independence, built from his deep curiosity, sense of wonder and Mary's model in childhood, also helped distance him from the 1819 divide in Congregationalism. That year Ralph adopted his middle name, "Waldo," and signed himself "R. Waldo Emerson," as Mary had addressed him nine years before.

Here was a new identity more interesting, and a voice more commanding, than the larger religious claims to authority that whirled about him.[40]

---

38 David Robinson, *The Unitarians and the Universalists* (Westport, CT: Greenwood Press, 1985), 4, 30; Cole, *MME*, 124-25; *Monthly Anthology* 2 (March 1805), 152 ff., 141; Sydney Ahlstrom, *A Religious History of the American People* (New Haven, CT: Yale University Press, 1972), 387, 393-96.

39 Robinson, *The Unitarians and the Universalists*, 30; *Letters of MME*, 445; *JMN* 2: 237.

40 *JMN* 3: 193; Allen, 47.

Yet his journal also reveals a young man whose maturity and self-confidence came only in fits and starts. Waldo's reserve persisted in his junior year. Rarely mentioning social occasions or fellow students in his journal, instead he drew heroic classical figures and male faces in profile as if they were imagined selves or ideal friends.

In fact, he was deep into puberty, what he later called "a passage from the sleep of the passions to their rage." Waldo's overt passion at seventeen took the form of longing for a true friend, guardedly confessed in his journal. "There is a strange face in the Freshman class whom I should like to know very much," he wrote in August, 1820. "He has a great deal of character in his features & should be a fast friend or a bitter enemy. His name is [Martin] Gay."

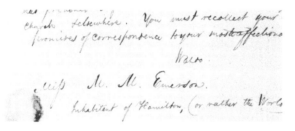

1.14 Early Emerson signature as "Waldo," 1821.

1.15 "Roman Phantasies of imagination and bad dreams," 1820, Emerson watercolor.

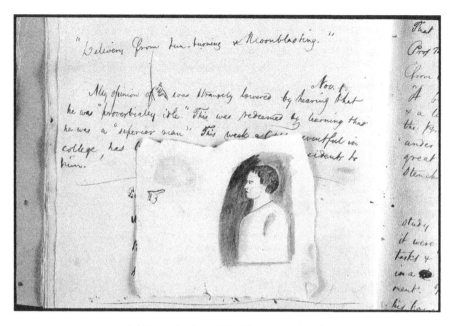

1.16 Martin Gay, 1820, Emerson sketch.

For months—often with the name left blank—he recorded exchanging glances with Gay. Gay's "cold blue eye" entered Waldo's thoughts a dozen times a day, leading him to speculate in verse about their different ambitions and destiny: "Perhaps thy lot in life is higher / Than the fates assign to me." This assumption reflected Waldo's insecurity about himself, registered in his simultaneous self-disparagement: "I find myself often idle, vagrant, hollow, and stupid." Such a lack of confidence evidently won out over his attraction to Gay, and the two never met. Despite chastising himself, Waldo still added to his self-profile, "I need excitement."[41]

Biographers differ in their interpretation of this apparently homoerotic declaration of love. Perhaps it was only the momentary crush of a teenage boy. Or perhaps his own awakening included acknowledgement of a homosexual inclination, otherwise kept silent amid his lifelong praise for the soul's bisexuality. Beyond dispute, however, was his unsuccessful struggle to bring admiration of Gay to any test for over two years, even after graduation from college. "Baby play" was Waldo's self-disparaging name for this unfulfilled flirtation. It was evidence of a profound inner

41   *JMN* 1: 22, 39, 40; 4: 348.

hesitation. Nearing nineteen, in mock address to a higher-ranking self, he described his heart as "[a] blank, my lord." "I have not the kind affections of a pigeon. Ungenerous and selfish, cautious & cold, I yet wish to be romantic." Waldo felt compelled to probe such an important matter to its emotional core. Even when his attraction to Gay was waning in 1822, he nevertheless found this "curious incident in the history of so cold a being . . . well worth a second thought." The explanation now seemed obvious to him: "From the first, I preferred to preserve the terms which kept alive so much sentiment rather than a more familiar intercourse which I feared would end in indifference."[42]

1.17 "Unfruitful land" of "Loggle," 1820, Emerson watercolor.

Expectation, for the vulnerable Waldo, was infinitely better than rejection. From now on, with a few notable exceptions, Emerson would shield his deepest feelings within a cold exterior. For this, he would regularly berate himself. Emotionally, he would remain timid and defensive and for a lifetime be reserved. This pronounced psychological trait was one reason, among others, for his slow pace in entering the social and political fray of

42 For differing interpretations of the incident, see Allen, 53-54, and Caleb Crain, *American Sympathy: Men, Friendship, and Literature in the New Nation* (New Haven, CT: Yale University Press, 2001), ch. 4. *JMN* 1: 54, 134; 2: 59.

coming decades. But intellectually, he was steadily building in confidence and self-assurance.

Becoming a True Philosopher

Waldo's intellectual courage took wing in his last two years at Harvard. Unremarkable before as a scholar, he began a new era in his junior year, by both using and ignoring Harvard's official course of study. He had hated and nearly failed mathematics, found no mentor comparable to Boston Latin's Gould, and performed without distinction in classrooms stressing recitation and rote learning. Increasingly, however, courses in philosophy confirmed the inward power that he had sought and Mary had encouraged. Until junior year, under Professor Levi Hedge, students had progressed from only logic to the seventeenth-century philosophy of John Locke, who saw knowledge as a system of ideas constructed from sense impressions of the outer world. But then Waldo's class began reading the newer views of the Scottish Common Sense School, especially Dugald Stewart, who affirmed a more intuitive morality and reasoning power in the mind itself. For Stewart, uniting sensory experience and prior mental power provided a new—indeed commonsensical—grounding in the world. By senior year, now under professor Levi Frisbie, Waldo took yet another step toward future beliefs by reading the English moral philosopher Richard Price. Mary had long sworn by Price and now quoted to the college senior lines that he was also hearing in class: "*Right* and *wrong* have had claims prior to all rites—immutable & eternal in their nature."[43] Moral principles did not simply arise from variable human experience but were written into the universe, directly empowering the mind. Such ethical thinking would become the backbone of Emerson's later reform work.

Not only was the young man maturing; times were also swiftly changing during his college years. In 1820, as Emerson later recalled, a "Movement" started to replace the "Establishment" at Harvard, exposing him to new ways of thinking that he made his own for life. While Frisbie instructed the students in philosophy, two young professors—Edward Everett in Greek and George Ticknor in French—introduced Germany's revolutionary

---

43   Rusk, *Life of Ralph Waldo Emerson*, 75-77, 79; Allen, 54-55; Ahlstrom, *A Religious History of the American People*, 355-56. Mary's dictum, *Letters of MME*, 139; identified as a quotation from Price and evidence of her continuing interest in him, Cole, *MME*, 167 (cf. 11, 124-25).

"higher criticism" from their recent studies abroad. They also honored students by lecturing at an adult level in the style of European professors. In response, Emerson recalled, he and his classmates developed critical "knives in their brain." This new scholarly method required examining literary texts, especially the Bible, through the lenses of historical context, multiple authorship, and linguistic study. Everett and Ticknor questioned traditional ideas, especially dogmatic, authoritative statements. Such a perspective also stimulated the imagination, and it was bound to appeal to Waldo's curiosity and creativity. His journal and college theme books began recording responses to lectures and elaborate notes for Harvard's prize essay contests, toward which Waldo was encouraged by lessons in rhetoric by another new professor, Edward Tyrell Channing, a brother of William Ellery Channing.[44]

Everett, Ticknor, and Channing were all commanding lecturers. As Waldo's friend William Furness recalled, "Rhetoric was all the rage in college . . . A finely turned sentence, a happy figure of speech, threw us into a spasm of enthusiasm. Edward Everett was a master in that line." Waldo, whose verbal "flash" was his forte, chiefly admired Everett at first, but then increasingly adopted Channing's new simplicity of style. Now was the moment when he might unite his formal education with informal reading "under the bench" and produce new writing of his own at home. The journal—his greatest feat of composition to date as well as a ready store of ideas for college essay contests—was begun not at Harvard but in his mother's parlor during a vacation. Mary was sitting nearby, doubtless the "witch . . . in the chamber" that his first pages invoked for aid.[45]

Referring to his pious aunt as a "witch" was no insult. Rather, Waldo was crediting her with supernatural gifts and alluding to their now serious, now light conversation about romantic poetry and the power of the imagination. Mary's self-education framed and gave meaning to his new learning at Harvard. In fact, for Waldo, she was not only "witch" but all-in-one "muse," "oracle," "Cassandra," and "weird woman," each title revealing nuances of her power to foretell his destiny and inspire him toward it. By 1821, transcribing her letters into his "Wide World" journals and college theme books, he attributed them primarily to "Tnamurya." The

44   W 10: 326, 329; Allen, 49-51.
45   Furness, "Random Reminiscences of Emerson," in *Emerson in His Own Time*, eds. Ronald A. Bosco and Joel Myerson (Iowa City, IA: University of Iowa Press, 2003), 186; McAleer, 55; *JMN* 1: 4. For the family group in Boston, see *L* 1: 89-91.

name, suggesting a figure of Eastern mystery, was Waldo's anagram for "Aunt Mary," perhaps to disguise her influence even from himself.

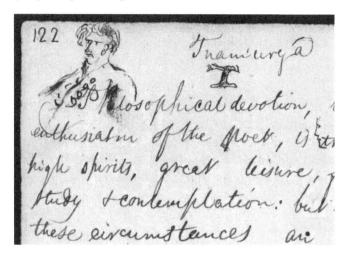

1.18 "Tnamurya," Emerson's anagram for "Aunt Mary," 1821.

"Tnamurya" not only encouraged him to become a "son of poetry" but also suggested how to begin. "If I were a Poet this night would inspire me," Mary wrote, then sketched out what she would describe. Or she urged his imagination to fly to her secluded mountain home in Maine, where "you might ... hear the songs of the grove echoed by the little Tritons of Neptune ... [or] people a sylvan scene with nymphs or fairies." As such fancies grew ridiculous, she shifted to higher purpose, urging withdrawal into nature and discovery of God's greatness through it.[46] Years ago, brother William had resisted such advice. Now her young protégé not only listened to, but also recorded, her wryly humorous and exalted words alongside his own.

In copying "Tnamurya's" letters, Waldo was immersing himself in ideas that explored a new philosophy. As a senior, writing on "The Present State of Ethical Philosophy" for the Bowdoin Prize, he asked Mary questions about both pre-Christian natural religion and the history of philosophical ideas. In dense, only partially decipherable responses, she laid claim to both idealism and a romantic theory of correspondence between soul and universe, quoting Richard Price and Mme. de Staël.

---

46   *JMN* 1: 333-34.

Fearing the contemporary love of "sensation rather than sentiment," she also urged Waldo toward a celestial poetry based on Plato and Plotinus, then ended her letter with the Hindu "Hymn to Narayena": "My soul absorbed one only Being knows / Of all perceptions one abundant source." She cited her beloved poets Milton, Byron, and Wordsworth as examples, defending solitude as the best way to resist mediocrity, "to form the eagle wings wh[ich] will bear one farther than suns and stars."[47] "Tnamurya's" words ranked so highly with Waldo that he included them in his journal's table of contents, at hand early and late, to draw upon for inspiration and re-quotation. He echoed the lines from Price and Staël in his senior Bowdoin essay, and those on solitude as late as *The Conduct of Life* (1860) .[48]

Mary, a devout force for "ancestral religion" in Waldo's life, also paradoxically opened the way for his heresies. Throughout his career he consistently and publicly acknowledged her first role, but her second, only privately. Two years after graduating from Harvard, Waldo described his aunt to a classmate as "an idolater of Nature," anxious to have him share her sublime landscape "as the temple where God & the Mind are to be studied & adored & where the fiery soul can begin a premature communication with other worlds." This devout idolatry pervaded Mary's letters and journals and foreshadowed themes that Waldo would develop thirteen years later in *Nature*. Also in 1823, he wrote her with an early concern about slavery, posing the "curious question" of why slaves suffered in a moral universe. She responded that the "tormentors" of slaves presented an even greater enigma, perhaps an "evil in the nature of things," echoing her Calvinist upbringing with its emphasis on original sin. This exchange, implying earlier conversations on such subjects as well, is the first surviving sign in Waldo of later abolitionist convictions, passionately shared with his aunt. Their Price-based affirmation of right and wrong as "immutable" universal principles demanded such justice. In 1836, as the antislavery cause was mounting in Massachusetts and among Concord women, Mary wrote to Waldo's wife Lidian, knowing that her abolitionist conversion would continue to influence him: "[T]hink that the revolutions of only half a century concentrate the great idea of man's greatness *as a man* . . . . [M]an

---

47   *JMN* 1: 334-35, 153-54; 2: 373-76; 2: 380-81 (cf. *Letters of MME*, 139-41, 143-44, 155-57, 182).

48   *JMN* 1: 251; Kenneth Cameron, *Transcendental Climate* (Hartford: Transcendental Books, 1963), 1: 12; W 6: 155-56; Cole, *MME*, 9-10, 164-70.

shall not thrive on the miseries of his brother!"[49] Waldo's internal drive to act would grow through more than a dozen years of family conversation.

In politics as in metaphysics, dialogue with Mary Moody Emerson enabled the emergence of Ralph Waldo Emerson's revolutionary views. After his star began to rise, he was asked what difference it would have made if Aunt Mary had not influenced his education. He answered, "Ah, that would have been a loss! I could better have spared Greece and Rome." On another occasion, he added, "I have no hour of poetry or philosophy, since I knew these things, into which she does not enter as a genius." He valued this obscure woman equally with the nation's famous men, but expressed such feelings only to his journal. In 1868, commenting on remarks made by his friend, the Boston critic Charles Eliot Norton, he asked, "What could Norton mean in saying that the only great men of the American past were Franklin & Edwards? We have had Adams & Channing, Washington, & the prophetic authors of the Federalist, Madison & Hamilton, and if he had known it, Aunt Mary."[50]

Around his quotation of Mary's ideas lay the "variety shop" of Waldo's journal. Turbulent with adolescent trials, it revealed an independent center of creativity, a theater for all his private musings, hopes, and literary experiments. Seemingly with an eye to a future biographer, he observed, "Thirty or forty years hence, if I should live so long, this book will serve as a nucleus for the association of ideas and may recall very vividly all the interest which attached to the projects and fancies of a young writer."[51] He lamented that his college studies, "however unsuccessful," kept him from plunging into the lore of chivalry and magic as he wished, except for the occasional watercolor of a Romantic landscape on one page and an assortment of towers, orbs, and unicorns on another. He would also jot down a song exhorting fellow students to empty their wine glasses, since "the tutors are near and the daylight's past," or compose a poem about

---

49 *Letters of RWE* 1: 137; *Letters of MME*, 176-77. On the longer development of Mary Moody Emerson's antislavery allegiance, first hinted at in 1805, see Cole, *MME*, 221; ibid., 237.

50 *Letters of RWE* 1: 133; Sanborn, *Transcendental and Literary New England*, 342-43; Cabot, *Memoir of Ralph Waldo Emerson*, 1: 30; *JMN* 16: 90. In 1869, Emerson did pay public tribute to his aunt in a lecture to the New England Women's Club, published as "Mary Moody Emerson" in the *Atlantic Monthly* 52 (1883): 733-45; in *W* 10: 397-433, he claimed she was a "representative life" of her age (399), leaving to his journal entries his much bolder historical and personal references to her.

51 *JMN* 1: 47, 184.

a hog which "drank swill from Pleasure's brimming cup / And grunted grunts of ecstasy."[52]

But Waldo's intellectual seriousness, increasing as he turned eighteen, was evident side by side with whimsy in his journal. Poems might appear with drafts of essays for college prizes. Here he quoted widely from Byron, Scott, Shakespeare, and dozens of other authors from his independent reading list. Two moral philosophers, French essayist Michel de Montaigne and the English writer-statesman Francis Bacon, father of the scientific method, especially won his respect. Three years later, Waldo would single out their essays, along with Alexander Pope's poetry, as models of the collected "wisdom of their times" that he hoped to emulate.[53] Such a framework of French and English realism, along with Mary's idealism, became part of his thinking for a lifetime.

Now two of his own attempts—his junior-year essay "Socrates" and senior-year "Dissertation on the Present State of Ethical Philosophy," both winners of second prizes in the Bowdoin competitions of 1820 and 1821—were pregnant with his developing core beliefs. At this early date, Waldo's ethical study affirmed a theme repeated in his future work: that philosophers from Plato to Bacon had shown the mind's ability to penetrate the universe and create a "SCIENCE of morality." Meanwhile, his fictional romances also hinted at lofty ambitions and explored the mysteries of inspiration, often in terms of a young man's relationship with an older woman. "The Magician" imagined a young hero encountering a witchlike woman of the forest. Another described how the prophetic mother of a fantasized New England founder, Foxcroft by name, instructed him to lay the foundation of nothing less than America's empire.[54]

Two poems Waldo wrote as a senior show his nationalistic pride and imaginative range as he moved thoughts from the private space of his journal to public performance. For the first, "Indian Superstition," he studied Robert Southey's "Curse of Kehama" among other works, noting to himself that "enlightened morality was taught in India" in the pre-Christian era of Manu, a semi-legendary Hindu lawgiver. A glimpse of both future reform and international interests lay in this comment. But his finished poem, read at the College Exhibition in April 1821, found no wisdom in Eastern religion. Rather, it conventionally faulted India's present

52 *JMN* 1: 10-11; 28; 1: 20 No. 35; 246-47; 274-75.
53 *JMN* 1: 395-99; 2: 265.
54 Rusk, *Life of Ralph Waldo Emerson*, 78, 80-83. *JMN* 1: 332-33; 1: 266-68; 337-39.

"thralldom" to superstition and expressed relief that "No Indra thunders in Columbian sky."[55] The poem's major interest was to point to the triumphal progress of culture through its migration westward to America.

A similar vision of greatness for America underlay his "Valedictory Poem," delivered as Class Day poet in July. This poem's deep personal and intellectual investment contrasted with his poem about India and made these lines his most resonant of any from his college years. Here Waldo mythologized his classmates as he likened their hopes to the "rapture" of young Columbus on first beholding the new world. His class of 1821 might achieve greatness by also listening, as did the Italian explorer, to the "oracles of Fate." He saw divine blessings falling on his generation as they had on Columbus and his men: "Earth, air, and heaven, which smiled benignant then / On those far travelers from the haunts of men, / With equal luster now look calmly on / This youthful band,—this goal which they have won; / Perhaps bear with them, in their counsels high, / The near fulfilment of old prophecy; / And we, perchance, may claim with joy to be/ The Ministers of Fate, the priests of Destiny." Consciously or not, Waldo was grandly projecting his own hopes to rank among America's "Ministers of Fate" and "priests of Destiny." Along with such lofty prophecies, however, his irrepressible humor emerged as the poem also recalled the ability of his class "to cheer, and to rebel" in the famous sophomore food fight.[56]

Yet Waldo did not cover himself with glory at Harvard, socially or intellectually. He stood dead center of his graduating class, thirtieth out of fifty-nine students in academic rank. He had been asked to be Class Day poet only after seven other seniors declined. Worse, the poem on which he had worked so hard apparently met with little enthusiasm. After its performance, he had to settle for a disappointing "conference part" at Commencement—a "stupid thing," as he wrote Sarah Bradford Ripley, all the more since the event was a popular state holiday, bringing crowds to the college. Affluent classmates like Josiah Quincy, whose father would be mayor of Boston and president of Harvard, celebrated with extended families at grand dinners and parties. But Waldo had only a small circle of his mother, his aunts Mary and Sarah, and brothers to meet him for the

55 *JMN* 1: 340; Cameron, "Young Emerson's Orientalism at Harvard," in *Indian Superstition* (Hanover, N.H: Friends of the Dartmouth Library, 1954), 13-14; von Frank, "Emerson's Boyhood and Collegiate Verse," 46-47.
56 Von Frank, "Emerson's Boyhood and Collegiate Verse," 49, 50, 56.

ceremony, with no festive dinner afterward. Apart from the question of academic honors, there was no money for grandeur.[57]

Leaving Cambridge in 1821, Emerson lacked self-trust and sure prospects, but his well-furnished imagination, grounding in academic learning, and maturing self-estimation offered a broad platform from which his revolutionary words would develop. Not until the early 1830s did he look back at Harvard and realize that, like Columbus heading toward America, he had been right to follow his own lead. "I was the true philosopher in college," he wrote, "and Mr. Farrar and Mr. Hedge and Dr. Ware the false, yet what seemed then to me less probable?"[58] The insight that these words expressed would be hard won over the next dozen years. Through such thoughts, however, Waldo would emerge a stronger prophet and prophet-in-action than anyone, except Aunt Mary, might have predicted.

57   Ibid., 55; E. W. Emerson, *Emerson in Concord*, 27; L 1: 101; McAleer, 61-64.
58   *JMN* 4: 293.

1.2 Becoming an American "Adam," 1822-1835

Wesley T. Mott

I have sometimes thought that in order to be a good minister it was necessary to leave the ministry. The profession is antiquated. In an altered age, we worship in the dead forms of our forefathers. Were not a Socratic paganism better than an effete superannuated Christianity?

Emerson, *Journal*, 2 June 1832

Emerson, still an uncertain eighteen-year-old when he graduated from Harvard College in 1821, in the next decade and a half would discover his purpose, his calling and his identity as a more clearly defined American. That sharper self-image, combined with his nascent Transcendentalist ideas, would define the pivotal reform role he would soon play in the country's mid-century era of enormous social change. The United States, only forty years old in 1821, was also in its adolescence, still forming its cultural and political identity at home and abroad. Both the country and Emerson shared high hopes and ambitions. Just the year before, the Missouri Compromise had attempted to settle sectional frictions arising from slavery, and the Monroe Doctrine in 1823 would soon announce the American hemisphere inviolate to further foreign claim. Many Americans, including Emerson, saw the hand of Providence at work when two great former presidents and earlier arch-rivals, Thomas Jefferson and John Adams—a sometime parishioner of Emerson's father whom Emerson also knew—both died on

http://dx.doi.org/10.11647/OBP.0065.02

July 4, 1826, exactly fifty years after they had signed the Declaration of Independence.[59]

Not that the event sealed a cultural unity between the states or even a sense of true nationhood. Only two years later, the election of Andrew Jackson ushered in momentous changes. Jackson, hero of the Battle of New Orleans, became the country's first president from the West, and also the first whose electors were chosen by popular vote, except in Delaware and South Carolina.[60] Democracy seemed to be in the ascendant. But political professionals—the boss system—increasingly manipulated these new voters. Jackson's two terms also saw increasing sectionalism in disputes over protective tariffs and arguments over the nature of the Union. However, the nation could hardly be totally self-occupied. European labor unrest, trade demands, and the international spread of epidemics such as cholera proved that the young United States could not insulate itself from the world simply by political proclamation.[61] More importantly, the Old World remained a cultural beacon. Romantic writers from Britain and the Continent deeply appealed to Americans, and exciting textual, cultural, even scientific study of texts, especially the Bible, in Germany drew bright graduate students in the arts and theology.

Yet a homegrown New World culture was taking shape, building on, even as it transformed, its colonial and Puritan past. The number of literate post-Revolutionary Americans was increasing, a product of both new public and private schools: Education reformer Bronson Alcott opened his experiment in childhood pedagogy in 1834, called the Temple School, located in Boston's Masonic Temple. The Second Great Awakening's evangelical churches and more liberal Christian denominations were also stimulating literacy, hoping to gain more educated followers. In Boston, the Unitarian Universalist Association was organized in 1825, and its great

---

59   When visiting Boston from his home in Quincy, John Adams occasionally worshipped at William Emerson's First Church. His son, John Quincy Adams, was a member of the church. Gay Wilson Allen, *Waldo Emerson: A Biography* (New York: Viking Press, 1981), 6-7. Waldo and his brother Edward visited Adams in Quincy in February 1825 to congratulate him on the election of John Quincy to the presidency. *The Journals and Miscellaneous Notebooks of Ralph Waldo Emerson*, 16 vols., eds. William H. Gilman, Ralph H. Orth, et al. (Cambridge, Mass.: Harvard University Press, 1960-1982), 3: 29, 35. Hereafter *JMN*.

60   Robert V. Remini, *Andrew Jackson*, vol. 2, *The Course of American Freedom, 1822-1832* (New York: Harper & Row, 1982), 145-47.

61   *The Complete Sermons of Ralph Waldo Emerson*, 4 vols., eds. Albert J. von Frank, et al. (Columbia, MO: University of Missouri Press, 1989-1992), 4: 42, notes 1-3. Hereafter *CS*.

pastor-theologian William Ellery Channing was preaching the liberating doctrine of "Likeness to God," a theme destined to be more popular in this new Garden of Eden than Adam's fall. The highly popular lyceum movement of public lectures—the forerunner of adult education—began at Millbury, Massachusetts, in 1826. Codifying an emerging national vocabulary was Noah Webster's *American Dictionary of the English Language* (1828).

Material changes in the country quickly developed along with ongoing social friction. The burgeoning population had been rapidly pushing westward. The Erie Canal's completion in 1825, giving inland access East and West, brought new wealth to the country, and epitomized both efficient transportation and regional cohesion. But this expansion included the forced relocation of Native Americans from historic tribal lands to lesser territories. North-South economic and racial tensions, moreover, had already begun to erupt. Nat Turner's unsuccessful slave rebellion in 1831 seized the attention of Americans everywhere. Only months before, abolitionist sentiment had started to take tangible shape: William Lloyd Garrison first published the *Liberator* in Boston in January 1831. Then exactly a year later, he founded the New England Anti-Slavery Society, and in 1833, he led in organizing the American Anti-Slavery Society in Philadelphia.[62] Channing published his powerful, theologically grounded *Slavery* (1835), and in the South, parallel movements started, especially among members of the Society of Friends, or Quakers. Closely observing the witness of certain Quaker leaders in New England, who were often protesters, Emerson was affected by their theology in action. He would be immediately touched by all these developments.

Seeking the Right Career to Suit His Temperament and Talents

As the United States aggressively expanded geographically and commercially, politicians and entrepreneurs often sounded a note of supreme confidence in the nation's prospects. Emerson was caught up in this same "can do"—or in 1830s terminology, "go-ahead"—spirit. But beneath the country's outward bravado, he also noted a moral crisis. As a

---

62 *Courage and Conscience: Black & White Abolitionists in Boston,* ed. Donald M. Jacobs (Bloomington, IN: Indiana University Press, 1993), 10, 17, 30, 80.

Christian steeped in classical Stoicism at home and school, Emerson's sense of the centrality of ethics in personal or public life had developed early and been sealed at Harvard. This felt philosophical position might have been at odds with the materialistic spirit of the times. Yet his ambition—a continuous theme in his journals of the 1820s—combined with his aunt Mary Moody Emerson's high hopes that he might become a great poet-prophet, gave him two linked imperatives: He must achieve both artistic and spiritual prominence as well as embody the good. This imperative to action soon forced him, though reluctantly at first, to enter America's array of social reform.

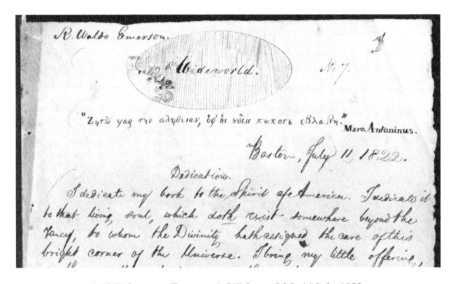

1.19 Title page, Emerson's Wideworld 2, 11 July 1822.

Alongside these lofty goals, however, arose familiar self-doubts that now fed his vocational uncertainty. Like most young adults, he focused on fundamentally unanswerable questions about the purpose and meaning of life, sounding now self-indulgent, now on the verge of despair. Throughout the 1820s, his journals are filled with musings about available life choices and his sometime worry that, were he to die at this age, the world would never remember that he had lived. In an impermanent, insecure world, he wondered what avenues might be open to a young man of his interests whose reserved temperament seemed to conflict with family and social expectations.

After Harvard, Waldo began teaching school, a route that his father had taken before settling on the ministry. Older brother William's school for girls in Boston was a natural place to begin, but Waldo soon became frustrated. In a letter profiling his life to a college classmate in early 1823, he wrote with wry self-effacement, "My sole answer & apology to those who inquire about my studies is—I keep school. —I study neither law, medicine, or divinity, and write neither poetry nor prose."[63] He went on to discuss academic studies, literature, and theology, revealing how deeply he missed the life of the mind. Then in December, William, preparing for the ministry, left for Germany to study "higher criticism" at the University of Göttingen. This emerging field of textual studies examined the Bible not as the inspired Word of God but as a cultural artifact whose meanings emerged in the contexts of history, literature, and anthropology. The religiously orthodox recoiled from such study, deeming it heretical. But the brightest young American divinity students welcomed the exciting scrutiny of scriptural texts for a spiritual reason: it was the soundest means of answering skeptical critiques of religion. Emerson, already familiar with this approach at Harvard and fascinated by William's first-hand reports, increasingly felt that he was wasting his time and talents.

For all his curiosity and avid reading, Emerson knew how to pace himself. Perhaps from early childhood, when his father expected him to read before he was even three, he had begun to develop a strategy of self-defense. If too much were asked of him, he would not do it, relieving himself of the demand. At Boston Public Latin School, Waldo did not earn the same high grades later achieved by his younger brothers Edward and Charles. And as we have seen, Waldo's Harvard record, though he had been a runner-up for essay and public speaking prizes, put him only in the middle of his class. In contrast, his brothers would both be first in theirs. No less able than they, Waldo read widely outside the required curriculum, a habit that meant he might put assignments second. It also reflected his independent streak. Following his own bent was evidently more important than achieving the highest class standing.

Besides, Waldo grew to be conscious of the benefit of relief from rigorous work. In July 1828, after Edward—overly assiduous in his high ambitions—had a temporary break-down, Waldo thought himself unlikely to follow suit: "I have so much mixture of *silliness* in my intellectual frame that I

---

63   *The Letters of Ralph Waldo Emerson*, 10 vols., eds. Ralph L. Rusk and Eleanor M. Tilton (New York: Columbia University Press, 1939, 1990-1995), 1: 127. Hereafter *L.*

think Providence has tempered me against this . . . Edward had always great power of face. I have none. I laugh; I blush; I look ill tempered; against my will & against my interest. But all this imperfection as it appears to me . . . is a ballast—as things go—is a defence."[64] In short, not measuring up to others' high standards, and openly showing it, protected him against trying to meet the world's demands, whether of his father long ago, his aunt Mary, his college, the institutional church, or eventually of society's unexamined dictums. In 1838, Emerson repeated the human need for diversion from daily work: "A man must have aunts & cousins, must buy carrots & turnips, must have barn & woodshed, must go to market & to the blacksmith's shop, must saunter & sleep & be inferior & silly."[65] Edward, and possibly Charles, under equal pressure to achieve, apparently did not find Waldo's path toward self-saving release.

Silliness aside, however, Emerson, approaching twenty-one, knew he needed to make a career choice. By mid-April 1824, he was finally able to lay out his plans and the reasoning behind them. Through independent reading, he would begin his "professional studies" for the ministry: "I deliberately dedicate my time, my talents, & my hopes to the Church." Waldo also knew that his lack of a competitive spirit kept him from careers in business, law, or medicine. "But in Divinity," he wrote, "I hope to thrive." Seven generations of his ancestors had been ministers, and Emerson felt a "passionate love for the strains of eloquence" that he attributed to traits inherited from his father and grandfather. He put it powerfully, "I burn after the 'aliquid immensum infinitumque' [something great and limitless] which Cicero desired." He specifically noted, "My understanding venerates & my heart loves that Cause which is dear to God & man—the laws of Morals, the Revelations which sanction, & the blood of martyrs & triumphant suffering of the saints which seal them." Still, painful self-consciousness plagued him. He felt timid and clumsy, and as so often before, he berated himself at his core: "What is called a warm heart, I have not."[66]

Despite the probable mismatch between pastoral duties and his distant, socially awkward personality, other aspects of the Unitarian pulpit enticed Emerson. Ever since the religious liberal Henry Ware, Sr. had been named Hollis Professor of Divinity at Harvard in 1805, New England

---

64   *JMN* 3: 137.
65   *JMN* 7: 6.
66   *JMN* 2: 237-41.

ministers had begun to subordinate scriptural and doctrinal exposition in favor of enhancing their own and their parishioners' "self-culture." An accomplished "liberal Christian" minister was expected to have broad cultural interests—to pursue scholarship and also to serve local institutions. Many prided themselves on their literary attainments; the Reverend Joseph Stevens Buckminster, known for his elegant sermons, was asked to preach the funeral sermon for Waldo's father in 1811. This new model of ministry appealed to Emerson. He might continue to explore his wide intellectual interests while aiming for uplifting literary performance.

William Ellery Channing, pastor of Federal Street Church, excelled all other Boston ministers as a model of the new preaching.

1.20 William Ellery Channing, 1857.

Emerson, hearing his sermon on revelation in October 1823, had admiringly noted his clear language and ability to convey "the pictures in his mind to the minds of his hearers." But he thought Channing's most valuable service was to properly relate nature and divine power. Creation might offer evidence of its creator, but the material world alone was unable "to kindle our piety & urge our faith." Though not ready to define nature as miraculous, Channing declared the experience of revelation, of sensing the presence of God, a natural happening. As Waldo carefully recorded, "Dr C. regarded Revelation as much a part of the order of things as any other event."[67]

---

67   *JMN* 2: 161.

Eloquence in the pulpit and on the public lecture platform loomed large in Emerson's imagination as a means to enhance his ambitions for influence, fame, and power. Political rhetoric had been crucial in defining the principles of the new nation, and in the 1820s lengthy speeches on commemorative occasions had become benchmarks of oratorical greatness. Inspired at Harvard by his classics professor Edward Everett, Emerson continued to admire the heroic content and impressive style of his public addresses on historical topics. Daniel Webster, elected to Congress in 1822, held Emerson spellbound with his eulogy to John Adams and Thomas Jefferson in early August 1826. "Never," Emerson wrote, "were the awful charms of person, manners, & voice outdone . . . . [I]n what was truly grand he fully realized the boldest conception of eloquence."[68] Though no politician and without ambition to become one, Emerson had done well in public speaking. The ministry not only suited his temperament and talents, it also allowed him to make widely known his ethical and moral concerns, with observations from a wide range of other fields.

Four years after graduating from Harvard College, in February 1825, Emerson entered its Divinity School as a middle student.

DIVINITY HALL, ERECTED IN 1826.

1.21 Divinity School, Harvard, 1840.

On and off since 1818, Emerson had continued to teach, including at his brother William's School for Young Ladies in Boston, which Waldo closed in late 1824 while William was studying in Germany; at a short-lived school that he himself opened in Chelmsford in September 1825; and for a time, at

---

68 *JMN* 3: 29.

his brother Edward's school in Roxbury. Emerson's habit of reading what he pleased continued: "My cardinal vice of intellectual dissipation—sinful strolling from book to book, from care to idleness, is my cardinal vice still; is a malady that belongs to the Chapter of Incurables."[69] At the same time, however, he faced a series of serious health problems. An eye ailment, making it impossible to read, first forced him to withdraw from formal study. Then he suffered from a painful hip condition, followed by an "aching" in the chest brought on by "exertion."[70] His physical complaints were not merely psychosomatic. Recent scholarship has confirmed what Emerson privately suspected: he was suffering from tuberculosis (or "consumption" in his day), a rampant nineteenth-century disease that became his family's curse.[71] Longstanding needs of his mother and of his ailing, mentally-challenged brother Bulkeley also pressed upon him: "My years are passing away," he wrote in his journal in March 1826. "Infirmities are already stealing on me that may be the deadly enemies that are to dissolve me to dirt and little is yet done to establish my consideration among my contemporaries & less to get a memory when I am gone."[72]

Yet Emerson's recurring sense of unworthiness and mortality could be swept aside by stunning flashes of insight, breeding confidence in his latent power. Paradoxically, he sensed this power as something beyond him, rooted in the "immortality of moral truth." It was an ethical lodestone, attracting his whole being, not merely his thought. In true Romantic fashion, he had tapped into a living force that transcended him and others as well as time and place. At the same time, it connected him and every sensitive person to the great minds of history. For Emerson, moral truth had become no abstraction or "vague name," but a passion and a real principle of personal strength.[73] Buoyed by these reflections, in late May, he ecstatically declared, "I feel that the affections of the soul are sublimer than the faculties of the intellect. I *feel* immortal. And the evidence of immortality comes better from consciousness than from reason."[74] Such trust in intuition—in the heart rather than the head—and in the inherent worth of the individual

---

69   *JMN* 2: 332.

70   *L* 1: 184.

71   See Evelyn Barish, "The Moonless Night: Emerson's Crisis of Health, 1825-1827," in *Emerson Centenary Essays*, ed. Joel Myerson (Carbondale, IL: Southern Illinois University Press, 1982), 1-16; incorporated in her *Emerson: The Roots of Prophecy* (Princeton, NJ: Princeton University Press, 1989).

72   *JMN* 3: 15.

73   *JMN* 3: 21.

74   *JMN* 3: 25.

attuned to a universal morality lay behind Emerson's later emphasis on self-reliance, more fully celebrated in his lectures of the next ten to fifteen years.

Determining and Unsettling Influences

Throughout his twenties, Emerson's two conflicting sides—the ambitious and the self-judgmental—continued to blend from their complex origins in his childhood. They were heightened by his habit of eclectic reading and by his continuing reliance on Mary's ideas and her interpretations of classical and contemporary authors. Waldo's early practice of copying Mary's letters and diaries into his journals gave him a permanent source of her thoughts. They were on tap to use in early sermons, and later, in lectures and essays. Sometimes he might give Mary direct or indirect credit. But other times, he might simply neglect to indicate that her very words were not his own. Emerson always held that "originality" was a misnomer, arguing that a mind recognizes wisdom in the works of others and rightly appropriates it. However one judges Emerson's use of Mary's texts, his thought was the product not of isolated genius but of collaboration, as will be seen more fully in Chapter 2.[75]

By temperament and education, Emerson put character and integrity first, so not surprisingly, social worth was at the heart of his boyhood exploration of personal identity as well as his later philosophical debates. Such sensitivity naturally remained at the forefront of his late teenage attitude toward the nation's festering social issue, slavery. Even though the Missouri Compromise of 1820, equally dividing the country into free and slave states, had sought to put a lid on constant sectional tensions over this issue, for decades they simmered nationally and, for Emerson, personally. Just days before the Compromise passed, his friend John Quincy Adams, then the country's Secretary of State, presciently noted in his diary, "Slavery is the great and foul stain upon the North American Union . . . A dissolution, at least temporary, of the Union, as now constituted, would be certainly necessary . . . The Union might then be reorganized on the fundamental principle of emancipation."[76]

---

75   See Phyllis Cole, *Mary Moody Emerson and the Origins of Transcendentalism: A Family History* (New York: Oxford University Press, 1998), esp. chaps. 7 and 8.

76   John Quincy Adams, 24 February 1820, *The Diary of John Quincy Adams, 1794-1845*, ed. Allan Nevins (New York: Charles Scribner's Sons, 1951), 228-29.

Slavery especially pressed on Emerson, who found the practice abhorrent but who shared many of the racial biases held by even the most educated northerners. For example, he mused about whether the races were created with "different degrees of intellect," which seemed "an indication of the design of Providence that some should lead, and some should serve." In the early weeks of November 1822, nineteen-year-old Emerson launched a lengthy, private pro-and-con debate with himself about slavery. He questioned whether this apparently natural human arrangement "can ever be pushed to the extent of total possession, and that, without the will of the slave?" After first giving his best arguments "*in behalf* of slavery," as he put it, he went on "to knock down the hydra." For now, he concluded that human inequality eluded rational explanation. But he had no doubt that slavery was "the worst institution on earth," insisting that "No ingenious sophistry can ever reconcile the unperverted mind to the pardon of *Slavery*." Indeed, he found it stunningly inconsistent that one could hold both religious beliefs and slaves. "A creature who is bound by his hopes of salvation to imitate the benevolence of better beings, and to do all the kindness in his power, fastens manacles on his fellow with an ill grace."[77] Although he would continue to explore the capabilities of different races and of women for some time to come, in the next few years Emerson's disgust with slavery per se would become more intense, and more public.

Emerson's Idiosyncratic Uses of Romanticism

In a Romantic era, Emerson and his generation were impatient with all types of rationalism and ripe for accepting felt knowledge about nature and human potential. On his own and through Mary, he had long been attracted to leading British and European Romantic writers. William Wordsworth's poetry, such as *The Excursion* (1815), had already appealed to Emerson by its emotional engagement with nature and its use of common everyday language. Then in 1829, James Marsh, president of the University of Vermont, published an American edition of English poet and essayist Samuel Taylor Coleridge's *Aids to Reflection* (1825). Coleridge described an enormously influential new model of the mind itself: For him, all humanity possessed both "Understanding" and "Reason" (both capitalized). "Understanding"

---

77   *JMN* 2: 43, 49, 57, 58.

was a lower faculty that engaged with material experience, and "Reason" a higher faculty that might intuit divinity. (Contrary to the usual use of these terms, Coleridge gave "Reason" the ability to imagine and feel in contrast to the observing, logical faculties of "Understanding.")

Finally, for Emerson and many of his circle, a deeply influential, anonymous Romantic voice appeared between 1827 and 1831 in a series of articles in the *Edinburgh Review* and *Foreign Review*. It spoke powerful— to some, merely bombastic—moral criticism, decrying the materialism of the age and calling for individual and social reform. This author also introduced the liberating insights of several Kant-inspired German idealists and Romantics, including Schiller and Goethe, as well as the Paris-born Mme. de Staël. Not until October 1832 would Emerson identify this bold essayist as the Scottish philosopher-historian Thomas Carlyle. In his own reading, now also endorsed by Carlyle, Emerson was most affected by the great humanist Goethe, who espoused an engaging pantheism, but above all stressed the authority of the individual.[78] The other German writers Emerson found in Carlyle variously advanced a more organic concept of human nature and the universe. Their common, dominant metaphor for the mind—a growing plant—would resonate with many American reform movements that, in varying degrees, Emerson came to support. For Emerson, Romanticism's assertion that "feelings" take precedence over "[b]are reason, cold as cucumber" was supremely attractive to him, as he wrote to Mary.[79] She had long encouraged such thinking, also supported by one aspect of the Scottish School of Common Sense taught at Harvard with which Waldo could agree: that moral law might be intuited.

At Harvard, too, Emerson had found a friend of similar spirit, Sampson Reed, who was three years older. In 1821, Emerson heard Sampson give his master's address, "Oration on Genius," and five years later extolled Reed's little book *Observations on the Growth of the Mind* as "a revelation . . . . It is remarkable for the unity into which it has resolved the various powers, feelings & vocations of men, suggesting to the mind that harmony which it has always a propensity to seek of action & design in the order of Providence in the world."[80] Reed, elaborating on the neo-Platonic notion of nature's correspondence with spirit, argued that God was not a distant

---

78   See Gustaaf Van Cromphout, *Emerson's Modernity and the Example of Goethe* (Columbia, MO: University of Missouri Press, 1990).

79   *L* 1: 174.

80   *JMN* 3: 45.

creator but an immediate presence that unifies and sustains perception and consciousness. "The mind must grow," Reed wrote, "not from external accretion, but from an internal principle."[81]

Reed also introduced Emerson to Emanuel Swedenborg, the eighteenth-century Swedish engineer turned religious mystic. Swedenborg had been the source of Reed's views of the physical world as a symbol of the spiritual—the nature-spirit interconnection that so appealed to Emerson. In turn, Reed's many articles for the Swedenborgian *New Jerusalem Magazine*, published in Boston from 1827, were additional sources from which Emerson came to know Swedenborg's views. As in all of his reading, however, Emerson took what he needed and discarded the rest. And he eventually came to regard Swedenborg, despite his reputation for mysticism, as too literal and mechanical in his interpretation of symbols. He began to think that the small Swedenborgian New Jerusalem Church in Boston was similarly reducing metaphor to doctrine, a process that he thought simply converted—and corrupted—insight into new theological dogma. No sect, Emerson later preached in 1831, had an exclusive claim to truth; no doctrine was "truth itself, but only as proceeding from truth."[82] This sort of critical thinking would underlie his steady questioning not only of theology and philosophy but of all institutional and social assumptions.

Six Years of Pastoring

Emerson's bouts with ill health during his time at Harvard Divinity School meant that he never formally graduated. But on October 10, 1826, his combined class work and independent theological study qualified him to be officially licensed, or "approbated," to preach. First, however, he followed a prescribed remedy for recovering from tuberculosis: prolonged exposure to sea air and sunshine. With funds from his Uncle Samuel Ripley, Emerson sailed south in late November. The distance and solitude of this first long trip away from his native New England proved creatively unsettling. True to form, personal and professional questions constantly preyed upon him, but in searching for answers, his sense of self and an idiosyncratic Romantic faith were taking shape. In Charleston, South Carolina, in early January, he

---

81 "Observations on the Growth of the Mind," *Sampson Reed: Primary Source Material for Emerson Studies*, compiler George F. Dole (New York: Swedenborg Foundation, 1992), 28.

82 Sermon CXI, *CS* 3: 127.

pondered the nature of Jesus in journal notes that would become the seeds of a later sermon. Humanity's "moral depravity" mocked the crucified Christ; nevertheless, Emerson felt that one may "enter into a sublime sympathy with him."[83] Emerson still felt his own inadequacy as a "moral agent," noting that a life of virtuous purpose seemed to be slipping away, and he frankly questioned his ability as a "young pilot" to guide others through the "shoals" of life.[84] Also unsettling was his ironic experience of participating in a Bible Society meeting in St. Augustine, Florida, while just outside the window he heard the shouts of a slave auctioneer. Emerson noted: "One ear . . . heard the glad tidings of great joy whilst the other was regaled with 'Going gentlemen, Going!'"[85] This cultural disconnection of morality from the market trading of blacks clearly remained alive in his consciousness before he publicly joined his ethical concerns with the cause of emancipation.

Despite these doubts about himself and his role in the church, Emerson's first exposure to Southern culture helped strengthen his self-confidence. At home, he wondered whether he could meet leadership challenges. In strange locales, thrown upon his own resources, he found it cathartic to meet others quite different from himself. On the first leg of his return voyage in late March, Emerson traveled with Achille Murat—a nephew of Napoleon, "a consistent Atheist," a man who owned a plantation outside Tallahassee and thus an experienced slaveholder.[86]

1.22 Achille Murat (1801-1847).

83   *JMN* 3: 63-64.
84   *JMN* 3: 72.
85   *JMN* 3: 117.
86   *JMN* 3: 77. On Emerson and Murat, see also Robert D. Richardson Jr., *Emerson: The Mind on Fire* (Berkeley, CA: University of California Press, 1995), 74-77, 225.

Despite heavy weather during the trip, the unlikely friends challenged each other in long conversations. Murat, the non-believer, responded to Emerson's ideas of liberal religion; and Emerson, hardly the intimidated provincial, gained confidence as he held his own and also quizzically admired this sophisticated companion who, shunning any faith, was yet evidently an ethical man, although he owned slaves.

In a famous phrase in "Self-Reliance" fourteen years later, he would call traveling "a fool's paradise."[87] But this trip was arguably life-saving; it improved his health, exposed him to a new world of believers and non-believers beyond Boston, and began to free him from certain self-doubts. Preaching at St. Augustine, Charleston, Washington, Philadelphia, and New York, he returned home with a stronger self-estimate, theological conviction, and renewed vocational purpose. Borrowing imagery from the psychological and maritime turbulence he had recently undergone, he now told his journal, "When the Sea was stormy the disciples awoke Christ. Let us do so. —"[88]

The Jesus awakening within Emerson, however, was not the conventional Christ, a mere mediator between God and humanity. This was clear when, once back in Boston and starting his career as a supply minister—substitutes for pastors on the odd Sunday—he gave a sermon in late June 1827 based on the Pauline text, "We preach Christ crucified" (1 Corinthians 1:23). Omitting the issue of Christ's divinity, he praised him for restoring humanity to God. He portrayed Jesus as a complete, exemplary man, who despite enduring agonies of persecution and suffering, accepted God's will and thus became history's great spiritual hero.[89] Emerson's focus on the combination of Stoic and God-directed courage in Jesus was a goad to himself and a criterion for his later biographical subjects. With conviction, Emerson now preached a feeling of impregnable spiritual centeredness. Already in March, writing from St. Augustine to Mary, he had hinted of such a sense: "[W]e can conceive of one so united to God in his affections that he surveys from the vantage ground of his own virtues the two worlds with equal eye & knowing the

---

87   *The Collected Works of Ralph Waldo Emerson*, 10 vols., eds. Alfred R. Ferguson, et al. (Cambridge, Mass.: Harvard University Press, 1971-2013), 2: 46. Hereafter *CW*.

88   *JMN* 3: 82.

89   *CS* 1: 85-92. See Mott, "'Christ Crucified': Christology, Identity, and Emerson's Sermon No. 5," in *Emerson Centenary Essays*, ed. Joel Myerson (Carbondale, IL: Southern Illinois University Press, 1982), 17-40; incorporated in Mott, *"The Strains of Eloquence": Emerson and his Sermons* (University Park, PA: Pennsylvania State University Press, 1989), 9-33.

true value of the love & praise of men challenges rather the suffrages [support] of immortal souls."[90] By the very act of discerning eternal truth, he believed, the hero overcomes the world's hypocrisy, pride, and viciousness.

Churches throughout eastern Massachusetts—including his father's former congregation, Boston's First Church—and into New Hampshire often called on Emerson to be their supply pastor. On Christmas Day 1827, in Concord, New Hampshire, he met the sixteen-year-old Ellen Tucker. She was beautiful, religious, poetically-inclined, vivacious, and fun-loving, but frail. Ellen was already clearly showing signs of consumption, a family malady, when they were engaged the following December. Within months, on March 11, 1829, the Second Church (Unitarian) in Boston's North End ordained Emerson its junior pastor to serve under the popular and eloquent Henry Ware, Jr. But the ailing Ware had to retire in July, the next year becoming a professor at Harvard Divinity School.[91] Emerson now became the sole minister of a venerable church that was once led by Increase and Cotton Mather and counted Paul Revere among its former members. On September 30, Waldo and Ellen were married in New Hampshire, and then took rooms near the church on Chardon Street.

1.23 Ellen Louisa Tucker at 18, 1829.

---

90   *L* 7: 159-60.

91   Sydney Ahlstrom, *A Religious History of the American People* (New Haven, CT: Yale University Press, 1972), 398, and William R. Hutchison, *The Transcendentalist Ministers: Church Reform in the New England Renaissance* (New Haven, CT: Yale University Press, 1959), 12.

1.24 Emerson at about 26, c. 1829.

Emerson's ministry in the late 1820s and early 1830s—long overshadowed by the emphasis on his more famous lectures and essays of a decade later—profoundly shaped him as a thinker and writer.[92] Although he based each sermon conventionally on a biblical text, Emerson admired Jesus as a deeply human prophet and was never rigidly dogmatic. Incorporating secular themes and allusions in his preaching, he made the most of the expressive freedom encouraged in the Unitarian pulpit and began to articulate themes he would revisit throughout his career: the importance of self-reliant character based on moral law, the dynamic quality of individual life within a limitless cosmos, the relationship of the citizen to the nation, and the ultimate value of discerning the truth for oneself. Above all, he was exploring the reality of the "God within," a concept he derived from widely diverse sources: Marcus Aurelius, the Pauline epistles, the French cleric Fenelon, and the Romantics, as well as from Mary and the Society of Friends' founder George Fox. As a supply minister in New Bedford in 1833-1834, he would be greatly impressed by the principle of "acquiescence," expressed by Quaker Mary Rotch, which would help him to clarify the God-dependence, or deep selfless quality of "self-reliance."[93] Later, mystic writers in the Islamic, Hindu, and Confucian traditions would strengthen

---

92 See David Robinson, *Apostle of Culture: Emerson as Preacher and Lecturer* (Philadelphia, PA: University of Pennsylvania Press, 1982); Mott, *"Strains"*; and Susan L. Roberson, *Emerson in His Sermons: A Man-Made Self* (Columbia, MO: University of Missouri Press, 1995).

93 *JMN* 4: 263-64, and Richardson, 157-63.

his sense of the omnipresence of a World Soul, another curb to excessive individualism.

Except for a few sermons prepared for purely ceremonial occasions, Emerson was preaching on topics that deeply mattered to him.

NEW BRICK, OR SECOND CHURCH,

1.25 New Brick, or Second Church, Boston, 1843.

He was also learning to address a live, intellectually demanding audience, tending to the congregation's pastoral needs, serving on several church committees, and generally becoming a public leader in a manner he had previously thought impossible. He also took on community responsibilities, acting as both chaplain of the State Senate and an elected member of the Boston School Committee. He extended his contacts and made friends, among them Abel Adams and George Adams Sampson, both merchants, parishioners at Second Church, and confidants whose decency persuaded Emerson that virtue and success in commerce were not necessarily incompatible.

The range of topics on which Emerson preached at Second Church and throughout the Northeast testifies to the flexibility allowed in the Unitarian pulpit. It also reflected Emerson's passionate quest to discover the unity of all knowledge, linking both heart and head, and thus blending belief with intellect. Never merely focused on theological matters, Emerson was fascinated by any subject vital, or even tangential to, right living: history, biography, the arts, or science. In Boston in 1827, he saw "a skilful experimenter lay a magnet among filings of steel & the force of that subtle fluid entering into each fragment arranged them all in mathematical lines & each metallic atom became in its turn a magnet communicating all the force it received of the loadstone."[94] In another sermon in mid-July 1829, he drew a spiritual analogy to this experiment: "If you introduce a magnet into a heap of steel-filings the rubbish becomes instantly instinct with life and order . . . The mind is that mass of rubbish . . . until its hidden virtue is called forth when God is revealed." Nature, "full of symbols of its Author," mirrors God's laws. Emerson is already moving beyond rigid Swedenborgian correspondences to a dynamic, organic concept of mind. Any sign, he insists, is "but a faint type of the power of this idea upon the soul of man." Reading nature symbolically is only a preliminary stage of revelation, for God "manifests himself in the material world . . . in the history of man . . . in our own experience."[95] In short, until we directly experience God, we are dead to other divine manifestations.

In this sermon Emerson makes an important break from traditional Unitarian norms for establishing authentic religious belief. Since ancient times, several spiritual traditions had sought laws in nature as evidence of God's handiwork. English philosopher William Paley's *Natural Theology* (1802) had been in wide currency for a quarter century as the standard work of "natural religion." Paley had presented an "argument from design." Invoking an old metaphor, he had concluded that the world, like a watch, implies a maker. Close study of such disciplines as anatomy and physiology, he reasoned, enabled one to draw inferences about God's nature and plan. This book and other works by Paley remained basic texts for Harvard undergraduates into the 1830s. Emerson, however, had come to regard Paley's kind of evidence as unconvincingly secondhand: it separated the laws of God from God's living power.

Emerson wrote his 1829 sermon on natural religion in a logical, reasoned way, carefully numbering his main points.[96] In style, his vision of intuitive personal experience as the best evidence of God differs from the scintillating, poetic, demandingly impressionistic manner of his later essays; nevertheless, it anticipates the primary thesis of his first book, *Nature* (1836). There he would argue that immediate, private perception

---

94 *JMN* 3: 93.

95 *CS* 2: 20-21.

96 Commentary on this sermon includes Mott, "From Natural Religion to Transcendentalism: An Edition of Emerson's Sermon No. 43," in *Studies in the American Renaissance 1985,* ed. Joel Myerson (Charlottesville, VA: University Press of Virginia, 1985), 14-26 (revised in chap. 3 of *"Strains")* and Laura Dassow Walls, *Emerson's Life in Science: The Culture of Truth* (Ithaca, NY: Cornell University Press, 2003), 159. For an extensive discussion of Emerson's interest in electromagnetism, see Eric Wilson, *Emerson's Sublime Science* (New York: St. Martin's, 1999).

itself could be divine revelation. In a later sermon with a more cosmic perspective, he reasoned that the vast scope of astronomy, far from undercutting religious belief, provides a corrective to narrow, idolatrous views of our place in the universe and of God's scope. Just as Copernicus had shown that the earth plays a subordinate, satellite role to the sun, so our world's microcosmic size in relation to an infinite universe should discourage spiritual and moral arrogance. Such a change in perspective does not threaten belief, Emerson argued, but rather stimulates a grander sense of God, not as a mere "governor," but as "an Infinite Mind."[97]

1.26 View of Boston from the South Boston Bridge, c. 1820-1829.

Whether preaching on the nature of Jesus or on scientific and moral law, Emerson tried to cultivate in his audiences an inner sense of the divine. But such awareness did not lead him to argue for passive introspection. Spiritual insight, he felt, must translate into daily, public activity. Their connection formed the bridge between ideals and reality that prompted him, even at this early date, to support abolition in principle, although he did not yet join that nascent movement. Emerson welcomed the radical antislavery minister Samuel J. May, later the father-in-law of his future friend Bronson Alcott, to speak from his Second Church pulpit. And in

---

97   Sermon CLVII, *CS* 4: 158.

April 1832—fifteen months after William Lloyd Garrison founded the Boston abolitionist newspaper the *Liberator*—Emerson preached a Fast Day sermon insisting on the moral obligation to resist government-sanctioned injustice. "Let every man say then to himself—the cause of the Indian, it is mine; the cause of the slave, it is mine; the cause of the union, it is mine; the cause of public honesty, of education, of religion, they are mine; and speak and act thereupon as a freeman and a Christian."[98]

Emerson's burst of directed energy and his growing confidence as a preacher developed alongside severe crisis and eventual tragedy. Throughout 1830, Ellen continued to suffer from lung hemorrhages. (Emerson's younger brother Edward, now in New York practicing law with William, was also showing tubercular symptoms.) On February 8, 1831, a numb Emerson recorded in both his journal and church records the death of his beloved wife.[99] On the 20th, crushed by "miserable debility," as he described his state, he groped for words to express his loss in a sermon on grief.[100] The loss of Ellen intensified his search for new, less doctrinal grounds for faith. "All is miracle," he asserted in his journal the month after her death, "& the mind revolts at representations of 2 kinds of miracle."[101] For a time, he mechanically carried on with his preaching and pastoral tasks, while every day walking the two miles to Ellen's tomb in Roxbury. After a year of this practice, in January 1832, he privately noted, "It is the best part of the man, I sometimes think, that revolts most against his being the minister." Eleven days later he challenged himself, "Write on personal independance [sic]."[102] Mary understood such deep malaise, yet anxious that the family's clerical tradition not be broken, she encouraged him to hold on to his noble profession.

But the depth of Emerson's torment is suggested by a stark journal entry of late March, well over a year after Ellen's death: "I visited Ellen's tomb & opened the coffin."[103] The act of viewing a deceased's remains, while not a common custom, was not particularly ghoulish or bizarre in New England.[104] Emerson described nothing more about the incident, either what he saw or felt.

---

98   *CS* 4: 115.
99   *JMN* 3: 226, *CS* 4: 302.
100 *JMN* 3: 226; Sermon CVII, *CS* 3: 101-05.
101 *JMN* 3: 242. On Emerson and the problem of Christian "evidences," see Mott, "*Strains*," 53-78.
102 *JMN* 3: 318, 320.
103 *JMN* 4: 7.
104 See Richardson, 3-5, and Ralph H. Orth, "Emerson's Visit to the Tomb of His First Wife," *Emerson Society Paper* 11 (Spring 2000), 3, 8.

But he had been meditating and preaching on mortality. Confronting once and for all the finality of Ellen's death, while simultaneously remembering her fervent belief in their reunion in an afterlife, Emerson asserted a belief in life here and now.[105] That summer, while thinking of what he might preach the next Sunday, he noted that true religion lies neither with church doctrines nor sacramental practices. Rather he strongly affirmed, "It is a life . . . a new life of those faculties you have. It is to do right. It is to love, it is to serve, it is to think, it is to be humble." In mid-September 1832, he was even more explicit on this theme, jotting down a motto, "'Think of living.' Don't tell me to get ready to die. I know not what shall be. The only preparation I can make is by fulfilling my present duties. This is the everlasting life." By opening up a new path beyond grief, this focus on the present could temporarily eclipse doubts about an afterlife.[106] The question of immortality, however, would be an unresolved issue about which he would speculate for the rest of his life.

Emerson now came to realize that except for the pleasure of writing sermons, pastoral duties no longer appealed to him. He filled his journal with fundamental doubts about his profession: "I have sometimes thought that in order to be a good minister it was necessary to leave the ministry. The profession is antiquated. In an altered age, we worship in the dead forms of our forefathers. Were not a Socratic paganism better than an effete superannuated Christianity?"[107] Emerson's concept of being "a good minister" shows both his insistence on integrity and a continuing appreciation of the prophetic role of preaching. But in the wake of losing Ellen, he now associated the ministerial vocation with an equally corrosive kind of death.

In early June, only two months after viewing Ellen's remains, Emerson invited leading members of the congregation to his house. He wished to explain his objections to administering the sacrament of Communion, and he took the opportunity to announce a radical idea: Why not simply dispense with the rite? On the 21st, a church committee sent him their report. It recognized that people of conscience differed over the nature of the Lord's Supper but stated that the church would not change its custom.[108] On the very same day, carrying William Sewel's *The History of the . . . Quakers* and the second volume of Thomas Clarkson's *A Portraiture of Quakerism*, Emerson left

---

105 Richardson states that "The loss that darkened his life also freed him. Ellen's death cut Emerson loose" (Richardson, 118).

106 *JMN* 4: 27; 40-41.

107 *JMN* 4: 27.

108 *CS* 4: 292-95.

with Charles to visit his oracle, Mary, on her farm in Waterford, Maine, with its inspiring mountain views. After going on to New Hampshire's impressive White Mountains with Waldo, Charles returned to Boston; Mary joined Waldo at Crawford Notch but departed abruptly. Left alone to ponder his literal and personal prospects, Waldo noted, "The good of going into the mountains is that life is reconsidered."[109] He was reconsidering nothing less than the painful and complex intersection of private, professional, and doctrinal issues. In this self-reexamination, Emerson must have found strength from the Quaker profiles he had in hand. Their idea of a divine "inner light" within every soul had fed his recent sermons on the "God Within," along with a favorite scriptural verse, Luke 17:21: "The kingdom of God is within you." Since at least 1825, his own inner light had made him look critically at Mary's repeated adulation of their common ministerial ancestors. He had then admitted, "It is my own humor to despise pedigree," declaring that "the dead sleep in their moonless night; my business is with the living."[110] Still, now that he was a responsible pastor, historical encouragement from leading Quakers who embodied moral independence and courage could only strengthen him in his inner debate over leaving the practice of his fathers.

Leaving His Pastorate

Under great stress and on the road that summer of 1832, Emerson developed a severe case of diarrhea that lasted on and off for months. Nevertheless, from this period of physical suffering and conflicted reflection, he emerged with new resolution. His journal entries make it clear that by mid-July, he was set on the course of leaving the ministry, breaking with Mary's ardent dreams for him to carry on the family tradition. Yet now, fondness overruled her earlier objections: She could only understand his decision and wish him well. She wrote to Charles, hoping that Waldo, "free from ties to forms & instruction may find the Angel who can best unite him to the Infinite." By his imagination alone, she thought he might experience a heartfelt infusion of Coleridge's "Reason," might, in short, intuit divinity.[111] In a sermon on September 9, 1832, now known as "The Lord's Supper," Emerson publicly stated the message he had given the church committee three months before: For scriptural, theological, and historical reasons, he could not in good conscience administer

---

109 *JMN* 4: 29. See also Cole, *Mary Moody Emerson*, 218.
110 *JMN* 2: 316.
111 Cole, *Mary Moody Emerson*, 219.

the sacrament of communion. In his view, Jesus did not intend this meal to be a perpetual observance. Once made so, Emerson argued, the rite shifts attention away from a direct experience of God's spirit to an exaggerated focus on the person of his mediator, Jesus. Furthermore, Emerson located the event as peculiar to a specific culture in a past time and place, and therefore inappropriate to modern Boston. Carefully researched and logical, the sermon was a forceful statement of Emerson's sense of the priority of spirit over a now meaningless ritual.

Beyond one church practice, however, Emerson's argument for his action arose from eighteen months of struggle with loss, grief, and his entire relationship with organized religion. Ending the sermon, he capped his long rationale with this forthright statement: "It is my desire, in the office of a Christian minister, to do nothing which I cannot do with my whole heart. Having said this, I have said all . . . That is the end of my opposition [to administering Communion], that I am not interested in it."[112] Two days later he wrote to the congregation formally requesting to be relieved of his pastoral charge.

Emerson had long chided himself for being cold and aloof. But his congregation had grown to love him, and seeking a compromise concerning communion, it entreated him to reconsider and stay. Even when Emerson stood firm, the vote to dismiss him (30 Yeas, 20 Nays, 4 Blanks) in late October expressed his congregation's reluctance to let him go, and they "Voted unanimously that the Salary of the Rev Mr Emerson be continued for the present." In fact, they even paid his last quarterly salary a few days early, on December 21.[113] Waldo, still ill and depressed, had talked of going to the West Indies to restore his health, but in early December, learning of a ship headed for Naples, suddenly decided to go to Italy on a trip that would eventually take him farther north in Europe, and finally to England and Scotland. When Waldo rapidly broke up his household on Chardon Street to sail for Europe, Charles wrote Mary, "[T]hings seem flying to pieces, and I don't know when they will again be put together and he [Waldo] harnessed in (what I think he requires) the labors of a daily calling."[114] On Christmas Day 1832, an ailing Emerson boarded the brig *Jasper* and set sail for Malta.

---

112 *CS* 4: 194.
113 *CS* 4: 296-97; *L* 1: 356n.
114 James Elliot Cabot, *A Memoir of Ralph Waldo Emerson*, 2 vols. (Boston, Mass.: Houghton Mifflin, 1887), 1: 174. See also John McAleer, *Ralph Waldo Emerson: Days of Encounter* (Boston, Mass.: Little, Brown & Co., 1984), 125-26, and Richardson, 127.

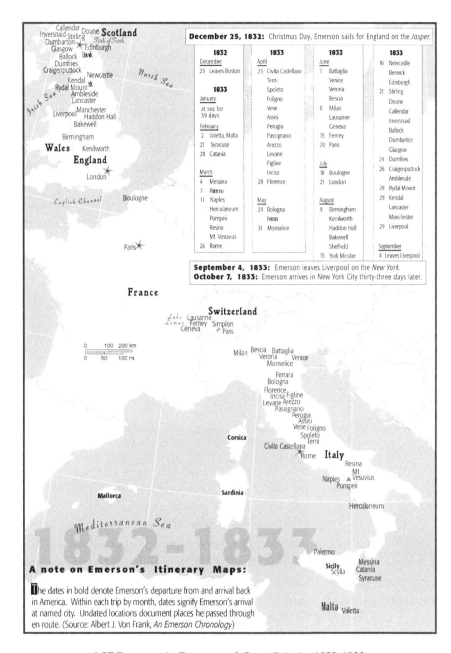

1.27 Emerson in Europe and Great Britain, 1832-1833.

Recovery and Renewal in Europe

With this dramatic exodus from Boston, Emerson started on his second life-altering journey, a nine-month tour of Europe. Like his shorter trip South six years before, this one strengthened him in body and mind, opening new intellectual, aesthetic, and emotional horizons. In Italy he visited ancient temples, catacombs, churches, monasteries, and museums. His New England eyes, used to the Puritan plain style, were overwhelmed by the Continent's centuries of monumental classic sculpture, painting, and architecture. After touring Syracuse, he proceeded to Naples, where he responded to its glories but also rejected certain "contemptible particulars." To a hotel's overdone splendors and the concern with proper dress, he challenged, "Who cares? Here's for the plain old Adam, the simple genuine Self against the whole world."[115]

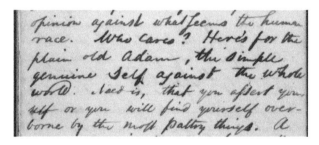

1.28 Journal entry: "Here's for the plain old Adam, the simple genuine Self against the whole world." 12 March 1833.

Emerson, approaching his thirtieth birthday and proud to stand for the uncomplicated integrity of New World values and tastes, would not be intimidated by the Old World's surface show.

Heading north, he visited Pompeii, before finally arriving in Rome, where for a month his aesthetic side luxuriated in views of the city's commanding architecture, art, and historic sites such as the Coliseum. At the Vatican's Sistine Chapel, he witnessed Pope Gregory XVI "bless the palms." "[W]hat a temple!" he declared of St. Peter's, whose incense-laden aromas pleased him and whose "immensity" awed him. Going out by moonlight to see Bernini's splendid piazza and fountain, his enthusiasm spilled into his journal: "how faery beautiful! An Arabian night's tale—."[116]

---

115 *JMN* 4: 141.
116 *JMN* 4: 152, 155-56.

1.29 Roman ruins, Emerson sepia watercolor, 1833.

He continued on to Florence, Milan, and Switzerland, then after five months arrived in Paris where he would stay for almost four weeks.

At first, Emerson was impressed with this "vast, rich, old capital." But after wandering about, he missed Italy's antiquities and was less impressed, remarking that Paris was "a loud modern New York of a place."[117] Yet the city's street scenes charmed him enough to record their details. And he absorbed certain antique riches at the Louvre while also bringing himself up-to-date on the latest European science by attending lectures at the Sorbonne. Then on July 13, a defining moment of the trip occurred on one of his visits to the Jardin des Plantes, or Jardin du Roi (King's Garden), also the site of the Museum of Natural History. Its vast arrangements of plants and array of animal skeletons by genus and species gave Emerson a sudden revelation: All nature was organically unified! He was so excited that he jubilantly wrote in his journal: "I feel the centipede in me—cayman, carp, eagle, & fox. I am moved by strange sympathies, I say continually 'I will be a naturalist.'"[118]

---

117 *JMN* 4: 196, 197.
118 *JMN* 4: 200.

1.30 Jardin du Roi, Paris, 1820, North-South view.

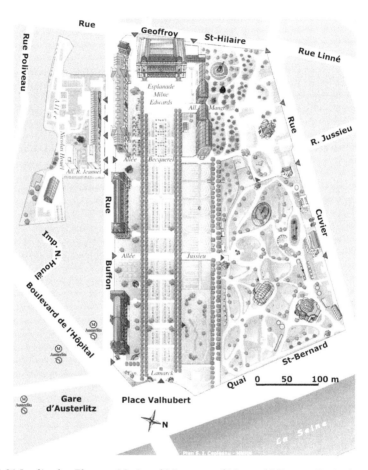

1.31 Jardin des Plantes, National Museum of Natural History, Paris, 2010, South-North view.

A week afterward in late July, having reached England, Emerson steamed up the Thames, finding "nothing surprizing" [sic] in a London familiar from "books & pictures & maps & traditions." After checking into his room at Russell Square, he stopped in St. Paul's Cathedral during a service. In his journal he jotted, "Immense city. Very dull city," but he admitted "an extreme pleasure to hear English spoken in the streets." He was also an eager tourist at Westminster Abbey, the House of Commons, Regent's Park, and the British Museum.[119]

Most importantly, Emerson paid visits to the great British writers whose ideas and works had been so influential in the United States. In early August, he met Coleridge (who was still in bed when Emerson arrived)—"a short thick old man" who "soiled" his neat clothing with snuff and declaimed against Unitarianism. Emerson found his conversation as difficult to follow as his writings.[120] He visited Warwick Castle en route to Edinburgh and Glasgow, and in late August, he arrived at the remote home of Thomas and Jane Carlyle in the hamlet of Craigenputtock.

1.32 Thomas Carlyle in his early 40s, late 1830s.

An elated Emerson called this a "white day in my years," signifying at once a climactic moment of perfection, startling clarity, and excitement. Carlyle's enthusiasm for Emerson was equally high, and he invited his new friend to stay the night. The Scot was a garrulous storyteller and opinionated, but Emerson liked the Carlyles from the start: "Truth & peace & faith dwell with them & beautify them. I never saw more amiableness than is in his

119 *JMN* 4: 204-05, 413-14.
120 *JMN* 4: 408-11.

countenance."[121] Despite increasing political and philosophical differences, their friendship managed to last for their lifetimes.

Two days later, Emerson visited the elderly Wordsworth, who lamented society's lack of "moral Culture." Commenting on the American scene, the aging poet surprised him with a paradox: For social cohesiveness, he thought that the United States needed a civil war. When they turned to assess leading writers, Emerson defended both Carlyle and Goethe. But on favorite examples in Wordsworth's own work, he apparently agreed with the old man's preference for poems that moved the heart. Wordsworth took his young visitor to see his garden, and they walked for a mile. Emerson saw "nothing very striking about his appearance," but thought him kind: "I spoke as I felt with great respect of his genius."[122]

Meeting these great men face-to-face, Emerson had been both impressed and sobered: They were quite human after all. He foresaw that "I shall judge more justly, less timidly, of wise men forevermore." Emerson especially thought that all of them lacked "insight into religious truth. They have no idea of that species of moral truth which I call the first philosophy."[123] The day after noting this, while waiting for the right weather before sailing home, Emerson added, "Glad I bid adieu to England, the old, the rich, the strong nation, full of arts & men & memories; nor can I feel any regret in the presence of the best of its sons that I was not born here. I am thankful that I am an American as I am thankful that I am a man."[124] When his ship left Liverpool for New York on September 4, 1833, Emerson had learned two priceless lessons. In Naples he had announced himself an American "Adam," dismissing European trumperies to represent, if imperfectly, a new set of ethics. Now he felt completely independent, freed from slavish adulation of even the leading minds of England.[125]

Two days later at sea Emerson wrote, "I like my book about nature & wish I knew where & how I ought to live. God will show me."[126] He was referring to nature as a world of facts for pursuing reality comparable to his similar search for truth in theological texts. Emerson's lengthy European tour had only strengthened his focus on that familiar Romantic trinity — Nature, Self, and God. The trip had not marked so much a turning,

---

121 *JMN* 4: 219, 220.
122 *JMN* 4: 222, 225.
123 *JMN* 4: 78, 79.
124 *JMN* 4: 81.
125 *JMN* 4: 236.
126 *JMN* 4: 237.

as a firming point. The arts and history of ancient cities had widened his perspective, and only strengthened, not shaken, his Yankee identity. Science in Paris had not sparked but rather rekindled his awareness of nature as a world for pursuing truth comparable to theology. And visiting the great literary figures of Britain had given him a strangely empowering revelation. Far from being in awe of these men as inaccessible titans, Emerson was measuring their biases and foibles as well as their virtues. Though he might learn from such geniuses, he recognized that they were, after all, men, and that his ideals and abilities were as fresh as theirs once had been. In his journal, safely letting slip more than a touch of youthful arrogance and native pride, Emerson allowed that he, the young American, had found these exemplars of European culture less sensitive than he to the ethical life.

Beginning a New Career in Boston, then Concord

Within days of his return to Boston in October, Emerson was invited by the Natural History Society to lecture on "The Uses of Natural History." In this first lecture of early November 1833 at the city's Masonic Temple, he drew on his Paris experience to argue that humans are "designed" to be natural historians.

Emerson pictured the benefits of studying nature as an upward spiral: Good health and practicality circled up to the inherent pleasures of knowledge, then turned higher to the ability of nature "to explain man to himself." He celebrated "that correspondence of the outward world to the inward world of thoughts and emotions, by which it is suited to represent what we think."[127] Emerson thus launched himself on a new career as a lecturer, gradually achieving fame in the United States and, later, abroad.

At the same time, although he had resigned his pastorate, Emerson never formally withdrew from the ministry, and was in demand once again as a supply pastor. For six years, until 1839, he preached frequently in Boston (including at Second Church), throughout Massachusetts, Maine, and even in New York City. From 1835 to 1838, he was virtually the regular minister for a rural parish in East Lexington. In fact, congregations in Waltham and New Bedford courted him with offers of full-time positions.

---

127 *The Early Lectures of Ralph Waldo Emerson*, 3 vols., eds. Robert E. Spiller, et al. (Cambridge, Mass.: Harvard University Press, 1959-1972), 1: 6, 23, 24. Hereafter *EL*.

MASONIC TEMPLE, BOSTON.

1.33 Masonic Temple, Boston, 1832.

In various guises, his major themes continued to be moral self-culture and the God within. Indeed, well into the 1840s, certain individuals and even some newspapers still addressed him as "the Rev. Mr. Emerson." By 1839, however, his preaching days were over, his transition from the pulpit to the lectern having been natural and seamless.[128]

In May 1834, Emerson's life was made at least somewhat easier when he received the first half of an inheritance from his wife's estate: $11,600, the equivalent in 2013 dollars of about $326,000. But Charles wrote William that the annual interest from this sum, $1,200 (about $33,700 in 2013), was insufficient for three (his mother, Waldo, and himself), especially since "Waldo does without a Profession." (He had only begun to lecture the previous fall.) Even after 1837, when Emerson received the second half of Ellen's inheritance, increasing his estate to about $653,000 in current dollars, he had to count on income from lecturing to fully provide for himself and his family.[129]

In 1834, however, Emerson was again beset by close personal loss. That summer, his close friend from Second Church, businessman George Adams Sampson, collapsed and died on his way to Bangor to join Emerson for a vacation. Emerson poured his grief into a memorial sermon for "our brother" at Second Church.[130] In attendance were Bronson Alcott and Elizabeth Palmer Peabody, who wrote that Emerson's preaching was so moving that she felt she knew Sampson as if she had been "his acquaintance on earth."[131] Then word came that on October 1, Waldo's brother Edward had died of consumption in Puerto Rico. His death, again a caution to Waldo about excessive work, combined with concern for his own health and a desire to leave fast-growing Boston for a place close to nature, led him a week later to move to the house in Concord, Massachusetts that his grandfather, the Reverend William Emerson, had built in 1770. It was known as the "Old Manse." Waldo had briefly stayed here as a child, as recounted earlier, and

---

128 The Boston *Daily Times*, January 30, 1846, for example, reported that "Rev. Ralph W. Emerson and Charles Sumner, Esq." were praised by the Massachusetts Anti-Slavery Society for boycotting the New Bedford Lyceum when it refused to admit blacks (2). For daily details of Emerson's preaching and lecturing engagements, see Albert J. von Frank, *An Emerson Chronology* (New York: G. K. Hall, 1994).

129 Henry F. Pommer, *Emerson's First Marriage* (Carbondale, IL: Southern Illinois University Press, 1967), 65. For monetary equivalencies, the latest figures available are for 2013; see Lawrence H. Officer and Samuel H. Williamson, "Measures of Worth"; and The Calculators: Relative Values U.S. $ at http://www.measuringworth.com/uscompare/

130 CLXVIII, *CS* 4: 221-28.

131 *L* 1: 417n.42.

had fond memories of this family manse. After enduring yet another family tragedy, he was emerging again from a period of crippling mourning with a determined will to live.

Drawn by J. W. Barber—Engraved by J. Downes, Worcester.
CENTRAL PART OF CONCORD, MASS.

The above is a northern view in the central part of Concord village. Part of the Court-House is seen on the left. Burying-ground Hill (a post of observation to the British officers in the invasion of 1775) is seen a short distance beyond. The Unitarian Church and Middlesex Hotel are seen on the right.

1.34 Concord Center, 1839.

Grief itself seemed to unlock a deep vein of creativity within Emerson. A dabbler in verse since childhood, he was now seriously writing poetry. While visiting Newton, Massachusetts, in early 1834, he composed an ode to the wild rhododendron, "The Rhodora," epitomizing spring. Unlike Keats's adulation of a man-made object to praise beauty in his classic "Ode to a Grecian Urn," Emerson's subject for the same purpose arises organically from nature, a rarely glimpsed wild shrub in Concord's swamplands with startlingly vivid, reddish-purple flowers. Its creator, he sees, is the same as his own, linking the flower—and its hidden potential—with himself: "Why thou wert there, O rival of the rose!/ I never thought to ask, I never knew;/ But, in my simple ignorance, suppose/ The self-same Power that brought me there brought you."[132] At his ancestral home, within a stone's throw of the Old North Bridge, where the Revolution began, he made progress on his revolutionary "little book" on Nature.[133] Along with this poetically

---

132 *CW* 9: 79.
133 See Merton M. Sealts Jr., and Alfred R. Ferguson, *Emerson's* Nature: *Origin, Growth, Meaning,* 2nd ed., enlarged (Carbondale, IL: Southern Illinois University Press, 1979).

philosophical manifesto, which would soon galvanize the attention of his own (rising) generation of restless idealists, came frequent walks in Concord's woods. With its longstanding family and patriotic associations, the village became home almost overnight, and Emerson's philosophical and daily delight with nature expressed itself in poetry. In the winter of 1834-1835, he composed "The Snow-Storm," its impressionistic style making it one of his more enduring poems. It captures the tumult of a blizzard by using the metaphor of a Romantic Creator—"the fierce artificer"—and of art itself—"the mad wind's night-work,/ The frolic architecture of the snow."[134]

In late January 1835, Boston's Society for the Diffusion of Useful Knowledge engaged Emerson to present a six-part series on biography, starting with a now-lost introductory lecture on the subject. It must have been like its successors on Michelangelo, Luther, and Milton, treating the lives of men of exceptional qualities "who had the advantage of rare cultivation."[135] His next lecture, on George Fox, focused on the Quaker's moral example as well as on his common humanity. Emerson's final figure was Edmund Burke, the Irish-born, eighteenth-century British politician and writer, a secular master of statesmanship and eloquence. Studying great lives, Emerson believed, was a means of understanding history and of challenging oneself.

In his private life, Emerson seemed to be moving toward conventional stability. In January, after having preached in Plymouth, where he met Lydia Jackson, orphaned daughter of a prominent businessman and a leading Sunday school teacher, he wrote to her, proposing marriage.

Though she frankly admitted that she was no housekeeper, Lydia—a year older than Emerson—promptly accepted. Intelligent and devout, she was known among family and friends as a fervent champion of animals and of the underprivileged, especially blacks and women. She was also given to visions. Though sometime earlier she had heard Emerson preach, Lydia had hardly met him when she imagined the two of them descending her family's staircase as husband and wife.[136]

---

134 *CW* 9: 90.
135 *EL* 1: 165.
136 McAleer, 201, and Richardson, 193.

1.35 Lydian Jackson Emerson at 56, 1858.

In early July 1835, for $3,500 (or on a national average, about $95,500 in 2013) Emerson purchased a large, handsome house on the Cambridge Turnpike. As far out of town as his grandfather's manse on the opposite side of Concord, the "Coolidge Castle," or "Bush," as he came to call it, was enlarged to accommodate not only his prospective wife and mother but also Charles, who had been practicing law in Concord, and Charles's betrothed, Elizabeth Hoar.[137]

Meanwhile, Emerson, proud of the role his ancestor the Reverend Peter Bulkeley had played in founding Concord in 1635, was glad to be asked to deliver an historical address on the occasion of its bicentennial. On September 12, 1835, he gave a carefully researched lecture, which eventually became his first noteworthy publication, *A Historical Discourse.*[138] His address celebrated "the ideal social compact," one that had united the strong-willed Puritans and endured during the Revolution, when, Emerson noted, a "deep religious sentiment sanctified the thirst for liberty."[139]

---

137 Richardson, 207-08, and McAleer, 207-08.
138 *A Historical Discourse, Delivered Before the Citizens of Concord, 12th September, 1835, On the Second Centennial Anniversary of the Incorporation of the Town* (Concord: G. F. Bemis, 1835). See *CW* 10: 17-54.
139 *CW* 10: 27, 43.

1.36 Emerson's house, "Bush," Concord, 1875, surrounded by pine trees he planted in 1836.

Two days after this address, Waldo and Lydia Jackson were married in Plymouth. She would have preferred to set up housekeeping in her family's historic seaside town, but he persuaded her of the virtues and charms of Concord. Emerson also asked her to add an "n" to "Lydia," making it "Lidian," possibly hoping to avoid the common New England pronunciation "Lydier Emerson," that typically inserted an "r" between two words that ended and began with vowels.[140] Lidian immediately devoted herself to a life of caring for her husband, increasing social concerns—particularly, at this moment, abolition—and a demanding household. In fact, on the first night the Emersons moved in, Waldo, exuberant over his purchase, invited a couple from Plymouth to spend the night. Lidian, initially aghast,

---

140 Richardson, 192, 611.

nevertheless dutifully managed.[141] Emerson's home for the rest of his long productive life, "Bush" would remain a constant center of high hospitality with constant comings and goings of family and a growing number of old and new friends.

In early November 1835, again in Boston, Emerson started a new ten-part lecture series on English literature. Great writers, he stated, express "the truths and sentiments in common circulation among us," and we approach them not as mere talented entertainers but as geniuses who were "obedient to the spirit that was in them."[142] With new confidence, Emerson was also offering a hopeful vision for himself: as someone who, like these classic figures, might express ideas about humanity's most central topics to a wide audience. Such a sentiment would raise expectations among his family, friends, and audiences—many still thought of him as a pastor— to use his lectures for reform matters. These anticipations would only increase as his reputation steadily grew alongside mounting unrest over slavery and women's rights. At thirty-two, he had minimized recurring self-doubt, boldly left his pastorate for lecturing, and was well on his way toward addressing the world as a compelling spokesman for a "new philosophy." Inspired by being resident on Concord's ancestral rebellious ground, Emerson would finish his testament to this fresh thinking—the manuscript that he would entitle *Nature*—in the coming months. Its basic ideas and their elaboration in landmark speeches that followed soon after would stir up the most sacrosanct traditions of Boston and eventually all of America. The next chapter explores the effect of these intellectual fireworks both on Emerson and on his increasingly turbulent country.

---

141 Ellen Tucker Emerson, *The Life of Lidian Jackson Emerson*, ed. Delores B. Carpenter (East Lansing: Michigan State University Press, 1992), 62.
142 *EL* 1: 230, 231.

PUBLIC AND PRIVATE REVOLUTIONS

2.1 The "New Thinking": Nature, Self, and Society, 1836-1850

David M. Robinson

There is victory yet for all justice; and the true romance which the world exists to realize will be the transformation of genius into practical power.

Emerson, "Experience," *Essays II*, 1844

Spokesman for the New Age

Leaving for Europe in late 1832, having resigned his pulpit and still in grief over the loss of his wife Ellen, Emerson sought to renew his severely tested faith and optimism. He began his recovery in an unexpected place, the Jardin des Plantes in Paris, where Antoine Laurent de Jussieu's Cabinet of Natural History presented an array of plants arranged by botanical classification. To Emerson's hungry eye, this display suggested interconnection, transformation, and all-encompassing unity, the verities that his recent crisis had brought into question. He saw vitality in this collection of living plants, the constantly transmuting yet interwoven processes of the natural world, a unified cosmos defined by its perpetual energy and unending metamorphosis. "I feel the centipede in me—cayman, carp, eagle, & fox," he wrote in his journal. "I am moved by strange sympathies, I say continually 'I will be a naturalist.'"[1] Before returning to America, he began to make

---

1   *The Journals and Miscellaneous Notebooks of Ralph Waldo Emerson*, 16 vols., eds. William H. Gilman, et al. (Cambridge, Mass.: Harvard University Press, 1960-1982), 4: 200. Hereafter *JMN*.

http://dx.doi.org/10.11647/OBP.0065.03

notes for a philosophy of nature, and on his arrival he began to fulfill his "naturalist" ambition with lectures on "The Uses of Natural History" and "Water" at the Boston Society of Natural History.[2] These early lectures, and the powerful insight that he experienced in Paris, became the foundation of his first book *Nature*, which established him as the exponent of an era of self-awareness and social renewal.

2.1 *Nature*, Emerson's first book, 1836.

With increasing clarity Emerson became aware that the tangible natural world could be the most accessible entry into an intangible realm of the spirit. For him, there could be no division between a scientific perspective and a religious one. Scientific advances strengthened his belief in a unified cosmos, the manifestation of a single force or energy. "Every natural fact is a symbol of some spiritual fact," he declared. To study the processes and development of nature was also to penetrate the transcendent laws that governed the spiritual and moral realms.[3]

---

2   For discussions of Emerson's visit to the Jardin des Plantes and its impact, see David M. Robinson, "Emerson's Natural Theology and the Paris Naturalists: Toward a 'Theory of Animated Nature,'" *Journal of the History of Ideas*, 41 (1980), 69-88; Elizabeth A. Dant, "Composing the World: Emerson and the Cabinet of Natural History," *Nineteenth-Century Literature* 44 (June 1989), 18-44; Robert D. Richardson, Jr., *Emerson: The Mind on Fire* (Berkeley, CA: University of California Press, 1995), 139-42; and Lee Rust Brown, *The Emerson Museum: Practical Romanticism and the Pursuit of the Whole* (Cambridge, Mass.: Harvard University Press, 1997). For the texts of his early lectures on natural history, see *The Early Lectures of Ralph Waldo Emerson*, 3 vols., eds. Robert E. Spiller, et al. (Cambridge, Mass.: Harvard University Press, 1959-1972), 1: 1-83. Hereafter *EL*.

3   *The Collected Works of Ralph Waldo Emerson*, 10 vols., eds. Robert E. Spiller, et al. (Cambridge, Mass.: Harvard University Press, 1971-2013), 1: 18 (*Nature*). Hereafter *CW*.

Although *Nature* did not conform to the expected format of a theological or philosophical treatise, Emerson's prose-poem explored the deepest religious questions, combining reasoned argument with poetic insight to decipher the natural world as a code of fundamental laws that defined the purpose of human experience. The full range of human awareness—observation, reason, aesthetic sensitivity, and emotion—was necessary to comprehend the bond between nature and the human. At the outset, Emerson recounted a dramatically revelatory moment "in the woods" in which he felt "uplifted into infinite space," and freed of "all mean egotism." His vision was transformed, and the natural and spiritual worlds opened to him: "I become a transparent eye-ball. I am nothing. I see all. The currents of the Universal Being circulate through me; I am part or particle of God."[4] In other passages, he seemed to become part of the natural world itself, speaking of "an occult relation between man and the vegetable," and proclaiming, "I expand and live in the warm day like corn and melons."[5] These were moments of unburdened freedom from material reality, but they were paradoxically triggered by a deep sensual immersion within it. Emerson's exuberant responsiveness to nature traversed the barriers between world and soul, each of which was encompassed in "the immutable laws of moral Nature."[6]

Such exuberance can be infectious, but it can also evoke wry amusement. Christopher Pearse Cranch, one of Emerson's most ardent devotees, seized on Emerson's weirdly striking images of the transparent eyeball and the occult vegetables for several gently satiric caricatures which circulated among friends in his day, but went unpublished until 1951.[7]

For helpful interpretive discussions of *Nature*, see Sherman Paul, *Emerson's Angle of Vision: Man and Nature in American Experience* (Cambridge, Mass.: Harvard University Press, 1952); Barbara Packer, *Emerson's Fall: A New Interpretation of the Major Essays* (New York: Continuum, 1992); David M. Robinson, *Apostle of Culture: Emerson as Preacher and Lecturer* (Philadelphia, PA: University of Pennsylvania Press, 1982); David Van Leer, *Emerson's Epistemology: The Argument of the Essays* (Cambridge: Cambridge University Press, 1986); Alan D. Hodder, *Emerson's Rhetoric of Revelation* (University Park, PA: Pennsylvania State University Press, 1989); and David Greenham, *Emerson's Transatlantic Romanticism* (New York: Palgrave Macmillan, 2012).

4   *CW* 1: 10.
5   *CW* 1: 10 and 35.
6   *JMN* 5: 203.
7   See Frederick DeWolfe Miller, *Christopher Pearse Cranch and his Caricatures of New England Transcendentalism* (Cambridge, Mass.: Harvard University Press, 1951).

"Standing on the bare ground, — my head bathed by the blithe air, & uplifted into infinite space, — all mean egotism vanishes. I become a transparent Eyeball."   *Nature.* p. *13.*

2.2 C. P. Cranch, caricature of Emerson's transparent eyeball, c. 1838-1839.

However odd they may have seemed, Emerson's evocations of his encounters with natural events suggested that thoughtful interactions with nature would awaken a fulfilling and purposeful life. But to activate this potential, one must renounce settled doctrines and conventions. "Let us demand our own works and laws and worship," he declared.[8] His sustaining faith was that every individual had access to a greater spirituality through contemplation, self-examination, and attention to the suggestions of the natural surroundings. "Who looks upon a river in a meditative hour and is not reminded of the flux of all things?" he asked. "Throw a stone into the stream, and the circles that propagate themselves are the beautiful

---

8   CW 1: 7.

type of all influence. Man is conscious of a universal soul within or behind his individual life, wherein, as in a firmament, the natures of Justice, Truth, Love, Freedom, arise and shine."[9]

Nature began as a hymn to the beauty of the woods and streams, but Emerson steered his argument toward the *transformative* beauty of nature, the capacity of creation to evoke a new energy within the human psyche. "All things are moral; and in their boundless changes have an unceasing reference to spiritual nature," he asserted in the chapter "Discipline," a pivotal chapter in his argument. Drawing on the eighteenth-century concepts of the moral sense, and a longer tradition of Platonic idealism, he depicted a cosmos whose deepest self-expression was concordant, harmonious action. "Every natural process is but a version of a moral sentence. The moral law lies at the centre of nature and radiates to the circumference. It is the pith and marrow of every substance, every relation, and every process."[10] Plato, and his many later followers, maintained that a deeper source of ideas gave the apparent world its material form. Plato was, as Robert D. Richardson explained, "the single most important source of Emerson's lifelong conviction that ideas are real because they are the forms and laws that underlie, precede, and explain appearances." Early discussions with his Aunt Mary Moody Emerson piqued his interest in Platonic idealism, and he was introduced to later versions of neo-idealism by his reading of the seventeenth-century English "Cambridge Platonists," Ralph Cudworth and Henry More.[11] His preferred contemporary writers,

---

9   *CW* 1: 18.

10   *CW* 1: 26. British ethical philosophers Lord Shaftesbury (1671-1713), Francis Hutcheson (1694-1746), and David Hume (1711-1776) principally developed the concept of the moral sense, an innate human capacity for moral discrimination and benevolent action. Hutcheson's work, in particular, directly influenced one of Emerson's key mentors, William Ellery Channing, minister of the Federal Street Unitarian Church in Boston. Closely connected to it was the concept of "self-culture," an important doctrine of Channing and other Unitarian thinkers of the generation preceding Emerson. For information on the tradition of Unitarian ethical thinking that shaped Emerson, see Daniel Walker Howe, *The Unitarian Conscience: Harvard Moral Philosophy, 1805-1861* (1970; reprint, Middletown, CT: Wesleyan University Press, 1988); and Robinson, *Apostle of Culture*.

11   See Richardson, 65-69; quotations from 65-66. Emerson withdrew Henry More's *Divine Dialogues* (1668) from the Boston Athenaeum on November 19, 1830. He acquired Ralph Cudworth's *The True Intellectual System of the Universe* (1678) on April 23, 1835. See Albert J. von Frank, *An Emerson Chronology* (New York: G. K. Hall, 1994), 54, 101. For further information on the Cambridge Platonists and their impact on American Unitarianism and Transcendentalism, see Daniel Walker Howe, "The Cambridge Platonists of Old England and the Cambridge Platonists of New England," in *American Unitarianism, 1805-1861*, ed. Conrad E. Wright (Boston, Mass.: Massachusetts Historical

the British Romantics William Wordsworth, Samuel Taylor Coleridge, and Thomas Carlyle, had also reformulated a version of Platonism, seeing it as a liberating alternative to the dry empiricism of John Locke and the skepticism of David Hume.[12] Emerson regarded the Romantics' resurrection of a modern form of idealism as a revolutionary turn in modern thinking, and as Barbara Packer noted, their powerful message, especially that of Carlyle, was a call to action. "If Carlyle preached a new gospel, how were his American disciples to put it into practice?"[13]

For Emerson, idealism breathed new life into the physical world, transforming it from lifeless matter into energy, and giving it vast religious dimensions. "Idealism saith: matter is a phenomenon, not a substance," he wrote in *Nature*, reaffirming his Parisian insight that creation was not static and unmovable but changing and malleable, a cycle of energies and interactions.[14] This leap from "substance" to "phenomenon" was crucial to Emerson because it resolved the dualism of body and spirit through the unifying agency of the event. To recognize that both matter and soul were continually revealed in the processes of nature was also to see those processes as expressions of a vital, evolving unity. "A spiritual life has been imparted to nature" and "the solid seeming block of matter has been pervaded and dissolved by a thought," he wrote.[15] He redefined religion as the enactment—the making real— of idealism, "the practice of ideas, or the introduction of ideas into life."[16] This is the reason that Emerson concluded *Nature* with a call to action. Proclaiming *Nature*'s ultimate message through the voice of an "Orphic Poet," Emerson emphasizes "building" rather than "seeing" or "understanding" as the conclusive wisdom. "Build, therefore, your own world," the Orphic Poet proclaims. "As fast as you conform your life to the pure idea in your mind, that will unfold its great proportions. A correspondent revolution in things will attend the influx of the spirit."[17]

Society and Northeastern University Press, 1989), 87-120.

12   For important studies of the impact of the British Romantics on Emerson, see Barbara L. Packer, *The Transcendentalists* (Athens, GA: University of Georgia Press, 2007), 20-45; Patrick J. Keane, *Emerson, Romanticism, and Intuitive Reason: The Transatlantic "Light of All Our Day"* (Columbia, MO: University of Missouri Press, 2005); and Greenham, *Emerson's Transatlantic Romanticism*.

13   Packer, *The Transcendentalists*, 40.

14   *CW* 1: 37.

15   *CW* 1: 34.

16   *CW* 1: 35.

17   *CW* 1: 45.

Concord Life and the Emergence of Transcendentalism

The ebullient mood of *Nature* and its message of world-building reflected the domestic and interpersonal world that Emerson was creating for himself in Concord.

2.3 Emerson house, 10 May 1903.

In October 1834 he relocated from Boston to Concord, where he had familial roots. He was drawn by its rural seclusion and ready access to the New England countryside.

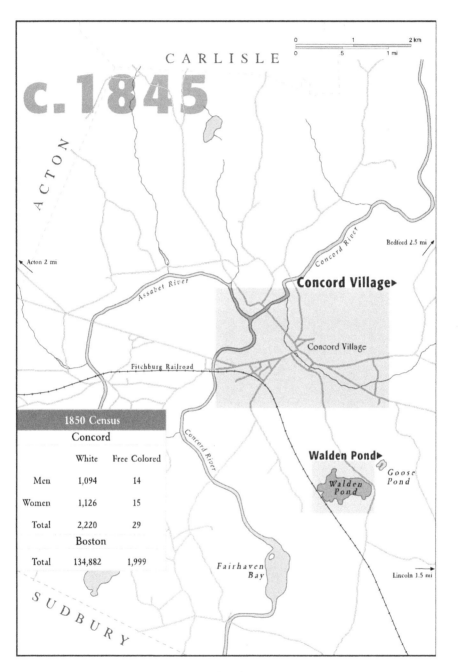

2.4 Concord and Vicinity.

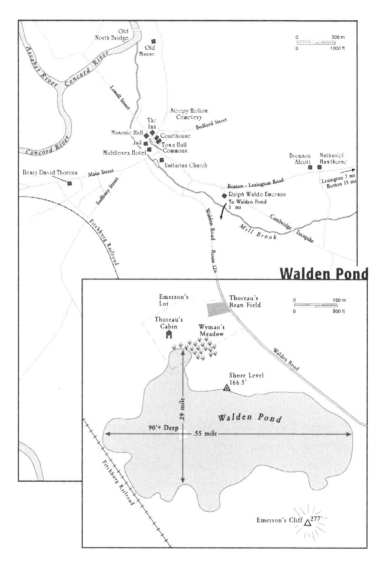

2.5 Concord Village and Walden.

There in 1835, he brought a new wife, Lydia Jackson of Plymouth, who had been following his career as pastor and lecturer. The first of four children, Waldo, was born in Concord in 1836, the month after *Nature* was published. As Bliss Perry explained in his still indispensable portrait of Emerson's domestic life, his neighbors "welcomed him as a true son of Concord into the ordinary life of the village. They put him on the School Committee. He taught in the Sunday School. He joined the Fire Company, and the Social Circle."[18] His home thus became not only a retreat for study and writing but a literary headquarters for the emerging American Transcendentalists. His door was open to frequent visitors, and through a combination of his Concord hospitality and his frequent forays into Boston, he built a network of like-minded friends. He played an important role in the gatherings of the "Transcendental Club," a group of rebellious Unitarian ministers who supported each other in dissent from what they regarded as the exhausted structures of their church. The club met thirty times in Boston, Concord, and other nearby places between 1836 and 1840, and became a rallying point for the Transcendental new views.[19] Even though he had resigned his Boston pulpit in 1832 before traveling to Europe, he resumed week-to-week supply preaching at a nearby church in East Lexington. This job required no ministerial duties except the one he preferred—preaching— and he had carefully preserved his stock of manuscript sermons (now held in the Houghton Library at Harvard). Throughout this busy Concord life Emerson continued to be remarkably productive and creative in his work as a "scholar."[20] He was a vigorous writer with a steely discipline, who conducted extensive correspondence and generated a continual flow of lectures, essays, and poems. Most crucially, he maintained a voluminous

18   Bliss Perry, *Emerson Today* (Princeton, NJ: Princeton University Press, 1931), 47. For an important study of the family context of Emerson's work and career, written from the perspective of women's history and family history, see Phyllis Cole, *Mary Moody Emerson and the Origins of Transcendentalism: A Family History* (New York: Oxford University Press, 1998).

19   For an informative study of the Transcendental Club, see Joel Myerson, "A Calendar of Transcendental Club Meetings," *American Literature* 44 (May 1972): 197-207. The origin of the name Transcendentalism seems to be obscure, but was most likely used first as a pejorative description. Emerson offered an explanation of the movement in his 1841 essay "The Transcendentalist" (*CW* 1: 201-16). For a thoughtful analysis see Charles Capper, "'A Little Beyond': The Problem of the Transcendentalist Movement in American History," *Journal of American History* 85 (September 1998): 502-39.

20   For a study of Emerson's long-developing conception of the scholar, one of his central concerns, see Merton M. Sealts, Jr., *Emerson on the Scholar* (Columbia, MO: University of Missouri Press, 1992).

journal that was the taproot of all of his work. He was able to accomplish all this, Bliss Perry explains, through "the long, inviolable mornings in his study," which began early and were sustained by "two cups of coffee and— it must be owned—a piece of pie."[21]

Foremost among his projects in the middle and late 1830s were annual winter lectures in Boston, performances that developed a local following and eventually enabled Emerson to expand his travels into other areas in the Northeast and the growing Midwest. His Boston lectures were a testing ground for his newest thinking, and served as the basis for the essay collections, published in the early 1840s, that became the cornerstone of his literary career. Two controversial public addresses at Harvard accelerated his rise as a public figure; these remain among his best known and most enduring cultural legacies. The first was a provocative address to the 1837 meeting of the Phi Beta Kappa Society, traditionally a celebration of "The American Scholar."

2.6 "American Scholar Address," 1837.

---

21   Perry, 54.

Emerson used the title as a vantage for critique rather than celebration, charging that "the spirit of the American freeman is already suspected to be timid, imitative, tame. Public and private avarice make the air we breathe thick and fat. The scholar is decent, indolent, complaisant."[22]

Applying the primary message of *Nature* to the literary and creative life, he urged original independence rather than passive compliance. While books were presumably the scholar's chief concern, Emerson called them dangerous when they stood in the way of independent thinking. "Meek young men grow up in libraries, believing it their duty to accept the views which Cicero, which Locke, which Bacon, have given; forgetful that Cicero, Locke and Bacon were only young men in libraries when they wrote these books." Each new generation, he argued "must write its own books," using the past for inspiration, but testing all received values against the conditions of the present. [23] "Books are for the scholars' idle times," he declared, cautioning against imitative, passive, or merely receptive reading that leads not to "Man Thinking" but instead to "the bookworm."[24] He urged the scholar—he might have said the "author," "the artist," or "the builder," or anyone of a creative and critical mind—to return to the primordial energy of nature to become original and authentic. "The one thing in the world of value, is, the active soul."[25]

As we view it now, this appears to be the moment when Emerson emerged into public prominence. Controversial to some of his listeners because of its hard-edged critique of American intellectual culture, "The American Scholar" was nevertheless memorable. As time passed," Richardson observed, "the talk became famous, even legendary."[26] He cites Oliver Wendell Holmes's enduring claim that "The American Scholar" was "our intellectual Declaration of Independence,"[27] a characterization that addressed America's deep-rooted sense of literary and artistic inferiority in the face of Europe. Emerson frankly disparaged the feebleness of

---

22   *CW* 1: 69.
23   *CW* 1: 56.
24   *CW* 1: 57 and 56.
25   *CW* 1: 56. For an important study of the background and impact of the address, see Kenneth S. Sacks, *Understanding Emerson: The American Scholar and His Struggle for Self-Reliance* (Princeton, NJ: Princeton University Press, 2003).
26   Richardson, 263.
27   Oliver Wendell Holmes, *Ralph Waldo Emerson* (Boston, Mass.: Houghton Mifflin, 1885), 115. For reactions to the address, see Bliss Perry, "Emerson's Most Famous Speech," in *The Praise of Folly and Other Papers* (Boston, Mass.: Houghton Mifflin, 1923), 81-112; John McAleer, *Ralph Waldo Emerson: Days of Encounter* (Boston, Mass.: Little, Brown & Co., 1984), 234-39; Sealts, *Scholar*, 97-110; Richardson, 262-65; and Sacks, 12-20.

American writing, a pursuit that seemed to falter "amongst a people too busy to give letters" serious attention.[28] When, unexpectedly, he received a second invitation to keynote a public event at Harvard, he was given the opportunity to assess the doctrines of Christianity and the state of the church, the most sacrosanct of his culture's foundations.

In the spring of 1838 the graduating students from Harvard Divinity School, the stronghold of New England Unitarianism, invited Emerson to speak at their commencement the next July. These beginning ministers numbered only seven, but the ceremony in the chapel at Divinity Hall was filled with close to a hundred alumni, faculty members, local pastors, friends, and family. Several key figures in the Unitarian establishment were there, including the erudite Biblical scholar Andrews Norton; Divinity School Dean John Gorham Palfrey, later prominent as an antislavery politician and historian; and Henry Ware, Jr., a Harvard faculty member who had been Emerson's predecessor and mentor in the pulpit at Boston's Second Church.[29] In "The American Scholar," Emerson had applied the principles of originality and direct experience to literature, scholarship, and action. In what became known as his "Divinity School Address," he measured religion and contemporary worship by this same standard. He argued that the religious spirit itself was being stifled by the routine performance of empty ceremony and rote creed.

Emerson called his listeners back to the "sentiment of virtue," an inherent "delight in the presence of certain divine laws." To assure them that he was not opening a conventional theological exposition, he explained that "these laws refuse to be adequately stated," but are instead revealed through direct experience, what we encounter daily "in each other's faces, in each other's actions, in our own remorse."[30] Such experience was, he believed, innate, the sign within us of the same ceaseless energy that coursed through nature. "This sentiment," he explained, "lies at the foundation of society, and successively creates all forms of worship. The principle of veneration never dies out."[31]

---

28   *CW* 1: 52.

29   On the background and setting of the Divinity School Address, see Conrad Wright, "Emerson, Barzillai Frost, and the Divinity School *Address*," in his *The Liberal Christians: Essays on American Unitarian History* (Boston, Mass.: Beacon Press, 1970); and Wright, "'Soul is Good, but Body is Good Too,'" *Journal of Unitarian and Universalist History* 37 (2013-2014): 1-20.

30   *CW* 1: 77.

31   *CW* 1: 79.

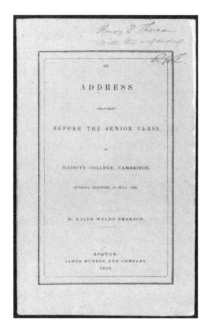

2.7 "Divinity School Address," 1838.

Emerson wanted to return the church and its ministers to the direct, experiential roots of religion and thereby free them from the hollow forms of belief and worship that were now too common. He audaciously rejected the significance of Biblical miracles, and explained Jesus's claim to be the son of God as an arresting metaphor for his sense of a divinity within every man and woman. Jesus demonstrated an inner spiritual power that was not unique, but potentially universal. "Alone in all history, [Jesus] estimated the greatness of man," Emerson maintained.[32] While he showed a reverence for Jesus, he by no means granted him a divine or supernatural character, as it was broadly understood in the 1830s.

Making himself more explicit, and more shocking, Emerson also denied the personhood of God in his description of the shortcomings of his religious tradition. "Historical Christianity has fallen into the error that corrupts all attempts to communicate religion. As it appears to us, and as it has appeared for ages, it is not the doctrine of the soul, but an exaggeration of the personal, the positive, the ritual. It has dwelt, it dwells,

---

32   CW 1: 81.

with noxious exaggeration about the *person* of Jesus. The soul knows no persons."[33] Uneasy with the theological use of anthropomorphic terms such as "Father," Emerson saw the personification of God as a false projection of limited human qualities onto an unfathomable power. His rejection of the personhood of God was one of his most disquieting ideas, inviting the strong criticism of his former ministerial mentor, Henry Ware. Ware insisted that an impersonal God lacked religious value. But Emerson held that to personalize God was to limit one's access to deeper sources of religious energy. Emerson sometimes used the word "God," in his journal and in his published work, but he constantly searched for other ways to express this originating energy: "Soul," "Over-Soul," "World Soul," "Spirit," "One," "Moral Sense," and "Moral Law." Emerson's conception of a continually developing deity corresponded with his belief in the potential for a continually growing spiritual awareness of the individual, and provided the basis for a revitalized spirituality, stripped of religious mythology and churchly traditions.[34]

Emerson himself was a product of the tradition that he was so frankly condemning. He revered the eloquent preaching of William Ellery Channing, whose landmark sermon of 1819, "Unitarian Christianity," had separated Unitarians from the Calvinist-grounded Congregationalism that had been New England's dominant theology for two centuries. The Unitarians dismissed the concept of original sin and affirmed the spiritual resources of every individual. They advocated a life of disciplined self-examination and continuing spiritual development. But Emerson's skepticism about Biblical miracles and Jesus as a supernatural figure touched sensitive points of Christian belief that were still dear to most Unitarians. He asked this graduating class—and by extension their professors and everyone gathered—not to accept these cherished precepts without intense scrutiny. Only through their witness to a direct experience of the holy might they preach with influence to their churches, and "convert life into truth."[35]

---

33 *CW* 1: 82.

34 On Emerson's stance of openness and change, his essay "Circles" (*CW* 2: 177-90) is of particular importance. See David M. Robinson, "Emerson and Religion," *Historical Guide to Ralph Waldo Emerson*, ed. Joel Myerson (New York: Oxford University Press, 2000), 165-67.

35 *CW* 1: 86.

2.8 Walden Pond from Emerson's Cliff, 1903.

While the "American Scholar" had ruffled some of its listeners, this attack on both Christian doctrine and church practice provoked a storm of controversy. A week after the address was published, a Boston newspaper brought out a stinging attack against it by Harvard's leading Biblical scholar, Andrews Norton, who himself had been a leader in the Unitarian break with Calvinism. A year later, at a meeting of Divinity School alumni, Norton expanded his attack on Emerson's Address with a fiery rebuttal, "A Discourse on the Latest Form of Infidelity."[36] Norton

---

36   For Norton's initial response, see Andrews Norton, "The New School in Literature and Religion," *Boston Daily Advertiser* (August 27, 1838), 2, http://bit.ly/1E9IslN; reprinted in Joel Myerson, ed., *Transcendentalism: A Reader* (New York: Oxford University Press, 2000), 246-50. For his address to the Divinity School alumni a year after Emerson's Address, see *A Discourse on the Latest Form of Infidelity* (Cambridge, Mass.: John Owen, 1839), excerpted with an informative discussion of the controversy, in Perry Miller, ed., *The Transcendentalists: An Anthology* (Cambridge, Mass.: Harvard University Press, 1950).

spoke for those Unitarians who viewed Emerson's ideas as a dangerously subversive abandonment of the key elements of Christianity. Cranch, ever loyal to Emerson, lost no time caricaturing Norton in an outrage and circulated the cartoon among his transcendentalist friends. Although ruffled, Emerson refused to engage his critics directly in public debate, rejecting a pamphlet war that would drain his energies for the campaign that he wanted to continue.[37]

Emerson believed that these conflicts were signs of much more than a theological schism. They registered a wider divergence of perspective and values in his culture, and they held the promise of a significant cultural transformation. "The two omnipresent parties of History, the party of the Past and the party of the Future, divide society to-day as of old," he argued in his series "Lectures on the Times, 1841-1842." He could feel the progressive currents of egalitarian change and predicted that "the present age will be marked by its harvest of projects, for the reform of domestic, civil, literary, and ecclesiastical institutions."[38] In this atmosphere of contending parties, Emerson and his allies recognized that stronger efforts to spread their views were needed, and that one of their most pressing needs was a journal of Transcendentalist opinion and artistic expression. In July 1840, Emerson, Margaret Fuller, George Ripley, and others launched a new quarterly, *The Dial*.

In its first issue, Emerson provided a rationale for the journal as a voice in "the progress of a revolution" in New England, challenging the adequacy of present forms of literature, religion, and education. Its sources would be innovative, as Emerson described them in "The Editors to the Reader," not the familiar work of established authors, but rather "the discourse of the living, and the portfolios which friendship has opened to us."[39] Fuller served as *The Dial*'s first editor, making her among the earliest American women to edit a literary journal.

---

37 For the reaction to the Divinity School Address, see McAleer, 247-65; Packer, *The Transcendentalists*, 121-29; David M. Robinson, "Poetry, Personality, and the Divinity School Address," *Harvard Theological Review*, 82 (1989): 185-99; Richardson, 295-300; and Lawrence Buell, *Emerson* (Cambridge, Mass.: Belknap Press of Harvard University Press, 2003), 165-69.

38 *CW* 1: 77.

39 *CW* 10: 96, 98.

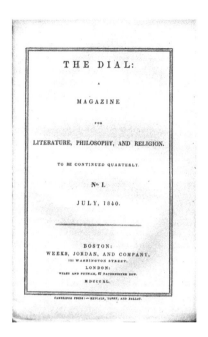

2.9 *The Dial*, wrapper, No. 1, July 1840.

The Dial became particularly important to aspiring poets such as Cranch, Jones Very, Ellen Sturgis Hooper, and Caroline Sturgis Tappan, whose work may not have been easily placed in more conventional journals. Access to *The Dial* was also vital for Fuller, whose work is now recognized as pioneering on several counts. Of particular importance were her 1841 essay "Goethe," the most perceptive early American critical assessment of this literary master, and her epochal defense of women's rights, "The Great Lawsuit." Fuller expanded this article into *Woman in the Nineteenth Century* (1845), a book that brought her to prominence and became a founding document for the women's rights movement in America. Thoreau's early essays on nature and Emerson's defining lecture on "The Transcendentalist" also first reached print via *The Dial*.[40] Bronson Alcott's "Orphic Sayings," aphoristic prose-poems that seemed impenetrably abstract to many readers, were among its most controversial pieces.[41] One

40   See Joel Myerson, *The New England Transcendentalists and the Dial: A History of the Magazine and Its Contributors* (Rutherford, NJ: Fairleigh Dickinson University Press, 1980).

41   On the reception of Alcott's "Orphic Sayings," see Joel Myerson, "'In the Transcendental Emporium': Bronson Alcott's 'Orphic Sayings' in *The Dial*," *English Language Notes* 10 (1972): 31-38.

of the magazine's most forward-thinking projects, jointly promoted by Emerson and Thoreau, was a series of "Ethnical Scriptures," translations of ancient Hindu, Buddhist, and Confucian religious texts. This pioneering effort disseminated knowledge about world religions, encouraging a modern, comparative view of Christianity, and suggesting its place as one faith tradition among the world's religions. Both Emerson and Thoreau remained keenly interested in Asian beliefs, finding links between their radical explorations in spirituality and these classic non-Western traditions. Although *The Dial* was publishing what we now recognize as historically important texts, its subscribers never exceeded about 300, and Emerson, busy with other matters, was finally forced to cease publishing it. But its four-year run had given his friends important encouragement and a common purpose in addressing America's need for a cultural revolution.[42]

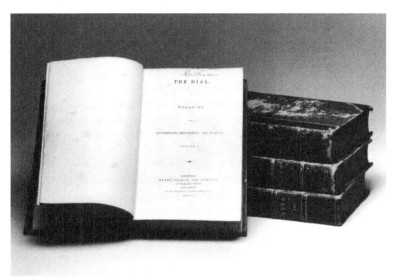

2.10 Emerson's four volumes of *The Dial*.

Emerson's ever-enlarging journal and his rich backlog of public lectures were the foundations for the work that would assure his place in the global literary canon: *Essays I* (1841). Characterized by its sharp-edged aphorisms and epigrammatic turns-of-phrase, this book established Emerson as a

---

42   Myerson, *N. E. Transcendentalists and the Dial*, 95, 96. For an overview of *The Dial*, see Susan Belasco, "The Dial" in *The Oxford Handbook of Transcendentalism*, eds. Joel Myerson, et al. (New York: Oxford University Press, 2010), 373-83.

stylistic innovator and an influential voice of wisdom and ethical guidance. He spoke directly to a rapidly shifting religious climate in which the findings of modern Biblical research and emerging science generated doubt and anxiety, and proposed fresh and revitalizing approaches to spiritual questions. He urged his readers to higher levels of integrity and ethical awareness, and offered them desperately needed freedom from tightly sanctioned limits on their thought and behavior. The best known of his remedies for doubt and anxiety was an essay that codified his own early struggle for self-acceptance and social confidence. He entitled it "Self-Reliance." "Trust thyself; every soul vibrates to that iron string." "Nothing is at last sacred but the integrity of your own mind." "What I must do, is all that concerns me, not what the people think." "Let us affront and reprimand the smooth mediocrity and squalid contentment of the times."[43] These and other lasting affirmations were vivid reminders of the code of courage and balanced self-possession necessary to resist modern society's crushing demands for acquiescence and conformity.

Emerson contended that the self-reliant individual gained strength not from external social approval but from inner resources—spiritual trust and recognition of the moral sentiment—that built and sustained character. Emerson's belief that the self was grounded in a greater Self discouraged egotism on the one hand, and social anarchy on the other. But such trust was hard to achieve and to retain. The distinctive tone of high confidence and optimism in his writings actually disguised his ongoing inner struggle with self-doubt and pessimism. "In the dark hours our existence seems to be a defensive war," he privately recorded in 1835, "a struggle against the encroaching All which threatens with certainty to engulf us soon, & seems impatient of our little reprieve."[44] This voice of insecurity stayed largely hidden in Emerson's speeches and published works, where he regularly put forward a self-assured and resolute persona. But a long history in his own experience with building courage lay behind "Self-Reliance," making his words apply first to himself, then to his readers.

"Self Reliance" was one of twelve essays in this first collection, which included subjects ranging from "History" to "Friendship" to "Art." Together they constitute a loosely structured theory of human culture and the ethical life. While "Self-Reliance" attained cultural significance through its articulation of

43   CW 2: 30, 31, 35. *Essays* was renamed *Essays: First Series* after Emerson published *Essays: Second Series* in 1844.
44   *JMN* 5: 28.

the presumably characteristic national value of individualism, its answering essay, "Friendship," has garnered wider recent attention, as readers of Emerson have come to recognize the social dimensions of his work more deeply. For Emerson, friendship and self-reliance are not mutually exclusive qualities. Each virtue depends on the other for its completion. Friendship must not be taken as a denial of self-reliance, Emerson cautions: "we must be our own, before we can be another's." But true friendship demands careful cultivation and what he terms "a long probation," or period of testing and trial. But its achievement stands as one of the greatest of human fulfillments, the sign of an aware and ethically purposeful life. Friendship is "the nut itself whereof all nature and all thought is but the husk and shell."[45] Emerson's discourse on friendship, with its careful analysis of interpersonal bonds, is a crucial indicator of the social trajectory of Emerson's work in the 1840s and 1850s, which is more directly engaged with the daily conduct of life, its social contexts, and the imperatives of political reform.

:
2.11 Emerson house, front hallway looking north.

---

45   *CW* 2: 124; 119. For a discussion of Emerson and friendship, see the essay collection *Emerson & Thoreau: Figures of Friendship*, eds. John T. Lysaker and William Rossi (Bloomington, IN: Indiana University Press, 2010).

2.12 Second floor nursery, Emerson house.

Self-Reliance and the Challenge of Reform

By the early 1840s Emerson was becoming more engaged in social criticism, developing a more relational theory of the self, and responding to the increasingly rancorous national political climate. Deep personal tragedy reinforced this shift of perspective. In January 1842, soon after the his success with the publication of *Essays I*, his first child Waldo, age five, developed scarlet fever and, within days, died.

"I comprehend nothing of this fact but its bitterness," he confided in his journal. "Explanation I have none, consolation none that rises out of the fact itself; only diversion; only oblivion of this & pursuit of new objects."[46] No stranger to disappointment, injustice, uncertainty, and loss, the death of the cherished Waldo affected him much more deeply than the earlier losses of his father, three brothers, and even his beloved first wife Ellen. Waldo's sudden absence jarringly refocused his attention on the meaning of life's major reversals. The loss accentuated the fragility of life and the tenuous stability of its moods and perspectives, and encouraged openness

---

46   *JMN* 8: 205.

and patience, virtues that clarified the limits of the self. Stunned by the loss, Emerson's grief-guided search for a response pointed him toward determined engagement in this world, and quickened his already discernible turn toward the pragmatic. Meaningful life and true character demanded purpose, will, discipline, stoical patience, and active involvement.[47]

2.13 Waldo Emerson, Jr. (30 October 1836-27 January 1841).

Compelling evidence of this change is Emerson's poem "Threnody," an elegy for Waldo written over many months. It registers Emerson's tortuous passage from blank despair to a renewed worldly purpose. His guide out of this morass is the voice of a "deep Heart" that responds to his personal pain with the assurance that death does not erase abiding values and affections: *"Hearts are dust, hearts' loves remain; / Heart's love will meet thee again."*[48] The poem's companion piece was "Experience," now

---

47   On Emerson's intellectual evolution, see Stephen E. Whicher, *Freedom and Fate: An Inner Life of Ralph Waldo Emerson* (Philadelphia, PA: University of Pennsylvania Press, 1953); Joel Porte, *Representative Man: Ralph Waldo Emerson in His Time* (New York: Oxford University Press, 1979); Packer, *Emerson's Fall*; and David M. Robinson, *Emerson and the Conduct of Life: Pragmatism and Ethical Purpose in the Later Work* (Cambridge and New York: Cambridge University Press, 1993).

48   *CW* 9: 295, 297.

regarded as the greatest of his essays. A complex meditation that blends surrealistic imagery with a succession of gripping voices and shifting moods, the essay records Emerson's voyage from numbed bewilderment to a tempered determination to rise "up again" and confront experience.[49] Strikingly candid in its portrayal of personal loss, "Experience" also sets the direction for the later public phase of his work. Beginning half-way up the stairway of life, Emerson depicts his dazed effort to find his way in a chaotic and misfortune-filled world. "Experience" poses a labyrinthine series of dilemmas in which the resolution of one adversity leads inevitably to another. In contrast with the earlier epiphany in the Jardin des Plantes, or the ecstasy of the transparent eyeball image of *Nature* (only eight years in the past), Emerson now dramatizes the loss of energy, desire, and self-confidence that darkens every purpose. His way forward is less to heal or redeem the private self than to envision the eventual emergence of a more communal justice. He calls for patience, resilient courage, and a conviction that "there is victory yet for all justice."[50] The antidote to misfortune is "the transformation of genius into practical power," the resolute application of one's intellectual resources and ethical commitments with reasoned, persistent effort.[51] Devastated by tragedy, Emerson turned mourning into a motivation for dedicated service.

This evolution toward a larger role in public affairs was not an easy one for Emerson. In 1838, concerned friends and family called on him to protest President Van Buren's order forcing the Cherokee nation to leave Georgia for the West. He wrote a blistering condemnation of the policy as a moral outrage to American civilization. But privately, he recorded his unhappiness at entering this debate over public policy, expressing his inner conflict between his literary calling and his sense of a citizen's public duty to advance progressive political causes.[52] As his stature as a public figure grew, so did his recognition of his responsibility to use his influence productively, especially as the national crisis over slavery and other abrasive issues intensified in the 1840s and 1850s. The revolutionary

---

49   *CW* 3: 49.

50   *CW* 3: 49. On the labyrinthine structure of "Experience," see Robinson, *Emerson and the Conduct of Life*, 58-70.

51   *CW* 3: 49.

52   Emerson's letter of protest is included in *Emerson's Antislavery Writings*, eds. Len Gougeon and Joel Myerson (New Haven, CT: Yale University Press, 2002), 1-5. Hereafter *EAW*. For an insightful discussion of the work and its context, see Richardson, 275-79.

currents of the 1840s in Europe also began to be felt in the United States, and as Larry J. Reynolds has shown, those ideas had a profound impact on Emerson, Margaret Fuller, Walt Whitman, and other American writers.[53] One important sign of the political turn among the Transcendentalists was a growing interest in the philosophy of Charles Fourier, a French utopian social theorist whose work was translated in 1840 by Albert Brisbane. Fourier's complex and sometimes bizarre theories focused on the formation of small communes or "phalanxes" that could create liberating alternatives to the competitive market economy. Emerson's friends George and Sophia Ripley urged him to join them in launching Brook Farm, one of the best known communal experiments of the era, but Emerson demurred. "I think that all I shall solidly do, I must do alone," he wrote to Ripley, remaining sympathetic but skeptical of communal alternatives to familial life.[54] In one sense he was right—the communes did not last long. Brook Farm, though a rewarding experience for many of its members, disbanded after six years in financial failure. Another close friend, Bronson Alcott, launched Fruitlands, an even more short-lived communal experiment that disbanded when facing its first winter.[55] Despite their clear failures as enduring institutions, these efforts were nevertheless valuable expressions of dissent, as Emerson recognized. Their formation signaled important opposition to the powerful new America that was coming into being.

The search for a more harmonious and cooperative form of social organization reflected a deep concern about the nation's hypocritical professions of democracy and its egregious social injustices. In an 1839 journal entry Emerson observed that "the number of reforms preached to this age exceeds the usual measure," an indicator, he believed of "the depth & universality of the movement which betrays itself by such variety of symptom." He offers a brief list of these oppositional groups, suggesting

---

53 Larry J. Reynolds, *European Revolutions and the American Literary Renaissance* (New Haven, CT: Yale University Press, 1988).

54 *L* 2: 370.

55 Albert Brisbane, *The Social Destiny of Man* (Philadelphia, PA: C.F. Stollmeyer, 1840). For a study of the rise of Fourierism in America, see Carl J. Guarneri, *The Utopian Alternative: Fourierism in Nineteenth-Century America* (Ithaca, NY: Cornell University Press, 1994). On Brook Farm, see Joel Myerson, ed., *The Brook Farm Book: A Collection of First-Hand Accounts of the Community* (New York: Garland, 1987); Richard Francis, *Transcendental Utopias: Individual and Community at Brook Farm, Fruitlands and Walden* (Ithaca, NY: Cornell University Press, 1997); Richard Francis, *Fruitlands: The Alcott Family and Their Search for Utopia* (New Haven, CT: Yale University Press, 2010); and Sterling F. Delano, *Brook Farm: The Dark Side of Utopia* (Cambridge, Mass.: Harvard University Press, 2004).

that they address almost every dimension of modern life: "anti-money, anti-war, anti-slavery, anti-government, anti-Christianity, anti-College; and, the rights of Woman."[56] But among these many reform efforts, the antislavery movement would quickly move to prominence, both in Emerson's thinking and on the national scene. One of the pieces that Emerson contributed to *The Dial* was an 1841 speech to the Mechanics' Apprentices' Library Association in Boston, entitled "Man the Reformer." Len Gougeon called attention to one moment in the speech in which Emerson lauded abolitionism for showing Americans their "dreadful debt to the Southern negro."[57] The goods produced by slave labor provided consumers in the North, even those opposed to slavery, with items of comfort and luxury. "We are all implicated, of course, in this charge," Emerson asserts. "It is only necessary to ask a few questions as to the progress of the articles of commerce from the fields where they grew, to our houses, to become aware that we eat and drink and wear perjury and fraud in a hundred commodities."[58]

Emerson remained an advocate of the reform movements, including antislavery, over the next few years, but a somewhat distanced one. He concluded *Essays: Second Series* with the 1844 lecture "New England Reformers," a text that Richardson describes as "calm and qualifying," and containing little mention of the antislavery movement.[59] A brief sentence near the end of that lecture, however, provides an important clue to his attitude about his public role as a spokesman for reform: "Obedience to his genius is the only liberating influence."[60] Emerson was reluctant to leave the path he had set for himself as a "scholar" of philosophy and literature.

---

56   *JMN* 7: 207. For an informative discussion of Emerson's relationship with the social reform advocates of his day, see two essays by Linck C. Johnson: "Reforming the Reformers: Emerson, Thoreau, and the Sunday Lectures at Amory Hall, Boston," *Emerson Society Quarterly: A Journal of the American Renaissance* 37 (4th Quarter 1991): 235-89 (hereafter *ESQ*); "'Liberty is Never Cheap': Emerson, 'The Fugitive Slave Law,' and the Antislavery Lecture Series at the Broadway Tabernacle," *New England Quarterly* 76 (December 2003): 550-92. For an insightful analysis of Emerson's complex and hesitant support of the women's rights movement, see Phyllis Cole, "Woman Questions: Emerson, Fuller, and New England Reform," in *Transient and Permanent: The Transcendentalist Movement and its Contexts*, eds. Charles Capper and Conrad E. Wright (Boston, Mass.: Massachusetts Historical Society and Northeastern University Press, 1999), 408-46.

57   Len Gougeon, "'Only Justice Satisfies All': Emerson's Militant Transcendentalism." *Emerson for the Twenty-First Century: Perspectives on an American Icon*, ed. Barry Tharaud (Newark, Del.: University of Delaware Press, 2010), 496.

58   *CW* 1: 147.

59   Richardson, 395.

60   *CW* 3: 167.

To put it more bluntly, he was wary of becoming enslaved to antislavery, and thereby losing what he felt was his particular voice and mission. Well after he had entered the antislavery effort unreservedly, he would express his misgivings in these arresting words: "I do not often speak to public questions;—they are odious and hurtful, and it seems like meddling or leaving your work. I have my own spirits in prison;—spirits in deeper prisons, whom no man visits if I do not."[61] But as the national political crisis over legal slavery simmered, he realized that the epitome of social injustice was the slave, the man or woman robbed legally of self-possession and the right to act and choose freely. The slaveholder had no right to oppress another individual who was by right his equal. The slave came to represent for him the greatest moral contradiction of modern civilization.[62]

A pivotal moment for Emerson came in the summer of 1844 when he was invited by the Concord Female Anti-Slavery Society to speak on the tenth anniversary of the abolition of slavery in the British West Indies. Urged onward at home by his wife Lidian, and by other women friends, he began to research the history of the slave trade as well as the British parliamentary debates and legislation leading to the abolition of slavery in the Caribbean. This assiduous homework resulted in one of his most stirring addresses in which he described the horrors of slavery in detail and made a powerful case, emotionally and intellectually, that slavery was a moral violation.[63] Emerson's reading had given him a wider understanding of the slave trade and of the physical conditions of slavery in the Caribbean, and had moved him to portray slavery, in vivid terms, as a viscerally moral

---

61 *EAW* 73.

62 For a discussion of Emerson's changing views of race, see Philip L. Nicoloff, *Emerson on Race and History: An Examination of English Traits* (New York: Columbia University Press, 1961), 123 and 142-46; and Gougeon, *Virtue's Hero*, 178-86.

63 "An Address . . . on . . . the Emancipation of the Negroes in the British West Indies," (also known as "Emancipation in the British West Indies" in earlier editions of Emerson's works) has become increasingly central to the Emerson canon. See *EAW* 7-34. Key essays in the burgeoning scholarly discussion of Emerson and antislavery include Gougeon, *Virtue's Hero*; Albert J. Von Frank, *The Trials of Anthony Burns: Freedom and Slavery in Emerson's Boston* (Cambridge, Mass.: Harvard University Press, 1998); Gary Collison, "Emerson and Antislavery," *Historical Guide to Ralph Waldo Emerson*, ed. Joel Myerson (New York and Oxford: Oxford University Press, 2000), 179-209; Phyllis Cole, "Pain and Protest in the Emerson Family," in *The Emerson Dilemma: Essays on Emerson and Social Reform*, ed. T. Gregory Garvey (Athens, GA: University of Georgia Press, 2001), 67-92; Len Gougeon, "Emerson's Abolition Conversion," *The Emerson Dilemma*, 170-96; Sandra Harbert Petrulionis, "'Swelling That Great Tide of Humanity': The Concord, Massachusetts, Female Anti-Slavery Society," *New England Quarterly* 74 (2001), 385-418; Gregg D. Crane, *Race, Citizenship, and Law in American Literature* (New York: Cambridge University Press, 2002); and Buell, *Emerson*, 242-87.

issue: "The blood is moral: the blood is anti-slavery: it runs cold in the veins: the stomach rises with disgust, and curses slavery."[64] The speech signaled an intensified concern with social and political issues, and was a major step in Emerson's adaptation of his identity as a scholar to that of an engaged public commentator and social critic.

International Fame and National Crisis

Increasingly in demand as a lecturer, Emerson traveled extensively on the expanding lyceum circuit, an important source of his income from the 1840s onward.[65]

His itineraries first focused on New England, expanding to the greater Northeast and the Middle Atlantic States, and then after 1850 following the nation's westward expansion to include frontier cities and towns. Conditions for travel were often arduous, and though some audiences were thirsty for culture, others were less than receptive. But Emerson persisted, combining a need for new audiences and continuing income with a desire to bring the life of serious thinking to all who would listen. Emerson clearly wanted to know his country, as his unremitting travels show. But he was a frank and incisive observer, and was often disappointed in what he saw. "Great country, diminutive minds," he noted with disgust in a June 1847 journal entry on "eager, solicitous, hungry, rabid, busy-body America." His lament for American culture centered on its scattered attention and aimless energy. "Alas for America as I must often say, the ungirt, the diffuse, the profuse, procumbent, one wide ground juniper, out of which no cedar, no oak will rear up a mast to the clouds! it all runs to leaves, to suckers, to tendrils, to miscellany. The air is loaded with poppy, with imbecility, with dispersion, & sloth."[66] A little over three months later he was on his way to a lecture tour in Great Britain, where his writings had gained a substantial following.

---

64 *EAW* 10. For Emerson's sources on the history of British abolitionism, see Joseph E. Slater, "Two Sources for Emerson's Fist Address on West Indian Emancipation," *ESQ* 44 (1966), 97-100.

65 For an informative account of Emerson's lecture career and his style and impact as a lecturer, see McAleer, 486-503; Richardson, 418-22; and the editors' "Historical and Textual Introduction" to *The Later Lectures of Ralph Waldo Emerson*, eds. Ronald A. Bosco and Joel Myerson (Athens, GA: University of Georgia Press, 2001), xvii-lxxi. Hereafter *LL*. For Emerson's detailed lecture travels year-by-year, see von Frank, *An Emerson Chronology*.

66 *JMN* 10: 79.

2.14 Emerson at 43, May 1846.

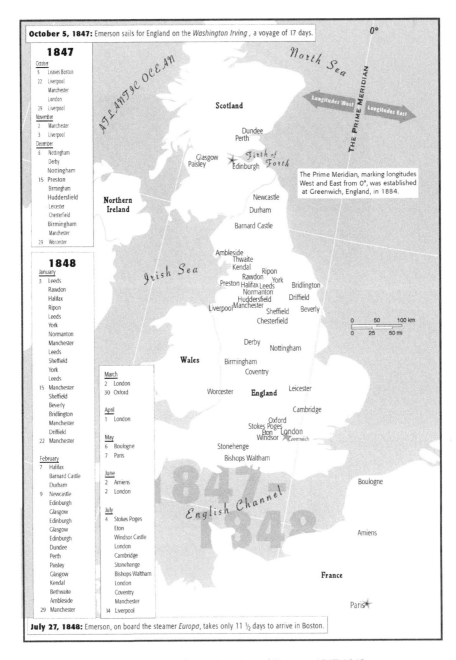

October 5, 1847: Emerson sails for England on the *Washington Irving*, a voyage of 17 days.

0°

1847

October
5   Leaves Boston
22 Liverpool
    Manchester
    London
29 Liverpool
November
2   Manchester
3   Liverpool
December
6   Nottingham
    Derby
    Nottingham
15 Preston
    Birmingham
    Huddersfield
    Leicester
    Chesterfield
    Birmingham
    Manchester
29 Worcester

1848

January
3   Leeds
    Rawdon
    Halifax
    Ripon
    Leeds
    York
    Normanton
    Manchester
    Leeds
    Sheffield
    York
    Leeds
15 Manchester
    Sheffield
    Beverly
    Bridlington
    Manchester
    Driffield
22 Manchester

February
7   Halifax
    Barnard Castle
    Durham
9   Newcastle
    Edinburgh
    Glasgow
    Edinburgh
    Glasgow
    Edinburgh
    Dundee
    Perth
    Paisley
    Glasgow
    Kendal
    Bethwaite
    Ambleside
29 Manchester

March
2   London
30 Oxford

April
1   London

May
6   Boulogne
7   Paris

June
2   Amiens
2   London

July
4   Stokes Poges
    Eton
    Windsor Castle
    London
    Cambridge
    Stonehenge
    Bishops Waltham
    London
    Coventry
    Manchester
14 Liverpool

North Sea

ATLANTIC OCEAN

Scotland

Dundee
Perth

Glasgow
Paisley
Edinburgh

Firth of Forth

Longitudes West — *Longitudes East*

THE PRIME MERIDIAN

Newcastle
Durham
Barnard Castle

The Prime Meridian, marking longitudes West and East from 0°, was established at Greenwich, England, in 1884.

Northern Ireland

Irish Sea

Ambleside
Thwaite
Kendal   Ripon
        Rawdon   York
Preston Halifax Leeds   Bridlington
        Normanton
        Huddersfield   Driffield
Liverpool Manchester
        Sheffield   Beverly
        Chesterfield

0   50   100 km
0   25   50 mi

Derby
        Nottingham

Wales   Birmingham
             Coventry

Worcester   **England**   Leicester

                            Cambridge

                    Oxford
            Stokes Poges
                Eton London
                Windsor Greenwich
Stonehenge
        Bishops Waltham

Boulogne

1847-1848

English Channel

Amiens

France

Paris

July 27, 1848: Emerson, on board the steamer *Europa*, takes only 11 ½ days to arrive in Boston.

2.15 Emerson in Great Britain and France, 1847-1848.

Obviously he was seeking new stimulation, and a respite from the monotonous mediocrity that defined American culture. The ten-month journey to Britain was an eventful and transformative one for Emerson. As Richardson so expressively put it, "England jolted Emerson. Everything seemed different, bigger, faster, heavier . . . . All was bustle and activity in England."[67] Lecturing in Liverpool, Manchester, and cities in the Midlands, he got a close look at England in the midst of its Industrial Revolution, and spoke to a varied audience that included workingmen's groups. He had Thomas Carlyle's assistance in London, and met literary celebrities such as Tennyson, George Eliot, and Dickens. Yet the England that Emerson visited was also an anxious nation, concerned about its own stability as it witnessed continental Europe erupt in political revolution in 1848. In a three-week interlude during the spring of 1848, he traveled to Paris where he witnessed the barricaded city in open revolution. He corresponded with Margaret Fuller, then in Italy, who had become an ardent proponent of the Italian *Risorgimento* led by Giuseppe Mazzini.[68] This tense political atmosphere kept him in constant thought about the divided, rancorous America to which he would return. In this sense, Emerson was a tourist with a double vision; he wanted to see and understand the new Britain that was rising as the world's greatest commercial and industrial power, and he also wanted the perspective that this other nation could give him on America. These questions were at the heart of his 1856 volume, *English Traits*, a work that combined descriptive aspects of the travel narrative with social analysis directed ultimately at the prospects of American advancement.

The future of America, he recognized, would be determined by how it responded to the slavery crisis, a question deeply rooted in the issue of race. Emerson's initial reaction to England's remarkable industrial growth and commercial power was to attribute it to the power of the Saxon "race." The category of race was a large one in the 1840s, much under scientific discussion, and it was a form of classification that included a variety of peoples, as Philip F. Nicoloff has written.[69] Drawn to racial explanations of British power initially, Emerson was forced to look into theories of race more deeply, and ultimately rejected one of the central ideas of the

---

67 Richardson, 441.
68 On Emerson's lecture tour in England, see von Frank, *An Emerson Chronology*, 218-37; McAleer, *Emerson*, 428-77; and Richardson, 441-56. On Emerson's experience in Paris, and Fuller's in Italy, see Reynolds, 31-36 and 54-78.
69 Nicoloff, 118-23.

day, the fixity of the races. "The limitations of the formidable doctrine of race suggest others which threaten to undermine it, as not sufficiently based," he wrote in the chapter on "Race" in *English Traits*. "The fixity or incontrovertibleness of races as we see them, is a weak argument for the eternity of these frail boundaries, since all our historical period is a point to the duration in which nature has wrought." In appealing to the vastness of historical time, Emerson dissolved the "frail boundaries" of racial division, and clarified the grounds of human equality upon which the essential moral objection to slavery rested.[70]

2.16 Emerson's study, 1972.

Emerson's English tour had another powerful impact on him. He saw not only the growing industrial economy of England, but also the history-making achievements of its scientists. The most crucial evidence of this impact can be found in the set of new lectures that he wrote and delivered in London in the early summer of 1848, "Mind and Manners of the Nineteenth Century." Addresses he heard by the prominent paleontologist

---

70   *CW* 5: 27. For a more detailed discussion of the impact of Emerson's tour of Great Britain and his thoughts on race and American politics, see Robinson, *Emerson and the Conduct of Life*, 112-33.

Richard Owen and the renowned theorist of electricity Michael Faraday stimulated Emerson to return to key questions that he had pursued in his own early natural history lectures, and in his first book *Nature*. Published from manuscript in 2001 in Joel Myerson and Ronald A. Bosco's edition of Emerson's *Later Lectures*, the "Mind and Manners of the Nineteenth Century" series has proven to be an extremely important addition to the Emerson canon. The lectures clarify the impact of modern science on Emerson's later thinking, bringing out a further dimension of his interest in the pragmatic, the material, and the empirical. This scientific bent, which Emerson sought to merge with his earlier commitment to idealism, evolved into a recurring project over the later phase of his career.[71]

2.17 Emerson's pocket globe (terrestrial and celestial).

---

71   *LL 1: 129-89.* On Emerson's London lectures see Laura Dassow Walls, "'If Body Can Sing': Emerson and Victorian Science," *Emerson Bicentennial Essays,* eds. Ronald A. Bosco and Joel Myerson (Boston, Mass.: Massachusetts Historical Society and University Press of Virginia, 2006), 334-66; David M. Robinson, "Experience, Instinct, and Emerson's Philosophical Reorientation," *Emerson Bicentennial Essays,* 391-404; and David M. Robinson, "British Science, The London Lectures, and Emerson's Philosophical Reorientation," in *Emerson for the Twenty-First Century: Globalism and the Circularity of Influence,* ed. Barry Tharaud (Newark, Del.: University of Delaware Press, 2010), 285-300.

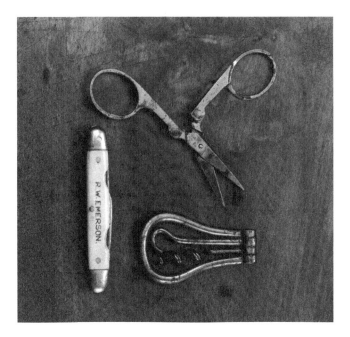

2.18 Emerson's penknife, bottle-opener/hook, and scissors.

2.19 Emerson at 45, 1848.

Emerson returned home in July 1848 to a nation in deepening political crisis over slavery. Once back, he acknowledged having allowed himself "freely to be dazzled by the various brilliancy of men of talent," but found himself in "no way helped."[72] The journey had, however, shown him America from a new critical perspective, and he would need that perspective in the coming decade.

2.20 Period Map of U.S. in 1848, railroad timetable.

Freshly appreciative of America as a young nation with hopeful ideas, he was also reminded of his nation's faults and areas of blindness. The political crisis accelerated on the 7th of March, 1850, when New England's most respected political figure, Daniel Webster, delivered the speech that enabled passage of the Fugitive Slave Law, an integral part of the Compromise of 1850. This law required the institutions, and the citizens, of the Northern states to cooperate in returning escaped slaves to their legal owners. Infuriated by this betrayal, Emerson watched as the law began to take effect and escaped slaves were returned to their bondage in the South.

72   *JMN* 10: 339.

2.21 Emerson at about 47, c. 1850.

In 1851, with "that detestable law" on his mind, he entered this pledge in his journal: "All I have, and all I can do shall be given & done in opposition to the execution of this law."[73]

---

73   *JMN* 11: 344.

2.2 Dialogues with Self and Society, 1835-1860

Jean McClure Mudge

"I was as a gem concealed;
 Me my burning ray revealed."

The Koran, as quoted by Emerson in"Love," Essays I (1841)

To appreciate the role that Emerson's inner life played in his translation of ideas into action, understanding his method of pursuing the truth is vital. In that quest, verbal exchange was primary. And dialogue, of course, depended upon words. Since boyhood, the Bible's opening claim, "In the beginning was the Word," had resounded in his young mind like an organ's deepest diapason chord. What did words mean? How close to the truth were they? Bored in church as a child, he had once said over and over, "'black,' 'white,' 'board,' etc., twenty or thirty times" until they became utter nonsense. Words were quite arbitrary, he realized, and were at least one level away from the tangible world. Here was "a child's first lesson in Idealism," as he put it, the sense of a reality beyond any concrete thing or imperfect name for it.[74]

---

74 *The Journals and Miscellaneous Notebooks of Ralph Waldo Emerson,* 16 vols., eds. William H. Gilman, et al. (Cambridge, Mass.: Harvard University Press, 1960-1982), 8: 30. Hereafter *JMN.*

http://dx.doi.org/10.11647/OBP.0065.04

Words as mere metaphors gained strength when nine-year-old Emerson started writing poetry. Later, his poetic perspective made Harvard's "higher criticism" of the Bible, or any text, all the more easy to accept. Language necessarily conveyed common meanings, but no word—casual or established—could define the truth for Emerson for all time. He also saw that body language, especially the face and eyes, could nuance speech or communicate wordlessly. Further, he came to appreciate that "the language of the street"—slang, double negatives, even oaths and cursing—was stronger and closer to vital life than proper speech. "Cut these words & they would bleed . . . ," he wrote.[75] Then as his lecturing career began, the limits of words took on new urgency. At the same time, close friendships forced him to explore his innermost being. In late 1839 and early 1840, he wrote the lectures on "Love" and "Friendship," placing them in the first half of his *Essays I* (1841). Though clearly wanting his feelings to be glimpsed, he long kept his very core a secret, even from himself.

Exploring Emerson's emotional life reveals that his public position as a Transcendental thinker ensconced in Concord's countryside encompassed private passions as fiery as his mind. Not fully understanding these himself, he had to come to grips with his feelings before he defined his goals as a lecturer. Recognizing himself in his heart of hearts was also essential before he entered the world of social reform. His earliest experiences with love and friendship had arisen in a relatively affection-free atmosphere, ruled by his dedicated but distant mother and aunt. Encouraged by their cool models, eight-year-old Ralph then built a stronger emotional and psychological wall after his father's death, adopting an inherited sense of privilege as well as duty that pushed away all but his brothers. By age eleven, when his excellent memory and oratory skills led a Concord storekeeper to put him up on a sugar barrel to recite for customers, he could genuinely feel superior—partial solace and compensation for the family's waning resources. Such performances help explain his unpopularity and quarreling with other boys, while he remained liked by adults, as his uncle Samuel Ripley noted.[76] Ralph's complex barrier of combined family position, responsibility, talent, and self-defense also grew from a desire to distinguish himself from his father's tarnished

---

75   *JMN* 7: 374. See also, John McAleer, "Emerson as Lecturer," *Ralph Waldo Emerson: Days of Encounter* (Boston, Mass.: Little, Brown & Co., 1984).

76   McAleer, 43.

reputation as a profligate spender and, for some, even a lady's man. (As seen in Chapter 1, after William Emerson's death, his wife and sister Mary rarely mentioned him.) Aloofness allowed Ralph to limit his chances to be offended, or to offend. When in his late thirties he was brought to face his "mask," as he himself called it, the process was slow and came about through intense Socratic dialogue.

In Emerson's day, dialogue, or conversation, was *the* popular mode for social interaction, a parallel on the everyday level of the era's rage for oratory. Boston's educated—meeting informally in each other's homes, bookstores, and increasingly in hotels—demanded quality thoughts from leaders in their midst, and among themselves. Superb conversation was noted between friends of both genders, often prompted by public speeches from such revered local figures as William Ellery Channing in the pulpit and Daniel Webster in the U.S. Senate. Margaret Fuller led more deliberate exchanges for women alone, occasionally attended by men, through private subscription to her "Conversations." So, too, did Elizabeth Peabody at her "Foreign Library" bookstore near Boston Common. As Emerson lectured his way toward stature in the 1830s, he mined private conversations, beginning with dialogues with himself, including dreams, as raw material for his public words. Often he would take whole sections from his journal—his "Savings Bank," as he called it—or from letters to friends to quote verbatim or re-work for his lectures. Both his journals and letters were often based on talks with friends on walks, at his dinner table, in his study, or gleaned from public speeches, more often than not given by men whom he knew. He carried on other conversations with stimulating printed sources, a "creative reading" stemming from his desire to use them in his lectures.[77] From journal to lecture, he further developed and revised his ideas-in-dialogue into published essays.

Lecturing as Conversation

Just home from Europe in the fall of 1833, thirty-year-old Emerson reinvented himself as a scholarly entrepreneur, a lecturer with high purpose. Self-defined in Italy as an American "Adam," he projected himself as the inaugurator of a new cultural start for the country. Freedom and

---

77   *JMN* 5: 233.

self-command, previously only for royalty or clergy before the Revolution, were now possible for all citizens. Every man and woman was a potential king or queen if s/he played the "iron string" of selfhood in harmony with God and Moral Law; this was, simply put, "ethics without cant."[78]

Emerson's inheritance from his first wife Ellen, fully in hand by 1837, was yet insufficient to support his financial needs, so he sold tickets for his talks and felt the compensation well deserved.[79] He read from prepared texts, but expected audiences to react, as his family had reacted when he practiced beforehand. He explained to Carlyle: "... I preach in the Lecture-Room and then it tells, for there is no prescription [proscription]. You may laugh, weep, reason, sing, sneer, or pray, according to your genius. It is the new pulpit, and very much in vogue with my northern countrymen."[80] Emerson began his lecturing career with a single appearance in Boston in November 1833, which in series format grew to seven the next year. By 1838, he was delivering thirty lectures per year, singly or as courses, largely in eastern Massachusetts and southern New Hampshire.[81]

Building on his preaching reputation, Emerson often surpassed his own standard for public speaking. Contemporaries reported, "His coming into the room had the magic of sunlight"; his smile made him "the translated inhabitant of some higher sphere"; and his deep baritone voice had "the appeal of silver trumpets." Even his eye seemed trumpet-like. Normally, he read quietly, hands folded, from a manuscript of about forty pages. But to emphasize a point, he would make a fist with his right hand, knuckles up, and come down with his forearm while shooting his audience "such a glance as no one ever saw except from Emerson: ... like the reveille of a trumpet." The fingers of his left hand seemed to let out energy, another profile testified: "He stands at an acute angle towards his audience, and limberly, and has barely a gesture beyond the motion of the left hand at his side, as if the intensity of his thoughts was escaping, like the electricity of a battery, at that point."

---

78 James Elliot Cabot, *A Memoir of Ralph Waldo Emerson* (Boston, Mass.: Houghton Mifflin, 1887), 1: 150, as quoted in McAleer, 487, http://catalog.hathitrust.org/Record/000389431
79 *JMN* 7: 312.
80 From Taylor Stoehr, *Nay-Saying in Concord* (Hamden, CT: Archon Books, 1979), 28; *The Correspondence of Emerson and Carlyle*, ed. Joseph Slater (New York: Columbia University Press, 1964), 171.
81 Robert D. Richardson, Jr., *Emerson: The Mind on Fire* (Berkeley, CA: University of California Press, 1995), 418.

2.22 Emerson at 45, 1848.

2.23 Emerson caricatures, *New York Tribune*, 6 February 1849.

Emerson's reserved, plain style contrasted with the era's flamboyant oratory. Yet he generated such spiritual excitement that a spoof of him in the *New York Tribune* only underlined his effect. Its four cartoons showed him with an axe chipping sparks off the world, dancing on his toes while emitting charges from hair and hands, grabbing a comet's tail for a ride, and swinging from a rainbow between earth and stars, a clear put-down to delight Gotham's empirically-minded readers. Nevertheless, with his high-minded message and deep penetrating voice, Emerson would become the country's most persuasive lecturer.[82]

By 1837, Boston educator Bronson Alcott saw Emerson's power as poetical rather than logical, his earthy language moving seamlessly into expressions of "loftiness" and "grandeur." He spoke of his "whip of small chords—delicate and subtle of speech, eloquent with truth," and predicted his friend's international success: "Emerson is destined to be the high literary name of this age."[83] Margaret Fuller, a powerful intellectual force among Boston's young, had earlier drawn spiritual strength from Emerson as a preacher, and now found his lectures subtly powerful and lyrically inspiring.[84] Even the uneducated flocked to him. A Mrs. Bemis of Concord never missed an Emerson lecture. Not understanding a word but undaunted, she "got the lesson from the tone and attitude of the man"[85]

After moving into his own house in Concord in 1834, Emerson came to nickname it "Bush," probably with reference to the forty-four pine trees he eagerly planted around it.[86] Bush became one of the centers for the Transcendental Club, begun by Emerson and Unitarian minister friends: his cousin George Ripley, George Putnam, and Frederic Henry Hedge. (It

---

82   Julian Hawthorne, *The Memoirs of Julian Hawthorne*, ed. Edith Garrigues Hawthorne. (New York: Macmillan, 1938), 94, 95; *Thoreau, Man of Concord*, ed. Walter Harding (New York: Holt, Rinehart, and Winston, 1960), 29, as quoted in Harmon L. Smith, *My Friend, My Friend: The Story of Thoreau's Relationship with Emerson* (Amherst, Mass.: University of Massachusetts Press, 1999), 6; Richardson, 195; McAleer, 493. *New York Herald Tribune*, Tuesday, 6 February 1849; reproduced in *Emerson's Prose and Poetry*, eds. Joel Porte and Saundra Morris (New York: Norton, 2001), 588.

83   A. Bronson Alcott, *The Journals of Bronson Alcott*, ed. Odell Shepard (Boston, Mass.: Little, Brown & Co., 1938), January, Week III, 1837, 81-82. Hereafter *JBA*.

84   Charles Capper, *Margaret Fuller: An American Romantic Life: The Private Years*, I (New York: Oxford University Press, 1992), 215-16, 237, 324.

85   McAleer, 153.

86   Megan Marshall, *Margaret Fuller: A New American Life* (Houghton Mifflin Harcourt, 2014), 119. The speaker of Emerson's poem "Good-Bye" (1847) happily forswears the world's vanities for his "own hearth-stone," where he is "in the bush with God— ." *The Collected Works of Ralph Waldo Emerson*, eds. Robert E. Spiller, et al. (Cambridge, Mass.: The Belknap Press of Harvard University Press, 2011), 9: 75-76. Hereafter *CW*.

was long called "Hedge's Club.") To emphasize their "new thinking" as distinct and to broadcast their rebelliousness from Harvard's establishment, the group's founding meeting was held in Cambridge on September 8, 1836, the same day the college celebrated its bicentennial.[87]

2.24 Harvard Bicentennial Celebration, 1836.

2.25 Emerson Dining Room.

---

87   Richardson, 245.

Other diverse, earnest, and well-read young Unitarian ministers came to join them, the group often gathering over dinner at Emerson's house. Like Emerson, they were largely fatherless, and thus felt all the more liberated to question tradition. But unlike him, as full-time pastors, they were wary and initially not as out-spoken as he in making their views public. In this loose membership, the non-clergymen Emerson and Alcott were the most radical, not counting Henry David Thoreau, who attended only sporadically. Alcott occasionally invited his teaching assistant, the insightful and well-educated Elizabeth Peabody, sister of Nathaniel Hawthorne's future wife, Sophia. Other women visitors were Ripley's wife, Sarah, Mary Moody Emerson, Elizabeth Hoar (fiancée of Emerson's brother Charles), and Margaret Fuller. This range of views insured fresh ideas would always be vigorously debated, even though the men dominated.[88]

2.26 Elizabeth Hoar with unidentified child, c. 1850.

Amos Bronson Alcott

Alcott, Thoreau, and Fuller were the three friends who most closely observed and seriously conversed with Emerson as his public persona took shape beyond the pastorate and his innermost identity was revealed, at least to himself. Four years older, Alcott came from a modest farming family near New Haven, Connecticut and was bright, sensitive, largely self-taught, a

88   Ibid., 245-49.

voracious reader, and a dedicated idealist.[89] A peddler in Virginia and the Carolinas for six years, he adopted his clients' genteel speech and manners. By 1828, he had begun teaching school in Boston, and heard Emerson preach for the first time the following year, judging him one of the "lesser glories of [Boston's] moral world," below the "pre-eminent" William Ellery Channing. In late January 1830, he again heard Emerson preach "a good sermon" on *"Conscience."*[90] After briefly teaching in Pennsylvania, Alcott returned to Boston in 1834, and with Elizabeth Peabody's help, started a small experimental school for pre-teen children at the Masonic Temple.

2.27 A. Bronson Alcott in his 40s, c. 1840s.

From this time forward, Alcott, hearing Emerson lecture rather than preach, was increasingly impressed with his content and style.[91] The two men also began exchanging visits between Boston and Concord. Meanwhile, Alcott published *Record of a School* (1835), Peabody's verbatim record of Alcott's Q & A sessions with his students on the subject of character. Emerson, on reading this testimony to infant wisdom, was captured by Alcott's sense of children as innocent souls only recently arrived from eternity — a

---

89   Frederick C. Dahlstrand, *Amos Bronson Alcott: An Intellectual Biography* (London: Associated University Presses, 1982), 17-18.

90   *JBA* 12, 19, 23.

91   On Emerson's Michelangelo lecture in 1835, Alcott remarked, "Few men — take nobler views of the mission, powers, and destinies of man than Mr. Emerson." *JBA*, 56.

sharp contrast to New England's residual ideas about original sin.[92] By mid-October 1835, Alcott's growing enthusiasm for Emerson approached hero-worship: he had become "a *revelation of the Divine Spirit*, an *uttering Word* [emphasis his]." In Concord, Alcott had a scintillating "intellectual and spiritual" conversation with Emerson and his family. Returning in late November, he correctly prophesied, "I shall seek [Mr. Emerson's] face and favor as a precious delight of life."[93] Alcott would always address his friend as "Mr. Emerson," reflecting his sense of their educational and social differences.

In February 1836, while still working on *Nature*, Emerson accepted Alcott's request to critique his draft essay, "Psyche or Breath of Childhood," a study of his daughters and their supposed proximity to the unseen world. Emerson suggested he rewrite this endless paean to Spirit, Life, or God, which Alcott did, but by August, though Emerson supported publication, Alcott had shelved the idea.[94] His attention was on a second book, *Conversations with Children on the Gospels*.[95] Six months before its publication, Peabody warned Alcott about including certain "unveiled physiological references"—birth and circumcision—as potentially incendiary. (In the fall, she left the school in protest, and Margaret Fuller replaced her.) When the book attracted heavy criticism, Emerson, Peabody, and Ripley came to Alcott's defense. But by 1838, his school much shrunken, he returned to "Psyche" and Emerson's criticism.[96]

In fact, some of Alcott's ideas had apparently found their way into Emerson's *Nature*.[97] In May 1837, Emerson, valuing his friend's thoughts, commanded Alcott to leave teaching and, in effect, adopt his own strategy, "Write! . . . the written word abides, until slowly and unexpectedly and in widely sundered places it has created its own church." But Alcott wanted to be an active teacher, and privately thought Emerson overestimated his talents.[98] Also, after his stay with the Emersons for a few days that May, he saw his host's distance from others, even, he charged, "using them for his own benefit and as means of gathering materials for his works." He

---

92 Dahlstrand, *Amos Bronson Alcott*, 130-31.
93 *JBA*, 58, 68-69, 70.
94 Dahlstrand, 145.
95 Emerson heard Alcott read his introduction, a summary of his Transcendentalist thought, with "pleasure," Alcott reported. *JBA*, 79.
96 Dalhstrand, *Amos Bronson Alcott*, 140-41; *JBA* 75.
97 *JBA*, 78
98 Ibid., 89, 90. Emerson quoted Alcott: "Every man, he said, is a Revelation, & ought to write his Record. But few with the pen." *JMN* 5: 98.

accused Emerson of being too idealistic and intellectual, too drawn to a perfect beauty rather than truth, too interested in effect and fame, in short, "A great intellect, refined by elegant study, rather than a divine life radiant with the beauty of truth and holiness. He is an eye more than a heart, an intellect more than a soul."[99]

Simultaneously, Emerson was privately noting the innate distance between any two persons, "Is it not pathetic that the action of men on men is so partial? We never touch but at points . . . . Here is Alcott by my door—yet is the union more profound? No, the Sea, vocation, poverty, are seeming fences, but Man is insular, and cannot be touched. Every man is an infinitely repellent orb & holds his individual being on that condition."[100] To be true to one's nature demanded solitude. By late January 1838, however, Alcott, who had recently repeated his complaints about Emerson, was momentarily warmed by his words as the two walked to his house. Alcott recalled his saying, " 'I know of no man of diviner faith in the soul, or who, amidst every hindrance, stands as firmly by it as yourself. Abide by yourself and the world shall come round to you at last.'"[101] In February, Emerson offered to pay for the publication of Alcott's "Psyche," but by June, after careful review, reversed his position. The problem, he said, was stylistic, "'Tis all stir and no go." Self-doubt made Alcott quickly accept his opinion, softened by Emerson's adding that it would be "absurd" to require the other man's work to be like his own. He welcomed "a new mind" with its "new style." Afterward, Alcott vowed that silence, living, and actual deeds would be his publication. He soon planned a series of adult conversation courses in several towns on topics such as "Free Will." But this idea only bore fruit years later when Alcott traveled west on several tours, then began the Concord School of Philosophy.[102]

Free of his critical role, Emerson tried to see his friend's true virtues, observing, "Alcott has the great merit of being a believer in the soul. I think he has more faith in the Ideal than any man I have known. Hence his welcome influence." Though a "wise woman," probably Fuller, had criticized Alcott for having too few thoughts, Emerson believed that Alcott's "distinguishing Faith," his "palpable proclamation out of the

---

99   JBA, 91.
100   JMN 5: 329. "Alcott by my door" meant the door to his study which was across the hall from the Emerson's guest room.
101   JBA, 99.
102   JMN 5: 506; JBA, 102-03; Dahlstrand, *Amos Bronson Alcott*, Chs. 11, 12.

deeps of nature that God yet is," separated him from "a countless throng of lettered men . . . ." A year later, Emerson even tolerated Alcott's distaste for books and lack of a formal education. Yet after closer company with Fuller and hearing Mary Moody Emerson's withering remark—"I am tired of fools"—Emerson was ready by December 1840 to come down hard, writing that "Alcott is a tedious archangel." The next year, he elaborated: "Alcott stands for Spirit itself & yet when he writes, he babbles."[103] When Alcott was about to depart for England in 1842, his trip paid for by Emerson, Emerson praised his inventive and limitless conversation. But his writings could not capture that verbal power. Emerson agreed with the *Boston Post* that Alcott's "Orphic Sayings," published in *The Dial*, "resembled a train of 15 railroad cars with one passenger."[104] On paper, Alcott could not take anyone with him.

From this time on, both men were reliably ambivalent about each other, but Emerson more so than Alcott. He found Alcott an "air-plant," moving from thought to thought, but also "brooding," producing "monotony in the conversation, & egotism in the character." Emerson exaggeratedly blurted: "I do not want any more such persons to exist."[105] Later, in 1849, in a semi-whimsical mood, he made two lists of heroes, the "Bigendians" and "Littleendians." On the first list were Plato and other historic figures he would treat in *Representative Men* (1850). Alcott headed the "Littleendians," while Emerson put himself and Thoreau, in that order, last on this list.[106] Yet in 1852, he revealed Alcott's importance to him: "It were too much to say that the Platonic world I might have learned to treat as cloud-land, had I not known Alcott, who is a native of that country, yet I will say that he makes it as solid as Massachusetts to me."[107] Between 1840 and 1848, Alcott came and went from Concord. In 1842, he generously remarked that Emerson's essays "Love" and "Friendship" had revived his ties to "Concordia" and returned him to "the realms of affection, a dweller in the courts of humanity."[108] In contrast, as Emerson's idealism increasingly encompassed the pragmatic, Alcott continued to serve as both an ascetic

---

103 *JMN* 7: 34, 177, 207, 539; 8: 118.

104 Ibid., 8: 210-11.

105 Ibid., 8: 213, 214.

106 Ibid., 11: 173.

107 Ibid.,13: 66.

108 Four years later at the Cliff, an overlook at Walden Pond, Alcott heard Emerson reciting lines that would be published in his *Poems* (1847). Alcott thought his friend "our first great poet," and listed him at the head of those Americans shaping a "new literature." *JBA* 160, 182.

model to admire and an unrealistic egotist to mourn—the tense basis of their ongoing friendship.

2.28 A. Bronson Alcott in his 70s, c. 1870s.

Henry David Thoreau

As with Alcott, Emerson's relationship with Thoreau ran the gamut between distance and affection, but for other reasons and with a very different emotional impact. True, Thoreau, like Alcott, came from a modest family. His father was a pencil-maker in Concord, and his mother took in boarders. Again like Alcott, Thoreau was intellectually untried. But he was more formally educated. Henry was a senior at Harvard in early April 1837, when at home in Concord on spring break, he walked from his house on Main Street to Emerson's on the Cambridge Turnpike for their first meeting. Emerson was immediately impressed. Fourteen years his junior, Thoreau could be the sort of "youthful giant," as yet unspoiled by having chosen a profession, that Emerson described as being "sent to work revolutions."[109] Thoreau returned to Harvard, read *Nature* and recommended it to others, then came back to Concord. Within a few months, Emerson's questions,

---

109 *JMN* 5: 293.

"What are you doing now? Do you keep a journal?" prompted Thoreau's first lines in his journal. Over twenty-four years, it grew to over two million words.[110]

Emerson suggested that Thoreau read classic works and criticized his first attempts in poetry and prose. They also took long walks and talked endlessly. Both slope-shouldered, the tall, lean "Mr. Emerson" with the short, stocky "Henry" would become a pair commonly seen en route to Walden Pond or other Concord haunts. In fact, Thoreau was so often with Emerson that he adopted Emerson's expressions and voice patterns, even imitating his pauses and hesitations.[111] After one walk-and-talk in early February 1838, Emerson noted, "I delight much in my young friend, who seems to have as free & erect a mind as any I have ever met." Thoreau had told him about a schoolboy friend, Wentworth, who had refused to bow to a Dr. Heywood, leading Heywood to clear his throat as Wentworth went by. The boy replied, "'You need not hem, Doctor; I shan't bow.'" [112] The story spoke to Emerson's emphasis on independence and revealed Thoreau's strong bias against authority. Such traits help explain why both men became idiosyncratic reformers, each in his own way.

Searching for a career, Thoreau took miscellaneous jobs and made several attempts to become a schoolteacher. Uninhibited in speaking to Emerson and uncertain of his future, his combative streak grew stronger. When roads and fences prevented his free movement across the countryside, he complained of being "hustled out of nature," as Emerson put it. Emerson, who owned two acres in Concord and, by 1845, would add forty-one more at Walden Pond, agreed that owning property was not the best arrangement. But "Wit & Worth," he wrote, were presumably in control, and "the bold bad man" was contained. He urged Henry to relieve his ire by expressing this "maggot of Freedom & Humanity" in "good poetry." But Thoreau thought that "not the best way; that in doing justice to the thought, the man did not always do justice to himself: the poem ought to sing itself: if the man took too much pains with the expression he was not any longer the Idea himself." Emerson agreed, "[T]his was the tragedy of

---

110 Henry David Thoreau, *Journal*, October 22, 1837; *The Heart of Thoreau's Journals*, ed. Odell Shepard (New York: Dover, 1961), 2.

111 McAleer, 336-37; Smith, 18; Thoreau's mother thought the influence was just the reverse, her angle on the matter was retold for years, much to Emerson's amusement. *JMN* 15: 489-90.

112 *JMN* 5: 452.

Art that the Artist was at the expense of the Man."[113] Thoreau, as idealistic as Emerson, was pressing his more fortunate friend to wonder, who owned nature?[114] From opposite poles, Alcott, the super-idealist, and Thoreau, the naturalist-protester against convention—both born to a lesser status than he—were squeezing Emerson to examine his thoughts.

But Thoreau entered into Emerson's world much more intimately than did Alcott. By the early 1840s, Emerson's overlapping worlds of new friendships, lecturing, publishing, and a growing family—a third child, Edith, would be born in late 1841—had become enormously demanding. Protégé Thoreau was a natural person from whom to seek help. Twenty-three years old, Thoreau had just endured the double pain of being rejected by the attractive young Ellen Sewall while winning the ire of another suitor of Ellen's, who happened to be his deeply admired older brother John. Henry needed to leave his tense family circle. Sensitive to his situation, on April 18, 1841, Emerson invited him to move into Bush. For the next two years, he occupied the small sleeping alcove at the top of the front stairs. Bringing his own desk, Henry came to Bush to write, to use Emerson's library, and to earn his keep as handyman.[115]

2.29 Thoreau's desk, flute, and sheet music.

---

113 Ibid., 7: 143-44.

114 Some years later, Emerson's poem "Hamatreya" (1847) opens with a list of neighbors—proud landholders all—and ends with Earth's triumph song over their remains. *CW* 9: 68-70.

115 Smith, 35-37.

He helped in the garden, orchard, barn, and with editorial chores for *The Dial* and other publishing matters. He also led Emerson on special excursions: After one enchanted moonlight row, Emerson dubbed him "the good river-god."[116]

Thoreau, joining the family when Waldo was four-and-a-half, Ellen two, Edith on the way, and remaining close after Edward's birth in 1844, rapidly became a beloved elder brother.[117] He so thoroughly charmed the Emerson children that they greeted him by grabbing his knees to plead for stories and songs, homemade toys, magic tricks, or for popped corn in a copper warming-pan. He would play his flute while they accompanied him on grass whistles he had made them (the best from the golden willow). Emerson more formally entertained his children and their friends in his study, or led them on Sunday afternoon nature walks.[118] Thoreau's capable hands, sprightly conversation, independence, and attention to the children could not help but impress Lidian as well.[119] Then in early January 1842, Henry returned home to nurse his brother John, ill with lockjaw (tetanus). John soon died. Afterward, deeply depressed, Henry withdrew into complete silence. Within weeks, equally swiftly, little Waldo died of scarlet fever. In despair, Emerson nevertheless had to leave home for a pre-arranged lecture tour, first for ten days, then for weeks. Though ill, Thoreau, who was needed in Emerson's absence, returned to Bush.[120]

Living in Concord for much of the rest of their lives, Emerson and Thoreau based their friendship on great mutual trust, dedication to both nature and transcendental truth, and admiration for each other's separate talents. But different views about nature and society, as well as personal tensions, were visible above this sure foundation. Emerson wondered how to promote Thoreau, whose writing, while free in style, seemed to have no new subjects. In September 1841, he noted, "I am familiar with all his [Henry's] thoughts—they are my own originally drest."[121] Thoreau's prejudice against the privileged was also a problem: He could hardly fit

---

116 *JMN* 7: 454.

117 Edward Waldo Emerson, *Henry Thoreau As Remembered By a Young Friend* (Boston, Mass.: Houghton Mifflin, 1917), 5: 1-6.

118 Mrs. Harriet E. Chapman, Concord, "Children's Reminiscences," *Boston Sunday Journal,* 24 May 1903, Emerson Family Papers, Houghton Library, Harvard, 1280.235 (707), Box 65.

119 Ellen Tucker Emerson, *The Life of Lidian Jackson Emerson,* ed. Delores Bird Carpenter (East Lansing, MI: Michigan State University Press, 1992), xlvi-xlviii.

120 Smith, 62.

121 *JMN* 8: 96.

well into Emerson's circle of well-bred friends, either in the Transcendental Club or the circle of Boston's young elite that Margaret Fuller soon brought him. (Fuller did not share Emerson's sense of Thoreau's promise; Alcott, in contrast, soon predicted his future success.) Thoreau's antagonism to authority and property may have also been directed at Emerson, his employer, lender, and literary agent. In turn, Emerson must have been ambivalent at least regarding Thoreau's clear appeal to Lidian and the children, a bond that was only strengthened by his own frequent absences. Their friendship was a struggle between two mutually proud, prickly, and even ornery men. When Emerson returned from lecturing in March 1842, however, Thoreau tried to read his cool reserve positively. Emerson, he reasoned, was shyly embarrassed by his affection for him. Thoreau wrote in his journal, "My friend is my real brother."[122]

At the end of July 1839, Thoreau showed Emerson a new poem, "Sympathy." Its subject was the handsome eleven-year-old Edmund Sewall, brother of Ellen, to whom Thoreau would unsuccessfully propose two years later. Edmund had spent a week with the Thoreaus that summer. "A stern respect," the poem narrates, held boy and man apart, a Platonic note continued to the end, where sympathy is defined as loving "that virtue which he is" and which his beauty speaks. Emerson had thought the poem "beautiful," the "purest strain & the loftiest, I think that has yet pealed from this unpoetic American forest."[123]

After Ellen's rejection, Thoreau played with journal-based fantasies about a same sex relationship, Platonic or otherwise, but firmly checked this avenue of affection as less desirable than marriage.[124] Undoubtedly, Thoreau and Emerson discussed the male and female characteristics that genius combined.[125] Their frequent chats may explain the few references to this subject in their journals. But a thread running through *The Dial*, particularly under Fuller's forceful leadership in its first two years, focused on romantic friendship. To this and later issues, Thoreau contributed his

122 Henry David Thoreau, *Journal*, vol. 6, March 20, 1842, MS, Pierpont Morgan Library, New York. Sentence added in pencil above inked line. Smith, 190n.40.
123 Henry David Thoreau, "Sympathy," *Collected Essays and Poems* (New York: The Library of America, 1984), 524; Smith, 28; Caleb Crain, *American Sympathy: Men, Friendship, and Literature in the New Nation* (New Haven, CT: Yale University Press, 2001), 202. Later, Emerson sent the poem to Ward, who apparently liked it. Crain, 211.
124 Smith, 35.
125 Emerson noted in 1839: "Men of genius are said to partake of the masculine & feminine traits." *JMN* 7: 310. In 1843, he wrote, "The finest people marry the two sexes in their own person." Ibid., 8: 380.

poems "Sympathy" and "Friendship," an essay on the Roman satirical poet "Persius," and translations of the Greek Anacreon's graceful poetry on the joys of wine and love, whose homoerotic intent Thoreau did not hide.[126] In short, by the spring of 1842, when he made the journal entry mentioned above, after eighteenth months in the highly charged atmosphere of Emerson's household of young guests (described in pages to come), Thoreau might have expected some natural affection from his host, patron, friend, and now brother. Until Thoreau's death, Emerson remained his close-but-distant benefactor, sometime promoter of his lectures and books, *A Week on the Concord and Merrimack Rivers* (1849) and *Walden* (1854), while also being his severest critic. He had extolled Thoreau in May 1839 for feeling "no shame in not studying any profession," but in 1851 complained that he lacked ambition: "Fault of this, instead of being the head of American Engineers, he is captain of a huckleberry party."[127] Emerson knew that Thoreau, like himself, sought wisdom, but thought his focus on action inadequate and recommended steady contemplation.[128] And Thoreau's independence, acerbic words, and solo experiment in a cabin at Walden Pond revealed his preference for nature over people. Emerson alleged that he felt just the opposite.[129] Further, he was not impressed with Thoreau's attitude toward art, Emerson's chosen profession. His young friend, he reported, once blotted "a paper with ink, then doubled it over & safely defied the artists to surpass his effect."[130] On Thoreau's apparent lack of "that power to cheer & establish [a relationship]," Emerson wrote, "As for taking [his] arm, I should as soon take the arm of an elm tree."[131]

On his side, Thoreau continued to extol Emerson in his journal in the mid-1840s; "There is no such general critic of men & things—no such trustworthy & faithful man.—More of the divine realized in him than in any."[132] Yet their tensions had led Thoreau to leave Bush in May 1843 to try his luck as a writer in New York, while tutoring Emerson's nephew, the son of William Emerson, on Staten Island. Unsuccessful and homesick, Thoreau wrote Emerson and Lidian a wry letter of high feeling, "But know, my

---

126 Crain, 235; Joel Myerson, *New England Transcendentalists and the Dial: A History of the Magazine and Its Contributors* (Rutherford: Fairleigh Dickinson University Presses), Appendix, 289-302; 314.

127 *JMN* 7: 201-02; 11: 400.

128 Ibid., 11: 15-16.

129 Ibid., 265-66.

130 Ibid., 10: 151.

131 Ibid.: 343.

132 Thoreau, *Journal* 2: Winter 1845-1846, 223.

friends, that I a good deal hate you all [including others, e.g., Hawthorne and Elizabeth Hoar] in my most private thoughts—as a substratum of the little love I bear you. Though you are a rare band and do not make half use enough of one another."[133] Thoreau returned home after only six months. Then in 1847-1848, while Emerson lectured in Great Britain, he readily accepted Lidian's invitation to move in as head-of-house and helper for ten months.

2.30 Lidian Jackson Emerson, c. 45,
with son Edward Waldo Emerson, c. 3, c. 1847.

2.31 Henry David Thoreau at 37, 1854.

---

133 Henry David Thoreau to Mr. and Mrs. R. W. Emerson, July 8, 1843, *The Correspondence of Henry David Thoreau*, eds. Walter Harding and Carol Bode (New York: New York University Press, 1958), 124.

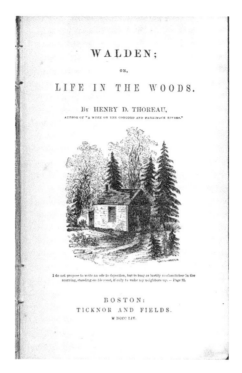

2.32 Title page, *Walden, or Life in the Woods,* 1854.

Emerson returned from this tour with a new sense of fame and elevation, affecting Thoreau in a doubly negative way. Though Thoreau occasionally lectured on his own subjects, he had not yet been published at thirty-one, and Boston's literary circles cruelly satirized him as Emerson's scrounging shadow. Thoreau was also taken aback when Emerson, feeling too involved in efforts to publish it, declined to review Thoreau's *A Week*; moreover, after it did not sell, he reversed his favorable opinion.[134] Thoreau naturally nursed both self-chastisement and resentment. At the same time, he rejected Emerson's efforts to restore an earlier, easier friendliness, resuming his hate-love mode. But Henry now also consciously feared that his friendship toward Emerson bore "the tendency and nicety of a lover."[135] With typical discipline, he resisted such niceties.

Ironically, Thoreau's erotic distancing mirrored Emerson's own self-isolation: Thoreau, like Emerson, felt he had to hide his true affections.

---

134 Smith, 112, 129-33.
135 Ibid., 142.

In Thoreau's case, his almost daily contact with the whole Emerson family demanded the utmost vigilance and restraint, a cover that often exacerbated his cantankerousness. Evidently unconscious of such behavior himself, he wrote in his journal the day before Emerson's fiftieth birthday in 1853, "Talked or tried to talk with R.W.E. Lost my time—nay almost my identity—he assuming a false *op*-position where there was no difference of opinion—talked to the wind—told me what I knew & I lost my time trying to imagine myself somebody else to oppose him."[136] Not long afterward, Emerson seemed to be referring to the same event, or one like it, but missed Thoreau's covert passion when he noted, "H[enry] seemed stubborn & implacable; always manly & wise, but rarely sweet . . . . "[Like Webster], H[enry] does not feel himself except in opposition. He wants a fallacy to expose, a blunder to pillory, requires a little sense of victory, a roll of the drums, to call his powers into full exercise."[137] Further encouraging Thoreau's disguise was his sympathy for Lidian, whom he had addressed as "sister" in 1843, and whom he knew had waited in vain for endearing expressions from Emerson both in England and after he returned home.

Yet despite these personal idiosyncrasies and philosophical differences, and despite Thoreau's own restraint, Emerson's high interest in Thoreau and admiration for his "mother wit" remained steady.

2.33 Henry David Thoreau at 39, 1856.

---

136 Thoreau, *Journal,* 6: 149.
137 *JMN* 13: 183.

After Thoreau's death in May 1862, only Emerson could have delivered a eulogy that combined such depth of insight, feeling, and perceptive criticism, ending, "wherever there is knowledge, wherever there is virtue, wherever there is beauty, he will find a home." [138] Thoreau had been one of Emerson's closest friends. Even when his feeling was masked in behavior suggesting the opposite, Thoreau had felt the same way about Emerson. [139]

Sarah Margaret Fuller

With the directed energy of a laser beam, and much more powerfully than either Alcott or Thoreau, Margaret Fuller first impressed, then came to pressure Emerson, forcing him to open up at his emotional center. Fuller was twenty-six, seven years younger than Emerson, when she met him in late July 1836, a year after Alcott and nine months before Thoreau. The highly educated first child of a Boston lawyer and former member of Congress, Fuller came to Concord for a brief first visit, but stayed for three weeks. Her conversational ability, dominating personality, and rich knowledge of classical and modern literature eclipsed her initially off-putting appearance and aggressive manner. Emerson, always drawn to beautiful women, noted Fuller's plainness, nasal voice, and constantly fluttering eyelids. Myopia made her squint, and overly tight corseting thrust her head unattractively forward. Margaret's reputation for intellectual pride and satirical put-downs was also well known.

On their first meeting, Emerson predicted that they would "never get far." But soon he was reading her parts of his as-yet unpublished *Nature*. After she left, he called her "very accomplished & very intelligent," even "extraordinary." The quick change was not so surprising. They had both recently suffered personal losses: Fuller's father in 1835, and Emerson's brother Charles just two months before they met. Other similarities more surely placed them on a par. Unlike Alcott and Thoreau, Fuller came from the same narrow slice of Boston's social elite as Emerson, knew poverty, and shared many friends with him, among them her cousin James Freeman Clarke and Frederic Henry Hedge.[140]

---

138 Emerson, "Thoreau," *Emerson's Prose and Poetry*, 411.
139 Smith, 170, 180.
140 McAleer, 324-25; JMN 5: 188; Joan von Mehren, *Minerva and the Muse* (Amherst, Mass.: University of Massachusetts Press, 1994), 226; Capper, 188, 265-66.

2.34 Margaret Fuller in her late 20s, c. late 1830s-early 1840s.

Over the next few years, Fuller rapidly moved into Emerson's inner circle through regular correspondence, more visits, her avid interest in his lectures, and her participation in the Transcendental Club. She also taught him German pronunciation and wittily delivered forbidden gossip. In addition, Fuller played to Emerson's distance from reformers in the late 1830s, when she safely flaunted her learning over female do-gooders, "Who would be a goody that could be a genius?"[141] The two soon called each other "Margaret" and "Waldo," Fuller establishing a first name basis with Emerson that Alcott, Thoreau, and even Lidian could not.[142] Less than a year after meeting Fuller, Emerson, while delighted with his first-born son Waldo—nearly six months old in April 1837—privately revealed his frustration with post-marriage reality: "The husband loses the wife in the cares of the household. Later, he cannot rejoice with her in the babe for by becoming a mother she ceases yet more to be a wife . . . at last nothing

---

141   *JMN* 5: 407.
142   McAleer, 327.

remains of the original passion out of which all these parricidal fruits proceeded; and they die because they are superfluous."[143] Fuller witnessed this new strain in Emerson's two-year-old marriage, itself based on the couple's understanding that his first wife Ellen would always remain, in death as in life, his "ardent love, all loves excelling."[144]

Nevertheless, Emerson's nicknames for Lidian showed either respect or teasing affection: "Asia," for her spiritual ascents and insights, and "Lidian Queen" or "Queenie," for staying in bed until noon—to avoid sunlight that might aggravate the after-effects of scarlet fever—as well as for her taste in fine furnishings and dress. But Emerson abhorred illness, and Lidian's frequent depressions did not help.[145] However, intelligent and poetic, she could be playful, feeding his need for silliness. Her "Transcendental Bible" wryly mocked his lofty ideals as self-serving. He thought her satirical scripture "a good squib" and "always laughed" when recalling it.[146] He also delighted in her "gift to curse & swear," allowing that "every now & then in spite of all manners & christianity," she might "rip out on Saints, reformers & Divine Providence with the most edifying zeal."[147] On marriage as an institution, Emerson was predictably ambivalent. But by 1850, he had softened his views, finding the married state to be a "good known only to the parties. A relation of perfect understanding, aid, contentment, possession of themselves & the world—which dwarfs love to green fruit."[148]

---

143 *JMN* 5: 297.

144 Emerson, untitled manuscript poem, September 1829, *Ralph Waldo Emerson: Collected Poems and Translations*, eds. Harold Bloom and Paul Kane (New York: The Library of America, 1994) 322, 606 (322n.13).

145 Emerson may also have named Lydia "Lidian" for her luxury tastes, high standards and piety that suggested the wealth and magnificence of Lydia, the ancient country in west-central Asia Minor (modern Turkey) on the Aegean, conquered by the Persians in 546 B.C.E. Writing Carlyle, Emerson described Lidian as "an incarnation of Christianity," adding that he called her "Asia," because she "keeps my philosophy from Antinomianism." This teasing honor alluded to their religious differences. Emerson wrote Lidian on February 19, 1838, the day after requesting release from his "charge" to preach in nearby Lexington: "But does not the eastern Lidian[,] my Palestine[,] mourn to see the froward [sic] man cutting the last threads that bind him to that prized gown & band[,] the symbols black & white of old & distant Judah?" Five months later on July 15, 1838, Emerson delivered his clergy-challenging "Divinity School Address." http://www.thefreedictionary.com/Lydians; *The Compact Edition of the Oxford English Dictionary* (New York: Oxford University Press, 1971), 1: 1684; *Correspondence of Carlyle and Emerson*, 2: 161; *L* 2: 113-14, as quoted in Gay Wilson Allen, *Waldo Emerson* (New York: Viking Press, 1981), 310.

146 Ellen T. Emerson, *The Life of Lidian Jackson Emerson*, ed. Delores B. Carpenter (East Lansing, MI: Michigan State University Press, 1992), xvi-xviii; 81, 83.

147 *JMN* 8: 88.

148 Ibid., 11: 213.

2.35 Emerson at about 50 with son Edward (c. 9) and daughter Ellen (c. 14), c. 1853.

What he truly sought was a lasting, stimulating, and compatible friendship, something that his heroes—Plato, Montaigne, and Bacon—had all so highly valued, but on his terms and suiting his schedule.

Fuller stood apart among Emerson's female friends and family for exuding fiery feeling as well as intellect. Emerson had known ardency only with Ellen. Both his mother and Mary Moody Emerson had lacked personal warmth. He later remembered that in contrast to Fuller's "great tenderness & sympathy," "M.M.E. has none."[149] With affection among friends one of her highest priorities, Fuller increasingly sought to pierce Emerson's

149 Ibid., 11: 259, quoted in Lawrence Buell, *Emerson* (Cambridge, Mass.: Harvard University Press, 2003), 88-89.

guarded emotions. In March 1838, his ideas, she said, were a "torch" to her own. She also drew him closer by dubbing him, "Sanctissime," Most Holy One, confessing to him her professional and personal troubles. Emerson could accept the role of hero-friend, but was bewildered by the role of priest-confessor. In mid-August, just after Fuller had made a brief visit, he noted the tragic disparity between "a gay dame of manners & tone so fine & haughty that all defer to her as to a countess . . . the dictator of society" and the reality of listening to her gnawing private woes from which she saw no release.[150] By 1839, however, Fuller was basking in Emerson's and others' acclaim for her translation of Eckermann's *Conversations with Goethe.*[151] Soon she was bringing him three select young friends. Epitomizing New England privilege, talent, learning, and sensitivity, their attention decidedly flattered him.

Emerson had attracted other youth on his own: Thoreau and Jones Very, with Ellery Channing (nephew of William Ellery Channing), Charles Newcomb, and C. R. Cranch soon to come. But beyond any others, Fuller and her special trio stimulated him to explore more deeply the meaning of Transcendental (ideal) love, friendship, and marriage. Already in June 1838, Fuller had introduced him to her artistic and poetic student, Caroline Sturgis, the twenty-year-old daughter of a partner in Bryant and Sturgis, a leading firm in the China trade. Sturgis, described as "very plain but with fine eyes," was an apt pupil of Fuller's spiritual guidance and wrote insightful, engaging letters. Then in July 1839, at a Boston art exhibit of Washington Allston's paintings, Fuller presented to Emerson the twenty-one-year-old Samuel Gray Ward, a handsome literary and artistic son of the American agent for Baring Brothers, English bankers for the Anglo-American trade.

Fuller had long been romantically drawn to Ward and believed that he reciprocated her feelings. In early October, she introduced Emerson to the stunningly beautiful twenty-six-year-old Anna Barker, daughter of a prosperous Quaker businessman from New Orleans.[152] Barker's regal appearance and demeanor impressed him as did her instinctive warmth and frankness. He noted, "She can afford to be sincere. The wind is not purer than she is."[153]

---

150 Von Mehren, 97-98; *JMN* 7: 48, quoted in Capper 247.
151 Von Mehren, 107.
152 Ibid., 50-51, 68, 82.
153 *JMN* 7: 260.

2.36 Samuel Gray Ward, before 1907.

Sturgis, Ward, and Barker were nothing less than a "necklace of diamonds about [Fuller's] neck," a phrase of Elizabeth Hoar's that Emerson soon repeated in describing Fuller as "the queen of some parliament of love." The title only emphasized Fuller's longstanding self-image as a queen.[154] Swept into her court, Emerson battled two sets of conflicting desires: the flattering company of these cultured young people and his need for solitude to think and write. At Harvard, he had fixed Martin Gay by eye but had exchanged only a few words with him at best. After Ellen's death, he guiltily recalled moments of treating even her coolly. In his second marriage, he and Lidian co-existed in parallel lives early defined by his nuptial demand, "You are in love with what I love." Emerson judged himself and anyone else to be "an infinitely repellent orb," as he had told Alcott, and repeated in his 1838 lecture "The Heart." In mid-November 1839, he wrote in his journal, "I dare not look for a friend to me who have never been one."[155] But the next day,

---

154   McAleer, 328; Capper, 264; Marshall, 119.
155   *JMN* 7: 298.

he again saw the virtues of his "churl's mask" of "porcupine impossibility of contact with men."[156]

The man behind this mask became clear only weeks later, and then to Emerson alone. Meanwhile, Fuller, sensing Ward's interest in her waning, increased her attack on Emerson's reserve. Her campaign, in fact, had begun in 1838, sharing art, literature, and her friends' intimate letters. Exploiting Emerson's eye for art,[157] Fuller sent him copies of Italian artworks collected by Ward (her "Raphael" or "Michel Angelo") during his tour of Europe (1836-1838).[158] In the summer of 1839, Fuller also gave Emerson novels infused with sex-role exchanges and romantic entanglements by risqué French novelists Honoré de Balzac, George Sand, and others. He had already read young Bettina von Arnim's highly-charged, fictionalized love letters to the fifty-eight-year-old Goethe.[159] Then in mid-October, Fuller told Emerson that Ward was in love with Anna Barker. A month later, she sent him two sets of letters, one between Ward and Barker, and the other, between herself and Sturgis. These revealed Fuller's complex range of maternal and paternal affections toward her three "children" (Ward called her "Mother") as well as her amorous feelings for them.[160]

While Fuller worked to break down Emerson's wall, his attention fell on Ward. Now that Ward and Barker were engaged, Emerson could cultivate Ward's friendship without jeopardy in this dangerously erotic small circle. The titles he gave himself and Ward reflect his view of their relationship: Ward was "Prince-of-the-Purple Island," the color signifying radiant enchantment, while Emerson scoldingly called himself "that Puritan at Concord."[161] Since early October, Ward had loaned Emerson more of his art collection.[162] One drawing especially caught his eye, a Roman relief of the sleeping nude Endymion, originally a handsome young shepherd or astronomer, watched over by Diana, the Roman goddess of the moon and hunt—successor to her original Greek counterpart Selene—represented by a dog. With one paw, the goddess leans on Endymion's shoulder. The other is caressingly poised over his head.

---

156 Ibid., 7: 30.
157 Ibid., 3: 270-71.
158 Crain, 201.
159 Capper, 258, 260-62, 326-27.
160 Von Mehren, 108, 111-12; Capper 325-26.
161 Von Mehren, 109; Richardson, 327.
162 Crain, 206-07; Capper, 327.

2.37 *Endymion*, drawing, c. 1830s.

In the Greek myth, Selene's desire that Endymion "never leave her," which kept her adoringly nearby even as he slept, makes her ask Zeus, Endymion's father, to grant him eternal youth and immortality. In other legends, Zeus asks Endymion to choose his future. He elects dormant youth and eternal life. The end result is the same: he is ageless and immortal, alive but asleep.

Endymion seems to have reflected both Emerson's sense of his unawakened emotions and his need for solitude. Long before, he had repressed his "animal spirits," professing to lack them, but he still yearned for the attentions of a Diana-like friend.[163] Yet that attention could not invade his creative meditative life. In mid-August, he noted in his journal that "every mortal" is tyrannized by the inescapable "rule" of a small company of men and women, leading one to dodge "behind a grave-stone at last . . . ."—clearly the equivalent of endless sleep. This thought reappears at the end of Emerson's later published poem "Manners" (1867): "Too weak to win, too fond to shun / The tyrants of his doom, / The much deceived Endymion / Slips behind a tomb." "Much deceived" may refer to his hope for transcendent, platonic relations with his young friends, betrayed by Ward and Barker's split from their idyllic quintet.[164]

Whatever the truth, *Endymion* united Ward and Emerson aesthetically. Only two days after Fuller's letters arrived, Ward wrote to present him with the drawing. Emerson answered the same day, "I am warmed at heart by your good will to me." He hung it in an honored place next to an engraving of Guido's *Aurora*, a wedding present from Carlyle.[165] The next day he wrote Fuller, stunned by the intimate letters in her packet. He felt himself "swimming" inside the liquid of "an Iris"—his own artistic eye—"knocked" about by a red light, and even blinded by a "casual" white one—a revelatory moment. "How fine these letters are! . . . They make me a little impatient of my honourable prison—my quarantine of temperament wherefrom I deal courteously with all comers, but through cold water." Emerson then almost shouted, "I should like once in my life to be pommelled back & blue with sincere words." He even stormed into his dining room, accosting Lidian and his mother with the novel idea that *he* should be writing such passionate stuff. Yet, ambivalent and guarding

---

163 *JMN* 7: 509.
164 http://en.wikipedia.org/wiki/Endymion_(mythology);   http://www.theoi.com/Titan/Selene.html; http://en.wikipedia.org/wiki/Diana_(mythology). Crain, 228; *JMN* 7: 211, 509; *CW* "Manners," 9: 499.
165 Crain, 211, 216-17.

his composure, he shied away: "I like no deep stakes—I am a coward at gambling."[166]

Now turned on by *Endymion* and these letters, Emerson explored his innermost self, but only in his journal, and then using a third-person pseudonym: "Rob was tender & timid as a fawn in his affections, yet he passed for a man of calculation & cold heart. He assumed coldness only to hide his *woman's heart*" [his emphasis].[167] Seven months later, on June 11, 1840, after revising "Love" for publication, Emerson elaborated the point, again to his journal, but now in the first person: "I [am] cold because I am hot—cold at the surface only as a sort of guard & compensation for the fluid tenderness of the core—have much more experience than I have written there [in "Love"], more than I will, more than I can write. In silence we must wrap much of our life, because it is too fine for speech, because also we cannot explain it to others, and because somewhat [somehow] we cannot yet understand."[168]

Emerson, stymied by the limits of his self-analysis, could at least name his "woman's heart" and its high heat, disguised by a cold exterior. He was not confessing to homosexuality. His lifelong devotion to Ellen attests to the opposite. And his close but chaste interest in Caroline Sturgis does the same.[169] Rather, both he and Fuller luxuriated in feeling psychologically male and female, the typical androgyny of geniuses according to Goethe.[170] Now, alone to himself, Emerson recognized his predominantly female sensibility (a trait that his friend Henry James, Sr. made public much later)[171] A male-dominant society required Emerson to keep that a secret. Biologically fully male, he readily married a second time. Only afterward did he protest the married state (awake or dreaming),[172] and

---

166 Capper, 327.

167 Emerson continued, "There is a play in which the sister is enamoured of her brother & when they embrace, she exclaims, "J'ai froid" [I am cold]. *JMN* 7: 321.

168 Ibid., 7: 368. In another self-observation of 1848, Emerson recorded, "The secret of Guy [his alter-ego from Harvard days], the lucky & famous, was, to conceal from all mankind that he was a bore. It was wonderful how often & how long by skilful dispositions & timings he managed to make it believed, by clever people, too, that he was witty & agreeable." *JMN* 10: 322.

169 In 1879, on the fiftieth anniversary of his marriage to Ellen, Emerson returned to the site of their wedding, Ellen's house in Concord, New Hampshire. Henry F. Pommer, *Emerson's First Marriage* (Carbondale, IL: Southern Illinois University Press, 1967), 98; Marshall, 170-71.

170 *JMN* 7: 310; 8: 175, 380. See also Capper, I, 261-62, 288-89.

171 Henry James, Sr., "Emerson," *Atlantic Monthly* 94 (1904), 743.

172 *JMN* 7: 544; 11: 213.

then only temporarily, as we have seen. Marriage and children doubly hid his female psyche as did his repeated disgust for "unmanly" words or deeds. Ultimately, his mask distanced him from anyone. Yet Fuller and her parliament of love had served to make Emerson as fully honest with himself as he could find words for.

2.38 Emerson Parlor with family tea service.

In late October 1839, he found an important reason to fault Fuller's "chronicle of sweet romance": "What is good to make me happy is not however good to make me write. Life too near paralyses Art."[173] This comment came from his working on first "Love" in 1839, then its companion, "Friendship," finished in 1840. In each essay, he was spelling out concrete applications of his philosophy arising from lessons learned from his young friends. To protect all parties, relationships had to be described abstractly. Abstraction was especially necessary in "Love," which he read as a lecture. The shorter of the two, this essay begins with a couplet from the Qur'an, "I was as a gem concealed; / Me my burning ray revealed." Thus Emerson alludes

---

173 Ibid., 7: 273, as quoted in Capper, I, 326-27.

to his new clarity about a "hot," socially unacceptable self, omitting any hint of his feminine side. In the essay proper, Emerson describes the keen fire of Eros at work between "maidens" and "youth"—as well as between older pairs, he, at thirty-six, cagily admits. His players remain heterosexual throughout, progressing from physical attraction and an assumed sexual union to spiritual beauty. Finally, he reaches a central paradox: "love, which is the deification of persons, must become more impersonal every day." The partners' mutual imperfections demand it, if the union is to last. From then on, their souls' trajectories are toward what Emerson calls a "real marriage," beyond sex, a higher love seeking virtue and wisdom.[174]

In contrast to "Love," Emerson begins "Friendship" with a poem that identifies a male addressee, ending, "The fountains of my hidden life / Are through thy friendship fair." The word "hidden" echoes Emerson's journal entries about "Rob" in December 1839 and his cold disguise in June 1840. But the essay drops the poem's male dialogue to speak to an audience of either sex: any and all friends must follow an immutable natural law of attraction and repulsion, an ebb and flow of interest and contact. He insists that the soul of each remains "alone in the world." However, the true friend, by conversation and correspondence, may come close, becoming "a beautiful enemy"—always desirable, but predictably other—"untamable, devoutly revered." For spiritual and practical reasons, the soul needs solitude to reap the harvest of elusive, intuitive insights that friends may either interrupt or prevent. Again, paradoxically, friends may "only be more each other's, because we are more our own." The dance of approach and withdrawal ideally enhances each, so that the essence of friendship is nothing less than to "deify" each other.[175] Near its end, "Friendship" repeats word-for-word Emerson's journal entry of December 22, "It has seemed to me lately more possible than I knew to carry a friendship greatly *on one side*, without due correspondence on the other."[176] ("On one side" is emphasized only in his journal.) He had apparently surmounted the paralyzing fear of unrequited love that he had known, beginning with Martin Gay.

Emerson's ideal of friendship, set by 1840, made his self-reliance all the more sure. Sturgis came closer, but as a cherished "child" and "sister," and he eventually steered her into marriage with a wealthy abolitionist

---

174 *CW* 2: 107, 109.
175 *CW* 2: 127.
176 Ibid.; *JMN* 7: 325.

friend, William Tappan.[177] He dealt with Fuller's direct assault by firmly turning her aside, if these words in his journal were meant for her: "You would have I love you. What shall I love? Your body? The supposition disgusts you."[178] Perhaps the two personal dangers he most feared were gluttony—from youth, he constantly weighed himself—and illicit sex, especially if threatened by force.[179] In Margaret's case, he described himself as forewarned, as if a voice had shouted, "*Stand from under!*" [Watch out below!].[180] Her aggression made an ostensibly cold fellow, he told her, a "cake of ice"—just the reverse of her desire.[181] After a time though, he wrote her, ". . . Be assured, dear Margaret, even though I may wear a churl's mask, I shall never go quite back to my old arctic habits. I shall believe that nobleness is loving, and delights in sharing itself."[182]

Lecturing as Sublimation

His true nature and scholarly needs increasingly clear to him, Emerson poured passion into his public words. On October 18, 1839, while enjoying *Endymion* and moving from writing "Love" to "Friendship," he assessed his first five years of lecturing:

> Adam in the garden, I am to new name all the beasts in the field & all the gods in the Sky. I am to invite men drenched in time to recover themselves & come out of time, & taste their native immortal air. I am to fire with what skill I can the artillery of sympathy & emotion. I am to indicate constantly, though all unworthy, the Ideal and Holy Life, the life within life—the Forgotten Good, the Unknown Cause in which we sprawl & sin. I am to try the magic of sincerity that luxury permitted only to kings & poets. I am to celebrate the spiritual powers in their infinite contrast to the mechanical powers & the mechanical philosophy of this time. I am to console the brave

---

177 Von Mehren, 220.

178 *JMN* 7: 400.

179 Emerson's Puritan and Stoic self-discipline coalesced in his habit of keeping his weight about 144-45 all his adult life; in 1844, he objected to the free sex of Fourieristic communitarianism: "I have observed that [sexual] indulgence always effeminates. I have organs also & delight in pleasure, but I have experience also that this pleasure is the bait of a trap." *JMN* 9: 115. See also, ibid., 9: 164.

180 R. W. Emerson, "Memoirs of Margaret Fuller Ossoli," *Emerson's Prose and Poetry*, 380.

181 *The Letters of Ralph Waldo Emerson*, ed. Ralph L. Rusk (New York: Columbia University Press, c. 1939-1995), 2: 352-53; McAleer, 332.

182 *L* 7: 400, 402; Crain, 228.

sufferers under evils whose end they cannot see by appeals to the great optimism self-affirmed in all bosoms.[183]

Less than a month later, Emerson noted that Fuller had written to say, ". . . she waits for the Lectures seeing well after much intercourse that the best of me is there." He immediately followed with self-criticisms about "a gulf," a "frigidity & labor of my speech" between himself and others, even in his own house.[184] And in mid-February 1840, Emerson berated himself for not transcending "coldest self-possession" in his recent Boston lecture series, "On the Present Age." Again he spelled out the sort of exhilarated energy he hoped to achieve on the platform: "I said I will agitate others, being agitated myself. I dared to hope for extacy [sic] & eloquence. A new theatre, a new art, I said, is mine. Let us see if philosophy, if ethics, if chiromancy [palmistry], if the discovery of the divine in the house & the barn in all works & all plays, cannot make the cheek blush, the lip quiver, & the tear start." He accused himself of failing to ignite this sort of intensity, merely delivering "fine things, pretty things, wise things—but no arrows, no axes, no nectar, no growling, no transpiercing, no loving, no enchantment."[185] His high aim demanded at least twenty hours of preparation per lecture. No wonder that in "Friendship," in process just now, he ends by treating valued friends like his books: "We must have society on our own terms and admit or exclude it on the slightest cause." Such constant exchange, he elaborates, might lead to "the vanishing of my mighty gods."[186]

Despite his self-criticisms, when Emerson was in top form at the podium, he could arouse listeners to an erotic state. Samuel Bowles, editor of the *Springfield Republican* and friend of Emily Dickinson and her brother Austin, wrote Austin: "[Emerson's lecturing] is pictures, landscapes, poetry, music, babies, and beautiful women rolled up in an hour of talk. It takes the place of making love in our young days." Others, Emerson simply held rapt. His daughter Ellen described one audience: "Not a word was lost, the whole company responded by movement, by smile, by breaths, by utter silence followed by some expressive sound from moment to moment through the whole lecture." [187]

---

183 *JMN* 7: 271.
184 Ibid., 301.
185 Ibid., 338-39.
186 *CW* 2: 126.
187 McAleer, 491; Richardson, 422.

2.39 Tickets to an Emerson lecture, 1861; ticket to the Concord School of Philosophy, 1888.

From his teens, Emerson drew and painted watercolors, so that his later self-portrait as a painter-lecturer is altogether natural: "I am & always was a painter. I paint still with might & main, & choose the best subjects I can. Many have I seen come & go with false hopes & fears, and dubiously affected by my pictures. But I paint on. I count this distinct vocation, which never leaves me in doubt what to do but in all times, places, & fortunes, gives me an open future, to be the great felicity of my lot." A few months later, he noted that the art of lecturing is instinctual and must come forth. Again, he is an artist, filled with "immortal ichor"—the ethereal fluid, instead of blood, that in classical mythology ran in the gods' veins. At its best, lecturing showed forth "these throbs & heart beatings" that allowed his ideas to "be ejaculated as Logos or Word."[188] Emerson's choice of spermatic action aptly expresses the physical pleasure that successful lecturing gave him.

Toward the beginning of his poem, "The Problem," written in early November 1839 at the height of his involvement with Fuller's young friends, Emerson used the image of a volcano to express an irrepressible, erupting Word from nature's center—his molten core. One painting he owned and kept in his front hall, an oil of Vesuvius erupting in 1794, symbolizes his felt situation.

---

188 *JMN* 9: 49, 72.

2.40 Vesuvius erupting, "Distruzione della Torre del Greco nel 1794".

As with Emily Dickinson, it expresses his sense of being "Vesuvius at Home," while, unlike her, also being involved in the world. In public, Emerson could safely let his private passions find an outlet. Face-to-face with even the closest of friends, he could not. But to his art, like the true Puritan Romantic that he was, he gave his full heart and mind, at his best arousing his listeners' deepest feelings. Not surprisingly, this intensity and its moving effect carried over to his later abolitionist and pro-feminist speeches.

Fuller, Emerson, and the Woman Question

Fuller led Emerson to unmask himself in private without altering his need for distance and solitude nor his vision of ideal love and friendship. But she did succeed in stirring his thoughts about women and their role in society. From 1840 to 1842, with Emerson's help, Fuller edited *The Dial*, a quarterly that brought to print topics similar to those of the now defunct Transcendental Club. Fuller was determined that *The Dial* would reflect "body" as well as "soul."[189] In that vein, she printed Sophia Ripley's article "Woman" in January 1841, a well-received piece that added to the other leading female voices speaking out on their future in the young democracy. Throughout the 1830s, Quaker female abolitionists, most notably the

---

189 Von Mehren, 142.

Grimké sisters and Lucretia Mott—whom Emerson later met—had both exemplified and advocated a fuller role for women in society. So, too, had educational pioneers such as Mary Lyon, who founded Mount Holyoke Female Seminary in western Massachusetts in 1837, the first institution of higher education for women anywhere in the world. That same year, in her *Society in America*, Harriet Martineau, a friend of Fuller's, criticized the shy conformity of most American women.[190] Such models provided vital context for the later work of women Transcendentalists like Ripley and Fuller.

Both women were building on Emerson's ideas. Lines from his essay "Love" of two years before are Ripley's main theme in "Woman." She denounced the current phrase "the sphere of women"—the household—as a restraint on female spiritual independence. In "Love," Emerson pointed to a prevailing "sensualism" in the education of young women that "withers the hope and affection of human nature, by teaching that marriage signifies nothing but a housewife's thrift, and that woman's life has no other aim."[191] More importantly, Emerson, after becoming editor of *The Dial* in 1842, printed Fuller's piece, "The Great Lawsuit," as the lead article in the July 1843 issue.[192]

2.41 Emerson at 40, silhouette, 1843. 2.42 Margaret Fuller at 36, 1846.

190 Ibid., 166; Elizabeth Alden Green, *Mary Lyon and Mount Holyoke: Opening the Gates* (Hanover, NH: University Press of New England, 1979), 169-70; Joel Myerson, *The New England Transcendentalists and the Dial* (London and Toronto: Associated University Presses, 1980), 202.
191 Von Mehren, 169.
192 Capper 2: 110.

Fuller's full title, "The Great Lawsuit: Man *versus* Men, Woman *versus* Women," alluded to the suffering of both genders under a patriarchal society's limits on individual hopes, especially that of women. By periodic, isolated self-study, she urged women to merge emotions with intellect. This echo of Emerson's firm habit became overt in Fuller's warning to women to know themselves before marrying. And then she directly quoted him: "Union is only possible to those who are units."[193]

Interestingly, at this very moment Fuller was distancing herself emotionally from Emerson, a detachment that he reciprocated. In summer 1844, writing in her journal, she charged him, "You stand for Truth and Intellect, while I, for Love and Life. I can no longer think of you as a father confessor. Instead, from now on, I will see you as a Sweet Child—Great Sage—Undeveloped Man!" The same year, when she accepted Horace Greeley's offer to write for his *New-York Tribune*, Emerson considered her another humanist lost to the "treadmill."[194] But far from deserting Transcendental thought, Fuller had been expanding its reach well beyond "The Great Lawsuit" by such novel means as interviewing women inmates in Sing-Sing Prison in upper New York State.[195] In 1845, she published a much more developed treatise, *Woman in the Nineteenth Century*. It was destined to become a font of inspiration to a host of contemporary leaders of the nascent women's movement and a landmark work in the history of women's studies.[196]

Asked to write an introduction to *Woman*, Emerson declined. Perhaps he felt too close to Fuller to be an unbiased judge. In truth, he thought her strengths lay in conversation, not writing. In 1843, he had observed, "[Margaret] has great sincerity, force, & fluency as a writer, yet her powers of speech throw her writing into the shade."[197] He was also busy preparing essays for his second collection.[198] In addition, only a few months before, he had publicly joined the abolitionist cause, evidently prioritizing that call above women's rights. Another factor may also have been in play: In 1838, he had noted in his journal that many reformers' self-righteousness put him off, "I hate goodies . . . . Goodness that preaches undoes itself . .

---

193 Von Mehren, 169.
194 Ibid., 184, 215.
195 Ibid., 189 ff.
196 Capper 2: 190-91.
197 *JMN* 8: 369.
198 Von Mehren, 194.

. . Goodies make us very bad . . . . We will almost sin to spite them."[199] In any reform, the key element for Emerson was the soulful energy of the affected parties, generated in enough numbers to become an irrepressible natural force. He said as much in his essay "Manners," on which he was then working. Despite noting a "new chivalry in behalf of Women's Rights" among men, he affirmed, "I confide so entirely in [woman's] inspiring and musical nature, that I believe only herself can show us how she shall be served."[200]

True to form, Emerson's sense of what women wanted and were due would become more acute, but at this moment he held rather conventional opinions. Such views strengthen the interpretation that his declaration of a "woman's heart" refers to his sensibilities, not his sexuality. He frequently honored women, especially his wives, for upholding society's highest virtues, honor, and laws.[201] Further, in random notes in his journals, he sympathized with women's plight, finding them in general to be slaves, which made the lives of intelligent women particularly tragic. In 1839, he noted, "Women see better than men. Men see lazily, if they do not expect to act. Women see quite without any wish to act." At other moments, he found women heedless of time; questionable writers; blind pawns in a monied culture; and sometimes dangerous sexual snares.[202] Clearly, he was somewhat conflicted on the subject. At the same time, his closest women friends encouraged him to pursue topics that might be, as he put it, "telescopes into the Future." Elizabeth Hoar urged that he work up "the rights of Woman."[203] As the women's movement gained momentum in the late 1840s and into the 1850s, Emerson slowly changed his views and forthrightly championed women's rights, but only on finding that a majority of women themselves favored the cause.

After Fuller's death in a shipwreck off Fire Island in 1850, as she was returning from Italy with her Italian husband and child, Emerson felt that he had "lost in her my audience."[204] It was more than that. Though Fuller was one of his best critics, he had also lost the principal mid-wife

---

199 *JMN* 7: 13.
200 *CW* 3: 88; Von Mehren, 195.
201 *JMN* 7: 96; 8: 380-81; 9: 191.
202 *JMN* 4: 306; 7: 388, 310; 9: 108. In 1845, as a random thought without context, Emerson expressed his sexual fears of women in verse: "Eve softly with her womb/ Bit him to death [full line space]/ Lightly was woman snared, herself a snare[.]" *JMN* 9: 164.
203 *JMN* 7: 48.
204 Ibid., 11: 258.

to his hidden self. For him, their relationship had approached his ideal in "Friendship." They had been "beautiful enemies."

Mature Lecturer and Founder of Clubs

Despite his need for isolated study, by 1850 Emerson's lecturing, publications (*Nature*, *Essays I*, *Essays II*, *Poems*, including *Representative Men*), and abolitionist speeches had made him one of the country's leading cultural figures and a major moral voice. In 1853, he extended his public conversations to the Mid-West. During the normal winter lecture season, despite never being robust and hating the cold, he endured bitter weather and rigorous travel, while also encountering the chill of listener impatience. In Beloit, Illinois, in early January 1856, when temperatures averaged twenty to thirty degrees below, Emerson knew that he needed both humor and variety to hold a hall. A year later, he also noted that the lecture circuit, no matter the location in America, had not become "the University of the people," as Alcott had idealistically hoped. Rather, it drew virtual children who required being coddled, adored, and, above all, entertained.[205]

Nevertheless, for appropriate audiences throughout the 1850s, Emerson continued to challenge them in some of his most demanding and important lectures: "Fate," "Power," "Wealth," "Culture," and "Worship."

2.43 Emerson at about 54, c. 1857, full-length in lecture suit.

---

205 Ibid., 14: 27-28; 168.

2.44 Emerson at about 54, c. 1857, seated.

In this pre-Civil War period, his lectures touched on philosophical aspects of the accelerating North-South tensions, while his antislavery speeches directly engaged ethics and politics. In one speech he said, "Americans were born to be propagandists of liberty—to each man the largest liberty compatible with the liberty of every other man. It is so delicious to act with great masses to great aims. For instance . . . the immediate or gradual abolition of slavery." The *National Anti-Slavery Standard* observed, "Mr. Emerson has given a fine anti-slavery lecture. Never was such a change, apparently, as from the Emerson of '45 to the Emerson of '55 . . . . People say, 'He is no more a philosopher, but a practical man.'"[206] In truth, he was now intermingling both ideal and real worlds, uniting them sometimes with paradoxical punch, as when he announced in "Fate": "Freedom is a necessity." His 1850s lectures appeared as *The Conduct of Life* —in 1860, less than a year before war broke out. For his friend, the writer and editor Charles Eliot Norton, this reminder to the nation of universal moral principles made Emerson's book the exact word needed in such perilous times.[207]

---

206 *Emerson's Antislavery Writings*, ed. Len Gougeon and Joel Myerson (New Haven, CT: Yale University Press, 1995), xliv.
207 McAleer, 619.

In this decade, Emerson sought to continue the conversations he had helped start in the 1830s with the Transcendental Club. The gentleman's clubs he had enjoyed in London and Paris in 1848 encouraged him to introduce a similar association at home. In 1849, with Ward, Alcott, and others, he began the Town and Country Club in Boston, which soon became the Magazine or Atlantic Club (publisher of the *Atlantic Monthly*), itself giving way to the Saturday Club by December 1854. It was also known as "Emerson's Club," its meetings scheduled to coincide with his Saturday mornings at the Boston Athenaeum. This small, all-male group of leading humanists and scientists—among them, Louis Agassiz, Oliver Wendell Holmes, Sr., and James Russell Lowell—met once a month during the winter for discussion and dinner.[208] Richard Henry Dana remarked at the club's first meeting, "Emerson is an excellent dinner table man, always a gentleman, never bores or preaches, or dictates, but drops & takes up topics very agreeably, & has even skill & tact in managing his conversation."[209]

In 1858, the Adirondack Club—the Saturday Club's summer substitute— sponsored an extensive camping trip for ten men, including Emerson, into the New York Lake District. An artist in the party, William Stillman, did an oil painting of the whole group, divided into smaller units.

Emerson stands alone in the middle.[210] Stillman's placement of Emerson suggests his central but removed position, even in moments of relaxed camaraderie. In 1848, in a journal entry on "The Beatitude of Conversation," Emerson had written from a similar center of one: "To talk with writers was a great pleasure," he noted; "the best heads" produce "the divinest wine." But their "economy" of listening only for ideas germane to their own work bothered him: "Each is apt to become abstracted & lose the remark of the other through too much attention to his own." He went on, "To escape this economy of writers, women would be better friends; but they have the drawback of the perplexities of sex."[211] Emerson's intricate relations with Fuller and her friends were experiences, ten years past, to which he

208 Besides Emerson and these three men, others in the club were Samuel Gray Ward, Benjamin Pierce, Richard Henry Dana, Jr., Edwin Percy Whipple, John Sullivan Dwight, Ebenezer Rockwood Hoar (Elizabeth Hoar's brother), Henry Wadsworth Longfellow, and John Lothrop Motley. *The Selected Letters of Ralph Waldo Emerson*, ed. Joel Myerson (New York: Columbia University Press, 1997), 395.

209 McAleer, 552; Von Frank, 299.

210 McAleer, 553; Von Frank, 244-45.

211 *JMN* 11: 28-29.

might well have been alluding, and reasons why the later groups he started, unlike the Transcendentalist Club, had no women members.

2.45 *The Philosophers' Camp in the Adirondacks,* 1858.

As a pre-Freudian Romantic, Emerson placed high value on his dreams. At twenty-eight he called them "test objects" to help us "find out the secrets of our own nature"; in short, they were useful as another sort of conversation partner. "All mystics use them," he wrote. Then and later, his dreams might be laced with threatening, even terrifying threads, suppressed by day. They combined a "double consciousness, a sub- & ob-jectiveness," as he put it. By 1857, he was declaring, "I owe real knowledge and even alarming hints to dreams . . . ." Nine years later, he was filled with marvel, evidently not for the first time, at the thought that he had authored both sides of his dream dialogues.[212] In 1869, over twenty years after referring to the "perplexities of sex" that women brought to conversation, Emerson described the following dream:

> I passed into a room where were ladies & gentlemen, some of whom I knew. I did not wish to be recognized because of some disagreeable task, I cannot remember what. One of the ladies was beautiful, and I, it

---

212 Ibid., 3: 321; 5: 475; 14: 169; 16: 49.

seemed, had already seen her, & was her lover. She looked up from her painting, & saw, but did not recognize me—which I thought was wrong—unpardonable. Later, I reflected that it was not so criminal in her, since I had never *proposed* [emphasis his]. Presently the scene changed, & I saw a common street-boy, without any personal advantages, walking with an air of determination, and I perceived that beauty of features signified nothing—only this clearness & strength of purpose made any form respectable & attractive.[213]

Emerson first appears to be the beautiful woman's lover. His undefined wish to be anonymous (hidden) is achieved: she doesn't recognize him. Then on consideration, as usual, he blames himself; he has not told her of his feelings. This scene dissolves to another. His eye is drawn to "a common street-boy," physically unremarkable, for his "clearness & strength of purpose." The boy's virtue strikes him rather than his beauty. This dream combines Emerson's androgynous sensibility and his sexual identity, making each distinct. In both "stories," he reaffirms a high ethical aspiration, a good in itself, but also a shield against hurt.

2.46 Emerson master bedroom.

213 Ibid., 16: 165.

2.47 Emerson's house coat (left) and preaching robe (right), in bedroom alcove.

In 1849, Emerson reassessed what he had done on moving to Concord: "I left the city, I hid myself in the pastures. When I bought a house, the first thing I did was to plant trees. I could not conceal myself enough. Set a hedge here, set pines there, trees & trees, set evergreens, above all, for they will keep my secret all the year round."[214] (This escape from authority by hiding himself was a pattern Emerson had followed since boyhood, when his father searched him out to make him swim.) The home that he had labeled "Bush," surrounded by this ever-higher growth, at least psychologically protected the secret he had known for nine years, his "woman's heart." Joined with a need to work alone, Emerson's desire to be concealed ironically increased

---

214 Ibid., 11: 130.

with his mounting fame as a lecturer and reformer, which reached its height immediately after the Civil War. Instead of living his passions privately, Emerson had poured them into public advice. The commands of his poem, "Give All to Love" (1847) are directly distilled from the ideals he had so fervently described in "Love" and "Friendship" just a few years before: "Give all to love; / Obey thy heart; / Friends, kindred, days, / Estate, good-fame, / Plans, credit, and the Muse,— / Nothing refuse. — Keep thee to-day, / Tomorrow, forever, / Free as an Arab / Of thy beloved . . . . Heartily know, / When half-gods go, / The gods arrive."[215]

---

215 *CW* 9: "Give All to Love," 179-80.

EMERSON THE REFORMER

3. Pragmatic Idealist in Action, 1850-1865

Len Gougeon

What great masses of men wish done, will be done.

Emerson, "Emancipation of the Negroes
in the British West Indies" (1844)

When Emerson entered the national scene in 1850 as a full-fledged reformer, he knew that America faced a dire moral threat. In September, the U. S. Congress passed a series of five measures, known collectively as "The Compromise of 1850." They were designed to ease growing sectional tension over slavery but only succeeded in increasing it, largely due to one measure, the Fugitive Slave Law. It allowed southern agents to enter Free States in order to seize escaped slaves who had sought refuge there. A long-dormant Constitutional provision that deliberately avoided mention of slavery would now be enforced: any "person held to Service or Labour in one State . . . escaping into another . . . shall be delivered up on Claim of the Party to whom such Service or Labour may be due."[1] During the decades following ratification, popular resistance in the Free States had effectively nullified this provision. Many of these states, including Massachusetts, had passed "Personal Liberty Laws" specifically designed to protect runaway slaves. In 1850, this law strengthening slavery outraged Emerson, especially because his own Senator Daniel Webster, a man he had

---

1   *Constitution of the United States,* Article 4, Section 2, http://www.archives.gov

http://dx.doi.org/10.11647/OBP.0065.05

once admired, played such a decisive role in its passage. Webster argued that he was merely trying to save the Union, but Emerson wondered at what cost. In the following decade, he became increasingly incensed both by the law and Webster.

The North-South Conflict in Historic Perspective

The passage of the Fugitive Slave Law was made possible by the South's preponderant power in the Congress. In part, Southerners came to hold this position through the effect of the Constitution's "three-fifths" provision: "Representatives . . . shall be apportioned among the Several States . . . according to their respective Numbers which shall be determined by adding the whole Number of free Persons . . . and . . . three fifths of all other Persons." The "other Persons," of course, were slaves.[2] Initially, Southerners wanted to count all slaves as citizens in order to increase their representation in the House and in the Electoral College. Northerners objected that since southerners generally insisted that slaves were property and not people, they should no more be counted as "citizens" than cows or horses.

A compromise was reached: five slaves would count as three citizens. Over the decades that followed, this "three-fifths compromise" allowed the South to predominate in Congress, promoting policies and laws that were actually dictated by relatively few men. In short, the government was run by an oligarchy, derogatorily referred to as the "slave power." Indeed, the Freesoiler John Gorham Palfrey, for whom Emerson would campaign in 1851, made this very argument in 1846. Writing in the *Boston Whig*, Palfrey held that the free citizens of the country, "amounting to some eighteen millions in number, are subjects of an oligarchy of about one hundred thousand owners of men. There are perhaps three hundred thousand slaveholders in the country," he noted. "Allowing for minors and women, probably not far from one-third the number are voters, and they administer our affairs."[3]

---

2   Ibid., Article 1, Section 2.
3   *Papers on the Slave Power: First Published in the Boston Whig, 1846,* pamphlet in the Birney Anti-Slavery Collection, Eisenhower Library, Johns Hopkins University. For more on the effects of the three-fifths clause, see Garry Wills, *"Negro President": Jefferson and the Slave Power* (Boston, Mass.: Houghton Mifflin, 2003).

Eventually, another major compromise with slavery became necessary in order to maintain a political balance between Free States and Slave States. When Missouri applied for admission to the Union as a Slave State in 1819, it threatened to upset the balance that had prevailed up to that time. The famous Missouri Compromise of 1820 provided that Maine, previously a part of Massachusetts, would enter the Union as a Free State at the same time as Missouri, thus preserving a national balance. However, the measure also forbade the creation of any new slave states from the territories of the Louisiana Purchase (1803). In the 1850s, the slave power's successful challenge to this provision exacerbated long-standing regional antagonisms, eventually leading to the Civil War.

Opposition to slavery increased steadily in the three decades leading up to that war. In the early 1830s, Boston emerged as a center for the growing antislavery movement. On 1 January 1831, William Lloyd Garrison published the first issue of the *Liberator*, destined to become America's most famous abolitionist newspaper.

3.1 William Lloyd Garrison at 28, 1833.

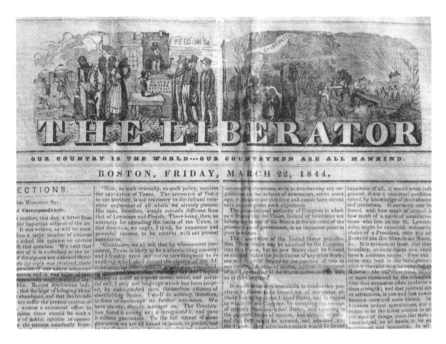

3.2 *The Liberator*, Friday, March 22, 1844.

A year later, he and nine others formed the New England Anti-Slavery Society.[4] Eventually this organization would attract a number of eloquent antislavery orators who would preach the cause of freedom and resistance to the slave power throughout the North. The most notable of these were Samuel Joseph May (Louisa May Alcott's uncle), Frederick Douglass, and Wendell Phillips. Women largely supported the antislavery movement, especially in the early years. Through fairs, picnics, bazaars, and the sale of gift books like *The Liberty Bell*, they raised money to keep the organization afloat and to subsidize Garrison's *Liberator*. Early on, talented women strengthened the movement by serving as editors, writers, and speakers. Among them were Maria Chapman, Sojourner Truth, and three Quaker women leaders: the Grimké sisters of South Carolina and Lucretia Mott of Philadelphia.

4   John L. Thomas, *The Liberator: William Lloyd Garrison, A Biography* (Boston, Mass.: Little, Brown & Co., 1963), 127, 141.

Emerson's Path into the World of Reform

At first, the skeptic in Emerson kept him apart from reforming "associations." He believed that reform could best be accomplished through the individual practice of "self-culture," his Transcendental term for moral self-improvement. Also, in the early years of the abolitionist movement, he found many of its proponents to be narrow, bitter, and self-righteous. After the abolitionist George Thompson visited his home in 1835, Emerson recorded the following in his journal.

> Thompson the Abolitionist is inconvertible; what you say or what might be said would make no impression on him. He belongs I fear to that great class of the Vanity-stricken. An inordinate thirst for notice can not be gratified until it has found in its gropings what is called a Cause that men will bow to; tying himself fast to that, the small man is then at liberty to consider all objections made to him as proofs of folly & the devil in the objector, & under that screen, if he gets a rotten egg or two, yet his name sounds through the world and he is praised & praised.[5]

But over the years, he came to admire and support many abolitionist leaders, including Mary Merrick Brooks, president of Concord's own Female Anti-Slavery Society. In fact, all the women in Emerson's household, beginning with Lidian in the 1830s, would become members of that Society.

Eventually, he would entertain several of these leaders in his home, including the Grimké sisters, Garrison, and Wendell Phillips. Phillips, Emerson came to feel, was one of the best orators of the age. Against protests by conservatives, he would argue successfully for Phillip's right to speak on slavery at the Concord Lyceum, a controversial topic even there. His admiration for Garrison, the most famous of the abolitionists, grew considerably over the years. In 1841, Emerson noted, "I cannot speak of that gentleman without respect."[6] He also considered Lucretia Mott a "noble woman," and described Frederick Douglass as a compelling example of the heroic "anti-slave."[7] Emerson's eventual alliance with these reformers came only after the slavery issue heated up and he began to appreciate their abolitionist efforts. Yet seeds for this shift lay in his earlier writings.

---

5   *The Journals and Miscellaneous Notebooks of Ralph Waldo Emerson*, 16 vols., eds. William H. Gilman, et al. (Cambridge, Mass.: Harvard University Press, 1960-1982), 5: 90-91. Hereafter *JMN*.

6   *JMN* 9: 134.

7   *JMN* 9: 132, *L* 7: 523; *JMN* 9: 125.

3.3 Lydian Jackson Emerson, about 55, c. 1850s.

When Emerson gave his "American Scholar" address in 1837, he assured his distinguished audience of Harvard alumni and students that "Action is with the scholar subordinate, but it is essential. Without it, he is not yet man."[8] Announcing a cultural revolution, his mission was change and

---

8   *The Collected Works of Ralph Waldo Emerson,* 10 vols, eds. Robert E. Spiller, et al. (Cambridge, Mass.: Harvard University Press, 1971-2013), 1: 59. Hereafter *CW.*

reform. The question was, how might someone such as himself, attuned to "the strains of eloquence," as he put it, actually act? Until the late 1830s and early 1840s, he felt that moral suasion and education were action enough. By "goodness calling to goodness," his speeches sought to open listeners to the divine voice within. He hoped that his message would lead individuals to an intuitive perception of universal moral law, which would then transform society. In this early view, change in the single soul had to come first.

By the mid-1840s, however, Emerson recognized that this strategy was simply not working. Far from improving, America was actually becoming more corrupt. Years before, he had warned about the dangers of materialism. Now the nation's commercial success had fostered what he called a "vulgar prosperity that retrogrades ever to barbarism."[9] In an 1846 poem, Emerson lamented, "Things are in the saddle, and ride mankind."[10] For him, the grossest example of this grasping after goods was the institution of slavery, long embodied by the South's "ownership" of Washington, D.C. Throughout the late 1840s, the Southern slave power threatened to grow exponentially. Soon after the Mexican War ended in 1848, Texas entered the Union as a large, new Slave State. Simultaneously, vast new territories acquired as a result of the war—territories that extended west to California and north to Utah—promised an even further expansion of the slave power. These national developments accentuated Emerson's moral and cultural distress. Consequently, beginning in the mid-1840s, his philosophy began to undergo a significant transition, as previously traced in Chapter 2. The "visionary ecstasy" of his earlier works gave way to a belief in "ethical engagement as a means of spiritual fulfillment."[11] As a result, Emerson became more and more involved in the major social issues of his day, especially slavery and, eventually, the women's rights movement.

Emerson's Landmark Steps as a Reformer

In Concord on August 1, 1844, Emerson delivered his first major antislavery address, "Emancipation of the Negroes in the British West Indies." It was

---

9   *CW* 1: 62.
10 "Ode: Inscribed to W. H. Channing," in Ralph Waldo Emerson, *The Complete Works of Ralph Waldo Emerson*, 12 vols., ed. Edward Waldo Emerson (Boston, Mass.: Houghton Mifflin, 1903-1904), 9: 76. Hereafter *W*.
11 David Robinson, *Emerson and the Conduct of Life: Pragmatism and Ethical Purpose in the Later Works* (Cambridge: Cambridge University Press, 1993), 3.

the tenth anniversary of that event, and the women in his family, along with their antislavery friends and cohorts, encouraged him to take this part. The recent aggressive growth of the slave power demanded a new tactic and Emerson's tone in the speech is decidedly militant. He denounced the creeping and insidious influence of slavery's "barbarities" on American civilization, and applauded the violent uprisings of the West Indian slaves who sought to win their freedom. "The arrival in the world of such men as Toussaint [L'Ouverture] and the Haytian heroes, of the leaders of their race in Barbadoes and Jamaica, outweighs in good omen all the English and American humanity."[12] In their quest for freedom, West Indian blacks demonstrated a moral superiority that set them above their "civilized" white oppressors. For Emerson, the rebellion of these long-suffering victims proved that the love of freedom was universal and irrepressible, a compelling moral principle that in itself guaranteed liberty's eventual triumph over oppression. Even abolitionism's considerable might paled before this dynamic and eternal moral force. "The anti-slavery of the whole world, is dust in the balance before this—is a poor squeamishness and nervousness; the might and the right are here: here is man: and if you have man, black or white is an insignificance."[13]

Young Frederick Douglass shared the platform with Emerson on this special day in Concord. In his book, *Narrative of Frederick Douglass, An American Slave, Written by Himself* (1845), Douglass would soon provide eloquent testimony of his own heroic struggle for freedom. When Emerson next spoke on West Indian Emancipation in August 1845, Douglass copied portions of his address into a personal notebook. Undoubtedly, he also read the *Liberator's* separate accounts of both this speech and Emerson's public refusal to address the New Bedford Lyceum in November 1845 to protest their racist membership policy.[14] Douglass's and Emerson's paths would cross many times as the abolitionists accelerated their antislavery efforts in the fifteen years before the Civil War. Douglass was especially taken with Emerson's idea of self-reliance and applied it to the black slaves' struggle to become free men. Beginning in the 1850s and into the 1890s, he repeatedly lectured on the topic "Self-Made Men."[15]

---

12   Ralph Waldo Emerson, *Emerson's Antislavery Writings*, eds. Len Gougeon and Joel Myerson (New Haven, CT: Yale University Press, 1995), 19. Hereafter *EAW*.
13   *EAW* 31.
14   Frederick Douglass Papers, Library of Congress; Len Gougeon, *Virtue's Hero: Emerson, Antislavery, and Reform* (Athens, GA: University of Georgia Press, 1990), 102-06.
15   Lawrence Buell, *Emerson* (Cambridge, Mass.: Harvard University Press, 2003), 256.

3.4 Frederick Douglass at about 29, c. 1847.

In the following year, Emerson accepted an invitation to deliver another address celebrating West Indian emancipation. In this second address, he attacked the bitter racism that was the primary justification for slavery. "What is the defense of Slavery," he asks. "What is the irresistible argument by which every plea of humanity and reason has hitherto been borne down?" The argument is summed up in one word, "*Niggers!*—a word which . . . is reckoned stronger than heaven." "They who say it and they who hear it," says Emerson, "think it the voice of nature and fate" proclaiming an inescapable "inferiority of race" that renders all the arguments of the reformer moot. Such an obscene fatalism strikes at the very heart of Emerson's Transcendentalist notion of cosmic justice, and he rejects it outright. "The only reply," he says, "to this poor, sceptical ribaldry is the affirming heart. The sentiment of right, which is the principle of civilization and the reason of reason, fights against this damnable atheism."[16]

16   *EAW* 35, 36, 37.

Emerson's new militancy grew throughout the balance of the 1840s. He accepted invitations to speak on the increasingly controversial topic of slavery, despite conservative opposition to the antislavery movement throughout New England.

3.5 Emerson at about 47, c. 1850.

Wealthy Northern textile factory owners depended on cheap Southern cotton to keep their mills profitably producing. These "gentlemen of property and standing," and others who indirectly gained from the institution of slavery, were determined to resist any movement that threatened a change in the economic status quo. As friction between the Slave and Free States grew following the Mexican War, the thirty-year-old Missouri Compromise became untenable. As a result, Congress attempted to defuse the situation with "The Compromise of 1850." For the North, the most onerous element of this compromise was most certainly the Fugitive Slave Law. Before, fugitive slaves who managed to escape to the North could be reasonably confident of freedom and security. But after 1850, agents from the South were allowed to enter Free States to recover the slave owner's human "property." Also, Northern commissioners were appointed to preside over hearings to determine if the accused was actually a fugitive slave. If the finding was "yes," the commissioner was paid a fee of $10 (or $288 today). If the finding was "no," he was paid only $5 ($144). The law also made harboring or aiding a fugitive slave a crime punishable by fine and imprisonment.[17]

Emerson was incensed at this grossly immoral effort to re-activate an earlier Constitutional requirement that to him had become a "dead letter." Such a backward development challenged his faith in moral progress. In his journal, he wondered how such a "filthy enactment" could have been "made in the 19th century, by people who could read & write." Like many other persons of conscience in the North, he vowed "I will not obey it, by God."[18]

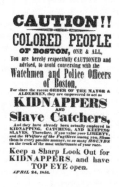

3.6 Boston broadside cautioning blacks, 4 April 1851.

In an open letter to his abolitionist friends, published in the *Liberator* on April 18, 1851, the eve of the Revolution's seventy-sixth anniversary, Emerson issued an unequivocal call for civil disobedience. He encouraged resistance to the law "in every manner, singly or socially, in private and in public, by voice and by pen—and, first of all, by substantial help and hospitality to the slave, and defending him against his hunters."[19] Despite the threat of fine and imprisonment, he and a small number of Concord neighbors agreed to provide aid and shelter to any runaway slave who should appear at their doors.[20] Concord's Underground Railroad, with Henry David Thoreau

---

17   Gary Collison, *Shadrach Minkins: From Fugitive Slave to Citizen* (Cambridge, Mass.: Harvard University Press, 1997), 75; http://www.measuringworth.com/uscompare/relativevalue.php

18   *JMN* 11: 412.

19   *EAW* 51.

20   Robert D. Richardson, Jr., *Emerson: The Mind on Fire* (Berkeley, CA: University of California Press, 1995), 496.

frequently serving as guide and conductor, eventually forwarded many runaway slaves to the safe haven of Canada.[21] Margaret Fuller's example undoubtedly encouraged Emerson's new militancy. Fuller, author of the proto-feminist work, *Woman in the Nineteenth Century* (1845) , had been in Italy since 1847. When its war for independence began in 1848, she covered the conflict as a foreign correspondent for Horace Greeley's *New-York Tribune*. Soon she fell in love with an Italian rebel, Giovanni Angelo Ossoli, and joined the revolution herself. First among her Transcendental circle to test its philosophy of reform in a violent struggle for liberty, and true to her radical nature, Fuller's dispatches from Rome glowingly reported on "these sad but glorious days" of conflict, and the bloody sacrifices of young Italian patriots.[22] Her example as a writer and active revolutionary in a war against oppression undoubtedly inspired her friends at home.

In the spring of 1851, not long after Emerson had begun his fight against the Fugitive Slave Law, one of its first victims, a young runaway named Thomas Sims, was captured in Boston. This event drew national attention. Despite abolitionists' vigorous protests against the rendition verdict of Judge Lemuel Shaw (Herman Melville's father-in-law), Sims was returned to bondage in Georgia from which he had so heroically escaped.[23] Emerson's outrage now reached a near fever pitch. He prepared to attack the new law in the most acerbic and bitter speech of his career, "Address to the Citizens of Concord" on May 3, 1851. Sims's return was accomplished with the assent and co-operation of some of Boston's most prominent citizens. Emerson was shocked by this capitulation of the educated elite to gross barbarity. "I thought none that was not ready to go on all fours," he jabbed, "would back this law."[24] Emerson here made concrete his earlier hopes that a higher moral law, one that ensured freedom to all humanity, would guide the public's actions. For him, the moral laws of the universe demand liberty for all humanity. Returning escaped slaves to bondage was clearly an obscene violation of this universal moral code. "A man's right to liberty," Emerson insisted, "is as inalienable as his right to life." He called upon his

---

21 Walter Harding, *The Days of Henry Thoreau: A Biography* (New York: Alfred A. Knopf, 1970), 195.

22 Margaret Fuller, *The Portable Margaret Fuller*, ed. Mary Kelley (New York: Penguin Books, 1994), 453.

23 Albert J. Von Frank, *The Trials of Anthony Burns: Freedom and Slavery in Emerson's Boston* (Cambridge, Mass.: Harvard University Press, 1998), 26-27.

24 *EAW* 56.

fellow citizens to defend this sacred principle, stating unconditionally, "If our resistance to this law is not right, there is no right."[25]

For Emerson, Daniel Webster, Massachusetts's gifted but conservative senator, was the chief villain.

3.7 Daniel Webster at 69, 1851.

By throwing his considerable weight behind the Fugitive Slave Law, in an alliance with Southern Congressmen, he had made this miscarriage of justice possible. Like many other Northerners, including Emerson's friend and fellow poet Oliver Wendell Holmes, Sr. , Webster had been willing to sell the region's conscience in the name of national unity and to preserve a comfortable material status quo. Once a younger Emerson had idolized Webster as a political orator second to none. His brother Edward had studied in Webster's law offices. Now, however, the senator's betrayal of Massachusetts's commitment to liberty turned his admiration to disgust. "The fairest American fame," Emerson asserts, "ends in this filthy law. Mr. Webster cannot choose but regret his loss . . . . Those to whom his name

---

25   Ibid., 57.

was once dear and honored, as the manly statesman to whom the choicest gifts of nature had been accorded, disown him." With uncommon ferocity, Emerson vividly depicts Webster as one who could not see the higher ideal because, as he puts it, "All the drops of his blood have eyes that look downward."[26]

On several occasions in the spring of 1851, Emerson repeated this speech, his first opposing the Fugitive Slave Law, in a stump campaign for his friend John Gorham Palfrey, who was running for a seat in Congress on the Free Soil ticket. Palfrey's bid failed, but Emerson's baptism in the fire of radical politics, something quite foreign to him as a scholar, illustrates his determination to respond to the moral emergency of the times. Throughout the speech, his militant insistence on civil disobedience as the only appropriate response to a grossly evil law did not go unnoticed in Boston's conservative press. "All that was waged against the law by Mr. Emerson," a writer for the *Boston Advertiser* (May 23, 1851) observed, "would have applied equally well to *any* law providing for the surrender of fugitive slaves." Therefore, according to this logic Mr. Emerson was actually attacking the "provision of the Constitution" upon which such laws were founded, a radical and dangerous course, indeed. "If the doctrines of his lecture were sustained and enforced in the Free States," the writer noted, "the Union would be infallibly severed." The writer spoke truer than he knew.

Emerson's direct involvement in Palfrey's campaign was, indeed, exceptional. By temperament and taste, he thought his best service was rendered from the lecture podium, not the political stump. That he made an exception for Palfrey demonstrates his commitment to the democratic process and the depth of his faith in the basic decency of "we the people." Still committed to the Transcendentalist ideal that all people were inherently divine, Emerson felt that when properly informed, their collective voice might become, quite literally, the voice of the divinity that is present in all of humanity. The obligation of government, he believed, was to implement the people's will. As early as his 1844 Emancipation address, he had observed that in a democracy, "What great masses of men wish done, will be done."[27] But that required an arduous and lengthy democratic process of free debate and discussion—reasoned discourse—to lift up, educate, and persuade the electorate toward their best interest.

---

26   Ibid., 65, 67.
27   Ibid., 28.

Not surprisingly, then, Emerson was most incensed by the slave power's practice of stifling free speech. A case in point was the Congressional "gag rule." This rule automatically tabled all antislavery petitions. Antislavery materials were deemed "incendiary" and an embargo was placed on their transmission through the Federal mails. Public discussion of the subject of abolition was forbidden for the same reason. For Emerson, these were the acts of a tyrannical oligarchy and were an unacceptable abridgment of the rights of a free people. Public dialogue and discussion, he felt, were essential in a democracy as the necessary antecedent to collective action.

While Emerson always insisted on the importance of self-reliance and the validity of intuitively perceived values, he came to see that it was important for individuals to connect with society in order to improve it. This change of emphasis matched an increasingly pragmatic vein in his idealism. Emerson makes this point explicit in his "Lecture on Slavery" (1855). "But whilst I insist on the doctrine of the independence and the inspiration of the individual," he notes, "I do not cripple but exalt the social action. Patriotism, public opinion, have a real meaning, though there is so much counterfeit rag money abroad under it, that the name is apt to disgust. A wise man delights in the powers of many people . . . . We shall need to call them all out."[28]

Bloodshed in the Run-up to War

Throughout the 1850s, tensions between Slave and Free States often erupted in violence. In 1854, Congress passed the Kansas-Nebraska Act, effectively nullifying the Missouri Compromise of 1820, which had specifically excluded slavery from the territories of the Louisiana Purchase. Vast new areas now lay open to settlement by pro-slavery advocates, potentially upsetting the balance between Free and Slave States.

Inhabitants of each new state were to determine whether they should be Slave or Free, a position opposed by antislavery reformers. The stakes were high; the South's Congressional hegemony was threatened and with it the future of slavery.

---

28   Ibid., 103.

3.8 Fugitive slave, Anthony Burns, 24,
returned to Virginia from Boston in 1854.

In Kansas, a virtual guerrilla war soon broke out between free farmers, immigrants from Massachusetts and elsewhere, and proslavery "Border Ruffians" from Missouri. When the Missourians wrecked the free-farmers' state capital at Lawrence, a fundamentalist abolitionist, John Brown of Connecticut, retaliated, leading a small band in murdering five proslavery settlers near Pottawatomie Creek. Northern newspapers reported in detail the growth of violence in what was now called "bleeding Kansas."

Meanwhile, conflict in the nation's capital reflected the territory's volatile events. In heated Congressional debates in May 1856, Massachusetts' abolitionist Senator Charles Sumner, elected to Webster's seat after his death in 1852, delivered a rousing, two-day speech, "The Crime Against Kansas." He strongly denounced the "slave oligarchy," calling it the "harlotry" that supported the proslavery faction, naming in particular South Carolina Senator Andrew P. Butler. Just three days later, Butler's irate nephew, Preston S. Brooks, a Congressman from South Carolina, brutally attacked Sumner as he sat at his Senate desk, repeatedly beating him with a cane until he was unconscious.

3.9 Senator Charles Sumner's caning in the U.S. Senate, 1856.

The attack so severely injured Sumner that it took him three-and-half years to recover.[29] This blatant brutality in the very halls of government outraged Emerson. Only four days after Sumner's beating, he addressed a Concord protest meeting, venting his anger: "I do not see how," he observed, "a barbarous community and a civilized community can constitute one state. I think we must get rid of slavery, or we must get rid of freedom."[30]

Clearly, the corruption of Southern slavery, with strong support from the North's commercial interests, was infecting the very fabric of the nation. For twelve years now, Emerson had spoken out against slavery, and had formed a virtual alliance with the abolitionists and their leaders, especially William Lloyd Garrison and Wendell Phillips. Their combined efforts, however, had not only failed to diminish the power of the institution within the federal government, they had failed to deter the potential of its legal expansion. Privately, Emerson confided to a friend, "If the Free States do not obtain the government next fall, which our experience does not entitle us to hope, nothing seems left, but to form at once a Northern Union & break the old."[31] The forces that would ultimately precipitate such a rupture were already in play.

All over Massachusetts, committees were being formed to raise money for relief and protection of the free farmers in Kansas. In June, a fund-raising event was held in Concord, and Emerson donated the substantial sum of fifty dollars (about $1,330 today). He also joined neighbors in signing a letter to the governor calling upon him to protect Massachusetts citizens in Kansas. In September, Emerson spoke at a Kansas relief meeting in Cambridge where he urged his listeners to "give largely, lavishly" to a fund that would be used to purchase Sharpe's rifles and other equipment necessary to defend freedom's cause in Kansas. For Emerson, as for many others, the time had come to meet force with force.

The nation was by now utterly polarized. The presidential campaign of 1856 pitted Democrat James Buchanan against Republican John Fremont. Buchanan won the election on a platform that supported both the Compromise of 1850 and the Kansas-Nebraska Act. The Republicans, meanwhile, continued to insist that Congress had the right to control slavery,

---

29   David Herbert Donald, *Charles Sumner* (New York: Da Capo Press, 1996), 295-96.
30   *EAW* 107.
31   Ralph Waldo Emerson, *The Letters of Ralph Waldo Emerson*, 10 vols., eds. Ralph L. Rusk and Eleanor M. Tilton (New York: Columbia University Press, 1939, 1990-1995), 5: 23. Hereafter *L*.

not the inhabitants of the territories. The U.S. Supreme Court's Dred Scott decision in March 1857 intensified the national debate. In this famous case, the court held that no person of slave descent or blood could be considered a citizen of the United States, and therefore had no standing in the courts. Furthermore, the decision declared that Negroes were generally regarded "as so far inferior that they had no rights which the white man was bound to respect."[32]

For Emerson, who had once declared that the role of government was to protect the "poor and the weaker party," the ruling was perverse. The very essence of American democracy was its dedication to the preservation of the principle of liberty for all. As recently as January 1855, in his "Lecture on Slavery," Emerson had insisted, "Every American will say, 'in the collision of statutes, or in doubtful interpretation, liberty is the great order which all lesser orders are to promote.'" For Emerson, American law should always seek to obtain for "every man the largest liberty compatible with the liberty of every other man." He advised, "No citizen will go wrong who on every question leans to the side of general liberty."[33]

3.10 Emerson about 51-52, c. 1854-1855.

---

32   Gougeon, *Virtue's Hero*, 231.
33   *EAW* 105.

The Dred Scott decision, following just three years after the passage of the Kansas-Nebraska Act and the proslavery victory in the presidential election the previous year, was apparently enough to convince Emerson that the federal government was now firmly in the control of forces opposed to freedom, equality, and justice. His militancy intensified, and he felt increasingly defensive. He confided in his journal a resolve to prevent this immoral plague from spreading: "We intend to set up & keep a *cordon sanitaire* all around the infected district, & by no means suffer the pestilence to spread."[34] This growing determination to forcefully resist the further expansion of slavery reinforced his support for the freedom fighters in Kansas.

In February 1857, John Brown, vilified in the South because of the "Pottawatomie Massacre," but considered a hero to many in the North, visited Concord to raise funds for his guerrilla partisans. He lunched with the Thoreau family, and in the afternoon was introduced to Emerson, who was immediately impressed by this forceful, imposing figure. Brown's later address at Concord's Town Hall reinforced Emerson's positive response, leading him to affirm his own growing militancy. "One of [Brown's] good points," he notes, "was the folly of the peace party in Kansas, who believed that their strength lay in the greatness of their wrongs & so discountenanced resistance." At the end of his stirring presentation, Brown vowed to carry on the struggle until the battle against slavery was won.

3.11 Heralds of Freedom, 1857.

34   *JMN* 14: 197.

Brown's final battle was not long in coming. In May 1859, again in Concord, he spoke at the Town Hall appealing for funds. Emerson, with many others, contributed to his cause. In October, he was still collecting money for him when word came that Brown, with only twenty-odd supporters, had attacked the Federal Arsenal at Harper's Ferry, Virginia. Their hope of arming and leading an insurrection of slaves throughout the South shocked many Brown supporters. It seemed a desperate and foolhardy attack by a small, untrained band on a much superior federal force that had no chance of success. Initially Emerson was also shocked, thinking Brown had "lost his head," but was soon praising his audacity, courage, and idealism. After two days of fighting, Brown and the other survivors were captured by troops led by Col. Robert E. Lee. They were charged with treason. While many condemned the violence and bloodshed suffered in the assault, Emerson continued to support his hero. In a lecture in November, titled simply "Courage," he spoke of Brown as "that new saint . . . who if he shall suffer, will make the gallows like the cross."[35]

For some, this allusion to Christ was pure blasphemy. After a highly publicized trial, in which Brown eloquently defended his action in the name of liberty and justice, he was condemned and sentenced to hang on December 2, 1859. The nation's torment over the cause for which he died only increased.

3.12 Emerson at 55, 1858.

---

35   W 7: 427.

3.13 John Brown at 59, 1859.

Conservatives in Massachusetts and throughout the country declaimed—as did the *Boston Post* that December—against the "anti-slavery fanatics" who supported Brown rather than the Constitution. Emerson had a different view. Before Brown's death, in a "Speech . . . to Aid John Brown's Family," he praised him as a "pure idealist" who believed in "the Golden Rule and the Declaration of Independence" as the proper guides to reform.[36] Repercussions from the raid continued to be felt: Southerners, long suspicious that the North was fomenting slave uprisings, appointed a Congressional committee to investigate the activities of a small group of Brown's supporters known as the "Secret Six." Emerson was not one of them, but his Concord neighbor, Franklin Sanborn, was. When federal agents from the committee arrived in Concord to arrest Sanborn in April 1860, a crowd of angry townspeople drove them off. Soon thereafter, a vigilance group was formed to protect any other citizens from such abuses. [37] At least at home, Emerson's "*cordon sanitaire*" was apparently taking shape.

The debate over slavery continued to intensify, and violence became even more common. Abolitionists, seen by many as largely responsible for this growing discord, were warned not to attempt further public meetings. Emerson was well aware of the growing danger but refused to

36   *EAW* 118.
37   Gougeon, *Virtue's Hero*, 256.

be intimidated. Privately, he exhorted himself: "Do the duty of the day. Just now the supreme duty of all thinking men is to assert freedom. Go where it is threatened, & say, 'I am for it, & do not wish to live in the world a moment longer than it exists.'"[38]

His resolution was soon to be tested.

3.14 Emerson at 56, 1859.

Lincoln's Election, the End of Southern Hegemony and Civil War

In November 1860, the Republican candidate Abraham Lincoln was elected President of the United States without a single Southern electoral vote. The national fault line now widened to a chasm. The South's slave oligarchy,

---

38   *JMN* 15: 111.

after dominating the federal government for decades, had been defeated. This sudden loss of power quickly prompted a reaction. In December, South Carolina issued a Declaration of Secession from the Union. In the months that followed, ten other Southern states did the same, soon forming the Confederate States of America. Emerson was elated. For some time, he had contemplated a Northern secession as necessary to resist slavery. The South's abrupt departure might be a first step in its eventual eradication. Once isolated and contained like a contagious disease, he was sure that slavery would die a natural death. The events of the day, as Emerson saw them, were "hastening the downfall."[39]

Conservatives in the North were upset by the prospect of the dissolution of the Union. A number of compromise proposals were discussed in Washington in hopes of resolving the crisis. Meanwhile, mob violence against abolitionists grew dramatically. In response, Wendell Phillips had taken to carrying a revolver in public, accompanied by a bodyguard of young volunteers. Yet he and his fellow abolitionists would not be silenced. They scheduled a public meeting for Tremont Temple in Boston on January 24, 1861. Phillips asked Emerson to be one of the speakers, and despite the strong likelihood that anti-abolition rowdies would attempt to disrupt the gathering, he accepted. Three loud cheers greeted him, followed by three counter cheers for the Union, along with catcalls from the rowdies. In the disorder, the police stood idly by. Yet according to the *Liberator* (February 1, 1861), Emerson was not intimidated, and he was in no mood for compromise. "As to concessions," he said, "we have none to make. The monstrous concession made at the formation of the Constitution is all that can ever be asked; it has blocked the civilization and humanity of the times up to this day." Calls rained down on him: "put him out," "dry up," "unbutton your coat." The situation became so chaotic that Emerson was forced to withdraw, and the meeting ended with the police clearing the galleries.[40] Yet Emerson felt that an important point had been made. In fact, he felt so strongly about it that he later noted in his journal, "If I were dumb [a mute], yet I would have gone & mowed & muttered or made signs."[41]

Attempts to forge a compromise with the Southerners ultimately failed. Lincoln, however, remained determined to preserve the Union at all costs. The die had been cast. The nation exploded into Civil War as rebel cannons

39   *JMN* 15: 91.
40   Gougeon, *Virtue's Hero*, 264-66.
41   *JMN* 15: 111.

fired upon Fort Sumter in Charleston, South Carolina on April 12, 1861. Emerson, like many others, was surprised by this dramatic development, but welcomed it. He had always believed that moral progress was inevitable, despite the corruption and resistance of some. The war, coming unexpectedly, confirmed his faith. "This revolution," he wrote in his journal, "is the work of no man, but the effervescence of nature . . . nothing that has occurred but has been a surprise, & as much to the leaders as to the hindmost. And not an abolitionist, not an idealist, can say without effrontery, I did it."[42]

While Lincoln had declared that the war was a struggle to restore the Union, Emerson had a much grander vision. For him, war was an opportunity to remove the cancer of slavery from the body politic once and for all, to heal the resulting wound, and to bring about a new birth of freedom and equality in America. With this, the original promise of the Founding Fathers could at last be fulfilled. At first, few shared this vision. Most expected a short conflict and a speedy restoration of the Union as it had been, under a firm federal authority. Emerson remained convinced, however, that an irrepressible "moral force" was at work. "If the war goes on," he noted in his journal, "it will be impossible to keep the combatants from the extreme ground on either side. In spite of themselves, one army will stand for slavery pure; & the other for pure freedom."[43] Events soon proved him right. When the inexperienced Union army suffered a catastrophic defeat in the first major battle of the war at Bull Run (Manassas), on July 14, 1861, it became clear to most that the South was determined to fight and that the war would be long and costly. Just days before the battle, Emerson delivered an address to the students at Tufts College, observing "the brute noise of the cannon has . . . a most poetic echo these days when it is an instrument of freedom and the primal sentiment of humanity."[44]

For Emerson, this "primal sentiment" was the moral force of the divine, the ultimate guide for those who would lead a just life. Following the Revolution, America had become nearly deaf to the dictates of this moral guide. The result was a corrupt, vulgar, and barbaric prosperity. America's moral education, its broad knowledge of right and wrong, had faltered. This knowledge, Emerson argued, and "the divine oracle which it ought to have

---

42   *JMN* 15: 405.
43   Ibid., 15: 145.
44   *The Later Lectures of Ralph Waldo Emerson: 1843-1871*, 2 vols., eds. Ronald Bosco and Joel Myerson (Athens, GA: University of Georgia Press, 2001), 2: 241. Hereafter, *LL*.

delivered, it has failed to deliver." "National calamities," like the present war, are the natural result.[45] Nevertheless, Emerson believed that America was on track to produce a more perfect democracy, one characterized by universal freedom and equality, the "inalienable rights" affirmed in the Declaration of Independence. In Washington in January 1862, he told an audience, "Our whole history appears like a last effort of the Divine Providence in behalf of the human race."[46] In this time of crisis, he felt it imperative to maintain a clear vision to guide the process: "Where there is no vision the people perish," he later affirmed to students at Dartmouth College.[47] Emerson was not about to let that happen.

Emerson, Lincoln, and Emancipation

For Emerson, the America promised by the Declaration was to be based on principles that today are considered the essence of liberal democracy: liberty, equality, and justice for all regardless of race, religion, or gender. And he saw the first giant step toward realizing these ideals to be universal emancipation. At the outset of his presidency, Lincoln had taken a decidedly different course. For personal and moral reasons, he may have wanted to free the slaves, yet political necessity led him to follow the more conservative Republican Party platform. It tolerated slavery where it already existed, but opposed its extension into the territories. At the war's start, Lincoln needed to hold not only Republican conservatives but also to keep four slave-holding "Border States" (Missouri, Kentucky, Maryland, and Delaware) loyal to the Union. Therefore, he resisted abolitionists' efforts to declare emancipation as a specific goal.

Complicating his position further, Lincoln believed that most emancipated blacks could never live free lives in this country because, as one historian describes it, "Wherever they went here, whites would oppress them, refuse them equal rights, want them to go. It was a fact of life they all had to face."[48] From early in his political career, this intolerance led Lincoln to support those who favored a colonization plan to remove freed blacks from America to Africa or the Caribbean.[49] He also recognized

45   *LL* 2: 242.
46   *W* 11: 299.
47   *LL* 2: 311.
48   Oates, Stephen B., *With Malice toward None: A Life of Abraham Lincoln* (New York: Harper Perennial, 1977), 312.
49   David Herbert Donald, *Lincoln* (New York: Simon & Schuster, 1995), 166-67, 221.

that racism was a bitter fact of life both North and South. Consequently, an emancipation declaration might demoralize Union troops who believed that they were fighting to restore the Union and not to free blacks. Indeed, many of them would have undoubtedly agreed with a soldier from New York who insisted in a letter home, "We must first conquer & then its [sic] time enough to talk about the *damn'd niggers.*"[50]

In the face of such bigotry, Emerson was determined to swiftly and repeatedly promote his vision of a free, racially diverse, and just American society. In a lecture appropriately titled "American Civilization," delivered first in Boston on November 12, 1861 and then at the Smithsonian in January 1862, he made his position clear. "The war for the Union is broader than any state policy of sectional interest," he insisted. The nation must be one, united on the basis of equal rights and justice for all. As it is, "The Union is not broad enough, because of slavery; and we must come to emancipation, with compensation to the loyal states. This is a principle. Everything else is an intrigue."[51] The address was later published in the *Atlantic Monthly* in April.

Strong opposition to emancipation also came from the conservative Democratic Party, which continued to have substantial influence in the North. Their motto was "The Constitution as it is, and the Union as it was." When Lincoln's proposal to abolish slavery in the District of Columbia (with compensation to the owners) was approved by Congress in April 1862, the party reacted predictably. Boston's Democratic newspaper, the *Courier*, referred to the measure as "a mortal blow to the Union . . . in spirit and effect." The writer complained that, except for the chance that the U.S. Supreme Court might declare it unconstitutional, "we should at once relinquish hopes, cherished through every discouragement, for the return for the country to its normal state under the Constitution."[52]

As the war dragged on, Lincoln was continually pressured by appeals from abolitionists and others in support of emancipation. But he was simultaneously worried about European intervention in the struggle, especially by the British whose strong commercial and social ties made them favor the South. (Even Emerson's friend, Carlyle, for example, was

---

50   James M. McPherson, *Battle Cry of Freedom: The Civil War Era* (New York: Ballantine Books, 1988), 497.

51   He would later repeat this presentation in Washington, D.C. in January.

52   Quoted in Gougeon, "'Fortune of the Republic': Emerson, Lincoln, and Transcendental Warfare," *ESQ: A Journal of the American Renaissance* 45: 3-4 (1999): 289.

bitterly racist, pro-slavery, and sympathetic towards the Confederacy.) Yet the support of British abolitionists and workingmen, as Lincoln was coming to see, might be won with a declaration of emancipation. Such a measure would give the Union cause the higher moral ground in the struggle. Soon after a technical Union victory at Antietam on September 17, 1862, Lincoln advised his Cabinet that when Congress convened in December, he intended to promote gradual and compensated emancipation in the loyal states, along with voluntary colonization. But in those states still in rebellion on January 1, 1863, "thenceforth and forever" all slaves would be declared free.[53]

Lincoln's Preliminary Emancipation Proclamation, announced just five days after Antietam on September 22, brought on a sharp, swift, and negative reaction, proving just how risky it was. Its effects threatened Lincoln's own carefully tended, tenuous coalition of Republicans, War Democrats, and border-state leaders. It also strengthened the peace element in the Democratic Party that was agitating for an end to the war through compromise with the slave power. Finally, it threatened to provoke a mutiny in the army. The situation was dire. As one distinguished scholar puts it, "During the hundred days after he issued the preliminary proclamation, Lincoln's leadership was more seriously threatened than at any other time, and it was not clear that his administration could survive the repeated crises that it faced."[54]

In these grim times, Emerson was one of the most prominent and formidable of Lincoln's supporters. With a distinguished career spanning three decades, he was now a cultural icon, an inescapable part of American public life.[55] For many in the North, he seemed to embody the Union's highest ideals.[56] Emerson had met with Lincoln twice, and with Charles Sumner after speaking on "American Civilization" at the Smithsonian Institution in January 1862. Emerson liked Lincoln immediately, describing the president as "a frank, sincere, well-meaning man."[57] When the war began, Emerson had been disappointed with Lincoln's priorities. He had put the cause of Union before emancipation, and seemed painfully slow

53   Oates, 319.
54   Donald, *Lincoln*, 377.
55   Richardson, 551.
56   Buell, 34.
57   Ralph Rusk, *The Life of Ralph Waldo Emerson* (New York: Columbia University Press, 1949), 414; *JMN* 15: 187.

in acting on this vital issue. However, when Lincoln finally issued his Preliminary Emancipation Declaration, Emerson was quick to applaud it.

Only three weeks after the announcement, Emerson celebrated the event in Boston in his address, "The Emancipation Proclamation." He heralded Lincoln's statement not so much for its actual effect—the vast majority of slaves in the South remained under the control of their rebel masters—but for the principle of freedom that it affirmed. "It is by no means necessary," Emerson asserted, "that this measure should be suddenly marked by any signal results on the negroes or on the rebel masters. The force of the act is that it commits the country to this justice,—that it compels the innumerable officers, civil, military, naval, of the Republic to range themselves on the side of this equity." Through his Proclamation, despite any reluctance he may have felt, Lincoln had contributed significantly to the progress of civilization in America. "Great as the popularity of the President has been," noted Emerson; "we are beginning to think that we have underestimated the capacity and virtue which the Divine Providence has made an instrument of benefit so vast. He has been permitted to do more for America than any other American man."[58] In time, Lincoln himself would come to see the Emancipation Proclamation as the crowning achievement of his administration.[59] The hearts and minds of many Americans, however, remained obdurate. It was to be Emerson's goal to win them over.

Just one month later, in his lecture "Perpetual Forces," Emerson not only endorsed Lincoln's preliminary steps, but also insisted that the principle be followed to its logical fulfillment. With the assured voice of a prophet, he offered a vision of the new American Republic that would emerge from this war. First and foremost, he insisted, "Leave slavery out," and "since nothing satisfies but justice, let us have that, and let us stifle our prejudices against common sense and humanity, and agree that every man shall have what he honestly earns, and, if he is a sane and innocent man, have an equal vote in the state, and a fair chance in society."[60] All of this—emancipation, equal opportunity, and suffrage—Emerson saw as the dictates of the "moral sentiment," an infallible guide to both personal and social life. Others were not so sure.

Lincoln himself had not yet articulated the notion of total emancipation. And Negro suffrage would never receive more than a limited and highly

---

58   *W* 11: 319, 317.
59   Herbert, 377.
60   *LL* 2: 300.

qualified endorsement from him.[61] Most Northerners, including the majority of Emerson's audience, shared these reservations. Following his impassioned address, a Democratic paper in Albany, the *Argus*, described Emerson's lecture as "a re-hash of his Abolition sophistry" and pointed out, "When he argued in favor of forcible emancipation, a few old ladies and gentlemen applauded; but when he insisted that the Negro should have 'an equal chance with the white man,' even they were indignantly silent."[62]

On the day when emancipation officially went into effect, January 1, 1863, Emerson was the first of several celebrities to speak to a huge gathering in Boston's Music Hall.

INTERIOR VIEW OF THE NEW MUSIC HALL, BOSTON.

3.15 Boston Music Hall, 1852.

Before the enthusiastic audience, he intoned the words of a poem he had just finished for the occasion, the stirring "Boston Hymn." He imagines the voice of God proclaiming freedom to all Americans, regardless of race. To

---

61   Oates, 424-25.
62   Quoted in *LL* 2: 288.

all those living in oppression, this Spirit—Emerson's embodiment of Moral Law—declares: "I break your bonds and masterships, / And I unchain the slave: / Free be his heart and hand henceforth / As wind and wandering wave." While ignoring the moral question, many Northern conservatives maintained that Lincoln's measure was unconstitutional and deprived honest citizens of their rightful "property." They insisted that at the very least compensation was due to the hapless slave-owner. Emerson had a different view: "Pay ransom to the owner, / And fill the bag to the brim. / Who is the owner? The slave is owner, / And ever was. Pay him."[63]

One observer that evening described Emerson's poem as "a hymn of Liberty and Justice, wide and strong, and musical," adding that his passionate lines "spell-bound the great assembly."[64] Eventually, the tides of war changed more favorably for the Union. Two great victories came in July 1863 with the costly triumph at Gettysburg and the fall of Vicksburg. Dedicating a Union cemetery at Gettysburg in bleak mid-November 1863, near the fields where so many had fallen only four months before, Lincoln's now-famous address took the nation another major step towards total emancipation. He defined the war as a struggle to establish equality, along with liberty, as the two most essential and defining American values. In effect, he was displacing the Constitution with the Declaration of Independence as the Republic's primary foundational document. He articulated this change succinctly in the twenty-nine-word prologue to his already brief speech: "Four score and seven years ago our fathers brought forth on this continent, a new nation, conceived in Liberty, and dedicated to the proposition that all men are created equal."

As intellectual historian Garry Wills has observed, Lincoln's Gettysburg Address set up a "dialectic of the ideal with the real," where a "nation conceived in liberty by its dedication to the Declaration's critical proposition (human equality) must test that proposition's survivability in the real world of struggle." For him, the president's interplay of ideals with reality registered how deeply he was influenced by "the primary intellectual fashion of the period, Transcendentalism."[65] The crowd departed from Gettysburg that day, according to Wills, "with a new thing in its ideological luggage, that new constitution Lincoln had substituted for the one they

---

63   *CW* 9: 382, 383.
64   Quoted in Gougeon, *Virtue's Hero*, 292.
65   Garry Wills, *Lincoln at Gettysburg: The Words That Remade America* (New York: Simon & Schuster, 1992), 103, 174, 105.

brought there with them . . . Lincoln had revolutionized the Revolution, giving people a new past to live with that would change their future indefinitely."[66] Emerson's direct and indirect influence undoubtedly had helped bring Lincoln to this momentous point.

Not everyone was pleased with the president's dramatic change. As earlier, when slavery was abolished in the District of Columbia, conservatives fretted that Lincoln was trampling on the Constitution, and they feared that a reconstructed America would differ greatly from what they had known. Of course, they were right. An article in the *Chicago Times* shortly after the address "quoted the letter of the Constitution to Lincoln— noting its lack of reference to equality, its tolerance of slavery—and said that Lincoln was betraying the instrument he was on oath to defend, traducing the men who died for the letter of that fundamental law."[67] Emerson, however, was delighted with Lincoln's bold action. He had earlier observed in *Representative Men* (1850), ". . . great action must draw on the spiritual nature. The measure of an action is, the sentiment from which it proceeds."[68] If Lincoln's declaration of equality did not comport with the letter of the Constitution, it was because the Constitution was out of sync with moral law. In a reconstructed America, this deficiency would be corrected. In his journal Emerson noted, "I speak the speech of an idealist. I say let the rule be right. If the theory is right it is not so much matter about the facts . . . The question stands thus, reconstruction is no longer a matter of doubt. All our action now is new & unconstitutional, & necessarily so."[69]

Emerson, Douglass, and Blacks in the Union Army

One of the most important steps in validating the concept of universal equality was to address Americans' pervasive, merely putative belief that Negroes were racially inferior. Many whites also presumed that blacks were docile and would not fight for their freedom. To disprove this notion, abolitionists prodded a reluctant federal government to allow them to take action on a final provision in Lincoln's Emancipation Proclamation allowing blacks to serve in the regular Union army. Emerson, Frederick Douglass, and many others joined forces in promoting enlistment in what

---

66   Wills, *Lincoln*, 38. See also Donald, *Lincoln*, 462.
67   Wills, *Lincoln*, 38.
68   *CW* 4: 154-55.
69   *JMN* 15: 301.

would be the Union's first, regular black regiment, the Massachusetts 54th. Emerson not only donated money to the cause; he also gave enlistment speeches aimed directly at young Negro men. In 1863, one such address elaborates the importance of the self-reliant "rise of the anti-slave," an idea articulated in his first emancipation speech almost twenty years before. "If war means liberty to you," he tells these young men, "you should enlist . . . If you will not fight for your liberty, who will? If you will not . . . the universe of men will say you are not worth fighting for. Go & be slaves forever & you shall have our aid to make you such. You had rather be slaves than freemen."[70]

The recruitment campaign was successful. So many young black men rushed to enlist, including Frederick Douglass's two sons, that a second regiment had to be formed.[71] The Massachusetts 54th would soon prove itself in a heroic though failed assault against the Confederates at Fort Wagner, South Carolina, on July 18, 1863.

3.16 Storming Ft. Wagner, 1863.

---

70   *JMN* 15: 210-11.
71   William S. McFeely, *Frederick Douglass* (New York: W. W. Norton & Co., 1991), 223-24. The second regiment was designated the Massachusetts 55th.

The regiment actually breached the defenses of the fort, but was thrown back, suffering 42% casualties. A short time later, in an address at Waterville College, Emerson observed that "War always exalts an age, speaks to slumbering virtue, makes of quiet, plain men unexpected heroes."[72] All questions about Negro courage were now answered. Emerson would formally memorialize the heroism of the 54th, and their gallant, young leader who was killed in the attack, Colonel Robert Gould Shaw, in one of his best-known poems. "Voluntaries" was published in the *Atlantic Monthly* in October 1863. The poem focused on the war's high stakes, universal human dignity and freedom, and celebrated the youth who died for this cause. Their sacrifice testified to the power of divinity in the heart of man: "So nigh is grandeur to our dust, / So near is God to man, / When Duty whispers low, *Thou Must*, / The youth replies, *I can*."[73]

3.17 Saint-Gauden's Robert Gould Shaw Memorial, 1884-1897, plaster cast of original.

---

72   *LL* 2: 316.
73   *CW* 9: 392.

Following the dramatic victories at Gettysburg and Vicksburg in July, many people hoped for a quick end to the war, but it was not to be. The Union armies soon became bogged down in a seemingly endless war of attrition. As casualties continued to mount, with the death toll reaching hundreds of thousands, many Northerners began to lose heart. A coalition of antiwar Democrats, sometimes called "Peace Democrats" or "Copperheads," began to emerge. They sought a negotiated end to hostilities and a restoration of the Union as it was, with slavery intact. Some war-weary citizens found this appealing. Meanwhile, Lincoln's popularity, always tenuous, began to sink. His policies on emancipation and his decision to allow the recruitment of Negroes offended many. There was also dissent in the Republican Party itself.[74] Emerson recognized how critical the times were. The nation had made great strides under Lincoln in reforming itself into the model democratic Republic that he had envisioned. A unique opportunity was at hand to fulfill the country's destiny. To lose that opportunity now, after so many sacrifices and so much bloodshed, would be a supreme tragedy that Emerson would do his utmost to prevent.

Emerson's "Fortune of the Republic" Speech (1863-1864)

In late November 1863, Emerson received a request to lecture in Brooklyn, New York, with the suggestion that he might speak on the topic of "American Politics."[75] But inevitably, he directed his words toward a much higher purpose. He titled his address, "The Fortune of the Republic." Asking for strong support of both the war and the president, Emerson's oration was a virtual stump speech for Lincoln's re-election. In a span of only two months, he delivered this stirring address no fewer than fourteen times.[76] In Emerson's view, during his nearly four years in office the president had evolved into the premier representative of America's democratic genius who, if re-elected, would lead America to fulfill the Declaration's promise of universal freedom and equality.

---

74 David Herbert Donald observes, "From time to time during the previous year, there had been talk of reelecting Lincoln in 1864, but for the most part it was desultory and not particularly fervent" (*Lincoln*, 474).

75 *L* 5: 340.

76 The speech was delivered between 1 December 1863 and 9 February 1864.

In "Fortune of the Republic," Emerson touched on themes that echoed, if they did not predate, Lincoln's. He specifically appealed to the nation's youth to commit itself to renew the country's founding ideals. "It is the young men of the land, who must save it: it is they to whom this wonderful hour, after so many weary ages, dawns, the Second Declaration of Independence, the proclaiming of liberty, land, justice, and a career for all men; and honest dealings with other nations." For Emerson, the United States was going through "a great revolution." It was "passing out of old reminders of barbarism into pure Christianity and humanity,—into freedom of thought, of religion, of speech, of the press, of trade, of suffrage, or political right." This new America was the ideal Republic promised from the start. Such a great achievement could not be accomplished without great sacrifices, and Emerson urged his audiences, as had Lincoln at Gettysburg, to endure the pain and continue the struggle. "For such a gain," he states, "one generation might well be sacrificed,—perhaps it will be,—that this continent be purged, and a new era of equal rights dawn on the universe. Who would not, if it could be made certain, that the new morning of universal rights should rise on our race, by the perishing of one generation,—who would not consent to die?" Eventually, according to the latest estimates, as many as 750,000 Union and Confederate soldiers would make the ultimate sacrifice, more than the combined fatalities of all the other wars fought by the United States to this day, in the painful struggle that resulted in a re-birth of the nation.[77]

Coincident with Emerson's repeated delivery of this speech, the situation on the battlefield significantly improved. On February 22, 1864, thirteen days after his final delivery of "Fortune of the Republic," the Republican Party re-nominated Abraham Lincoln, and on Election Day, November 8, a large majority voted for Lincoln's second term. Shortly afterward, Emerson, who had always believed that the people in a crisis would make the right choice, wrote to a friend expressing "joy of the Election." "Seldom in history," he observed, "was so much staked on a popular vote.—I suppose never in history."[78]

In Lincoln's re-election, the North expressed its resolve to prosecute the war to a successful conclusion. But he did not live to see it. With final victory in sight, Lincoln's assassination in April 1865 made Andrew Johnson

77   EAW 140, 146-47, 153; Guy Gugliotta, "New Estimate Raises Civil War Death Toll," Science Times Section, New York Times, April 3, 2012, D1.

78   L 5: 387.

president. As the Reconstruction Era began, Johnson's administration would be both difficult and controversial. But liberal historical forces put in play by Lincoln and urged on by Emerson, Charles Sumner, and the Radical Republicans eventually led to the enactment of laws that would change forever the complexion of American democracy. The most important of these are the Thirteenth (1865), Fourteenth (1866) and Fifteenth (1870) Amendments to the Constitution. These amendments destroyed slavery forever, established the principle of equal protection under the law, and guaranteed universal manhood suffrage, regardless of race. Such dramatic changes laid the groundwork for the South's renewal in the Reconstruction Acts of 1867. However, regional racist groups, epitomized by the Ku Klux Klan, virulently resisted these changes throughout the period of Reconstruction and later. Their efforts were countered only by the social revolution of the Civil Rights Movement of the 1960s, quickly followed by a renewed Women's Movement. The voices of blacks and women in the twentieth century once again built upon the ideas that Emerson had championed a hundred years before.

Emerson on Women's Rights

The Women's Movement did not evoke Emerson's passions to the pitch and participation of abolition; nevertheless, he early, even inevitably, gave it his support. His advocacy for women's causes, beginning later than his antislavery efforts, followed a similar trajectory. With both, he began with a troubled concern, moved to a forceful but limited commitment, and ended in robust support of legal guarantees.

In many ways, the feminine element was a key aspect of Emerson's Transcendentalist philosophy, and the primary stimulus in his career as a reformer. In fact, as seen in Chapter 2, like Goethe and other gifted thinkers, he sensed within himself the presence of both genders, even recognizing that in his deepest soul, he harbored "a woman's heart." Not surprisingly, then, he felt that the feminine qualities of "sentiment," as well as "feeling" and "intuition," were central and vulnerable. They provided the connecting link to "that Over-Soul within which every man's particular being is contained and made one with all other; that common heart, . . . to which all right action is submission."[79]

---

79   *CW* 2: 161.

Reflecting certain social assumptions of his day, Emerson believed that women are by nature closer to their affective side, while men incline toward the rational.[80] Male or female, a person's feminine side would principally guide them toward right living. Emerson notes in his address "Woman," first delivered at the Second Annual Women's Rights Convention in 1855, "But the starry crown of woman is in the power of her affection and sentiment, and the infinite enlargements to which they lead."[81] Such "infinite enlargements" are the "divine laws" that guide our lives and absolutely condemn slavery. Slavery, like any injustice, was incompatible with the "moral sentiment."

As noted earlier, since the early 1830s, women had thrown themselves into the antislavery movement, often spearheading the activities of local units such as Concord's Female Anti-Slavery Society, active since 1835. By the late 1840s, successful participation in this liberating cause led them to organize for their own rights, culminating in a landmark convention at Seneca Falls, New York in 1848.[82] After this historic national gathering, they formed activist groups throughout the nation. As the virtual center of the abolitionist movement, Massachusetts had more than its share. In August 1850, Paulina Wright Davis sent Emerson a copy of a call for a women's rights convention to be held in Worcester, Massachusetts, and attached to it a handwritten note requesting "the sanction of your name and your personal attendance."[83] Davis no doubt sought out Emerson because of his increasingly active role in the antislavery movement and hoped for a similarly sympathetic response to the women's rights cause.

Emerson was well aware of women's special contributions to the antislavery movement, admiring, as we have seen, both the Quaker abolitionist Lucretia Mott and the British social reformer and antislavery advocate Harriet Martineau. His wife Lidian, mother Ruth, and aunt Mary Moody Emerson were all early activists in Concord's Female Anti-Slavery Society.[84] These relatives, Thoreau's mother and sisters (also members of

---

80   For a comprehensive discussion of the importance of the affective, feminine element in Emerson's thought and life, see Len Gougeon, *Emerson & Eros: The Making of a Cultural Hero* (Albany, NY: State University of New York Press, 2007).

81   *LL* 2: 23.

82   For details on this important gathering, see *The Birth of American Feminism: The Seneca Falls Women's Convention*, eds. Virginia Bernhard and Elizabeth Fox-Genevese (St. James, NY: Brandywine Press, 1995).

83   Quoted in Gougeon, "Emerson and the Woman Question: The Evolution of His Thought," *The New England Quarterly* 71 (Dec. 1998), 573.

84   Phyllis Cole, "Pain and Protest in the Emerson Family," in *The Emerson Dilemma: Essays*

the society) and others, had urged Emerson to give his "Emancipation in the British West Indies Address" in August 1844. Emerson's response to Davis's request at this time shows a commitment to women's rights but one tempered by concerns about both women and society. His letter states in part:

> The fact of the political & civil wrongs of woman I deny not. If women feel wronged, then they are wronged. But the mode of obtaining a redress, namely, a public convention called by women is not very agreeable to me, and the things to be agitated for do not seem to me the best. Perhaps I am superstitious & traditional, but whilst I should vote for every franchise for women, —vote that they should hold property, and vote, yes & be eligible to all offices as men—whilst I should vote thus, if women asked, or if men denied . . . these things, I should not wish women to wish political functions, nor, if granted assume them. I imagine that a woman whom all men would feel to be the best, would decline such privileges if offered, & feel them to be obstacles to her legitimate influence.[85]

Emerson's reservations here have nothing to do with the right of women to vote, hold property or public office, or generally enjoy the full benefits of citizenship. Rather, he fears that a public role might debase, or even erase, femininity's high virtues.

As one biographer notes, Emerson "hoped that women would not after all wish an equal share with men in public affairs," for "his imagination balked when he pictured women with masculine aggressiveness wrangling in public." Another suggests that in this matter Emerson's views were very similar to Margaret Fuller's. He notes that Fuller had written in "The Great Lawsuit," the forerunner of *Woman in the Nineteenth Century* (1845), "Were they [women] free, were they wise fully to develop the strength and beauty of woman, they would never wish to be men, or man-like."[86] Despite these concerns, however, Emerson did support the convention's principles, telling Davis, "At all events, . . . you are at liberty if you wish it to use my name as one of the inviters of the convention."[87]

The following year, 1851, when Lucy Stone asked him to participate in another women's convention, Emerson again declined, saying he was at work on a biography of Margaret Fuller, who had tragically died in May

---

    on Emerson and Social Reform, ed. T. Gregory Garvey (Athens, GA: University of Georgia
    Press, 2001), 80.
85   *L* 4: 229-30.
86   Rusk, *Life of Emerson,* 370; Richardson, 533.
87   *L* 4: 230.

1850. In his journal he continued to express support for the principles of the women's movement: "I think that, as long as they have not equal rights of property & right of voting, they are not on a right footing." He also noted, "For the rest, I do not think a woman's convention, called in the spirit of this at Worcester, can much avail. It is an attempt to manufacture public opinion, & of course repels all persons who love the simple & direct method."[88]

Yet as Emerson's antislavery advocacy strengthened in the 1850s, women's rights advocates naturally continued to appeal to him on behalf of their cause. In June 1855, Paulina Davis again invited Emerson to participate in the Second Annual New England Women's Rights Convention to be held in late September, stating that its planners unanimously looked to Emerson as a natural ally in their fight. "From your well known antecedents we have taken it for granted that your heart is with us, and that you have a message which will aid, cheer, and strengthen us in progress toward perfect freedom and the highest right."[89] This time Emerson accepted, encouraged no doubt by the convention's roster of major speakers: Wendell Phillips, Thomas Wentworth Higginson, Lucy Stone, Caroline Dall, Antoinette L. Brown, and Susan B. Anthony. Phillips and Higginson had become prominent figures in the antislavery movement, and Dall was a protégée of Margaret Fuller's.

For feminist scholars, Emerson's "Woman" address has always been somewhat problematic. One points out that Emerson "voiced no pain and no protest."[90] And at least one activist of the time, Elizabeth Oakes Smith, negatively compared Emerson's treatment of the topic with that of more outspoken advocates. "Emerson," she said, "was one that did not seek contest, did not snuff the battle with the heat of the war-horse, like Wendell Phillips."[91] Another feminist critic, however, notes that "In the second half of the essay, if contemporary readers can bear through, they will find Emerson stating an agenda of women's rights radical even for the late nineteenth century, much less for its midpoint."[92] A brief overview of the speech suggests that this interpretation is correct.

At the outset, Emerson reiterates his belief in the importance of female "sentiment." "Plato said, 'Women are the same as men in faculty, only less

---

88   *JMN* 11: 444.
89   Quoted in Gougeon, "Woman," 579.
90   Cole, "Pain and Protest," 84.
91   Ibid.
92   Armida Gilbert, "'Pierced by the Thorns of Reform': Emerson on Womanhood," in *The Emerson Dilemma*, 98.

in degree.' But the general voice of mankind has agreed that they have their own strength; that women are strong by sentiment; that the same mental height which their husbands attain by toil, they attain by sympathy with their husbands. Man is the will, and Woman the sentiment."[93] Once again, Emerson stresses the absolutely essential power of sentiment to express humanity's intuitive strength and divinity. With this power, women fundamentally help shape society. Simply put, he believes that "Woman is the power of civilization."[94] In more public roles, Emerson fears, women might lose this sensitivity.

However, Emerson acknowledges the generating role played by women's participation in the antislavery movement, a sympathetic involvement leading naturally to demands for a greater share of rights for themselves. He notes, "One truth leads in another by the hand; one right is an accession of strength to take more. And the times are marked by the new attitude of woman urging, by argument and by association, her rights of all kinds, in short, to one half of the world: the right to education; to avenues of employment; to equal rights of property; to equal rights in marriage; to the exercise of the professions; to suffrage."[95] On all of these controversial issues, Emerson is in complete agreement with the radicals. Women, he insists, "have an unquestionable right to their own property. And, if a woman demands votes, offices, and political equality with men . . . it must not be refused."

While acknowledging the justice of their cause, Emerson continues to hesitate over endorsing the public exercise of these rights by women. His fear is both for them and for society. In support of his position, he references the expressed desires of the "best women," presumably the most sensitive and moral. "They," he argues, "do not wish these things. These are asked for by people who intellectually seek them, but who have not the support or sympathy of the truest women: and that, if the laws and customs were modified in the manner proposed, it would embarrass and pain gentle and lovely persons, with duties which they would find irksome and distasteful."

Emerson also maintains that most women now do not really "wish this equal share in public affairs. But it is they, and not we, that are to determine it. Let the laws be purged of every barbarous remainder, every barbarous impediment to women. Let the public donations for education

---

93   *LL* 2: 19.
94   *LL* 2: 18.
95   *LL* 2: 25.

be equally shared by them. Let them enter a school, as freely as a church. Let them have, and hold, and give their property, as men do theirs. And, in a few years, it will easily appear whether they wish a voice in making the laws that are to govern them."[96] Ultimately, Emerson is advocating a form of gradualism in the growth of women's rights. First there must be equal education and property rights, and then equal voting rights, if women so wish. Overall, however, Emerson clearly defers to women themselves: *they* alone must dictate the process and final outcome.

Contemporary reactions to Emerson's speech, like critical reactions today, were mixed. Paulina Davis, however, was delighted. Writing after the address, she thanked him "for the good service done to our Cause."[97] Feminist Caroline Dall concurred: "It did not trouble me that some of the papers thought it doubtful, whether you were for us or against us. That was only because they were too heavy to breathe that upper air. Neither was I inclined to quarrel with your estimate of woman *per se*, though it differs somewhat from my own. In the lowest sense—it has been true of the best women of the past. In one far higher, it may be true of the best that are to come. That they are fully capable of becoming 'innocent citizens' was all we needed you should admit."[98]

On December 2, 1860, Emerson repeated his "Woman" address before the Parker Fraternity, an informal Boston social club for young men, but otherwise offered no further formal public statement on the woman question for fourteen years. However, he maintained an interest in the movement, and his support would become stronger as women continued to express what they wanted. After Caroline Dall's address on women's rights to a joint committee of the Massachusetts legislature on February 12, 1858, Emerson sent her his compliments.[99]

Emerson had never questioned the justice of rights for women, but had worried that public life might have a negative effect on women. Their actions as well as their words eventually changed his mind. Women's contributions to the campaign against slavery and their unselfish labor throughout the Civil War impressed him. He also now saw that such activism only increased women's sympathetic capacities. Emerson was

---

96   *LL* 2: 26, 28.
97   Quoted in Gougeon, "Woman," 584.
98   Quoted in Helen Deese, "'A Liberal Education': Caroline Healey Dall and Emerson," in *Emersonian Circles: Essays in Honor of Joel Myerson*, eds. Wesley T. Mott and Robert E. Burkholder (Rochester, NY: University of Rochester Press, 1997), 248.
99   Deese, "A Liberal Education," 249.

well aware of the invaluable service rendered by women through the Sanitary Commission, as nurses, administrators, and inspectors; through the Freedman's Bureau, as teachers of emancipated slaves; and through various home-front organizations that provided the Union army with supplies ranging from clothing to bandages. Not surprisingly, one of the most active of such sewing groups was Concord's, in which all the Emerson women took part. In his 1863 address, "Fortune of the Republic," Emerson observed that ". . . the women have shown a tender patriotism, and an inexhaustible charity."[100] Unquestionably, the women in his own household helped to shape Emerson's sense of the contemporary female's will to participate in the larger society. His wife Lidian was an eager advocate of women's rights, and his daughter Edith was in favor of the movement, too. Only Ellen, possibly the voice of the "best women" that had earlier fed his ear, was opposed.[101]

Post-Civil War, the women's suffrage movement gained momentum. With slavery now abolished, reformers focused attention on a campaign to liberate American women. The similarities between the two causes seemed obvious to many. Harriet Beecher Stowe's article in *Hearth and Home* on "The Woman Question" noted, "The position of a married woman, under English common law, is, in 'many respects, precisely similar to that of the Negro slave.'"[102] Women's rights activists resumed their appeal for Emerson's support. He now responded without reservation. His 1867 Phi Beta Kappa lecture at Harvard, "Progress of Culture," praised the women's movement as a sign of America's continuing advancement. "The new claim of woman to a political status," he said, "is itself an honorable testimony to the civilization which has given her a civil status new in history." The progressive development of women's rights, envisioned in his 1855 address, had matured. "Now that by the increased humanity of law she controls her property, she inevitably takes the next step to her share in power."[103]

In a speech before the New England Woman's Suffrage Association in Boston in May 1869, Emerson offered no qualifications on women's rights. "The claim now pressed by woman," he declares, "is a claim for nothing less than all, than her share in all. She asks for her property; she asks for her

---

100 *EAW* 152.

101 Richardson, 534.

102 Quoted by Joan D. Hedrick, in *Harriet Beecher Stowe: A Life* (New York: Oxford University Press, 1994), 360.

103 *W* 8: 208.

rights, for her vote; she asks for her share in education, for her share in all the institutions of society, for her half of the whole world; and to this she is entitled."[104] At the same meeting, the Association named Emerson their vice-president. For the rest of his life, Emerson remained committed to the women's cause. One scholar notes that in the 1860s and 1870s, he became "an icon of the suffragist leaders."[105] In a memorial address following his death in 1882, Julia Ward Howe remembered his steadfast support over the years. She concluded, "He was for us, knowing well enough our limitations and short-comings, and his golden words have done much both to fit us for the larger freedom, and to know that it belongs to us."[106]

Emerson and Racism

Despite Emerson's long career as an outspoken advocate for universal human rights, some critics have accused him of racism. One of the earliest works to make this claim is Philip Nicoloff's *Emerson on Race and History* (1961). This study is based almost exclusively on the author's reading of Emerson's *English Traits* (1856). In the nineteenth century the term "race" was used to describe what were considered to be the defining characteristics of various groups of people. The distinctions were not limited to color. Thus, even among Caucasians, various "races" were identified, such as Saxon, Celt, Norman, etc. Today, we would consider such distinctions as cultural or ethnic, but in Emerson's time they were seen as genetic and deterministic. Thus, Robert Chambers in *Vestiges of Creation* (1844), a work that Emerson knew well, holds that Caucasians had reached a higher level of evolution than non-Caucasians, whose development was "arrested" at an earlier evolutionary stage. Other scientists, such as Robert Knox in *Races of Men* (1850), insist that "human character, individual and national, is traceable solely to the nature of that race to which the individual or nation belongs." For Knox, "race is everything."[107] Some of Emerson's statements in *English Traits* appear to reflect this view. In that work, he comments on the progenitors of the English "race," the Celts and the Saxons by asking:

> It is race, is it not? that puts the hundred millions of India under the dominion of a remote island in the north of Europe: Race avails much, if that be true,

104 This speech was later reported in detail in the *Boston Post*, 27 May 1869.
105 Gilbert, 103.
106 From the *Women's Journal* (6 May 1882), quoted in Gougeon, "Woman," 592.
107 Robert Knox, *Races of Men: A Fragment* (Philadelphia, PA: Lea & Blanchard, 1850), 7.

which is alleged, that all Celts are Catholics, and all Saxons are Protestants; that Celts love unity of power, and Saxons the representative principle. Race is a controlling influence in the Jew, who, for two millenniums, under every climate, has preserved the same character and employments. Race in the negro is of appalling importance.[108]

Statements such as this, coupled with an examination of the various racial theories of the time, many of which Emerson examines in his journals, leads Nicoloff to conclude that Emerson believed that race was a determining factor in human life. He suggests that Emerson believed that "races which lacked primitive energies, whose blood was pale and diluted, or whose capacity for 'refinement' was otherwise 'arrested,' did not achieve a true national status, and were exterminated rather than civilized." And he adds, "Such apparently would be the fate of the Negro." While this conclusion may appear stark, Nicoloff insists that when "his intellectual environment [is] considered, Emerson never became more that a relatively mild 'racist.'"[109] Later critics have been much more severe. Louis Simpson, for example, asserts that Emerson "was fundamentally a white supremacist and never free from a degree of Negrophobia."[110] Even harsher is Nell Irvin Painter who, in her recent *The History of White People* (2010), castigates Emerson as "the philosopher king of white race theory."[111]

All of this appears rather anomalous, indeed, in light of the record of Emerson's crusade against slavery, and the racism that supported it, that is outlined in this chapter. That record, however, did not come to light until the 1990s and, hence, was not available to either Nicoloff or Simpson. Painter's work, however, was published in 2010, after a more complete and balanced record of Emerson's position on race had become well established. One is left to conclude that she simply chose to ignore it. The result is a study that, as far as her two chapters on Emerson are concerned at least, is riddled with significant factual errors and striking omissions. For example, Painter contends that "Emerson had little to say about black people" despite his numerous antislavery addresses in which he celebrated, defended, and encouraged them. She also implies that Emerson's racial views were similar to those of his racist friend Thomas Carlyle, but the private and public record

108 *CW* 4: 26.
109 Phillip Nicoloff, *Emerson on Race and History: An Examination of English Traits* (New York: Columbia University Press, 1961), 127, 128, 124.
110 Lewis P Simpson, *Mind and the American Civil War: A Meditation on Lost Causes* (Baton Rouge, LA: Louisiana State University Press, 1989), 53.
111 Nell Irvin Painter, *The History of White People* (New York: W.W. Norton & Co., 2010), 151.

shows them to be diametrically opposed. She also claims that Emerson never advocated suffrage "for either white women or black people of any sex," while the public record, as indicated above, clearly shows that he did both.[112]

Better-informed scholars who have written on Emerson and race have concluded that he was actually staunchly opposed to the racist theories of his day, on both moral and scientific grounds. The notion of a fixed and determinate reality that denied the possibilities of human development and growth ran against his most fundamental beliefs. As indicated in his early essay "Circles" (1841), Emerson always insisted, "There are no fixtures in nature. The universe is fluid and volatile." Recognizing this, his fundamental goal was always to challenge conventional beliefs that sought to stifle this progressive flow. His ultimate desire was to "unsettle all things."[113] The universe, he believed, is moral at its core. Thus, any theory of law or science that attempts to visit upon any group of people a damning determinism is clearly out of sync with that moral law. Like slavery itself, theories of deterministic racial inferiority are simply inconsistent "with the principles on which the world is built."[114] Those principles constitute a divine and "Higher Law," hence his declaration, noted earlier, that the deterministic racism expressed in the word "*Niggers*" is a "damnable atheism." Later, he condemned the Supreme Court's infamous Dred Scott decision, which held that "The black man has no rights which the white man is required to respect," as a "blasphemy [that] . . . does not honor the moral perceptions of the people."[115]

On the scientific side, his journals show that Emerson was very much aware of the pernicious race theories of his day. His weighing of them there has led some critics to accuse him of racism. However, as more discerning critics have shown, though he studied these theories, ultimately he rejected them.[116] He came to see the classifications of races as "mutable" rather than fixed. All "races," he believed, were actually changing and evolving in a

---

112 Ibid., 185, 154-64, 185.
113 *CW* 2: 179, 188.
114 *EAW* 86-87.
115 *LL* 2: 140.
116 In 1853, for example, he records the following from another author: "The brute instinct rallies & centers in the black man. He is created on a lower plane than the white, & eats & kidnaps & tortures, if he can. The Negro is imitative, secondary, in short, reactionary merely in his successes, & there is no origination with him in mental & moral sphere" (*JMN* 13: 198). For a detailed and informed discussion of these racial theories and Emerson's rejection of them, see Laura Dassow Walls, *Emerson's Life in Science: The Culture of Truth* (Ithaca: Cornell University Press, 2003), 166-87.

process of amelioration that depended on what one scholar calls "racial assimilation and amalgamation."[117] Thus, he observed as early as 1846 that "Nature loves to cross her stocks. A pure blood, Bramin on Bramin, marrying in & in, soon becomes puny & wears out. Some strong Cain son, some black blood must renew & refresh the paler veins of Seth."[118] This belief, as David Robinson has pointed out, reinforced Emerson's commitment to antislavery, a commitment that was "grounded in a larger conception of the evolution of human society through an expanding egalitarianism and inclusiveness."[119] This commitment persisted throughout his long career. In the post-Civil War period, Emerson celebrated the "fusion of races and religions" in America in his 1867 "Progress of Culture" address. It was here, as noted above, that he also applauded "the new claim of woman to a political *status*."[120] Clearly, for Emerson, equality was not bounded by race or gender.

Emerson's attitude on race is probably best summed up in his 1878 address re-visiting "The Fortune of the Republic." Here, once again, Emerson insisted that the principle of equality, above all others, should be the defining characteristic of American society. In this presentation, which was one of his last public lectures, he summarized his vision of the new America that he hoped would arise from the ashes of the Civil War. "The genius of the country has marked out our true policy," he notes, "opportunity. Opportunity of civil rights, of education, of personal power, and not less of wealth; doors wide open. If I could have it, —free trade with all the world without toll or custom-houses, invitation as we now make every nation, to every race and skin, white men, red men, yellow men, black men; hospitality of fair field and equal laws to all."[121]

The Centrality of Reform to Emerson's Message Then and Now

Throughout his long career as a visionary reformer, Emerson identified with the lowly, the oppressed, and the despised. Such empathy lay in his

---

117 Ian Finseth, "Evolution, Cosmopolitanism, and Emerson's Antislavery Politics." *American Literature* 77: 4 (2005), 731.
118 *JMN* 9: 365.
119 David M. Robinson, "'For Largest Liberty:' Emerson, Natural Religion, and the Antislavery Crisis," *Religion & Literature* 41: 1 (March 2009), 5.
120 *CW* 8: 108.
121 *W* 11: 541.

loyalty to the "moral sentiment," and no doubt to his childhood memories of extreme poverty and its painful social consequences. He firmly believed that "only that state can live, in which injury to the least member is recognized as damage to the whole."[122] For a lifetime, he insisted on the divine oneness of humanity and the infinitude of the private man. This vision included everyone, an unchanging perspective even as his strategy for reform shifted. Emerson's early role of moral advisor, coaxing his audiences to heed their inner moral voice and reform first themselves, then society, did not meet the country's needs, North or South, as the century reached a mid-point. From 1850 until the early post-Civil War period, Emerson entered the political fray to revolutionize America.

Even before the 1850s, his tactics were changing. From personal transcendent ecstasy, his focus widened and spoke to tangible, pressing problems. With his eyes still on the horizon and focusing on large human concerns, his lectures and essays yet revealed the influence of the mounting crises immediately facing him. In contrast to his earlier, more purely philosophical lectures and essays, Emerson's political speeches against slavery and for women's rights directly confronted the issue of racial and gender equality. In the process, Emerson transformed himself from a local ethical advocate and preacher to a national prophet. He became the heroic man of action he himself had called for in his 1837 "American Scholar" address. In a period of increasing turbulence, violence, and conflict, the nation needed a calm and assured voice to guide it through its greatest crisis since the Revolution. Emerson provided that voice. His ideal republic drew from the Declaration of Independence rather than the Constitution for its principles of universal freedom, equality, and justice.

Emerson's vision proved to be revolutionary both for him and for the country. As a union of states and as a culture, the America that emerged from the Civil War was radically different from what it had been only a few years before. In keeping with Emerson's belief that "one truth leads in another by the hand; one right is an accession of strength to take more," the freedoms that were introduced then led to yet other social revolutions in the twentieth century, finally bringing African Americans the right to be treated like all other citizens and also enfranchising women. Of course, the struggle still continues. As Emerson well knew, the perfect society is always just beyond the horizon.

---

122 Ibid., 11: 352.

EMERSON'S EVOLVING EMPHASES

4.1 Emerson at 64, 1867.

4. Actively Entering Old Age, 1865-1882

Jean McClure Mudge

Within, I do not find wrinkles
& used heart, but unspent youth.

Emerson, *Journal*, June 1864

Emerson's capacities after the Civil War, often seen as diminishing, in fact gained a surprising new life.

He carried on with multiple tasks at an amazing level, considering his gradual loss of memory, possible mini-strokes, and even Alzheimer-like symptoms. Until his very last years, he maintained his ability to reason. This he put to good work, vigorously bringing his pre-war thinking to bear upon his post-war purpose and activities. His thought-in-action illustrates how fully he continued to make Transcendentalism a social tool of great practical worth in his seventeen remaining years after Appomattox.

In this period, too, he evidently reached an almost complete resolution of the lifetime tension between principle and prejudice he had felt concerning blacks and women. From nature's given moral law, he sincerely believed that both groups were due freedom and just treatment. But as a privileged white male, he had long carried on an inner debate about the given mental capacity of all but exceptional blacks and about the natural social and political place of women. Pro and con private conversations could mire him in hesitant ambivalence. Even as he spoke publicly and passionately for emancipating blacks and for new privileges for women,

http://dx.doi.org/10.11647/OBP.0065.06

his private biases about both groups persisted. And though he knew each party needed outside help, he was hoping they themselves would exhibit the evident truths he sought and thus persuade him en masse of both their capabilities and desires. In fact, as both groups largely adopted his ideas about self-reliance, this eventually happened. Until such time as that liberation occurred, however, his self-questioning on these issues could not stop. Some might find this incessant debate a mark of his integrity.

Emerson was nearly sixty-two when the Civil War ended and arguably at the pinnacle of his career. Never a man of rest or resignation, he continued to extend his understanding of oppression and freedom beyond his own class and gender. In May 1865, he made a list of projects Americans should be doing: ". . . break down prisons, capital punishment, slavery, tariff, disfranchisement, caste . . . abolish laws against atheism . . . [and] be just to women, in property, in votes, in personal rights."[1] With considerable remaining vitality, Emerson followed his own counsel, helping set a course for the continuing civil rights and feminist movements still with us today.

Continuing an Energetic Agenda

A sense of life's swiftness and unpredictable end had long been a hallmark of Emerson's daily consciousness, only heightened in his sixties and seventies. At twenty-three, recuperating from tuberculosis in St. Augustine, Florida, he had mused about the best use of his last days, even then accepting death's imminent reality as part of life's natural evolution. Forty years later, in 1866, Emerson read his poem "Terminus" to Edward, who later remembered that his father, "so healthy, so full of life and young in spirit," had startled him with "his deliberate acknowledgment of failing forces and his trusting and serene acquiescence." Edward added, "I think he smiled as he read."[2] Emerson had cultivated that serenity for decades. Though he did not publish "Terminus" until 1867, he had begun drafting it in his forties.[3] Before then, he had survived the deaths of numerous close

---

1   *The Journals and Miscellaneous Notebooks of Ralph Waldo Emerson*, 16 vols., eds. William H. Gilman, et al. (Cambridge, Mass.: Harvard University Press, 1960-1982) 15: 469. Hereafter *JMN*.

2   Edward Emerson, *Emerson in Concord: A Memoir* (Boston, Mass.: Houghton Mifflin, 1889), 183.

3   Albert J. von Frank, *An Emerson Chronology* (New York: G. K. Hall, 1994), 426; Robert D.

family members: his father, two brothers, his first wife, and his firstborn child. Keeping his own terminus in sight had always helped Emerson direct his aims and energy.

Such an attitude was invaluable as aging brought physical and mental challenges. In addition to relatively minor hearing and dental problems,[4] he began to suffer in the late 1860s from obsessive behavioral symptoms similar to early Alzheimer's disease as well as progressive aphasia and memory loss. These suddenly worsened after a fire nearly destroyed his home in July 1872. Shortly afterward, Ellen vividly captured his change, writing to Edith, "Poor man how he struggles for words! The simplest escape him."[5] The fire, according to Ronald Bosco, "while not fatal to Emerson, was effectively so."[6] Afterward, his speech seemed more limited, his memory issues more pronounced. Possibly he had suffered a series of strokes. Whatever his medical condition, Emerson's expression was more affected than his comprehension, and with Ellen's assistance, he was able to continue reading his lectures until the year before he died. In 1869, he complained in his journal that "Memory . . . volunteers or refuses its informations at *its* will, not at mine," though a few months later he noted some "compensation" for its failures in "increased power & means of generalization."[7]

In the mid-1860s, Emerson plunged himself into a heavy schedule of effective participation in the major matters of his day, continuing to write, lecture and speak out for reform. He was riding on the sense of high energy he had felt in June 1864, "Within, I do not find wrinkles & used heart, but unspent youth."[8] That wellspring propelled him through his last years of new writing and publications, busy lecture schedules, and teaching at Harvard as well as travel to California, Europe, and Egypt. He steadily published new articles, poems, and four books: *May-Day and Other Pieces* (1867), *Society and Solitude* (1870), a poetry collection with Edith (*Parnassus*, 1874), and, with Ellen and his close friend James Elliot Cabot as editors, *Letters and Social Aims* (1876).

Richardson Jr., *Emerson: The Mind on Fire* (Berkeley, CA: University of California Press, 1995), 554.

4   Von Frank, *Chronology*, 481, 486.

5   Ellen Emerson, *The Letters of Ellen Tucker Emerson*, 2 vols., ed. Edith E. W. Gregg (Kent, OH: Kent State University Press, 1982), 1: 691.

6   *The Collected Works of Ralph Waldo Emerson*, 10 vols., eds. Robert E. Spiller, et al. (Cambridge, Mass.: Harvard University Press, 1971-2013) 8: clx, xl. Hereafter *CW*. See also A. B. Paulson's "Emerson and Aphasia," *Language and Style: An International Journal*, 1: 1 (Winter 1968): 155-71.

7   *JMN* 16: 145, 172.

8   Ibid., 15: 416.

In fact, Emerson's lecturing career reached an apex only after the war, a record made possible in part by his habit always reading his lectures, and also because he either repeated his favorites or the most popular ones. In 1865, he spoke seventy-seven times as far west as Milwaukee, a remarkable effort especially in the winter months. Two years later, he excelled that record by three lectures, this time reaching Kansas.

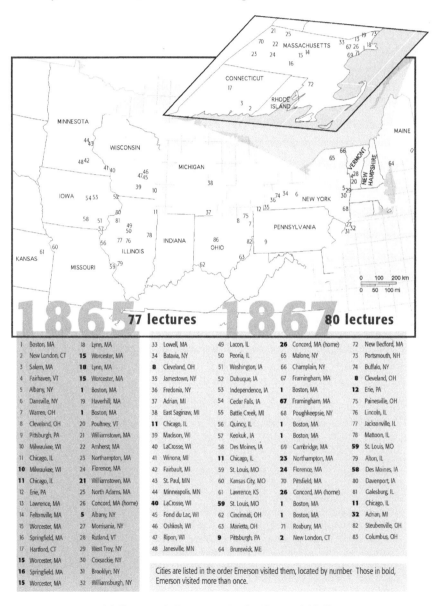

1	Boston, MA	18	Lynn, MA	33	Lowell, MA	49	Lacon, IL	26	Concord, MA (home)	72	New Bedford, MA
2	New London, CT	**15**	Worcester, MA	34	Batavia, NY	50	Peoria, IL	65	Malone, NY	73	Portsmouth, NH
3	Salem, MA	**18**	Lynn, MA	**8**	Cleveland, OH	51	Washington, IA	66	Champlain, NY	74	Buffalo, NY
4	Fairhaven, VT	**15**	Worcester, MA	35	Jamestown, NY	52	Dubuque, IA	67	Framingham, MA	**8**	Cleveland, OH
5	Albany, NY	**1**	Boston, MA	36	Fredonia, NY	53	Independence, IA	**1**	Boston, MA	12	Erie, PA
6	Dansville, NY	19	Haverhill, MA	37	Adrian, MI	54	Cedar Falls, IA	**67**	Framingham, MA	75	Painesville, OH
7	Warren, OH	**1**	Boston, MA	38	East Saginaw, MI	55	Battle Creek, MI	68	Poughkeepsie, NY	76	Lincoln, IL
8	Cleveland, OH	20	Poultney, VT	**11**	Chicago, IL	56	Quincy, IL	**1**	Boston, MA	77	Jacksonville, IL
9	Pittsburgh, PA	21	Williamstown, MA	39	Madison, WI	57	Keokuk, IA	**1**	Boston, MA	78	Mattoon, IL
10	Milwaukee, WI	22	Amherst, MA	40	LaCrosse, WI	58	Des Moines, IA	69	Cambridge, MA	**59**	St. Louis, MO
11	Chicago, IL	23	Northampton, MA	41	Winona, MI	**11**	Chicago, IL	**23**	Northampton, MA	79	Alton, IL
10	Milwaukee, WI	24	Florence, MA	42	Fairbault, MI	59	St. Louis, MO	**24**	Florence, MA	**58**	Des Moines, IA
11	Chicago, IL	**21**	Williamstown, MA	43	St. Paul, MN	60	Kansas City, MO	70	Pittsfield, MA	80	Davenport, IA
12	Erie, PA	25	North Adams, MA	44	Minneapolis, MN	61	Lawrence, KS	**26**	Concord, MA (home)	81	Galesburg, IL
13	Lawrence, MA	26	Concord, MA (home)	**40**	LaCrosse, WI	**59**	St. Louis, MO	**1**	Boston, MA	**11**	Chicago, IL
14	Feltonville, MA	**5**	Albany, NY	45	Fond du Lac, WI	62	Cincinnati, OH	**1**	Boston, MA	**32**	Adrian, MI
15	Worcester, MA	27	Morrisania, NY	46	Oshkosh, WI	63	Marietta, OH	71	Roxbury, MA	82	Steubenville, OH
16	Springfield, MA	28	Rutland, VT	47	Ripon, WI	**9**	Pittsburgh, PA	**2**	New London, CT	83	Columbus, OH
17	Hartford, CT	29	West Troy, NY	48	Janesville, MN	64	Brunswick, ME				
15	Worcester, MA	30	Coxsackie, NY								
16	Springfield, MA	31	Brooklyn, NY								
15	Worcester, MA	32	Williamsburgh, NY								

Cities are listed in the order Emerson visited them, located by number. Those in bold, Emerson visited more than once.

4.2 Emerson's Lecturing Peak, 1865 and 1867.

These strenuous western tours had to be suspended in 1868, but that same year he lectured extensively throughout New York and New England. And in November and December 1871, refreshed by his trip to California that spring, he pressed himself to travel west again to lecture in Illinois and Iowa.[9] From the next year onward, however, after embarrassing Ellen by twice reading the same page during a lecture, Emerson increasingly relied on her help when he spoke.

4.3 Ellen Tucker Emerson at 21, 1860.

In 1876, for his first and only foray into the South, the two travelled to Thomas Jefferson's University of Virginia. Abolitionism had hardly won him many Southern supporters, so his reception was unsurprisingly mixed, when not decidedly negative. Still, despite his weak voice and a noisy

---

9   Von Frank, *Chronology*, 401-13, 427-39, 478.

inattentive audience, some listeners took his words as "a sign of re-union," Ellen reported to Lidian, adding—no doubt to hearten her mother—that one had avowed, "It was fit that Virginia should hear the Sage of the North." As late as 1879, he delivered selections from his essay "Memory" when his own had greatly diminished. And a year before he died, in February 1881, Emerson was able to read remarks about his friend Carlyle to the Massachusetts Historical Society.[10]

Besides lecturing to the very end, Emerson took on a brand-new occupation as a Harvard academic soon after the war. Though the college had shunned him for nearly thirty years, it could no longer ignore his stature in America and abroad. In 1866, it awarded him an honorary Doctor of Laws degree and the next year elected him to the Board of Overseers.

4.4 Emerson at 65-66, c. 1868-1869, with grandson, Ralph Waldo Forbes,
and the boy's paternal grandfather, John Forbes.

---

10 *Letters of ETE* 1: 658; 2: 212. See also, John McAleer's "The Virginia Immolation," *Ralph Waldo Emerson: Days of Encounter* (Boston, Mass.: Little, Brown & Co., 1984), 633-39; von Frank, *Chronology*, 524, 530.

4.5 Emerson at about 73, c. 1876 with son Edward and Edward's son.

He also served on several committees, examined students in Greek, and, in 1870 and 1871, prepared and delivered a new lecture series for a philosophy course entitled "Natural History of Intellect," a subject that had long interested him. By this time, his philosophical odyssey toward emphasizing the complete unity of matter and mind—the basis of his pragmatic Transcendentalism—was clear in a statement from his second lecture, "The Transcendency of Physics": "I think no metaphysical fact of any value which does not rest on a physical fact, and no physical fact important except as resting on metaphysical truth."[11]

From Harvard's prestigious platform, Emerson also directed continuing attention to the war's significance. Even before becoming officially linked to the faculty, he had given an address at the college's Commemoration Day in 1865, stressing that the conflict's moral meaning "gave back integrity to this erring and immoral nation."[12] One of his postwar priorities was to

11   Richardson, 536.
12   *The Complete Works of Ralph Waldo Emerson,* 12 vols., ed. Edward Waldo Emerson (Boston, Mass.: Houghton Mifflin, 1903-1904), 11: 320. Hereafter *W*.

memorialize that lesson on campus. For nine years he raised funds, helped plan the construction of Memorial Hall, and attended its dedication in June 1874. That same year, as proof that his reputation as an educator was now widely established in the English-speaking world, the University of Glasgow invited him to be a candidate for its rectorship.[13]

To be sure, teaching combined with aphasia took its toll. By early 1871, Emerson's Harvard course had exhausted him, and he accepted the invitation of John Forbes (daughter Edith's father-in-law) to travel to California on the new transcontinental railroad. On arrival, he was overwhelmed by the climate and landscape. He wrote to Lidian, ". . . if we were all young, —as some of us are not,—we might each of us claim his quarter-section of the Government, & plant grapes & oranges, & never come back to your east winds & cold summers."[14] San Francisco's spectacular bay even inspired him to write exuberant, Whitman-like lines: "Golden Gate: named of old from its flowers./ Asia at your doors & S. America./ Inflamed expectation haunting men."[15] He traveled from the coast to Yosemite, where he rode and hiked with one of the west's most promising young naturalists and writers, John Muir.

4.6 Redwood "Samoset," Mariposa Grove, Yosemite, 1871 or after, John Muir drawing.

---

13   *The Letters of Ralph Waldo Emerson*, 10 vols., eds. Ralph Rusk and Eleanor Tilton (New York: Columbia University Press, 1939-1994), 6: 258-60. Hereafter *L*.

14   *L* 6: 152.

15   *JMN* 16: 237.

4.7 Emerson house leather fire bucket, 1794.

The fire at "Bush" the next year prompted another recuperative trip, this time to Europe and Egypt with Ellen. From October to May, they traveled through England, France, Italy, and Egypt, then back again. Although Emerson declined invitations to lecture, he enjoyed the privileges of international renown, greeting old friends Carlyle and Herman Grimm and meeting new ones, among whom were John Stuart Mill, Robert Browning, John Ruskin, William Gladstone, and Max Müller.[16] Rejuvenated, he exulted in his journal, ". . . the feeling of free adventure, you have no duties,—nobody knows you, nobody has claims, you are like a boy . . . . For the first time for many years you wake master of the bright day, in a bright world without a claim on you;—only leave to enjoy."[17] Ellen sometimes fretted that Emerson "would rather sit quite still in the parlour"[18] than go sightseeing. But these quiet intervals doubtless encouraged his genuine eagerness to meet new people.

---

16   *Letters of ETE* 2: 10-87; *JMN* 16: 284-92.
17   *JMN* 16: 292.
18   *Letters of ETE* 2: 18.

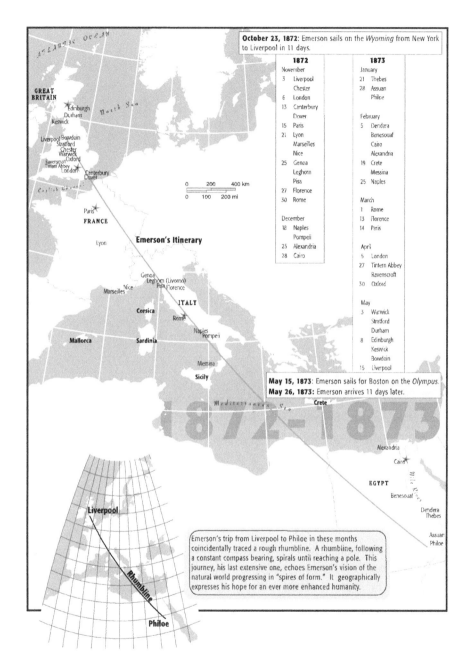

October 23, 1872: Emerson sails on the *Wyoming* from New York to Liverpool in 11 days.

1872		1873	
November		January	
3	Liverpool	21	Thebes
	Chester	28	Assuan
6	London		Philoe
13	Canterbury		
	Dover	February	
15	Paris	5	Dendera
21	Lyon		Benesouaf
	Marseilles		Cairo
	Nice		Alexandria
25	Genoa	19	Crete
	Leghorn		Messina
	Pisa	25	Naples
27	Florence		
30	Rome	March	
		1	Rome
December		13	Florence
18	Naples	14	Paris
	Pompeii		
25	Alexandria	April	
28	Cairo	5	London
		27	Tintern Abbey
			Ravenscroft
		30	Oxford
		May	
		3	Warwick
			Stratford
			Durham
		8	Edinburgh
			Keswick
			Bowdoin
		15	Liverpool

Emerson's Itinerary

May 15, 1873: Emerson sails for Boston on the *Olympus*.
May 26, 1873: Emerson arrives 11 days later.

Emerson's trip from Liverpool to Philoe in these months coincidentally traced a rough rhumbline. A rhumbline, following a constant compass bearing, spirals until reaching a pole. This journey, his last extensive one, echoes Emerson's vision of the natural world progressing in "spires of form." It geographically expresses his hope for an ever more enhanced humanity.

4.8 Emerson's Trip to Great Britain, Europe, and Egypt, 1872-1873.

Revising Ideas for Postwar Action

A fundamental factor keeping Emerson active as he aged was his expectation that he would continue to change. In 1872, he noted, "Our first view is only a guess"; inevitably, we must "give the greater heed."[19] This comment, hardly surprising for one long attuned to nature's constant metamorphoses, came as he was adjusting his ideas about blacks and women. They were finding their own voices, in part by adopting his argument for self-reliance, and were adding to America's diversity, ever greater as waves of immigration increased in those years. The country was pointed firmly in the direction of a more democratic society. In Chapter 3, Len Gougeon showed Emerson's steady progress in becoming a leader in this change. Nevertheless, he was still plagued by certain biases, a public-private divide going back to his youth, and a penchant for remaining his own type of reformer.

Despite his commitment to human freedom, Emerson had lagged behind close family members in becoming an active abolitionist.[20] In the early 1820s, he had posed to himself two opposing natural facts: on the one hand, ". . . all men are born unequal in personal powers," and on the other, slavery was an unnatural "hydra" that must be "knock[ed] down."[21] Despite advocating justice for all, he conflated racial difference with racial inferiority, as did many of his peers. He wrote in a journal entry of the late 1830s, "I think it cannot be maintained by any candid person that the African race have ever occupied or do promise ever to occupy any very high place in the human family."[22] This conflict between principle and prejudice sporadically erupted, even while he was becoming one of the country's most prominent voices against slavery. After the war, traces of it remained. One 1866 journal entry reads, "The way to wash the negro white is to educate him in the white man's useful & fine Arts, & his ethics."[23] But publicly and privately, he was adamant about voting rights for freedmen and insightful about the reasons for obstacles to blacks occupying a "very high place." Nor did he spare himself among those who might fail to think otherwise. In 1867, addressing the white establishment of which he was so solidly a part, he wrote in his journal, "You complain that the negroes are

---

19   *JMN* 16: 271.
20   Lawrence Buell, *Emerson* (Cambridge, Mass.: The Belknap Press of Harvard University Press, 2003), 148.
21   *JMN* 2: 49, 42.
22   Ibid.,12: 152.
23   Ibid.,16: 19.

a base class. Who makes & keeps them so . . . but you, who exclude them from the rights which others enjoy?"[24]

Before the war, Emerson was similarly ambivalent about what was natural to women, his private opinions evident in his public lectures. Though he had supported a host of rights for women in 1855, including the vote, he felt that women in general had not yet expressed a preference to work outside the home, stating, "[I do] not think it yet appears that women wish this equal share in public affairs."[25] This concern continued despite his having promoted women for inclusion in the all-male Transcendental Club eighteen years before. In 1837, only the second year of the club's existence, he had invited Margaret Fuller, Elizabeth Hoar, and Sarah Ripley to dinner before the club was to meet at his house. Correctly, it turned out, he thought their ethical influence and intellectual conversation would lead to their swift acceptance into the club. Soon other women were included.[26] Three years later, he encouraged Fuller to be the first editor of *The Dial* and to sign her lead article for the premier issue with her own name.[27] Yet not until after the war did Emerson begin to worry less about public life diminishing women's invaluable civilizing power.

Emerson's well-known wariness of certain types of reformers also lingered long after he had entered the abolitionist fray. In 1839, Lidian observed that she "scarce ever saw the person upon whom the suffering of others made so real [an] impression."[28] But his struggle to find the best, most honest response to that suffering spawned a complex, prolonged inner dialogue. Lawrence Buell suggests that he repeatedly refused to join reformist groups because he felt "himself . . . unusually susceptible to peer pressure" and feared endangering his self-reliance.[29] That may have been true, but he was equally torn by the spectrum of quality among reformers. In an 1844 journal entry, he had labeled "the abolitionists with their holy

---

24   Ibid., 16: 55.

25   Emerson, Ralph Waldo, "Woman," *The Later Lectures of Ralph Waldo Emerson 1843-1872*, eds. Ronald A. Bosco and Joel Myerson, vol. 2 (Athens, GA: University of Georgia Press, 2001), 28.

26   Richardson, 266; von Frank, *Chronology*, 126.

27   Megan Marshall, *Margaret Fuller: A New American Life* (Boston, Mass.: Houghton Mifflin Harcourt, 2012), 151.

28   Lidian Jackson Emerson, *The Selected Letters of Lidian Jackson Emerson*, ed. Delores Bird Carpenter (Columbia, MO: University of Missouri Press, 1987), 82.

29   Buell, 243. *JMN* 9: 134; *JMN* 9: 102. Sandra H. Petrulionis, *To Set This World Right: The Antislavery Movement in Thoreau's Concord* (Ithaca, NY: Cornell University Press, 2006), 42.

cause . . . an altogether odious set of people," while simultaneously finding Wendell Phillips, Frederick Douglass, and William Lloyd Garrison quite worthy of his public support.[30] Such inconsistencies continued well into the 1850s. In Concord in 1856, just days after Charles Sumner's beating at his Senate desk, he had declared, "I think we must get rid of slavery, or we must get rid of freedom."[31] Yet the very next year he could privately note that narrow-minded abolitionists, while "logically right," were "bitter sterile people" and "not better men for their zeal."[32] Notably, he excluded from this group the violently resolute abolitionist John Brown, whom he heralded as a true Transcendentalist, while backing him with fiery fundraising speeches and hard cash. Perhaps he had made up his mind in 1858, when he denounced Massachusetts politics as "cowardly" and demanded to know, "Why do we not say, We are abolitionists of the most absolute abolition, as every man that is a man must be?"[33] But as the private comments previously quoted demonstrated, he questioned the native abilities of blacks.

Emerson, too, had always wondered whether advocating the freedom of others was either appropriate or effective. In his 1844 address "On the Anniversary of the Emancipation of the Negroes in the British West Indies," he had described "the anti-slavery of the whole world" as "dust in the balance" before this uprising of "their race," led by the Haitian slave Toussaint L'Ouverture. He had urged his audience to the same sort of start in self-reliance: "I say to you, you must save yourself, black or white, man or woman."[34] In other settings, this insight made him quick to praise and support the able who rose to leadership, but reticent to speak for them. As a nascent feminist and privileged white male, he knew the irony of self-displacement in his argument.[35]

The conflict between Emerson's basic values and his unsettled attitudes on race and gender had gradually eased with his increased emphasis on concrete action. In "Experience" (1844), he announced his intent to turn from the "intellectual tasting of life" to "muscular activity." He ended the

30 *JMN* 9: 120.
31 *W* 11: 247, as quoted in Len Gougeon, *Virtue's Hero: Emerson, Antislavery and Reform* (Athens, GA University of Georgia Press), 221.
32 *JMN* 14: 166.
33 Ibid., 197.
34 *CW* 10: 325.
35 Christina Zwarg, *Feminist Conversations: Fuller, Emerson, and the Play of Reading* (Ithaca, NY: Cornell University Press, 1995), 259.

essay by declaring that ". . . the true romance which the world exists to realize, will be the transformation of genius into practical power."[36] Eight years before in *Nature*, he had described that romance in more personal terms: he was a "lover" who sought "intimate Unity" with nature.[37] This solo emphasis continued in his "American Scholar" address (1837), in which the lover of truth is one for whom "action is "essential" but "subordinate."[38] In contrast, "Experience" dismissed the "pedantries" of thought in favor of action. The romance had become more collective.[39] *Nature* had sought "unity in variety" for the single soul,[40] while "Experience" committed him to be nature's agent in making that goal a social fact. Emerson thus affirmed that he would "settle myself ever the firmer in the creed, that we should not postpone and refer and wish, but do broad justice where we are, by whomsoever we deal with."[41] Such a heartfelt pledge had emerged from his deep and prolonged mourning for the swift death of young Waldo in 1842, as described in Chapter 2. His son's death jolted Emerson afresh into making his ideals reality. But he knew this change would take time and require a more mature blend of perseverance, calm, and conviction. In "Experience," he urged himself as much as anyone else: "Patience and patience . . . we shall win at the last . . . there is victory yet for all justice."[42]

In a parallel demonstration of patience, this watershed work of 1844 did not lead to an immediate reversal of Emerson's arch individualism, his private social biases, or his aversion to joining certain reformers whom he found "odious." It would take the Compromise of 1850 with its Fugitive Slave Act to make him furious over what the South's slave power was doing to the North and to accelerate his public statements as an abolitionist. Ten years later, in the spring of 1860, he even joined the crowd of Concord neighbors who fended off U.S. Senate deputies sent to arrest his friend Frank Sanborn, John Brown's fervent supporter. For years, prominent feminists had eagerly solicited him to speak at their conventions, and as noted, by 1855 he began to accept their invitations. Against this background of increasing reform activity, in 1851 he had begun a new series of lectures

---

36   *CW* 3: 34, 49.
37   Ibid., 1: 10, 27.
38   Ibid., 59.
39   Ibid., 3: 34.
40   Ibid., 1: 27.
41   Ibid., 3: 35.
42   Ibid., 48-49.

that focused on the "practical question of the conduct of life."[43] Delivered over the next nine years, these lectures became the essays he titled *The Conduct of Life* (1860).

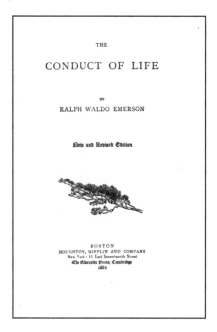

THE

CONDUCT OF LIFE

BY

RALPH WALDO EMERSON

New and Revised Edition

BOSTON
HOUGHTON, MIFFLIN AND COMPANY
New York: 11 East Seventeenth Street
The Riverside Press, Cambridge
1889

4.9 *The Conduct of Life*, title page, revised edition, 1889.

In 1870, twenty years after first giving this lecture series and five years into Reconstruction, Emerson commented to a friend, "In my works I like the articles 'Fate' and 'Worship' in my 'Conduct of Life' very well."[44] It is not difficult to see why. At that moment, he was preparing a course at Harvard with the title, "Natural History of Intellect" (1870-1871). The intellect had been a major theme of "Fate" in its argument for freedom. ("So far as man thinks, he is free.") More broadly, in 1870 Emerson thought the country was in great need of spiritual renovation. In "Worship," he had explored a fresh definition of authentic belief, motivated by the churches' predominant failure to oppose slavery in the 1850s and by his desire to restore an educated basis for belief in a scientific age. Despite his

---

43 Ibid., 6: 1.
44 Pendleton King, "Notes of Conversations with Emerson" (1884), eds. Ronald Bosco and Joel Myerson, *Emerson in His Own Time* (Iowa City, IA: University of Iowa Press, 2003), 132.

own fascination with science, in this essay he had argued that empirical investigation had its limits. As always, he believed that felt knowledge was the deepest avenue to coming as close as we might to ultimate truth.

All of *Conduct's* essays reflect his mid-career shift toward making his philosophy count in practice. But in "Fate" and "Worship" especially, Emerson married familiar ideals with his urgent need to find realistic solutions to the dramatic social, political, and religious upheavals of the 1850s.[45] As was his custom, he had doubtless deliberately ordered the essays' arrangement in *Conduct*.[46] "Fate" he put first and "Worship" sixth, even though the latter had pre-dated the former as a lecture. Apparently, when he collected his lectures, Emerson judged that intervening chapters on the worldly topics of power, wealth, culture, and behavior were necessary to prepare readers for "Worship." Both "Fate" and "Worship" also frequently mention a core Emersonian topic: character, a subject that had been of primary importance to him for some time. His first "Character" had appeared in *Essays II* (1844). His second essay with the same title, much more than a revision of the original, was written in 1865 and published the next year. Comparing the two "Characters" once again reveals Emerson's evolution toward pragmatic Transcendentalism, the second essay drawing on themes explored in "Faith" and "Worship." These three essays coalesce Emerson's first concerns in his later years: freedom, faith, and moral law, together making a virtual platform for his thought and action from the war's end to his own.

Close reading of each essay is essential to understanding Emerson's meanings, so often expressed in the allusive language of the heart. His preference for this impressionistic style had only strengthened after the 1840s. It was then that he was first drawn to Eastern mysticism, becoming fascinated by the Persian Sufi poets, especially Hafiz and Saadi. By 1864, he was applauding their "inconsecutiveness" and lack of unity. These virtues matched his long-sought goal in writing: to reflect nature's constant change, irregularities and mysteries. In addition, both of Emerson's expressed strengths—imagination and intuition—and his Romantic philosophy made him share the Persians' suspicion of pure reasoning and logic, and

---

45   Barbara Packer, Historical Introduction, *CW* 6: xvii.
46   Without a doubt, *Conduct's* essays were selected and arranged as assiduously as had been *Essays II* (1844) and his two collections of poems (1847 and 1867). Joseph Slater refers to Emerson making four "organizational outlines" for *Essays II*, Historical Introduction, *CW* 3: xxvii; for his detailed attention to the order of his published poems, see von Frank, *CW* 9: xc.

its authoritative result, religious orthodoxy. For similar reasons, he had criticized Unitarianism. Quite readily, then, he found a stylistic home in "the loose and irrecoverable ramble of the Oriental bards."[47] Emerson may have deliberately imitated their style—discursive, sometimes illogical, and often allusive. Nevertheless, his major concepts in "Faith," "Worship," and the two versions of "Character" together reveal a loose package of pragmatic idealism that defined his post-Civil War active life.

Both "Fate" and "Worship" deal with morality and ethics, long Emersonian subjects but now applied directly to contemporary issues. At eighteen, his prize-winning essay at Harvard, "The Present State of Ethical Philosophy," had brought the weight of historical ethics to bear on reforming the self.[48] In college, too, he had already decried the "plague spot of slavery,"[51] though he had taken no action against it. Years later, frustrated by the apparent futility of public protest against the Fugitive Slave Act (1850), the Kansas-Nebraska Act (1854), and slavery's swift extension into the northwest territories (1850s), he had begun exploring new ways to meld the ideal with the actual, emphasizing national reform, "performance,"[49] in short, practical results.

Never a man to force his ideas on others, he had nevertheless become convinced that, as he states in "Worship," "To make our word or act sublime, we must make it real."[50] Emerson had delivered "Worship" for the first time in Pittsburgh on 1 April 1851,[51] coincidentally only two days before the seventeen-year-old Thomas Sims was arrested in Boston under the Fugitive Slave Law.[52] In late December, months after official Boston had ordered Sims' forced return to Georgia, Emerson made "Fate" a standard part of this lecture series.[53] While not a direct attack on slavery, his argument in this essay nevertheless allows for only one conclusion: enslavement anywhere is unnatural because it denies freedom. A free humanity has the power, even the duty, to end it.

Given its national context, the mere title "Fate" hints of Emerson's sense of impasse in effecting peaceful reform and his fear of impending civil war.

47   Von Frank, *CW* 9: lxxii, lxxxiii-lxxxv.
48   Emerson, Ralph Waldo, "The Present State of Ethical Philosophy," in *Edward Everett Hale, Ralph Waldo Emerson, Together with Two Early Essays of Emerson* (Boston, Mass.: American Unitarian Association, 1902), 97-135, 131.
49   *CW* 6: 23.
50   Ibid., 120.
51   Von Frank, *Chronology*, 265.
52   *CW* 6: xli.
53   Ibid., xlv.

Could there be any way to redirect America from an imminent North-South conflict? Always taking the largest view possible, Emerson's true hope was clear in "Worship," where he had argued, ". . . the real and lasting victories are those of peace, and not of war."[54] But now, at the beginning of "Fate," he makes public a question that in 1833 he had only asked of himself, "How shall I live?" [55] With only a few strokes, he broadly outlines his argument to come: within the "irresistible dictation" of fate, there is also "liberty, the significance of the individual, the grandeur of duty, the power of character."

Another question propels him forward, "What to do?"[56] He frames an answer with a silent nod to the classic debate of determinism vs. free will, and as always, with nature as his touchstone. But in contrast to *Nature* fifteen years before, he no longer extols creation's beauty and beneficence. Rather, he emphasizes the rough, rude, totally unsentimental ways of "Providence," repetitively highlighting its disasters—from diseases to earthquakes, volcanoes to climate change—that coolly, indiscriminately sweep humanity aside. Genetics, too, he finds, limits humanity's range of face, physique, temperament, and character. Emerson illustrates this determinism with reference to familiar persons, political events, and new fields of inquiry—such as statistics.[57] Fate's apparent hegemony in everything—"matter, mind, and morals" (even high and low justice appear fixed)—appears a "limitation . . . impassable by any insight of man . . . ."[58] Then he turns the tables on "Providence."

Fate, Emerson declares, also has "its lord," its limit. Power is its opposing force: "If Fate follows and limits power, power attends and antagonizes Fate." This force that contests fate, he says, is nothing less than humanity's capacity to rise above its physical nature and become "a stupendous antagonism, a dragging together of the poles of the Universe." In creating us as we are, nature has given us the power to challenge it. We share in its great "lightning," the generating energy of the whole cosmos. More precisely, Emerson argues that human thought, "the spirit which composes and decomposes nature" for good or ill, allows us to challenge the tangible world—from "sandstone . . . to sea and shore . . . ." The union of thought and free will makes this possible.

---

54   Ibid., 119.
55   Ibid., 1.
56   Ibid., 2.
57   Ibid., 3-11.
58   Ibid., 11-12.

Emerson then unfurls his simple but arresting paradox: ". . . freedom is necessary." He elaborates: ". . . a part of Fate is the freedom of man. Forever wells up the impulse of choosing and acting in the soul. Intellect annuls Fate. So far as man thinks, he is free."[59] To pit humanity against its creator, nature itself, inspires "a fatal courage," he acknowledges, but we can supersede such conflict by our creativity, a parallel to nature's. This is possible in moments when "the inward eye opens to the Unity in things, to the omnipresence of [moral] law . . . ." Then, "We are as lawgivers; we speak for Nature, we prophesy and divine." Repeating himself, but in fresh ways, Emerson wends his way to state that thought and will "must always have coexisted." And the will he describes is "not mine or thine, but the will of all mind." He likens it to a great wind that blows through the soul releasing it from selfishness into a "universe of souls" driven by "the Right and Necessary." And "Right," universally applied, also makes us free. In fact, Emerson insists, "Whoever has had experience of the moral sentiment cannot chose but believe in unlimited power. Each pulse from that heart is an oath from the Most High." What is more, "the inward eye" of insight must fuse with "the moral sentiment" of affection to propel the will. Lacking men of such will, he notes, ". . . the world wants saviours and religions."[60]

Yet again thought can come to the rescue, Emerson argues, since ". . . every jet of chaos which threatens to exterminate us, is convertible in intellect into wholesome force. Fate is [simply] unpenetrated causes." For proof, he turns first to man's accomplishments in science and then to the humanities. Steam, he points out, once a powerful physical threat, was converted to useful energy in the hands of Watt and Fulton. Their counterparts in politics have harnessed "higher kinds of steam" to come up with justice, a version of controlled power. Justice, as a leveling principle, satisfies everyone, he asserts, replacing a mountain of hierarchical might with "the most harmless and energetic form of a State" —a clear allusion to democracy. [61]

Emerson then elaborates on "how fate slides into freedom, and freedom into fate," while optimistically connecting fate with inevitable progress and pointing to its most efficient instruments: great men. He gives a long list of such models from Goethe to Adams to Rothschild. Such figures

---

59   Ibid., 12-13.
60   Ibid., 16.
61   Ibid., 18-19.

lead Emerson naturally to character, where, in essence, he announces that a man's destiny or "fortune" depends on his allotted degrees of thought, will, and moral sentiment. Momentarily conflating thought and morality, he uses a homespun metaphor to state: "History is the action and reaction of these two, Nature and Thought,—two boys pushing each other on the curb-stone of the pavement. Everything is pusher or pushed: and matter and mind are in perpetual tilt and balance, so."[62] Later, he returns to the same paradox, using fate and freedom as alternative names for nature and thought. Experienced simultaneously, the two are a "double-consciousness." A familiar circus act illustrates his point: "A man must ride alternately on the horses of his private and his public nature, as the equestrians in the circus throw themselves nimbly from horse to horse . . . ."[63] This duality of the determined with the free in us is what Emerson means by "the Blessed Unity," or its identical twin, "the Beautiful Necessity."

Again, Emerson does not preach abolitionism head on. Unlike the average reformer, his apology for free will's coexistence with nature's inevitability gives his argument the largest possible framework. Early on in "Fate," he obliquely criticizes slavery, mentioning ". . . —expensive races— race living at the expense of race." [64] Nor does Emerson hide his prejudices. His "scale of races" puts Anglo-Saxons at the top, while he approves of English, French, and German colonization, and commiserates with the plight of "Jew," "Indian," and "Negro." He also affirms two statements by an author, whom he finds otherwise objectionable, but who has produced "charged" and "pungent" truths: first, "Nature respects race, and not hybrids"; second, "Detach a colony from the race, and it deteriorates to the crab." To illustrate the latter point, Emerson asserts that German, Irish, and Negro immigrants have "a great deal of guano in their destiny." [65]

Emerson lapses into bias, but he is speaking of the present. Looking ahead, he announces that "soon or late" fate will inevitably strike to bring about justice, hinting of future radical change.[66] And after he has established human power as a partial check to destiny, he delights in the progress of the races as a major example of nature's constant improvement. Eight years before Darwin's *Origin of the Species*, Emerson is, in effect, publicly arguing

---

62   Ibid., 23.
63   Ibid., 25.
64   Ibid., 4.
65   Ibid., 8-9.
66   Ibid., 11.

for evolution. (He had glimpsed the idea in Paris in 1833, when comparing classified museum specimens displayed at the King's Garden.) Now he writes, "The first and worst races are dead. The second and imperfect races are dying out, or remain for the maturing of higher. In the latest race, in man, every generosity, every new perception, the love and praise he extorts from his fellows, are certificates of advance out of fate into freedom."[67] In 1856, in *English Traits*, Emerson had already noted that pure races were a myth, and that many people were of obvious mixed ancestry. He had even remarked, "The best nations are those most widely related; and navigation, as effecting a world-wide mixture, is the most potent advancer of nations."[68]

"Worship," in contrast to "Fate," takes up slavery in its opening poem. Emerson sings of an unidentified man who "to captivity was sold, / But him no prison-bars would hold . . . ." Only at the poem's end is the man revealed as "Jove"—the Romans' supreme god. Emerson's last lines allude to the essay's overarching blend of ideal and tangible worlds: "Draw, if thou canst, the mystic line, / Severing rightly his from thine, / Which is human, which divine."[69] Though "Worship" was written before "Fate," Emerson reverses their chronology in *The Conduct of Life*. Evidently drawing on actual reactions gleaned in the ten years he had been reading both essays as lectures, he describes "Worship" as a response to the claims of "some friends" that "Fate" and two other essays in *Conduct*, "Power" and "Wealth," had overly reflected "the evil of the times," and possibly even encouraged atheism.

Emerson essentially refutes such charges as nonsense. If he needs to play "devil's attorney" to argue points, he will. Then, he unequivocally declares, "I have no infirmity of faith . . . Nor do I fear skepticism for any good soul." He would "dip my pen in the blackest ink, because I am not afraid of falling into my inkpot." In short, he feels no danger in becoming tainted by exploring any evil. Using a multitude of "I's" and "we's" to affirm that he speaks of himself and such resources, Emerson admits to holding "different opinions at different hours," but states that ultimately and always, he stands "at heart on the side of truth." In effect, he commands, bring on doubt and questioning: "We may well give skepticism as much line as we can. The spirit will return, and fill us. It drives the drivers. It counterbalances any accumulations of power." To emphasize this superiority of higher truth

---

67   Ibid., 19.
68   *CW* 5: 27.
69   *CW* 6: 106.

over human criticism, Emerson makes a single paragraph of a line from Edward Young's religious meditation, *Night Thoughts*: "'Heaven kindly gave our blood a moral flow.'" [70]

Once again, this grounding ethical thread in "Worship" typifies Emerson's post-"Experience" direction: to emphasize the interpenetration of unseen and seen worlds, spirit and matter, soul and body, belief and science. It is their intricate and intimate marriage that allows him to use scientific evidence to support the spiritual life. "We are born loyal," he announces. That is, we are made to be communal, a natural human pattern that he found epitomized by the Shakers. Equally, he insists, "We are born believing." Despite the rise and fall of particular religions, supposedly necessary to the health of their cultures, humanity continues to go on bearing beliefs, he says, "as a tree bears apples." So foundational is faith, as revealed by personal "self-poise" and "rectitude," that these qualities permeate "every particle" of creation. Later, Emerson will refer to this phenomenon as "the intimacy of Divinit . . . in the atoms." [71] At this moment, he presents the natural givenness of belief as a ringing aphorism, "God builds his temple in the heart on the ruins of churches and religions." [72]

From the empirical evidence of the birth and decline of religions that he has just documented, Emerson offers a definition of true religion, or worship, as the "flowering and completion" of culture. From cannibals to crusaders, Indians to Pacific Islanders, he illustrates the universal link between faith and culture, colorfully making his point by featuring the Norse King Olaf's forced conversion of hapless Eyvind by putting a pan of bursting coals on his stomach. Turning to the present, he replaces this semi-whimsy with dead seriousness. In this "transition period," when faiths that once "made nations" are expiring, he finds "the religions of men . . . either childish and insignificant, or unmanly and effeminating." In sum, he charges that the churches have separated religion from morality.

Emerson's critique follows on the many months of turmoil in Boston and its environs, described earlier, when citizens had been bitterly divided over Webster's role in the Compromise of 1850 and the enforcement of its Fugitive Slave Law in Massachusetts. By the time of its publication in 1860, "Worship" included much more evidence of the North's inner frictions over slavery than was available when he first wrote it. Not surprisingly, then,

---

70   Ibid., 107.
71   Ibid., 123.
72   Ibid., 107-08.

he puts "slave-holding and slave-trading religions" near the top of the churches' failures, only third behind know-nothingness and "scortatory" (lewd) behavior. He extends his critique into other religious practices then current, lambasting "peacock ritualism, the retrogression of Popery . . . the squalor of Mesmerism, the deliration of rappings [seances, in which even Lidian was participating] . . . thumps in table drawers [superstition], and black art." With no "religious genius" to "offset the immense material activity," [true] religion, he laments, "is gone." Soon afterward he asks, "What proof of infidelity, like the toleration and propagandism of slavery?" [73]

Yet despite this deluge of decay, Emerson re-introduces his earlier apology for humanity's persistent "moral sense." It is a principle, he says, an "undescribable [sic] presence, dwelling very peacefully in us, our rightful lord: we are not . . . to work, but to be worked upon; and to this homage there is a consent of all thoughtful and just men in all ages and conditions." The benefit, Emerson expansively states, will be "vast and sudden enlargements of power." To activate this moral sentiment, ethics rather than theology, the simple exercise of "motherwit" (immediate moral perception) is a more reliable and lasting guide. Before, he admits to having "groped" to explain the spiritual as something invisible. Now he insists, "The true meaning of *spiritual* is *real*; that law which executes itself, which works without means, and which cannot be conceived as not existing [his emphases]." Emerson dares his audiences to turn from sentimentalism to realism, allowing the "simple and terrible laws," visible or invisible, to be released throughout nature and rule.[74] Further on, he argues that this reality, inescapable and tangible, is like pervasive, natural electricity: the world is " a battery," and every atom is "a magnet" where God's divinity (power) appears in "every particle." [75]

These references to science are not accidental. Emerson wanted to assimilate the leading intellectual pursuit of his day, one he had long avidly followed, into his celebration of human thought and universal moral law. But for him, science—knowledge of the physical world—could never be the highest authority. Beyond empirical fact, Emerson argues, the spiritual actually exists as an ideal model, for which he had given a cornucopia of names over the years: God, Over-Soul or World-Soul, the Infinite, Universal or Higher Law—or even Higher Fact. In "Worship," that model becomes

---

73   Ibid., 109-11.
74   Ibid., 113-14.
75   Ibid., 118.

Questioner, Giver, untitled Thought or Power, and superpersonal Heart. In pursuing this spiritual unity, Emerson anticipates C. P. Snow's mid-twentieth-century, strict separation of science and religion, with which he would have quite disagreed. His disagreement would be all the more emphatic because he foresaw the "scientism" of our day, the absolutist claim that the scientific method, instead of being one avenue to knowledge, is the exclusive route to all truth—a belief held as firmly in some secular circles as any religious fundamentalism.

In this vein, Emerson critiques his era's faith in an array of material improvements—from chemistry to the steam-engine, galvanic battery, and sewing machine—but "not in divine causes." It is "short sight," he says, to "limit our faith in laws" to those of gravity, chemistry, botany, etc. He argues that they "do not stop where our eyes lose them," and advises his readers to "push the same geometry and chemistry up into the invisible plane of social and rational life, so that . . . in a boy's game or in the strifes of races, a perfect reaction, a perpetual judgment keeps watch and ward." Once again, he alludes to slavery, when he insists that moral law supersedes injustice.[76]

In this way, Emerson has been carefully preparing for his conclusion, a full-blooded call from the heart to imbue science with moral character. Earlier he had quoted Blaise Pascal, the seventeenth-century French mathematical prodigy, who at nineteen had invented the mechanical calculator and was simultaneously a physicist and devout Christian. Emerson discovered Pascal in college and afterward always highly praised him.[77] Apparently quoting from memory, he misstates Pascal's exact words when he writes, "The heart has its arguments, with which the understanding is not acquainted." Pascal's original in *Provincial Letters* (1656-1657) had punned on the word "reasons": "The heart has its reasons which reason knows nothing of."

---

76 Ibid., 116-17.

77 At twenty-three, Emerson had noted humanity's untrustworthiness, including reason (corruptible by pride). Then he wrote, "It is the leading idea of Pascal's Religious Meditations to contrast what is grand & pitiful in human nature." This practice, evidently already Emerson's habit, arose from his need to treat "the *whole* of Man," who being "a lopsided thing," could only be justly viewed by weighing his two sides (*JMN* 2: 390). In Spring (?) 1859, he remarked, "Now & then, rarely comes a stout man like Luther, Montaigne, Pascal, Herbert, who utters a thought or feeling in a virile manner, and it is unforgettable" (*JMN* 14: 277). Then again, in April-May 1864, "We said, that ours was the recuperative age. Pascal is one of its recoveries, not only the essay on Love, but the pure text of the Pensees" (*JMN* 15: 52).

Emerson's error in quoting Pascal probably arose from his familiarity for some twenty years with Coleridge's famous distinction of "Reason" and "Understanding." Coleridge—somewhat confusingly for readers today—had defined *reason* as the higher faculty of imagination, intuition, and sympathy to contrast with *understanding*, the lower faculty of observation and analysis. But as early as 1824, when twenty-one-year-old Emerson had newly decided on the ministry, he was substituting "heart" for Coleridge's intuitive "reason," and reading his analytic "understanding" as the "reason" to which Pascal refers. In his journal, Emerson noted, ". . . the highest species of reasoning upon divine subjects is rather the fruit of a sort of moral imagination, than of the 'Reasoning Machines' such as Locke & Clarke & David Hume."[78] Just weeks after delivering his "Lord's Supper Sermon" and soon to resign from his pastorate, he must have had Pascal in mind when he favored his own authority over Christ's and even God's, asking himself, "Why then shall I not go to my own heart at first?"[79] As he ends "Worship," Emerson uses "knowledge" in Pascal's sense of the heart's wisdom, surpassing logic: "When [a man's] mind is illuminated, when his heart is kind, he throws himself joyfully into the sublime order, and does, with knowledge, what the stones do by structure."[80]

Emerson believes he has described "a faith which is science," because he has united mind and matter within every atom. Spirit and the world are, in effect, one reality. He had envisioned this unity in *Nature*. But in "Worship," that unity is tighter and more complete; the two realms are essentially identical. And their combination, he finds, has another virtue: it will discourage false religious poses. (Universalizing this point, he quotes Muhammad: "There are two things which I abhor; the learned in his infidelities and the fool in his devotions.") The "new church founded on moral science," Emerson writes, will return humanity to its "central solitude," with only "the nameless Thought, the nameless Power, the superpersonal Heart" as company.[81] This is not a throwback to individualism. At the essay's start, he had taken man's social nature as given. And as he said in 1854, ". . . surely our education is . . . to know . . . that self-reliance, the height and perfection of man, is reliance on God."[82] Now he assumes that

---

78   *JMN* 2: 238.
79   Ibid., 4: 45.
80   *CW* 6: 128.
81   Ibid.
82   "The Fugitive Slave Law," *Emerson's Antislavery Writings*, eds. Len Gougeon and Joel Myerson (New Haven, CT: Yale University Press, 1995), 84.

character may parallel the unity of spirit and matter in atoms, and, through exceptional individuals, infuse society with "superpersonal Heart."

The theme of character so courses through both "Fate" and "Worship" that his revised version of "Character" (1865) makes it a natural third party to them. In this essay's first version (1844), he had written from a lofty perspective above everyday conflict, abstractly defining character as "an extraordinary and incomputable agent" that draws men toward the natural and universal "moral order." He had further defined character as a solely individual matter: "Character is nature in the highest form," true to itself and shunning social convention. His brief reference to religion also stressed private experience: ". . . it [is] more credible," he had written, "that one man should *know heaven* . . . than that so many men should know the world.'[83] Emerson's first "Character" was decidedly transcendental and addressed to the single soul.

In contrast, the second "Character," written at the height of his lecturing career in 1865, is more concrete and communal. Communality, in fact, grounds his aim: to focus on the moral sentiment as the worldwide source of true faith. Painstakingly and at length, he unpacks its evident nature, its pervading presence in all humanity, and its relationship to character. Emerson might have entitled the essay "The Moral Sentiment" instead of "Character," if he had not wanted to show that ethically-motivated, self-confident and gifted men are the essential means to accomplishing authentic good in the world.

With this intent, Emerson explores the meaning of faith, described in "Worship" as a scientific phenomenon occurring in all times and cultures, but now clarified in its social context. He begins with a trumpet-like declaration: "Morals respects what men call goodness . . . [what] they agree to honor as justice, truth-speaking, good-will, and good works." Rather than focus on the single soul, he writes of associations of men, who jointly arrive at the urge to right action and thereby "recommend themselves to each other." Immediately, he applies the concept of mutual benefit to politics, slightly misquoting Jeremy Bentham's dictum: ". . . the object of the state is the greatest good of the greatest number."[84] As he had in "Fate," Emerson notes the centrality of free will to morals, then cautions against

---

83   *CW* 3: 34.
84   *CW* 10: 447. Bentham's basic Utilitarian axiom is, ". . . the greatest happiness of the greatest number" measures "right and wrong." Jeremy Betham, Preface, *A Fragment on Government* (1776), 2nd paragraph.

undue private exercise of this liberty should it infringe on others' rights. He invokes Kant's moral imperative, based on what the German philosopher had called the "universal laws of nature." Kant had written, "Always act according to that maxim whose universality as a law you can at the same time will" and which is the "only condition under which a will can never come into conflict with itself . . . ."[85] This rule, Emerson goes on to say, is the work of "universal mind," a "sense of Right and Wrong" that belongs to everyone. Dormant in bad men, it is still there in all. For him, as for Kant, it is simply "the reason of things," or nature's gift.[86]

Such thinking expands our loyalties and desires, Emerson argues. Beyond personal satisfaction, we feel a wider commitment to others. "No one is accomplished whilst any one is incomplete. Weal does not exist for one, with the woe of any other."[87] In this way, the moral sentiment centers men "at the heart of Nature . . . where all the wires terminate which hold the world in magnetic unity,—and so converts us into universal beings." Echoing "Worship," Emerson combines scientific and religious language as he suggests that this encompassing ethical sense is intimately related to the mind, determining its sanity as well as its greatness. Equivalent to Truth, Power, Goodness, and Beauty, the moral sentiment uses us, he argues, as mere "passing agents" of its superior illumination.[88]

Once more, Emerson calls upon history to support his argument, listing the terms past generations have given this powerful force: "the light, the seed, the Spirit, the Holy Ghost, the Comforter, the Daemon, the still, small voice, etc . . . ." Such witnesses to its presence lead Emerson to yet another delicious paradox: the moral sense "creates a faith which the contradiction of all mankind cannot shake, and which the consent of all mankind cannot confirm." At once acknowledging morality's mystery and its calm existence "above all mediation," Emerson cites its declaration-as-command, *"I am"* [his emphasis], as a "revelation" to consciousness made known to all men in every generation.[89]

At last Emerson closes in on his title theme by insisting that "you and I and all souls" do not *receive* this "Eternal [Truth]" so much as *live in* it [my emphases]." That indwelling, in fact, defines our humanity, and

---

85 Immanuel Kant, *Foundations of the Metaphysics of Morals,* trans. Lewis White Beck (Berlin: 1902-1938), 437.
86 *CW* 10: 448.
87 Ibid., 449
88 Ibid., 450.
89 Ibid.

specifies how we participate in effecting morality: "The soul of God is poured into the world through the thoughts of men."[90] The better the men, the better their ideas, thus their acknowledged leadership. Here Emerson calls on his notion of a few great men, born with "no weakness of self" nor "impediment to the Divine Spirit" to become "the apparition of gods among men . . . ."[91] A political allusion makes his point concrete: "Great men serve us as insurrections do in bad governments," giants above "a whole nation of underlings." Finally, well into his essay, he introduces the topic of character per se, defining it as steadfastness, self-knowledge, and balance, all inspired by "a will built on the reason of things."[92]

No longer appealing to the single soul, Emerson asserts that such admirable men will go beyond "pure vision" to model morality in action for the rest of mankind. He further states that the "private or social practices" developed to honor that sentiment, ". . . we call religion."[93] In brief, religion is the moral sense on which we found our faith institutions with their laws, creeds, and beliefs. Over time, however, they may become corrupt and perverse through the influence of fallible men. Religions that might have once been true, thus inevitably become false. Emerson surveys this decline from purity, ending with special attention to Christianity. At first a protest movement, the church has morphed into a hierarchical tradition encrusted with dogmas and rituals. Emerson traces this hindrance to truth in various historical national religions through the Reformation, up to and including even liberal Unitarianism. Over and against this historical development were individuals—perhaps especially notable atheists, such as Voltaire— who in their forthrightness became morality's true torchbearers.

But the future, not the past, is Emerson's interest, and he foresees unknown "religious revolutions" on the horizon upsetting longstanding accepted theologies. Such changes are expected and do not worry him: "All the victories of religion belong to the moral sentiment."[94] He has already praised atheist and pagan ethicists, from Socrates to Voltaire, for being suggestive guides to right living in contrast to Christianity's clerics, whom he accuses of demanding allegiance to their dogmas and creeds. For him, these ancient pagans and modern atheists excel the churches of his day in

---

90   Ibid., 451.
91   Ibid., 452.
92   Ibid., 453.
93   Ibid., 454.
94   Ibid., 455-59.

being exemplars of Jesus's protest movement for justice. His high hope is that humanity will return to the same enduring "pure morals . . . not subject to doubtful interpretation, with no sale of indulgences, no massacre of heretics, no female slaves, no disfranchisement of woman, no stigma on race."[95] In these words, perhaps to soften his message for predominantly Protestant readers, Emerson alludes to the Reformation's brave sixteenth-century rebels. He even goes on to allow that the churches, so blind to slavery before the war, have since promoted a host of practical reforms: helping society's outcasts, educating the ignorant, and supporting government-sponsored nursing and teaching programs in Washington, D.C. Shortly after the war ended in 1865, Emerson joined the First Unitarian Church of Concord for the fellowship, perhaps, and for its awakening social activism. As far as belief was concerned, he remained resolutely removed, describing himself in an 1870 journal entry: ". . . in this republic . . . every citizen has a religion of his own—is a church by himself—& worships & speculates in a quite independent fashion."[96]

Character remained such a vital topic to Emerson in 1865 because of its lynchpin role, rising above all legislation, in reconstructing a nation where all men and women might be free. If America were to be born anew after the war, he thought, it would have to substantially amend its Constitution to disallow slavery. As early as 1862, long before the surrender at Appomattox, he had anticipated the need for such sweeping changes, writing in his journal, "All our action now is new & unconstitutional, & necessarily so."[97] Three years later in the revised "Character," he acknowledged the dangers of such radical change, observing that a person of character does "not ask . . . even for the assurance of continued life." He had also broadly resolved the opening frustration of "Fate" over the failures of individual and collective reformers. Now, even as he faced Reconstruction and its uncertainties, he took strength in this thought: "To a well principled man existence [itself] is victory," because "he feels the immensity of the chain whose last link he holds in his hand, and is led by it." That chain is, of course, moral sentiment, so sure and trustworthy a guide for men of character that they should put no other value—praise, happiness, even life itself—before this "spirit" that has "all."[98] Despite Emerson's nod to the churches' wartime and postwar

---

95   Ibid., 457-58, 460.
96   Ibid., 462; von Frank, *Chronology*, 401; *JMN* 15: 301.
97   *JMN* 15: 301.
98   *CW* 10: 464.

return to ethical service, this new "Character" was too controversial in its praise of pagan wisdom and its critique of the churches for even the liberal *Atlantic Monthly*, which he had helped found. But sure of his argument, he delivered this lecture five times on his 1865 lecture tour, and published it the following year in the *North American Review*.[99]

Exercising a Pragmatic Idealism

"Fate," "Worship," and Emerson's second "Character" together cover the essential concepts of his later thought that prompted his leadership in two organizations started soon after the war's end: the Free Religious Association (FRA) and the Radical Club. In 1867, at the inaugural meeting of the FRA, he spoke as a founding member, and the same year, was among the first to join the Radical Club. Active in both groups until just three years before his death, he served multiple terms as a vice-president of the FRA and regularly took part in the club's conversations. Both association and club, formed to include non-Christians and Christians alike and to connect spirituality to active reform, naturally sought out a person of Emerson's cultural and reform stature to join them. In turn, their calmness of tone appealed to him. William James Potter, president of the FRA, described its "chief function" to be "a voice without a hand," which "puts us in most honorable company," naming Socrates, Jesus, and then "our own Emerson."[100] Beyond Emerson, the two organizations shared a number of other members, including Octavius Brooks Frothingham, James Freeman Clarke, John Weiss, Thomas Wentworth Higginson, and David Wasson.[101] Youth had always been Emerson's first audience, and many members in both groups were young Unitarian ministers, such as Frothingham and Clarke, who had long admired him. Like Emerson, they were seeking a "naturalized, post-Christian, and universal understanding of human spirituality." They also urged that religious institutions prioritize social change.[102]

---

99 Von Frank, *Chronology*, 419.

100 William James Potter, *The Free Religious Association: Its Twenty-Five Years and Their Meaning: An Address for the Twenty-fifth Anniversary of the Association, at Tremont Temple, Boston, May 27th, 1892* (Boston, Mass.: Free Religious Association of America, 1892), 19.

101 Richard A. Kellaway, "The Free Religious Association," Unitarian Universalist Collegium: An Association for Liberal Religious Studies. 22 July 2013, http://www.uucollegium.org, p. 8; Julia Ward Howe, *Reminiscences: 1819-1899*, chapter 13, 18 July 2013, http://www.perseus.tufts.edu

102 David Robinson, "The Free Religion Movement," *The Oxford Handbook of*

The FRA and the Radical Club crystallized in the aftermath of a rift that had divided the 1866 National Conference of Unitarianism (which Emerson did not attend). Within this already liberal community, a splinter group of radicals had proposed that Unitarianism "declare itself a thoroughly nonsectarian organization . . . thereby explicitly affirming the right of many member congregations to identify themselves outside the Christian fold."[103] After this proposal failed to carry, the disappointed radicals formed the two groups the following year. Cyrus Bartol, a founding member of the FRA and the club, described them as inevitable outcomes of the convention, noting that the Radicals ultimately opposed "any final wording" in favor of free and open investigation of spiritual experience.[104] The club's historian, Mary Sargent, who with her husband John Turner Sargent hosted many meetings in their home, wrote that a common desire was "for larger liberty of faith, fellowship, and communion."[105] Similarly, Potter described the FRA as a reform effort aimed at "the utmost liberty for thought in matters of religion." Both groups affirmed, in Potter's words, "the human mind itself as the seat of ultimate authority in the discovery and holding of truth."[106] Emerson's insistence in "Worship" on the heart's reasons—a felt measure exceeding logic—would have led him to qualify any full endorsement of this statement.

The larger FRA pursued actual reforms more intently than the Radical Club. Potter named "one of the most obviously practical interests of religion" to be "working not only for the alleviation of misery, but for the prevention and cure of moral evil, the removal of oppressive burdens, and the opening to each and all of free opportunity for the best use of their faculties and life." Many members, such as Frank Sanborn and Julia Ward Howe (sister of Emerson's younger friend, Sam Ward), had been abolitionists and particularly wanted to see the status and rights of blacks assured during Reconstruction.

Transcendentalism, ed. Joel Myerson, Sandra Harbert Petrulionis, Laura Dassow Walls (New York, Oxford University Press, 2010), 617.

103 David Robinson, *The Unitarians and the Universalists* (Westport, CT: Greenwood Press, 1985), 107.

104 Cyrus A. Bartol, "Radicalism," *Radical Problems* (Boston, Mass.: Roberts Brothers, 1872), 98-118, 110.

105 Mary Sargent, *Sketches and Reminiscences of the Radical Club of Chestnut Street, Boston* (Boston, Mass.: James R. Osgood & Co., 1880), x.

106 Potter, *Free*, 21, x.

4.10 Julia Ward Howe at 42.

On the FRA's twenty-fifth anniversary in 1892, Potter noted its roots in the war and in establishing the Freedmen's Aid and Educational Societies. He also commented on the close ties between abolition and women's freedom, all evidence of a wider "great awakening of rational thought and of the higher moral sentiments and humane activities" in the postwar period.[107] The FRA also did more public outreach and education than the club. It published a newspaper called *The Index*, held large public meetings, and supported the efforts of the Freedmen's Aid Society to advance the literacy of freed blacks.

In contrast, the Radical Club, like the Transcendental Club of over twenty years before, was a small circle that met in members' homes for private, more academic discussions.[108] Themes of pre-war Transcendentalism

---

107 Ibid., 6, 7, 22.
108 According to Julia Ward Howe, "Mr. Emerson objected strongly to newspaper reports of the sittings of the Radical Club . . . sent to the New York Tribune by Mrs. Louise Chandler Moulton" on the grounds that they "interfered with the freedom of the occasion." *Reminiscences*, 290.

entered their free-ranging talk. That emphasis could diminish the importance of religious reform issues dear to certain members who also belonged to the FRA, such as prewar activist John Turner Sargent.[109] The Radical Club instead focused on comparative religion, science, and culture. Emerson began the first meeting with remarks on religion. He stressed the agreement of the world's leading sacred writings about the cosmos, and specifically praised the insights of Eastern religions.[110] In the following discussion, however, some members questioned this celebration of Eastern texts. With clear consternation, Julia Ward Howe remarked on "the anti-Christian twist that prevailed in the Radical Club."[111] Nevertheless, this first debate, ranging widely over history, culture, and reform, was lively and friendly.[112] And Howe continued to attend later meetings.

4.11 View of Boston, July 4, 1870.

Religion was also Emerson's subject at the FRA's first meeting in 1867, when he encouraged this diverse group to rouse the church from its "checked, cribbed, confined" torpor. Once again, he noted ". . . worship finds expression" in "good works . . . only on the basis of active duty." For him, the Civil War was such a good work: "The soul of our late war . . .was,

---

109 David Pettee, "John Turner Sargent," Unitarian Universalist Association, 16 July 2013, http://www25.uua.org
110 Sargent, *Sketches*, 4.
111 Howe, *Reminiscences*, chapter 13.
112 Sargent, *Sketches*, 7-20.

first, the desire to abolish slavery in this country, and secondly, to abolish the mischief of the war itself, by healing and saving the sick and wounded soldiers" through the "sacred bands of the Sanitary Commission."[113] In 1869, he addressed the FRA again, glad that "a more realistic church" was emerging, one aligned with a science accepting "Divinity in the atoms" instead of resorting to supernatural theism. This was the modern, scientifically informed church he had called for in "Worship," giving him an opportunity to reaffirm that ". . . the moral sentiment speaks to every man the law after which the Universe was made."[114]

Assessing Reconstruction

Emerson felt that the Union's triumph in 1865 had irrevocably rid the nation of slavery, writing in his journal, "This victory . . . will stay put." Further, he was glad "that the rebels have been pounded instead of negociated [sic] into a peace." Yet he was well aware of the hurdles to enacting and enforcing emancipation: "The problems that now remain to be solved are very intricate & perplexing, & men are very much at a loss as to the right action." Only six months after the war's official end, he also worried about achieving his vision of national transformation: "We hoped that in the Peace, after such a war, a great expansion would follow in the mind of the country; grand views in every direction,—true freedom in politics, in religion, in social science, in thought. But the energy of the nation seems to have expended itself . . . and every interest is found as sectional as before." His list of indictments spared no one: "The Episcopal church is baser than ever, . . . the Democrat as false & truckling; the Union party as timid & compromising, the scholars pale & expectant, never affirmative."[115]

   More positively and closer to home, his journal now showed little trace of his former ambivalence about the capabilities of blacks. He wrote with forceful clarity, "The obvious remedy is to give the negro his vote." In fact, he had more confidence that "the negro will learn to write & read" to qualify for voting "before the [poor and uneducated] white will." Furthermore, he doubted the moral potential of any class of white southerner. Their wartime "cruelty & malignity" repulsed him. On a mild rampage, he charged them not only "with starving prisoners of war . . . massacring surrendered men,"

---

113 *W* 11: 479, 480.
114 Ibid., 485, 486.
115 *JMN* 15: 77-78, 459.

and "burning cities," but also with biological warfare in "attempts to import the yellow fever into New York" and with such barbaric practices as "cutting up the bones of our soldiers to make ornaments, & drinking-cups of their skulls." Northerners were in another category of concern: "If we let the southern States in to Congress, the Northern democrats will join them in thwarting the will of the government."[116]

Nevertheless, two months before Lincoln's assassination, on February 1, 1865, Congress had passed the Thirteenth Amendment abolishing slavery, and the states ratified it on December 18 of that year. The Fourteenth Amendment, granting due process and equal protection under the law to former slaves, followed in 1866, and the Fifteenth Amendment, giving voting rights to all men regardless of "race, color, or previous condition of servitude," came three years later.[117] The last two amendments, ratified in 1868 and 1870 respectively, meant that all three became law within only five years, remarkably fast given the fierce controversy they evoked. These liberal reforms were first threatened by a trio of pivotal events in April 1865: Lee's surrender five days before Lincoln's assassination and Andrew Johnson's succession to the presidency. Johnson was a southern Democrat hostile to the agenda of universal suffrage. When southern states rushed to block the amendments and to pass the first Jim Crow laws, a virtual war broke out between the president and the combined forces of radicals and abolitionists.[118]

In quick order, Emerson deplored Johnson's leadership as a "disastrous mistake" and hoped his fellow New Englanders would "go to the polls, to put a check on our mad President."[119] Early in 1868, Johnson, having narrowly escaped impeachment, remained in office to oppose the Fourteenth Amendment. In June that same year, Emerson privately made his position clear: "The Negro should say to the government, your principle is, no tax without representation; but as long as you do not protect me at home & abroad, you do not give me the value for which I have paid." Only with Grant's election to the presidency a few months later did the agenda for Reconstruction seem assured. Emerson counted Grant among "the few stout & sincere persons . . . that encourage your heart from day to day."[120]

---

116 Ibid., 65, 458, 459, 471-72.
117 Constitution of the United States, Amendments XIII, XIV, XV, http://www.archives.gov
118 Gougeon, *Virtue's Hero*, 320.
119 *JMN* 16: 27; *L* 5: 477.
120 *JMN* 16: 115, 142.

By deft management of his infirmities during this time, Emerson remained involved in affairs near and far. From Baltimore in January 1871, he wrote Lidian of his visits to "General Howard's Freedmen's Institute, an important college for colored men" (now Howard University) where he was eagerly pressed into an impromptu address.[121] In his absence, Lidian collected a constant stream of fan letters as well as requests for articles. In 1872, she wrote him in Europe, "Letters keep coming for you—mostly for autographs. The 'drummer' of the 'Index,' [the FRA's newspaper] wishes you to send him instead of the money . . . an article for that wise paper. The Independent wants one."[122] Before that, he had kept in touch with friends at memorials, funerals, and special events.

Emerson's testimonies on these occasions enlarge the record of his postwar thinking and attitudes. In his speech at the Concord service for Lincoln on April 19, 1865, the town's annual date to commemorate the Revolution, he described the president's assassination as singularly tragic and globally significant. With cosmic overtones, he likened Lincoln's murder to "an uncalculated eclipse over the planet . . . because of the mysterious hopes and fears which, in the present day, are connected with the name and institutions of America." Still, he saw Lincoln's achievements as cause for "a song of triumph, which even tears for his death cannot keep down." Projecting his own feelings about responsible self-reform, he praised Lincoln as a man who "grew according to the need."[123] Two years later, at the funeral for his friend George Luther Stearns, Emerson recounted the personal sacrifices Stearns had made for the abolitionist cause, often working at a pace that "so effectually banished him from his own house, that his children asked their mother who this man was that came there on a visit."[124]

Five days after Stearns' funeral in 1867, again on April 19, Concord's hallowed commemoration day, Emerson stood on the common to dedicate a thirty-foot granite obelisk, the Soldier's Monument, to forty-four Concord men who had died in the war and helped bring about what he claimed was the country's second Revolution.

121 L 6: 195.
122 Lidian Emerson, Selected Letters, 286-87.
123 W 11: 307, 308, 311-12.
124 CW 10: 468.

4.12 Civil War Memorial, Monument Square, Concord, Mass., 1867.

This patriotic note prefaced a much deeper call for the moral reconstruction he had outlined in "Faith," "Worship," and "Character." Addressing the whole nation, in effect, he admitted that the North's "own theory and practice of liberty had got sadly out of gear." Nevertheless, he called the Union soldiers "as much missionaries to the mind of the country, as they were carriers of material force." He singled out George L. Prescott, who "had grown up in this village from a boy," and who in three years of service had risen from lieutenant of Concord's company G of the 5th Regiment to colonel of the 32nd Massachusetts Volunteers. He then movingly quoted from letters, notes, and battle reports of rank-and-file Concord recruits to honor their aborted youthful sweetness, tender feelings, homesickness, and suffering. He shared the "gloom" of his neighbors, especially those "who can hardly read the names on yonder bronze tablet, the mist so gathers in their eyes." He noted as well that "three of the names are of sons of one family," Asa, John, and Samuel Melvin. Concluding, Emerson did not forget those survivors, unnamed on the obelisk, who "put just as much at hazard as those who died."[125]

By the mid-seventies, Emerson was making few such public addresses. But in the spring of 1874, he served as pallbearer at the funeral of his close friend Charles Sumner. This death led him to reminisce in his journal, "For Sumner's merit, go back to the dark times of 1850 & see the position of Boston & its eminent men." [126] Earlier, in 1865, he had remembered his friend's energetic response to Webster's betrayal in 1850-1851: "Sumner & his valiant young contemporaries" made "their views not only clear but prevailing . . . & drove Mr Webster out of the world." Four years later, he had been pleased that Sumner was assembling his papers, believing they would form "the history of the republic for the last 25 years, as told by a brave, perfectly honest & Well instructed man."[127] Sumner had been Emerson's political alter ego, a prime candidate to epitomize the contemporary ethical leader envisaged in "Character" (1865).

4.13 Charles Sumner in his 50s, photograph, c. 1860s.

125 Ibid., 471, 472, 473, 475, 483-84; yankeeancestry.tripod.com/concordcwm.html.
126 Ralph L. Rusk, *The Life of Ralph Waldo Emerson* (New York: Charles Scribners' Sons, 1949), 490. *JMN* 16: 300.
127 *JMN* 15: 76; 16: 478.

Posthumous tributes to Emerson, generally ignored by his biographers, measure the long and wide shadow of his influence. A few months after his death in 1882, Julia Ward Howe, speaking at the Concord School of Philosophy, recalled her changing estimate of Emerson. Early on, he had seemed to be "a more charming personification of Satan . . . universally laughed at . . . in high society." Later, she saw something else: "He had a look of power that did not show itself in the garb of power. Who can give us that look of inward meaning again?" On this same occasion, Ednah Dow Cheney noted that at Sumner's funeral Emerson had forgotten the "brave words" he had spoken about the senator's notorious beating in the Senate in 1856. But she noted that a black man in South Carolina "had remembered them as they were reported in the newspapers of the time," saying "how they had been an inspiration and a strength to him ever afterward."[128]

Two years later, the school again sponsored an occasion of formal tributes to Emerson, published as *The Genius and Character of Emerson* (1885). Speakers included FRA and Radical Club members, abolitionists, and feminists who heralded Emerson's long-term legacy to both history and politics. Among them, Julia Ward Howe once more perceptively noted that Emerson's "great sensitiveness to the rights and claims of others, sometimes made him a waiter where others dashed headlong into the fight." She particularly applauded "his indignation . . . at the great wrongs which have disgraced our social and political history" and the power of his response: ". . . a single shaft from his bow flew far and hit the mark." George Willis Cooke exuberantly connected Emerson's literary and reform careers, naming him "the literary interpreter of [an] America" that "brings together the races of the world as no nation or time ever did before." Cooke also argued, "If the anticipations of Emerson were in any degree correct, the literature representing America will have in it the spirit of freedom and equal rights."[129]

In May 1903, Concord's leading men's club, the Social Circle, of which Emerson had been a venerable member, celebrated the centenary of his birth. At this event, Moorfield Storey, Edward Emerson's Harvard classmate and an old family friend, honored Emerson for his "most valuable lessons" about human dignity, namely "that every man, . . . white, brown or black, had his right to his chance of success, and it followed that no other man

---

128 Julia Ward Howe and Ednah Dow Cheney, "Reminiscences," in Bosco and Myerson, *Emerson in His Own Time*, 113-14.

129 *The Genius and Character of Emerson: Lectures at the Concord School of Philosophy*, ed. Frank Sanborn (Boston, Mass.: James R. Osgood & Co., 1885), 133, 292, 299, 313, 332, 333.

had a right to take that chance."[130] Such lessons were more influential than Emerson could have known: in 1909, Storey, a white man, became the first president of the National Association for the Advancement of Colored People.

Within weeks of the Social Circle's event, the FRA sponsored the Emerson Memorial School, held in Concord and Boston from July 13-31. It was one of the most lengthy and influential posthumous tributes to Emerson, unique in focusing solely on his reform work. For eighteen days, lectures by thirty scholars and activists were so scheduled that hundreds of educators from many parts of the country, already in Boston for a conference of the National Educational Association, could also attend. Emerson's abolitionism was a prominent topic, surveyed by William Lloyd Garrison's lecture, "Emerson and the Anti-Slavery Movement" and Moorfield Storey's "Emerson and the Civil War."[131] To prepare his remarks, Storey had borrowed Emerson's "Liberty" notebook, a collection of his notes on slavery and abolition. Unreturned to the family, this revealing manuscript was effectively lost in his own papers until it was rediscovered in 1964, years after their deposit in the Library of Congress.[132] The Memorial School lectures also documented Emerson's work for women's rights. Anna Garlin Spencer, daughter of the abolitionist Nancy Garlin and a prominent activist for women, lectured on "The American Woman's Debt to Emerson." Spencer praised Emerson's liberal support "without regard to distinctions of sex . . . race, or inheritance" and also "the strongly radical position" he had taken on women's rights in 1855.[133]

Adding to Women's Rights

In late 1839, thirty-six-year-old Emerson revealed to his journal a tightly kept secret. His mask of cool deliberation hid just the opposite: a tender

---

130   "Speech of Moorfield Storey," *The Centenary of the Birth of Emerson as observed in Concord, May 25, 1903*, http://www.archive.org

131   "The Emerson Centennial Memorial School at Concord and Boston, July 13-31, 1903" (Boston, Mass.: Free Religious Association, 1903).

132   Gougeon, *Virtue's Hero*, 344, 345. In light of the notebook's discovery, Emerson's antislavery record came to full light for the first time. See *JMN* 14: 373 and John C. Broderick, "Emerson and Moorfield Storey: A Lost Journal Found," *American Literature* 38: 2 (May 1966): 177-86.

133   "A Tender Tribute Fittingly Paid by Anna Garlin Spencer," *Boston Evening Transcript*, 16 July 1903.

"woman's heart" (his emphasis).[134] At first he projected this perceived vulnerability onto an imagined "Rob" and so kept it at a distance. Even after owning up to it, however, Emerson was baffled: he was thoroughly male and already the father of two children. But this clandestine, feminine side of Emerson helps to shed more light on his announced preference for study and lecturing over the reformer's platform. It also illuminates an aspect of the tension he felt between his principles and biases, especially concerning women's rights, and the near resolution of that inner debate after the war.

It is true that Emerson and Margaret Fuller, following Goethe's idea of genius as androgynous, had flattered themselves that their psyches exhibited both masculine and feminine traits. But that was aesthetic, mutual congratulation among friends. The world into which Emerson threw himself as a lecturer during the 1830s and 40s was a male-dominated society with women secondary at all levels. He could not afford to be identified with females, however he admired them as friends, who were so stringently marginalized outside the home. That state of affairs was why he pitied women in general, criticized people whom he considered "effeminate," and so often extolled "manly" virtues. Living in Concord since the 1830s, Emerson had been surrounded by family and neighbors who were abolitionist leaders and activists, most of whom were women.[135] Many, in his view, were overly sentimental and too singularly focused on abolition, including his wife Lidian.[136] Though he entirely agreed with their antislavery position, he did not want to be linked to what he saw as their defects and those of certain others, especially one-note, sometimes self-aggrandizing reformers—nor did he want to expose his tender feminine heart.

Although Emerson's 1844 Concord address on slavery announced his entry into the abolitionists' cause and alluded to women's self-reliance, it was not until the South's virtual march North to enforce the Fugitive Slave Act of 1850 that he fully responded to the call of abolitionists and women. In his view, Daniel Webster, New England's greatest politician and orator, had disgraced himself. Male issues—sectional rivalry, political power, pride, and honor—now combined with women's high moral concerns to dominate the daily news. Emerson could express his "woman's heart" and

---

134 See fuller discussion, Ch. 2, Part 2.
135 Petrulionis, 15-19.
136 *JMN* 5: 382.

all its sympathetic passion with less fear of a feminized taint. And in 1855, at the Woman's Rights Convention in Boston, he began to do so, extending his work to abolition's natural corollary—women's rights. In fact, at this early date, among many other privileges for women, he openly endorsed female enfranchisement, with a sly reference to its potential benefit to his own interests: ". . . certainly all my points would be sooner carried in the state, if women voted."[137]

Emerson had had one proviso about those rights: that women should not operate in the public sphere lest their crucial civilizing influence be lost. This restraint was partly based on his view of the given nature of females, but it also arguably reflected his need to protect his "woman's heart" by being a scholar-critic above the hurly-burly of politics. After the war, that protection was increasingly unnecessary. In "Character" (1865), he built upon Goethe's belief "'that pure loveliness and right good-will are the highest manly prerogatives, before which all energetic heroism . . . must recede,'" by swiftly attributing these "manly" virtues to women. And he added, "In perfect accord with this, Henry James [Sr.] affirms, that 'to give the feminine element in life its hard-earned but eternal supremacy over the masculine has been the secret inspiration of all past history.'"[138] Such high judgment by a respected friend whose gaze covered, as he put it, "all past history," allowed Emerson to accept his hidden heart, completing this important aspect of his private revolution. An aging man, his inner life no longer a society liability urging him to restraint, he was freed from convention and from himself to promote the rights that women wanted, and for the reason they gave: because they wanted it.

Emerson's psychological release coincided with his wider recognition of women's impressive public record during the war. By 1865, they had proven their indispensable effectiveness as nurses, educators, vital volunteers, and leaders in activist organizations. In 1862, he had seen his young neighbor Louisa May Alcott volunteer to nurse the wounded in Washington D.C., an experience fictionalized in her *Hospital Sketches* (1863). He also admired Lucretia Mott, the pioneering Quaker abolitionist who in 1840, ignoring prohibitions against women, had attended the World Anti-Slavery Convention in London. With domestic help, Mott had successfully integrated motherhood and family life with her public career. With Emerson, she, too, helped found the FRA after

---

137 "Address at the Women's Rights Convention, 20 September 1855," *LL* 2: 26.
138 *CW* 10: 464. James had earlier remarked on Emerson's feminine side. See Ch. 5, 37; Henry James, Sr., "Emerson," *Atlantic Monthly* 94 (1904), 743.

the war. In addition, Lidian's influence as a reformer—lessening Emerson's sense of her excessive sentimentality—was both powerful and constant.

Emerson's opinions about women and their public and private roles were now moving toward more complete alignment. In 1862, his "American Civilization" address at the Smithsonian repeated his point in "Woman" of seven years before: the influence of good women was at the root of civilization. Only three years later, when the New England Women's Club formed, it immediately offered him honorary membership. (At this club, he would read the first draft of his essay about Mary Moody Emerson.)[139] In 1865, too, he privately critiqued Hawthorne for the "dismal mask" he had cast over Fuller's "rich & brilliant genius" in his novel *The Blithedale Romance* (1852), based on Brook Farm. In other journal entries from 1866 onward, Emerson reassessed his relationships with Margaret Fuller and Mary Moody Emerson while also reexamining the public importance of their works. He asked himself, "What could [Charles Elliot] Norton mean in saying that the only great men of the American past were Franklin & Edwards? We have had Adams, & Channing, Washington, & the prophetic authors of the Federalist, Madison & Hamilton, and, if he had known it, Aunt Mary." He added both women to "my own list of thinkers & friends," noting "MME's journals shine with genius, & Margaret Fuller's Conversation did." In May 1872, he reported reading his aunt's manuscripts "to Hedge & Bartol on Friday evening . . . nearly a hundred years since she was born."[140]

Beyond these two closest female intellectuals in his life, Emerson reappraised the general contribution of contemporary women to the public good. In 1867, in his Phi Beta Kappa address at Harvard on "The Progress of Culture," he listed first "the new claim of woman to a political *status*" among post-war "ethical . . . innovations [his emphasis]."[141] Two years later in Boston, Emerson gave an untitled address, a revision of "Woman," on the anniversary of the New England Woman's Suffrage Association, at which time he became one of its vice-presidents. Another post-war address similar to these two, "Discours Manqué. Woman," was perhaps never delivered. But Emerson's choice of title, connoting a lack

---

139 *CW* 10: 397; T. Gregory Garvey, *The Emerson Dilemma: Essays on Emerson and Social Reform* (Athens GA: University of Georgia Press, 2001), 107, 113 n.20.
140 *JMN* 16: 90, 94, 259, 274.
141 *CW* 8: 108.

or failure, reveals his sense that the vote and other rights for women had failed to receive adequate attention.[142]

In this period of renewed interest in women's rights, Emerson met the eighteen-year-old poet Emma Lazarus at Sam and Anna Ward's home in New York in February 1868.

4.14 Emma Lazarus at 38.

She gave him a signed copy of her *Poems and Translations* (1867) and sought his advice. He warmly welcomed her. Though younger than any woman who had approached him, he no doubt saw her as yet another potential genuine American voice. Most of his protégés—with the exception of Whitman—had been local and part of his own Transcendental literary culture. Lazarus, from a prominent and wealthy Jewish family of New York City, represented a socially foreign world to Emerson. But in featuring non-Christian religious texts in *The Dial* over twenty years before, he had proved himself open to other faiths. A decade before meeting Lazarus, on Anna Ward's conversion to Catholicism, he had assured her, "To old eyes, how supremely unimportant the form under which we celebrate the Justice, Love, & Truth,—the attributes of the Deity & the Soul!"[143] That Lazarus was a Jew would not be an issue for him.

Emerson and Lazarus began a correspondence that lasted until his death. He soon wrote her to encourage but also criticize certain verses as "too youthful, & some words & some rhymes inadmissible." In addition,

142 *LL* 2: 16-18.

143 Von Frank, *Chronology*, 440-41; *L* 6: 7; *Letters of ETE* 2: 228; *Letters* 5: 143, 144. Emerson kept any misgivings to himself, omitting from his letter to Anna: "I must lament the chance-wind that has made a foreigner of you, whirled you from the forehead of the morning into the medievals, again."

he found fault with her "tragic & painful" endings. Two months later, he was a more impressed mentor, simultaneously self-deprecating and playfully arrogant as well as open to her criticism. He called himself "a shut up dilatory correspondent," but one who, "appointed your professor, . . . should be very stern & exigeant, & insist on large readings & writings, & from haughty points of view." By habit, he referred to the "true lover of poetry" as male and relied "on your being docile." But typically, he asked Lazurus to think for herself, wishing to see her "own results." This advice he paired with his other favorite caution: avoid excessive book-learning. "Books," he wrote to her in June, were "introductory only"—better to hear what "you have found therein, . . . or still better if you have found what I have never found, & yet is admirable to me also." In April 1870 he included his own work, chiding her "overestimate of the little book of 'Society &c" (*Society and Solitude*, 1870) .[144] Rather, he invited parity between them, his requirement for serious discussions of poetry.

Educated in Greek and Latin classics and familiar with current Continental writers, Lazarus had the intellectual background for that equality. She also had stamina to match Emerson's, responding to his frank criticism with diligent revision. She did so twice in 1869, reworking her poem "Admetus" after Emerson judged its "feeble lines & feeble words" inadequate for a promised submission to the *Atlantic*. And he declined to allow her to dedicate it to him, arguing that would prejudice his promotion of it. Though Lazarus never won his approval, she featured the poem in her collection *Admetus and Other Poems*, free there to dedicate it to Emerson (for which he thanked her).[145] Eight years after they had met, in August 1876, he invited Lazarus to spend a week in Concord with the family. By then, his conversation and memory were sharply limited, but her company energized him. Ellen described the two as "a novel spectacle . . . she got answers out of him that I should have declared he wouldn't give."[146]

Lazarus was the first and youngest of four poets who honored Emerson at the Concord School of Philosophy in 1884. The sonnet she wrote for the occasion draws the obvious parallel to their relationship: "As, when a father dies . . . so do we gather round thy vacant chair . . .

---

144 *L* 6: 6-7, 11, 21, 114.
145 Ibid., 6: 75, 83, 90, 144.
146 *Letters of ETE* 2: 225.

for the love we bear, / Not for thy fame's sake."[147] On the same occasion, Julia Ward Howe applauded Emerson's independence in speaking out "for Woman Suffrage more than once with sober weight and earnestness," and in recognizing the "character and intelligence of the women" who had asked him for public support: "Mr. Emerson considered these women as of a rank to commend any views concerning their own sex which they might adopt."[148]

Other women also benefited from Emerson's warm support. At the Concord School of Philosophy in 1880, Emerson overheard Elizabeth Peabody chide young student Kate Douglas Wiggin for her wind-tossed hair, advising that to "be a real student" she should wear it "drawn back smoothly." Despite his aphasia, Emerson quipped, "'I have seen smoother heads with less in them.'"[149] On larger matters, Wellesley College president Caroline Hazard, speaking at Emerson's centennial in 1903, extolled his feminist advocacy and expressed "the affection and gratitude which I have—which all women must have—for the work which Mr. Emerson did for women." She also praised "his splendid message of the dignity of the person," applied to the young generally, as having "an especial force to the young women of to-day."[150] A full generation after his death, Hazard's testimony indicates Emerson's lasting influence in encouraging female self-confidence and rights. Such support had been a major factor, with New England women leaders at the cutting edge, in the founding of the National American Woman Suffrage Association in 1890. In turn, the association's efforts led to the Nineteenth Amendment, ratified in 1920, sixty-five years after Emerson's "Woman" had advocated the right it guaranteed: female enfranchisement.[151]

---

147 *Genius and Character*, 215. Lazarus's most famous sonnet, "The New Colossus," was written a year after Emerson's death, and was not placed on the base of the Statue of Liberty until 1903, sixteen years after her own death. http://xroads.virginia.edu/~cap/liberty/lazarus.html

148 *Genius and Character*, 309.

149 Kate D. Wiggins, *Autobiography*, Bosco and Myerson, *Emerson in His Own Time*, 246.

150 "Speech of Carol Hazard," ibid., 221-22.

151 http://en.wikipedia.org/wiki/National_Woman_Suffrage_Association; http://www.ourdocuments.gov/doc.php?flash=true&doc=63

Answering Terminus

4.15 Emerson at 70, 1873.

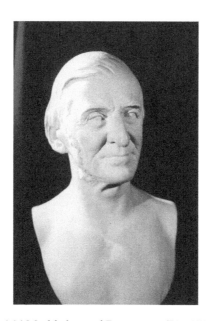

4.16 Marble bust of Emerson at 76, 1879.

Emerson's repeatedly-stated belief in nature's flux shaped his view of death, including his own: ". . . early hints are given that we are not to stay here, that we must be making ready to go;—a warning that this magnificent hotel and conveniency we call Nature is not final. First innuendoes, then broad hints, then smart taps, are given, suggesting nothing stands still in nature; that the creation is on wheels, in transit, always passing into something else, streaming into something higher; that matter is not what it appears."[152] This sort of thinking and his admiration of the Persian poets made him conceive of his poetry as a "Chasing with words fast-flowing things."[153] From this perspective, the final version of his "Terminus" (1867) should be read.

> It is time to be old,
> To take in sail:—
> The god of bounds,
> Who sets to seas a shore,
> Came to me in his fatal rounds,
> And said: 'No more!
> No farther shoot
> Thy broad ambitious branches, and thy root.
> Fancy departs: no more invent,
> Contract thy firmament
> To compass of a tent.
>   . . . .

Emerson's youthful awareness of a final limit to his days meant that for over a lifetime he had been thinking about the poem that finally became "Terminus." The record shows that writing it took him at least twenty years.[154] Such a long genesis helps explain his crisp opening of three

---

152 CW 8: 1-2, quoted in von Frank CW 9: l-li.
153 Emerson's Poetry Notebook, quoted in von Frank, CW 9: li.
154 Parts of Emerson's first lines date from his journal entry in 1846 ("I grow old") and from an 1847 letter ("to live within bounds" and to take "in sail") (von Frank, CW 9: xci). In the 1850s, he wrote a short fragment entitled "Terminus": "For thought & not praise;/ Thought is the wages/ For which I sell days,/Will gladly sell ages,/ And willing grow old, Deaf, & dumb, & blind, & cold,/ Melting matter into dreams, Panoramas which I saw/ And whatever glows or seems/ Into substance into Law[.]" See "Terminus," Emerson: Collected Poems and Translations, eds. Harold Bloom and Paul Kane (New York: Library of America, 1994), 419. Emerson's third collection, Selected Poems (1876), assembled with much help from others, contained no newly written poems. Von Frank, CW 9: xciv.

swiftly rendered lines: "It is time to be old, / To take in sail: —": Emerson is face-to-face with Fate, "the god of bounds." With a thundering "No more!" this god issues a cascade of commands, first cancelling Emerson's chief incentives, ambition and imagination, then prescribing what he must now do: "Contract thy firmament / To compass of a tent." He must also ration energy's " failing river," and, still honoring "the Giver," focus his remaining days on maturing "unfallen fruit" — projects undertaken but not yet completed. This deity of limit then allows Emerson ten full lines to "curse, if thou wilt, thy sires." He does indeed, blaming them for being among poets "deaf and dumb" and among "gladiators" — front-line reformers — "halt and numb." Yet as he had said in "Fate," ". . . freedom is necessary." Fated to give a ready yes to this god's "if thou wilt," Emerson has already escaped its power, and flies forward even more freely.

Proclaiming "As the bird trims her to the gale, / I trim myself to the storm of time / I man the rudder, reef the sail," he pledges that he will above all, "Obey the voice at eve obeyed at prime." Unmistakably, this is obedience to the "Ought" announced in *Nature* thirty years before, now become the voice of free will in "Fate" and the moral sentiment of "Worship" and "Character." The voice had told him then and continues to say, "'Lowly faithful, banish fear, / Right onward drive unharmed; / The port, well worth the cruise, is near, / And every wave is charmed.'"[155]

Emerson's choice of a poem as the means of facing his own mortality might have been predicted. Encouraged by Mary Moody Emerson, he had long envisioned becoming a prophetic poet. Certain poems realize that ambitious hope. The best lines in "Terminus" alone contradict his sense of being a poetic failure. In addition, his essay "The Poet" of twenty-three years before had been a uniquely inspirational analysis of what makes a modern poet, and his lectures often championed the scholar-poet as a "liberating god." Emerson was this scholar-poet par excellence. But ironically, it was his avid followers — Whitman, Dickinson, Frost, Stevens, and others — who surpassed him in quantity and quality of poems and in the convention-breaking style he advocated. Then and now, Emerson's deepest and widest success lies in having made his revolutionary thinking permeate the world

---

155 Young William Dean Howell's appreciation of "Terminus" in the *Atlantic Monthly* (1867) gives the poem an enduring and perceptive reading: "'Terminus' has a wonderful didactic charm, and must be valued as one of the noblest introspective poems in the language. The poet touches the reader by his acceptance of fate and age, and his serene trust of the future, yet is not moved by his own pathos" (von Frank, *CW* 9: xciii).

in prose infused with poetry. His lasting aphorisms succinctly capture that gift. One such saying in "Experience" (1844) anticipates his final arrival in "Terminus": "To finish the moment, to find the journey's end in every step of the road, to live the greatest number of good hours, is wisdom."[156]

4.17 Emerson at 76 with family on east side of "Bush," 1879.

---

156 *CW* 3: 35.

EMERSON'S LEGACY
IN AMERICA

5. Spawning a Wide New Consciousness

Jean McClure Mudge

This is my boast that I have no school & no follower. I should account it a measure of the impurity of insight, if it [my thought] did not create independence.

Emerson, *Journal*, 1859

On the lecture circuit, Emerson was a provoking charmer—a conscious persona he projected for what he called his new "art" or "theater." This style was vital to his goal: to speak "fully, symmetrically, gigantically . . . not dwarfishly & fragmentarily." Such an ambition required his most felt, practiced expression to touch, incite, and challenge. In 1844, someone was overheard to say, "The secret of his popularity is that he has a *damn* for everybody."[1] But Emerson deliberately irritated to inspire change. Most who heard him—whether comprehending, baffled or offended—were magnetized.

In 1868, James Russell Lowell, assessing the effect of Emerson's lecturing—his appearances would soon total 1,500 over four decades[2]— called him America's "most steadily attractive lecturer."

---

1   *The Journals and Miscellaneous Notebooks of Ralph Waldo Emerson*, 16 vols, eds. William H. Gilman, et al. (Cambridge, Mass.: Harvard University Press, 1960-1982), 9: 78 (hereafter *JMN*), as quoted in Albert J. von Frank, *An Emerson Chronology* (New York: G.K. Hall & Co., 1994), 1: 188.

2   Robert D. Richardson, Jr., *Emerson: The Mind on Fire* (Berkeley, CA: University of California Press, 1995), 418.

http://dx.doi.org/10.11647/OBP.0065.07

5.1 James Russell Lowell at 49, 1868.

5.2 Emerson's top hat, [n.d.].

Lowell professed, "We do not go to hear what Emerson says so much as to hear Emerson." The man seemed to *be* his message. Lowell described a typical audience as swept by a "rustle of sensation" as Emerson's "pithier thought, some keener flash of that humor . . . played about the horizon of his mind like heat-lightning . . . ." Lowell particularly pointed to Emerson's talent to raise "the supreme and everlasting originality of whatever bit of soul might be in any of us . . . ."[3] The real secret of his popularity, then, lay in inciting audiences to their deepest imaginative and spiritual possibilities.

This gift reflected the thoroughly modern aspect of Emerson's revolutionary message. From his first published words in the 1830s— *Nature*, "The American Scholar," and "The Divinity School" addresses— he had invited fresh views on any inherited matter, encouraged experimental thinking, and, in general, reflected his own intention of absorbing the world's chaos with the combined eyes of an inquisitive child and a cultured critic. His essay "Circles" expanded his key view of physical reality as constant flux, but guided by a higher spirit whose essence was moral law. This sense of a given contradiction at the heart of life—nature's ceaseless state of transition under an abidingly ethical World Soul—made ambiguity, paradox, and irony unsurprising to him.

Seized by the exciting fluidity of his "new philosophy," Emerson wanted to share it, yet avoid making disciples. He dearly valued friends of intellectual quality and true affection. But as seen in Chapter 2, his essays "Love" and "Friendship" (1841) clearly reflected his sense of the limits of even the most intimate personal relationships. He needed to keep his core self as private as possible, and he wanted to guard his working time. Above all, he would cultivate no disciples. Emerson told his journal, "This is my boast that I have no school & no follower. I should account it a measure of the impurity of insight, if it did not create independence."[4] He would encourage those attuned to morality's natural law and already confident self-starters, certainly not worshippers or sycophants. From near and far, however, disciples came, and by blossoming beyond him, fulfilled his primary wish. A. Bronson Alcott, Margaret Fuller, and Henry David Thoreau had formed

---

3   James Russell Lowell, "My Study Windows" (1971) in *Emerson in His Own Time*, eds. Ronald A. Bosco and Joel Myerson (Iowa City, IA: University of Iowa Press, 2003), 53-57.

4   *JMN* 14: 258.

a first nucleus. Afterward, five leading figures—Abraham Lincoln, Walt Whitman, Emily Dickinson, William James, and Frank Lloyd Wright— caught Emerson's fire, refashioning and adding to his thought in politics, poetry, philosophy, and the arts.

Abraham Lincoln (1809-1865)

Emerson's influence on Lincoln reached a climax at a crucial time, just as Lincoln was considering emancipation in the year 1862. For at least nine years before, and probably earlier, Lincoln had known about Emerson. In contrast, Emerson first took note of Lincoln only after he had won the Republican presidential nomination in 1860, registering the news, as he put it, "coldly and sadly."[5] Lincoln continued to champion the Union over emancipation, while Emerson had rapidly become one of its foremost advocates. Though both men opposed slavery, they were on different timetables, and for separate reasons, toward its abolition. Emerson's measured advancement of this cause would shortly bring them face to face. In retrospect, their encounter seems almost inevitable.

Lincoln's exposure to Emerson probably came first through the library of his law partner William H. Herndon, or "Billy," as Lincoln called his young fellow Kentuckian. In 1844, the two began their practice in Springfield, Illinois, the same year that Emerson joined forces with the abolitionists in his Concord speech and published *Essays II*. Lincoln and Herndon shared literary tastes, and both belonged to an informal "Poetical Society."[6] In an age of strong, even fierce regional loyalties, Herndon avowed that he regularly "turned *New Englandwards* for my ideas—my sentiments—my education." Drawn to leading thinkers, he was particularly interested in the Transcendentalists.[7]

Herndon kept his growing library in the office he shared with Lincoln, and would later list Emerson first among world-class writers to be found there. He reported, "Mr. Lincoln had access to all such books as I had and frequently read parts of the volumes, such as struck his fancy.

---

5   John McAleer, *Ralph Waldo Emerson: Days of Encounter* (Boston, Mass.: Little, Brown & Co., 1984), 569.

6   Interviews of James H. Matheny by W. H. Herndon, 1865-1855; Lincoln favored Shakespeare, Byron, and Burns, *Herndon's Informants: Letters, Interviews, and Statements about Abraham Lincoln*, eds. Douglas L. Wilson and Rodney O. Davis (Urbana, IL: University of Illinois Press, 1998), 470.

7   David H. Donald, *Lincoln* (New York: Simon & Shuster, 1995), 100-01.

I used to read to him passages in the books that struck me as eloquent, grand, poetical, philosophic, and the like."[8] Herndon also subscribed to abolitionist newsletters, among them the *National Anti-Slavery Standard*, *Emancipator*, and *National Era*, in the first of which Lincoln would have regularly been able to read positive reviews of Emerson's abolitionist addresses. He collected speeches of leading East Coast abolitionists. Friends sent him Garrison's *Liberator*, to which Emerson contributed.[9] In addition, Herndon "kept on my table" speeches by notable abolitionists— Parker, Giddings, Phillips, Sumner, Steward, and others, as well as antislavery histories and biographies. When he found "a good thing, a practical thing, I would read it to Lincoln. I urged him along as fast as I could."[10] Lincoln did not comment on his partner's favorite authors,[11] but he had had every opportunity to know about Emerson before he came to town.

That happened in 1853. From January 10-12, Emerson launched his lecturing in "the West" in Springfield, reading "The Anglo-Saxon," "Power," and "Culture" in the state House of Representatives. He stayed in what he called a "cabin" with a group of Illinois legislators, familiar to Lincoln from his days as a state legislator in the 1830s. In the 1840s, he had served as a U. S. Congressman.[12] From their encouragement and Herndon's, as well as his own curiosity, Lincoln may have heard all three of Emerson's lectures, but if only one, it was probably "Power." Its second sentence would have intrigued a man of Lincoln's high ambition: "Who shall set a limit to the influence of a human being?" After the lecture, he may even have shaken hands with Emerson at a dinner in the Senate Chamber.[13]

---

8   Emanuel Hertz, *The Hidden Lincoln: From the Letters and Papers of William H. Herndon* (New York: The Viking Press, 1938), 116.

9   See references to the *National Anti-slavery Standard* in *Emerson's Antislavery Writings*, eds. Len Gougeon and Joel Myerson (New Haven, CT: Yale University Press, 1995), 231; William Herndon to Jesse W. Weik, 28 October 1885, *Hidden Lincoln*, 96.

10 Ibid.

11 Donald, 168.

12 Von Frank, *Chronology*, 281; McAleer, 457; *Lincoln Day By Day: A Chronology, 1809-1865*, ed. Earl Schenck Miers (Washington, D.C.: Lincoln Sesquicentennial Commission, 1960), 2: 91. Hereafter *Lincoln Day by Day*.

13 *The Collected Works of Ralph Waldo Emerson*, 10 vols., eds. Robert E. Spiller, et al. (Cambridge, Mass.: Harvard University Press, 1971-2013), 6: 28. Hereafter *CW*. *Lincoln Day by Day*, 91.

5.3 Abraham Lincoln at 45, 27 October 1854.

Seven years later in 1860, both men were at the peak of their careers and on the road to emancipation, though by quite different routes. Lincoln became an abolitionist in 1854, ten years after Emerson, when Senator Douglas introduced the Kansas-Nebraska Bill. By his eloquence and character, Lincoln became his circle's leader. But according to Herndon, he was "too conservative for some of us . . . and yet I stuck to Lincoln in the hopes of his sense of justice and eternal right."[14] Lincoln had always been politically wary on racial matters, a position only reinforced by winning the presidency without any Southern support. Separatism clearly threatened. He thus took his first duty as chief public servant to be the preservation of the country as a whole, with its slave-tolerant Constitution. He would not prioritize abolition. On the analogy of the human body, Lincoln argued that the life (unity) of the country was essential to the existence of any part. [15] In contrast, by 1860, the independent scholar Emerson had been a

---

14   Herndon to Weik, 28 October 1885, *Hidden Lincoln*, 96.
15   Abraham Lincoln to A. G. Hodges (April 4, 1864) and to Charles D. Robinson (August

strenuous abolitionist for sixteen years. His 1844 Concord speech had been angry enough. But when the Compromise of 1850 reinforced the Fugitive Slave Law, he spoke in white heat against the "slave power." After war broke out in April 1861, Emerson, principled and firm, pressed for freeing the slaves immediately. Lincoln, beyond his official and political scruples, hoped to enlist both the Border States and former slaves to the Union side, and waited for a better military moment to press for such a change.

For abolitionists, that wait seemed interminable. In the first year of fighting, the North suffered huge setbacks while also failing to take opportunities against the South. Impatient abolitionists took their issue to Lincoln's doorstep through the Washington Lecture Association (WLA), one of emancipation's most active arms in the still slave-owning District of Columbia. From mid-December 1861 to April 1862, the WLA—one of whose leaders was Emerson's friend, Massachusetts Senator Charles Sumner—sponsored a marathon, twenty-two-part lecture series on emancipation, held in the Smithsonian Institution, the capitol's largest public hall. With Congress in winter session, speakers attracted the capitol's political and social elite with an average attendance of over 1,000.[16]

Just weeks before Emerson spoke, Horace Greeley, editor of the *New-York Tribune*, the country's most widely distributed newspaper, had seized his moment to roundly criticize Lincoln, who was seated behind him on the platform. He first questioned Lincoln's reversal of Maj. Gen. John C. Fremont's grant of freedom to all slaves in Missouri. Then turning to face Lincoln, Greeley demanded that ending slavery must be the "sole purpose of the war." The audience loudly applauded. Lincoln did not join in. Nor did he attend any other lectures in the series, including Emerson's. But he did meet privately with later speakers.[17]

Before leaving for Washington on 31 January 1862 for his turn in the series, Emerson was clearly primed to go, writing in his journal, "It is impossible to extricate oneself from the question in which your age is involved. You can no more keep out of politics than you can keep out of the frost."[18] Eagerness, however, did not make him confrontational. Unlike

17, 1864), *The Collected Works of Abraham Lincoln,* ed. Roy P. Basler (New Brunswick, NJ: Rutgers University Press, 1953), 281-83, 499-502.

16　Michael F. Conlin, "The Smithsonian Abolition Lecture Controversy: The Clash of Antislavery Politics with American Science in Wartime Washington," *Civil War History* 46: 4: 301, 303, 304, 305, 310, 311.

17　Ibid., 312-13.

18　*JMN* 15: 182.

Greeley, Emerson came to Washington in an irenic mood, perhaps calmed by the high tone of his title, "American Civilization." Beginning with a rhetorical search to define civilization, he finally settled on "the evolution of a highly organized man, brought to supreme delicacy of sentiment, as in practical power, religion, liberty, sense of honor, and taste."[19] Emerson elaborated on this theme, emphasizing morality as the great prize of civilization. He also announced the state's highest goal: to secure "the greatest good of the greatest number" (John Stuart Mill's refinement of Jeremy Bentham's utilitarian maxim). The "greatest number" for Emerson, of course, included the slaves, or 12.5% of the population in 1860.[20]

Turning to slavery, Emerson charged the South with vitiating the greatest good by "denying a man's right to his labor." He argued that humanity's first purpose was to work, "the visible sign of his power." The South's institution (or as he put it, "destitution") of slavery had stolen this most basic function from blacks and set back civilization's progress. The South had become an oligarchy as compared to the North's democracy. "Servile war" had been the result. In this situation, Emerson now presented the government, in effect Lincoln, with a challenge. Civilization required heroic, practical action. In this "new and exceptional age," Emerson proclaimed, "America is another word for Opportunity." A frugal Yankee himself, he was appealing to business-oriented America, rightly or wrongly stressing that for some decades slavery had proven to be quite unprofitable.

Once again taking the long view, Emerson brought his speech to a climax by announcing, "Emancipation is the demand of civilization. That is a principle; everything else is intrigue. This . . . progressive policy, — puts every man in the South in just and natural relations with every man in the North, laborer with laborer." Briefly summarizing familiar reasons for emancipation, he then posed a fresh and realistic option: Congress, whose duty was the country's military defense, could independently issue an edict abolishing slavery, "and pay for such slaves as we ought to pay for." This move would bring slaves near and far into the North's armies. Yet the only permanent solution, Emerson acknowledged, would be an executive

---

19   "American Civilization," April 1862, CW 10: 394.
20   Emerson could have read Mill's nuanced version of Bentham's utilitarianism in Fraser's Magazine, serially published in 1861, in which Mill made quality more important than quantity in defining what was good. Also, Bentham's phrase had originally been, "the greatest good *for* the greatest number" [italics mine]. John Stuart Mill, http://www.iep. utm.edu/milljs/. Of a total U.S. population of 31,443,321, nearly 4 million, or 12.5%, were slaves. https://en.wikipedia.org/wiki/1860_United_States_Census

proclamation of emancipation, permissible to the president in wartime. He added, "The power of Emancipation is this, that it alters the atomic social constitution of the Southern people." It would let poor whites, as well as blacks, earn wages for their labor, and therefore help unify society. Emerson followed with a crucial point: "Emancipation removes the whole objection to union." Freeing the slaves, he argued, would only strengthen Lincoln's first aim in fighting the war! True to form, Emerson added a moral note, "The measure at once puts all parties right." Justice would then come to any race—"white, red, yellow or black."

Emerson's ending illustrates how fully he had applied his Transcendentalism to the major social issue of his day and solidified his transformation into a pragmatic idealist. Simultaneously, he had elevated Lincoln, rather than chastised him. "Nature works through her appointed elements; and ideas must work through the brains and the arms of good and brave men, or they are no better than dreams."[21] Beyond Emerson's flattery, Lincoln would have seen his clever, convincing point: socially and economically, emancipation would help preserve the Union. Emerson had shown Lincoln how his private preference for abolition might now be joined with his long-sought goal of keeping the nation together.

Only forty-eight hours after Emerson's speech, on February 2 and 3, 1862, he found himself in the White House being introduced to Lincoln by Charles Sumner. As Emerson shook hands with Lincoln, he knew that his friend Moncure Conway, a Southern abolitionist minister transplanted to Boston, had spoken two weeks before at the Smithsonian. Conway had predicted that immediate emancipation would start a slave revolt, greatly weakening, maybe fatally wounding, the South. Afterward, Lincoln had told Conway, "I think the country grows in this direction daily, and I am not without hope that something of the desire of you and your friends may be accomplished."[22]

Emerson was also aware that the president, not having heard his speech, at best only knew its essence. But rather than discuss emancipation, the two simply assessed each other. They had much in common. Both were great readers, fond of poetry and Shakespeare. Both were also ambitious public servants, close students of power who deeply wished to be remembered widely and well. But Emerson's role as a free-lance lecturer

---

21   *CW* 10: 410.
22   Conlin, 317; Gay Wilson Allen, *Waldo Emerson: A Biography* (New York: Viking, 1981), 612.

allowed him more independence than Lincoln. Lawyer-president Lincoln had to adjust conflicting parties, including his private views, to pragmatic, legal solutions. In his thinking, Emerson was revolutionary; Lincoln was much more conservative. Lincoln, always ready with stories and jokes, was also more social than the distant Emerson. Furthermore, strong sectional differences underlay their encounter: Emerson's Northeastern privilege and formal education sharply contrasted with Lincoln's Western raw energy and self-culture.

Emerson recorded that Lincoln—always ready to disarm—had begun their conversation with this mischievous sally: "'O Mr Emerson, I once heard you say in a lecture, that a Kentuckian seems to say by his air & manners, 'Here am I; if you don't like me, the worse for you [Emerson's emphasis].'"[23] Lincoln, the humble Kentuckian now president, was effectively saying, "So?" Perhaps both laughed—Lincoln, because he usually did so after such a tease, and Emerson because he no doubt took the tease as playful self-defense. But he might have corrected the president. In "Power," rather than denigrating Westerners, Emerson applauds their health, energy, and strength, especially in politics. They are free, robust models of his vaunted self-reliance.[24]

Emerson judged Lincoln at first hand straightforwardly and well: "The President impressed me more favorably than I had hoped. A frank, sincere, well-meaning man, with a lawyer's habit of mind, good clear statement of his fact, correct enough, not vulgar, as described; but with a sort of boyish cheerfulness, or that kind of sincerity & jolly good meaning that our class meetings on Commencement Days show when telling our old stories over. When he has made his remark, he looks up at you with great satisfaction, & shows all his white teeth, & laughs."[25] Five days after they met, Lincoln ordered Emerson's *Representative Men* from the Library of Congress.[26] Though his chosen figures were all of the Old World, the

---

23   *JMN* 15: 187. Although the printed version of Emerson's lecture "Power" does not mention Kentuckians, it does extol the raw energy of the rough, ready, even coarse Western men (the "Hoosier, Sucker, Wolverine, Badger") versus pampered, elite Americans (like himself).

24   *CW* 6: 33.

25   *JMN* 15: 187. The next year, Emerson privately noted Lincoln's coarseness and lack of taste but counted his proven virtues—directness and honesty—more important. *Emerson in His Journals*, ed. Joel Porte (Cambridge, Mass.: Harvard University Press), 511.

26   Entry for 7 February 1862, The Lincoln Log, http://www.thelincolnlog.org/Results.aspx?type=CalendarDay&day=1862-02-07; *Lincoln Day By Day*, 3: 93.

first chapter, entitled "Uses of Great Men," would have impressed the pragmatic Lincoln. Emerson recognized individuals as truly great only if they benefited the common good, and went on to say, "Great men exist that there may be greater men," a comment that would have appealed to Lincoln's capacity for humility.

In April, the *Atlantic Monthly* published Emerson's speech with a newly added coda. In it, Emerson again praised Lincoln, this time for his recommendation to Congress in early March for government-supported compensation to any state that enacted a gradual end to slavery. For Emerson, Lincoln had expressed, as he put it, "his own thought in his own style. All thanks and honor to the Head of State!" Claiming that the whole country applauded the move, Emerson urged that emancipation follow right away. At the same time, he clearly understood Lincoln's delicate position, ending, "More and better than the President has spoken shall, perhaps, the effect of the Message be, —but, we are sure, not more or better than he hoped in his heart, when, thoughtful of all the complexities of his position, he penned these cautious words."[27]

Lincoln, an *Atlantic* reader, could not have missed this April issue. Perhaps he read it before indicating that he wished to sign a bill abolishing slavery in the capitol, which he did on April 5. Two days later he signed a treaty with England to suppress the African slave trade (which became an act that he signed on July 11). But Lincoln's timing in making public any change in the war's goals still depended on the fate of military events. Union reversals continued, keeping Lincoln, as in previous months, daily immersed in war strategies and tactics. The lack of troops was always a problem. A stream of domestic and foreign business also continued. Nevertheless, all along, Lincoln was moving toward what Emerson and others had urged: the use of his executive power in wartime to negate the constitutional protection long given to slavery.[28]

On June 19, Lincoln secretly read a draft Emancipation Proclamation to his vice president, Hannibal Hamlin, while the North continued to suffer severe setbacks and heavy casualties. He did not sleep well and was observably "weary, care-worn and troubled." A month of similar pressures

---

27 Emerson, "American Civilization," *Atlantic Monthly* (April 1862), 502-11. See Cornell University Making of America, http://ebooks.library.cornell.edu/cgi/t/text/pageviewer-idx?c=atla;cc=atla;rgn=full%20text;idno=atla0009-4;didno=atla0009-4;view=image;seq=0508;node=atla0009-4%3A14; also *Lincoln Day by Day*, 3: 98.

28 Doris Kearns Goodwin, *Team of Rivals: The Political Genius of Abraham Lincoln* (New York: Simon & Schuster, 2005), 462-63.

went by. Then on July 22, Lincoln read his draft of the proclamation to the cabinet. He also issued an executive order that included two items that Emerson had been urging since January: pay for black workers if used by Union troops, and compensation, too, to their former owners, for any of their property, including slaves.[29] Then at summer's end came the "Northern victory" at the battle of Antietam, Maryland. In Lee's first attempt to move Southern troops into the North, he was repulsed and retreated, but only after 6,000 had died and 17,000 were wounded. Neither side won. Even though Lee had been forced to withdraw, McClellan failed to pursue him into Virginia.[30] Nevertheless, the *New York Times* heralded the battle as a turning point for the North: Southerners had been forced to flee Union territory.

Five days later, on September 22, Lincoln—evidently ready to go— released his preliminary Emancipation Proclamation. In effect, it annulled the Fugitive Slave Law and promised compensation to those slave-owners who had been loyal to the Union throughout the rebellion. In addition, Lincoln announced that on January 1, 1863, a hundred days hence, he would declare "forever free" the slaves in all the states that were still in arms against the North.[31] To his journal, Emerson exulted, "Great is the virtue of the Proclamation. It works when men are sleeping, when the Army goes into winter quarters, when generals are treacherous or imbecile."[32]

Then began Emerson's role as one of Lincoln's greatest promoters, immeasurably enhancing the president's prestige and political fortunes. Just days after the proclamation, Emerson spoke at a Boston abolitionist rally, enthusiastically calling it "a poetic act," advancing both "catholic" and "universal" interests. He equated the proclamation with landmark events in the nation's history from the planting of America, to the Declaration of Independence, to the end of British slavery in the West Indies. Lincoln's "capacity and virtue" made him nothing less than an "instrument" of "Divine Providence," Emerson declared. He continued, "[Lincoln] has been permitted to do more for America than any other American man." Moreover, this "dazzling success" eclipsed Lincoln's previous delay and

---

29 *Lincoln Day By Day*, 3: 104, 105, 126,127-28, 129.

30 Antietam Battle Description, http://www.civilwarhome.com/antietam.html; Goodwin, 468-69, 481.

31 *Lincoln Day By Day*, 3: 141; Preliminary Emancipation Proclamation, September 22, 1862, http://www.archives.gov/exhibits/american_originals_iv/sections/preliminary_ emancipation_proclamation.html

32 *JMN* 15: 291.

any weaknesses Emerson had earlier noted. The president now epitomized "endurance, wisdom, magnanimity." Emerson then offered his highest praise, connecting the president's *realpolitik* with Transcendentalism in a single sentence: the Proclamation had delivered Americans "from our false position," planting citizens on "a law of Nature . . . ." Lincoln had in effect become Emerson's first "Representative Man" of the New World. In a less lofty style, the president remarked on Sept. 28: "The North responds to the proclamation sufficiently in breath; but breath alone kills no rebels."[33]

Lincoln had not only adopted key abolitionist points that Emerson had presented in January and April, but apparently had also absorbed Emerson's point of view as well as his tone, perhaps even his expression. In the president's annual message to Congress on December 1, 1862, he repeated his assent to swift emancipation, but from a new perspective, opposite to what it had been a year before. His first inaugural address had looked to the past—to the Constitution and the Union. Now, announcing that the war's goal was to end slavery, Lincoln spoke of the present and future in the style of Emerson. (His message, equivalent to our current State of the Union address, thus intended to mold public opinion, was widely printed and discussed.)[34] In *Nature* (1836), Emerson had rhetorically asked, "Why should not we also enjoy an original relation to the universe?" Twenty-six years later, Lincoln's affirmation, "As our case is new, so we must think anew, and act anew" resounds with Emerson's question. Lincoln's talents made this December message fully his own, but his words echo the coda to Emerson's "American Civilization": "Our whole history appears like a last effort of the Divine Providence in behalf of the human race." Eight months later, Lincoln concluded his remarks, sounding Emerson's liberty note and secularizing his phrase about the last effort of providence: "In *giving* freedom to the *slave*, we *assure* freedom to the *free*— . . . We shall nobly save, or meanly lose, the last best, hope of earth."[35]

Less than a year after they met, Emerson and Lincoln came together in spirit to celebrate January 1, 1863, Emancipation Day. In Boston, over

---

33   Emerson, "The President's Proclamation," *CW* 10: 435; *Lincoln Day By Day*, 3: 142.

34   James M. McPherson, *"We Cannot Escape History": Lincoln and the Last Best Hope of Earth* (Urbana, IL: University of Illinois Press, 1995), 1-2; Ronald C. White, Jr., *The Eloquent President* (New York: Random House, 2005), 171, 177, 181.

35   White, Appendix 7: "[Lincoln's] Annual Message to Congress, December 1, 1862," 383. Three years later, Emerson's lasting recognition of Lincoln's shift led him to extol the president, often criticized for his rustic crude ways, for exhibiting "a grace beyond his own, a dignity, dropping all pretension & trick, and arrives . . . at a simplicity, which is the perfection of manners" (*JMN* 15: 465).

6,000 gathered in two of the city's largest venues, Tremont Temple and the Music Hall. At the Music Hall, the Boston Symphony struck up Beethoven's "Consecration of the House" overture as Emerson—with Longfellow, Whittier, Oliver Wendell Holmes, Sr., and Harriet Beecher Stowe (Frederick Douglass was at the Temple)—waited for word to come from Washington that Lincoln had, in fact, signed the Emancipation Proclamation. At ten o'clock that night, a telegraphed message confirmed the fact. Emerson, first on the program, read a just-finished poem, "Boston Hymn." Boston, he said, was to abolition as Concord had been to independence. His poem "Concord Hymn" of 1836 had celebrated the Revolution. Now, twenty-five years later, his "Boston Hymn" was consecrating emancipation, but with an important difference: "Concord Hymn" had been *Emerson's* song; "Boston Hymn" he made *God's*. Near its end, he has the divine voice command, "Pay ransom to the owner, / And fill the bag to the brim. / Who is the owner? The slave is owner, / And ever was. Pay him." Electrified by his lines, Emerson's long pent-up audience—including at least a few blacks—rose, wildly shouting and singing.[36]

In the proclamation's final form, Lincoln had made a single, but momentous change: blacks could now officially serve in the Union army.[37] The North-South balance of power stood to shift enormously. Emerson and his friends quickly seized their chance and helped form two black regiments in Massachusetts. Later, in a speech he repeatedly gave, "Fortune of the Republic," Emerson virtually campaigned for Lincoln's reelection in 1864. But when Lee surrendered on April 9, 1865, Emerson found Grant's terms too lax. He also feared that Lincoln's desire to return the South peacefully to the Union and thus not impose retributions would allow northern Democrats to help the South undermine the North's victory.

Yet Lincoln's assassination, just five days later, brought Emerson back to his former praise. At Concord's annual commemoration of the Revolution, he noted Lincoln's virtues, in particular his sense of humor: It was ". . . a rich gift to this wise man. It enabled him to . . . meet every kind of man, and every rank in society; to take off the edge of the severest decisions; to mask his own purpose and sound his companion; and to catch with true instinct the temper of every company he addressed . . . ." Emerson continued, warmly celebrating Lincoln as this "aboriginal man," this Kentuckian, this

---

36   CW 9: 381-84; Goodwin, 499-500; McAleer, 573-74; Allen, 618.
37   Abraham Lincoln, "The Emancipation Proclamation, January 1, 1863," http://www.4uth. gov.ua/usa/english/facts/funddocs/emanc.htm

first middle-class president for "this middle class country." Finally, he mused on what providence (nature or fate) revealed in Lincoln's passing. "[W]hat if it should turn out that [Lincoln] had reached the term . . . and what remained to be done required new and uncommitted hands . . . and that Heaven . . . shall make him serve his country even more by his death than by his life?"[38] Emerson may have often pondered that question when passing Lincoln's portrait in his upstairs hallway, where it still hangs today.

5.4 Abraham Lincoln at 56, c. 1865.

Walt Whitman (1819-1892)

In 1842, Whitman first heard Emerson's speech, "Poetry of the Times"—a study for his seminal lecture "The Poet." Afterward, he immersed himself in Emerson's words. Thirteen years later, in 1855, Emerson was the most prominent critic among the few who welcomed Whitman's *Leaves of Grass*.

---

38 Emerson, "Remarks at the Funeral Services Held in Concord, April 19, 1865," W 9, Miscellanies; http://www.RWE.org

Despite the book's increasing popularity over the next twenty-five years, especially among a small avant garde, most critics kept attacking its free rambling style, earthiness, and shocking sensuality. Even Emerson, who was no prude, implored Whitman to temper his challenges to convention. Whitman in turn could be disappointed with Emerson, but never lost his loving loyalty to this first and major mentor. At the end of his life, he kept at hand an unframed photograph of Emerson. A dozen or so times, his young friend and secretary Horace Traubel rescued it from the floor. He described the portrait, "Emerson at his best: radiant, clean, with that far-in-the-future look which seemed to possess him in the best hours."[39] The photograph's shifts between table and floor suggest that the failing Whitman enjoyed studying it as a reminder of his debt to one so different from himself in background and education but so like him in soul.

By his eleventh birthday in 1830, Whitman, from a modest but large East Long Island family, had had all the formal education he would receive. His family moved to Brooklyn for a time, but when they returned to the country, the early teenage Walt, now trained as a printer's apprentice and compositor, stayed on in New York City. Its catastrophic fires of 1835, however, sent him back to Long Island where he wrote for newspapers and taught school. Then, in 1845, Brooklyn again became the family home. Like Poe, Whitman's combative nature meant that he would be in and out of jobs that also included building and contracting. But early access to a lending library had given him the habit of wide, voracious reading. His job experience also made him sympathetic with workingmen and liberal causes, a tendency reinforced by his family's political radicalism, Quakerism on his mother's side, and the highly politicized, brawling world of journalism. But Whitman much preferred literary writing to reporting. By the early 1840s, he had published standard essays, semi-autobiographical short stories, and routine, rhyming poetry. They all reflected his generally depressed late adolescence.[40]

Then in early March 1842 came Emerson on his second lecture trip to New York City.[41] Twenty-year-old Whitman reported his speech on "Poetry

39   Walt Whitman to Horace Traubel, *Intimate with Walt: Selections from Whitman's Conversations with Horace Traubel, 1888-1892*, ed. Gary Schmidgall (Iowa City, IA: University of Iowa Press, 2001), 218.

40   Jerome Loving, *Walt Whitman: The Song of Himself* (Berkeley, CA: University of California Press, 1999), 32-42, 39, 50-51; see also Gay Wilson Allen, "Whitman Chronological Table," *The New Walt Whitman Handbook* (New York: New York University Press, 1975), xi-xvii.

41   Emerson first lectured in New York in 1840, before he was widely published; Whitman

of the Times" for the *New York Aurora*: "The Transcendentalist had a very full house on Saturday evening." Then he summarized Emerson's most arresting points: "He said that the first man who called another an ass was a poet. Because the business of the poet is expression—the giving utterance to the emotions and sentiments of the soul; and metaphors." Whitman declined "to do the lecturer great injustice" with further comment, but ended by claiming he had heard "one of the richest and most beautiful compositions, both for its matter and style, we have ever heard anywhere, at any time." Emerson had outlined the poet's power, his tools, and his present and future roles. Like James Russell Lowell, Whitman felt his best self had been called forth. Afterward, he reviewed Emerson's remaining five lectures in this series. In one review, he tried to compare Emerson and Kant's philosophies; of Emerson's last lecture, "Prospects," he noted, "We should not be surprised if he made a good many converts in Gotham." Whitman was clearly one.[42]

Besides these known direct encounters, from 1842 until Whitman began writing *Leaves of Grass* in the early 1850s, Emerson's ideas were readily available both in print and in person. Margaret Fuller reviewed her friend's *Essays II* (1844) in the *New-York Tribune* in 1845; "The Poet" had headed that collection. During this time, too, Whitman's pieces in leading New York journals and as editor and book reviewer of the Brooklyn *Daily Eagle* in 1846-1847 led him to explore authors who had fed Emerson's Transcendentalism: Carlyle, Coleridge, Goethe, George Sand, and Schlegel. His reactions foretold the encompassing, free-ranging, frank writer he would become.[43] Then in 1843 and again in 1850, Emerson gave two lecture series in New York City, each of nine parts, the first in February 1843 (one lecture was repeated in Brooklyn) and another series in January and March 1850 (three were also given in Brooklyn). In February 1852, Emerson's comments on "Power" for the People's Lectures at New York's Broadway Tabernacle would again have stimulated Whitman's ambitions. Finally, the outspoken Freesoiler Whitman, as idiosyncratic an abolitionist as Emerson, would have eagerly heard him speak on "The Fugitive Slave Law" at the New York Anti-Slavery Society, on March 7, 1854. Whitman later recalled attending either this lecture or Emerson's "American Slavery" on February 6, 1855, also for the Society.[44]

---

   was on Long Island, not to return to Manhattan until 1841. Von Frank, 151, 169-70; Loving, 50.

42   Gay Wilson Allen, *Waldo Emerson* (New York: Viking Press, 1981), 400-01.

43   Justin Kaplan, *Walt Whitman: A Life* (New York: Simon & Schuster, 1980), 128, 172, 173.

44   Von Frank, 179-80, 252-55, 272, 294; Loving, 158.

Other cultural forces shaping Whitman strengthened the appeal of Emerson's themes. Emerson's self-reliance worked hand-in-glove with the individualism and stand-alone psychology that Alexis de Tocqueville described in *Democracy in America* (1835-1840). The enormously popular pseudo-science of phrenology—reading character by cranial bumps—with its motto of "Self Made or Never Made" fascinated Whitman. Emerson, Daniel Webster, and Henry Ward Beecher all had their heads "read."[45] Then, too, Manhattan's new daguerreotype galleries probably provided the image Whitman used when he wrote "Pictures" in 1853-1854, a preliminary study to *Leaves*. In the "gallery" of his mind, Whitman housed images of historic and contemporary places and people. Among the latter easily hung on his walls was the "tall and slender" Emerson standing "at the lecturer's desk, lecturing."[46]

Whitman's familiarity with Emerson was so deep that by age thirty-five, when he came to publish his slim green volume on or near 4 July 1855—its gilt title *Leaves of Grass* auspiciously sprouting roots—he sent Emerson a copy, as if to please a primary mentor.

5.5 Walt Whitman at 34-36, 1853-1855.

45   Kaplan, 148-49.
46   Loving, 158.

He later reportedly admitted, "My ideas were simmering and simmering, and Emerson brought them to a boil."[47] Emerson's response in a letter of July 21 overflowed with enthusiasm. This "wonderful gift," he felt, was nothing less than "the most extraordinary piece of wit & wisdom that America has yet contributed." Reading it gave him "great joy" for its "free & brave thought" as well as for its "courage of *treatment*," a sign of "large perception." "I rubbed my eyes a little to see if this sunbeam were no illusion," Emerson admitted, "but the solid sense of the book is a sober certainty." A few months later, the elated Whitman printed the whole letter, without permission, in the *Tribune*. More, for the spine of his second 1856 edition, he quoted from this letter again: "I greet you at the / Beginning of A / Great Career / R. W. Emerson." In its pages, Whitman responded to Emerson's letter with one of his own, calling him "Master." He never admitted any wrongdoing in printing Emerson's endorsements, nor did the mildly miffed Emerson ever complain to him. Rather the reverse: Emerson sought out Whitman in December 1855, calling on him in Brooklyn after giving a lecture there. The two then walked the three miles to Manhattan for dinner at the Astor House.[48]

Five years later, in mid-March 1860, Whitman again met Emerson, this time in Boston. On the home turf of "proper Bostonians," two young radical publishers were bravely bringing out a third, expanded version of *Leaves*. In Whitman's humble rented room and on Boston Common, Emerson—who did most of the talking—tried to persuade him "for the sake of the people" to remove his most sexually explicit "Children of Adam" poems. Emerson felt they would prematurely draw moralistic fire, be banned in Boston, and diminish Whitman's potentially broad appeal. Whitman knew that Emerson spoke to protect and promote him, not to defend New England respectability. But he adamantly refused to censor himself: "What does a man come to with his virility gone?" he asked. His *Leaves* of 1860, unlike contemporary versions of the Bible and Shakespeare, remained unexpurgated—except for the removal of earlier letters from or to Emerson. As the two went off to dine at the American House, Whitman had already taken the independent stance Emerson would have hoped for. He had become his own man.[49]

---

47   Whitman to John T. Trowbridge, quoted in Richardson, 527-28.
48   Loving, 189-90, 209-11.
49   Ibid., 240-41; Richardson, 528-29; Kaplan, 251.

Afterward, a certain cooling between the two occurred. They both championed nature and the natural man—soul and body—as filled with meanings that transcended this world. But the patrician-scholar Emerson emphasized "Soul, Soul, and more Soul," while the laborer-singer Whitman proclaimed himself to be first "the poet of the Body," and then "the poet of the Soul." In "Song of Myself," "Walt Whitman" sang with unabashed pride of being a "turbulent, fleshly, sensual, eating, drinking and breeding" self.[50] In contrast, Emerson had long ago sternly repressed his deepest desires for both sexes, a stance belied by his repeated regret for lacking "animal spirits." Face to face with the uninhibited Whitman, these emotions could flash through Emerson's restraint. More than once, Whitman recalled, Emerson had said, "'I envy you your capacity for being at home with anybody in any crowd.'" And at another moment, Emerson seemed to probe both his private desires and *Leaves*'s openly androgynous ones by asking him, in Whitman's words, "'Don't you fear now and then that your freedom, your ease, your nonchalance, with men may be misunderstood?'" Whitman posed a counter question, "'Do you misunderstand it?' He put his hand on my arm and said: 'No: I see it for what it is: it is beautiful.'"[51]

Emerson's envy of Whitman's sexual frankness, however, may well have helped turn his earlier irritations into at least mild antagonism. Also, Emerson's friends, heavy with anti-Whitman prejudice, must have affected him, though he did not share their ethical scruples. (Earlier, he had written that the poet he was looking for would speak with words not used in polite society.) In 1856, one friend in his circle could not hide self-righteousness behind a little joke: the *Leaves'* author "had every leaf but the fig leaf."[52] In 1860, Lidian (with Alcott's wife and Thoreau's mother) shunned Whitman in Concord, forcing Emerson to meet him in Boston.[53] Though Emerson had sent Alcott and Thoreau to see Whitman, his first exuberance was already subdued in 1856 when he wrote Carlyle: "One book, last summer, came out in New York, a nondescript monster which yet had terrible eyes and buffalo strength, and was indisputably American."[54] Emerson seems

---

50   Cf. Emerson's "American Scholar" with Whitman's "Song of Myself" 21, line 422; 24, line 498.
51   Whitman probably did not exaggerate Emerson's response. Otherwise young Traubel, often critical of Whitman's hyperbole, would have challenged him. Whitman to Traubel, 217.
52   *JMN* 14: 74.
53   Loving, 470; Allen, 666-67.
54   Loving, 209.

to have been torn in his estimate; for him, *Leaves* was a cross between the "*Bhagavad Gita* and the *New-York Tribune*,"[55] inspiration married to mere reportage.

In 1863, Whitman, searching for a job in the office of Secretary of State William Seward, sought and received a letter of recommendation from Emerson that characterized his writings as "in certain points open to criticism."[56] Not surprisingly, Whitman did not use the reference. The same year, Emerson wrote in his journal under the heading "Good out of evil," "[O]ne must thank Walt Whitman for service to American literature in the Apalachian [sic] enlargement of his outline and treatment."[57] "Apalachian" values Whitman's frontier-like breadth as it also hints of cultural limit. Then, in 1874, Emerson published a poetry anthology, *Parnassus*, which did not include Whitman—or himself, for that matter. Meant for family parlor readings, it was produced with the help of Emerson's daughter Edith, no fan of Whitman's. And the anthologies of the poetry establishment—collections of poems edited by Bryant, Whittier, and others—also omitted Whitman.[58]

Meanwhile, after 1860, the isolated Whitman kept promoting himself as America's best present and future poet. By 1867, he brought out a larger *Leaves* in a fourth edition. In 1871, when a fifth version, also enlarged, appeared, Emerson's opinion must have reached Whitman through a mutual friend: "I expect—him—to make—the songs of the—nation—but he seems contented to make the inventories."[59] No wonder Whitman found Emerson's lectures in Baltimore and Washington the next year stale—"the same themes as twenty-five years ago."[60] And in 1880, on the celebration of Emerson's seventy-seventh birthday, in "Emerson's Books (The Shadows of Them)," Whitman acknowledged Emerson's pioneering role in pressing for "freedom and wildness and simplicity and spontaneity," but he found that excessive culture had kept him several removes from true, organic nature. In short, Emerson was too refined.[61] Yet just the next year, Whitman, who was in Boston to work on the last edition of *Leaves*, visited Concord. He went to a family dinner at Emerson's, invited by a now welcoming

---

55 Paul Zweig, *Walt Whitman: The Making of the Poet* (New York: Basic Books, 1984), 8.
56 Whitman to Traubel, *Conversations*, ed. Gary Schmidgall , 221.
57 *JMN* 15: 379.
58 Richardson, 570; Loving, 361-62; Kaplan, 354.
59 Kaplan, 353.
60 Allen, 653.
61 Loving, 395.

Lidian. Once again, Whitman was drawn by Emerson's mere presence, the constant cheerfulness of his last years only augmenting his personal aura.[62] A decade later, as Whitman neared his own death, he recalled Emerson's distancing dignity, yet how "free, easy, liquid" he had always been with him.

5.6 Walt Whitman at 68, 1887.

Whisking away decades of strain, Whitman's lasting memory of Emerson was of his "phenomenal sweetness."[63] Emerson's photo, constantly loose on his table or floor, spoke of Whitman's ongoing loyalty to his first master.

Emily Elizabeth Dickinson (1830-1886)

In stark contrast to Whitman, there is no record that Emily Dickinson ever met Emerson, or even heard him lecture. But it is highly likely that she did. In the thirty years from 1849 to 1879, Emerson spoke in the Connecticut

---

62   McAleer, 647-48; Loving, 408-09.
63   Schmidgall, ed., 216, 218.

Valley seven times, and Dickinson lived her entire life in that valley, in Amherst, Massachusetts, a town of only about 3,000.[64] She certainly knew about his appearances from family, friends, and the local press. Despite this lack of sure encounter, Emerson greatly influenced Dickinson's work, as has been widely acknowledged. But it has not been noted that he gave her the self-confidence, direction, and model of solitude that inspired her very destiny. Dickinson would come to epitomize Emerson's ideal of the solitary scholar-poet at home.

When Emerson began lecturing near Amherst, eighteen-year-old Dickinson was just awakening to her poetic potential. That talent was evident to Benjamin Newton, her father's law student, who began tutoring her after her single year at Mt. Holyoke Seminary.

5.7 Emily Dickinson at 16, 1846.

Newton had come to Amherst in 1847 from Worcester,[65] near Boston and Cambridge, within the swirl of theological dust kicked up by Emerson's "Divinity School Address" less than a decade before. A Unitarian, he

---

64   Amherst was even smaller; this average also includes inhabitants of nearby towns. Edward W. Carpenter, *The History of the Town of Amherst* (Amherst, Mass.: Carpenter & Morehouse Press, 1896), 604. Ref. kindness of Tevis Kimball, Special Collections, Jones Library, Amherst.

65   Alfred Habegger, *My Wars Are Laid Away: The Life of Emily Dickinson* (New York: Random House, 2001), 216.

appears to have wholly embraced Emerson, and Emily soon considered him an "elder brother" who "became to me a gentle, yet grave Preceptor, teaching me what to read, what authors to admire, what was most grand or beautiful in nature, and . . . a faith in things unseen . . . ." In late 1849, Newton returned to Worcester, but sent Emily a letter with a copy of Emerson's *Poems* (1847).[66] It would not have been hard for Dickinson to wrap Emerson with the same awe and affection that she felt for Newton. Years later, Dickinson recalled that Newton, ill with tuberculosis, had told her "he would have liked to live till I had been a poet." Among her handful of intimates, Newton was the first to make her heady—like Santo Domingo rum that "comes but once," she later said—with a sense of her promising power. His words echoed in her mind for years.[67]

Emerson's history in western Massachusetts actually predated Dickinson's birth by seven years. In late August 1823, he had set off on foot from Cambridge to inspect the new Amherst College. "The infant college is an Infant Hercules," he noted.[68] Four years later, Emerson spent two weeks in nearby Northampton as a supply preacher to the new Second Congregational Society. (His hosts Judge Joseph and Mrs. Anne Jean Lyman had led a break with the town's First Church. Mrs. Lyman, wrote a friend, exclaiming, "O Sally! I thought to entertain a 'pious indigent,' but lo! An angel unawares!")[69] Over twenty years later in February 1849, when Emerson returned to lecture in Northampton (again staying with the Lyman's), he came with the reputation of a renegade pastor with dangerous theological and social views. Despite the new fame he had gained as a lecturer abroad just the year before, the Amherst group that attended found him literally insupportable. According to the *Hampshire Gazette*, "The large

---

66   Emily Dickinson (ED) to Jane Humphrey, January 23, 1850, *The Letters of Emily Dickinson*, 3 vols., eds. Thomas H. Johnson and Theodora Ward (Cambridge, Mass.: The Belknap Press of Harvard University Press, 1958), 1: 84-85; hereafter *EDL*; Habegger, 314.

67   ED to Thomas Wentworth Higginson, June 7, 1862, *EDL* 2: 408. See also, Jay Leyda, *The Years and Hours of Emily Dickinson*, 2 vols. (New Haven, CT: Yale University Press, 1960), 1: lxv.

68   *JMN* 2: 182. Emerson added: "Never was so much striving, outstretching, & advancing in a literary cause as is exhibited here." He further noted that "there is a daily exhibition of affectionate feeling between the inhabitants & the scholars, which is the more pleasant as it is so uncommon." See also, Leyda 1: xxxi. Among the College's founders was Samuel Fowler Dickinson, Emily's grandfather; Noah Webster, author of America's first dictionary; and Lucius Boltwood, the future second husband of Emerson's cousin Fanny; https://www.amherst.edu/aboutamherst/facts/history

69   Susan Inches Lyman Lesley, *Memoir of the Life of Anne Jean (Robbins) Lyman* (Cambridge, Mass.: 1876), as quoted by Elise Bernier-Feeley, Local History and Genealogy Librarian, Forbes Library, Northampton, Mass., e-mail to author, 21 May 2007.

party of gentlemen and ladies from Amherst, who graced Mr. Emerson's lecture with their presence, not only omitted, but when reminded of the omission, declined to pay the entrance fee of 12 1/2 cents [or $3.77 in 2013 dollars]."[70]

The provocative Emerson had doubtless challenged their Calvinist theology and anti-abolitionist views. Amherst College had been founded to train conservative Congregationalist ministers. Racially, a town-gown consensus reigned too. In the 1830s, the president and faculty had retracted their early encouragement of student abolitionists, probably due to a violent backlash against the antislavery movement in the state and generally throughout New England. In 1835, William Lloyd Garrison had been paraded through Boston's streets with a noose about his neck. By the early 1840s, the administration, fearing for the future, effectively quieted campus antislavery protest.[71] The town either encouraged this move in the first place, or followed suit.

It was probably Benjamin Newton, still in Amherst, who promoted curiosity about Emerson, persuading Edward Dickinson and his family to attend the lecture. Quite possibly, the group included Emily's close friend, future sister-in-law, and poetry-lover, Susan Huntington Gilbert—like Newton, an early Emerson enthusiast. Emerson's remarks might easily have goaded Edward Dickinson—conservative, parsimonious, and prickly—into refusing to pay. In contrast, Emily would have found Emerson's liberating ideas vital to her own. His example would have encouraged her resistance to joining the church, already begun at Mount Holyoke and continuing at home during Amherst's series of revivals. Her father overrode his usual criticism of the average sermon to join the church in spring 1850, but Emily would never become a member, even though for a time she continued to attend services.[72]

Until 1849, Emerson had been a distant hero in print. Now he might be met face-to-face, especially since his revolutionary thoughts were igniting her own. But Dickinson neither directly presented herself to, nor credited, Emerson. As with all central subjects, she skirted the matter of anyone's influence, claiming never to "consciously touch a paint, mixed

70 Leyda 1: 155; http://www.measuringworth.com/
71 Jake Maguire, "Anti-Slavery Men: The Anti-Slavery Societies at Amherst College," http://www3.amherst.edu/~thoughts/contents/maguire-slavery.html
72 Richard Sewall, *Life of Emily Dickinson*, 2 vols. (New York: Farrar, Straus, and Giroux, 1974), 1: 4, 162; 2: 336; Habeggar, 242.

by another person— ."[73] The intensity of her admiration may have made her shy. However, her markings in his works make his influence clear. In the copy of Emerson's *Poems* that Newton gave her, heavy "X's," probably Newton's (none like them appear in her other books), are found next to five poems in the Table of Contents: "Each and All," "The Problem," "Goodbye," "Woodnotes I," and "Dirge." Her typical marks, vertical light pencil lines, appear next to seven poems. Her choices omitted two of Newton's, while she added four of her own. Among these seven, Emerson's "The Sphinx" strengthened her sense of truth's final mystery and suggested a poetic strategy of indirection. Dickinson might have wondered if his "Each and All" overstated when it found the world "perfect and whole." She had heard too many sermons to the contrary. But "The Problem" named her own theological dilemma: A soul, innately drawn to spiritual things, yet rejects the uniform of traditional faith. Emerson's advice "To Rhea," to return unrequited love with disinterested god-like devotion, spoke to Dickinson, already familiar with spurned affection from both sexes. As she herself would soon do, Emerson's "Rhodora" exclaimed over nature's beauty and power. And "the public child of earth and sky" of his "Woodnotes II" resonated with Dickinson's sense of being a lone child at home in Amherst's woods and swamps. Unmarked poems in this same collection also clearly struck her. Dickinson's "I taste a liquor never brewed —" (1860) directly echoes Emerson's "Bacchus." And his poem "Humble-Bee" spoke to her self-image of being small and attracted to summer's heat. She too was an "insect lover of the sun."[74] For truth and belief, life, love and nature, Emerson was calling a natural follower.

Even before Emerson's poems, his *Essays I* and *II* of a few years earlier had come to Dickinson, either by way of Newton or Sue Dickinson. Writing a memoir for her children in 1892, Sue remembered Emerson's visit to Amherst in 1857: "For years I had read him, in a measure understood him, revered him, cherished him as a hero in my girl's heart, till there grew into my feeling for him almost a supernatural element . . . ."[75] For her early

---

73   Emily Dickinson to Thomas Wentworth Higginson, August 1862, *L* 2: 415.

74   Jack L. Capps, *Emily Dickinson's Reading, 1836-1886* (Cambridge, Mass.: Harvard University Press, 1966), 61, 114; "I taste a liquor never brewed—", *The Poems of Emily Dickinson*, ed. Thomas H. Johnson, 3 vols. (Cambridge, Mass.: The Belknap Press, 1963), 1: *P* 214, 149. Hereafter *P*. ED to Mrs. J. Howard Sweetser, early May 1883, *EDL* 3: 775.

75   Susan H. G. Dickinson, MS, "Annals of the Evergreens" in "Society in Amherst Fifty Years Ago," 1892, Dickinson Papers Box 9 (Susan H. G. Dickinson), Houghton Library, Harvard University.

adoration and identification with Sue, Emily might well have said these words herself. All the more because Sue, singled out by teachers as a gifted student of poetry, regularly shared with Emily her growing library of European and English Romantics and a complete collection of Shakespeare. As late teenagers and young adults, Sue, Emily, and her brother Austin had also exchanged their own poems and belonged to a Shakespeare Club, secretly reading his unedited work and that of other "modern literati" that Edward Dickinson disdainfully outlawed. No doubt Emerson was such an outlaw, making his essay "The Poet" all the more alluring. For Emily, Sue's continuing habit of loaning her books and magazines as they grew older, explains her pencil markings not only in Sue's copies of Emerson's *Essays*, but also in *The Conduct of Life* and *Miscellanies*, all editions of the early 1860s.[76]

As Dickinson became familiar with Emerson in print, she could not have escaped notice of him in the local press. In fact, a February 1850 issue of the Amherst College literary monthly, the *Indicator*, featured both a valentine she had written and a review of Emerson's latest book, *Representative Men*.[77] Emily's prose-poem—a rollicking, madcap experiment possibly sent to the editor, George Gould, a friend of hers as well as Austin's classmate—was anonymous, but its style revealed her identity. Gould's review of Emerson's *Men* called him an "erratic genius and brilliant oddity," reprehensible for his "complete antagonism" to Christianity, yet he confessed to being "quickened and strengthened by communion with a master-mind."[78] These words would have sped Dickinson to Emerson's first chapter, "Uses of Great Men," to find this uplifting conclusion: ". . . great men exist that there may be greater men." Twenty-six years later, she gave *Representative Men* to a friend, calling it "a little Granite Book you can lean upon."[79]

On three occasions in the 1850s—when Dickinson was stirred with unsettling thoughts about her place, powers, and identity—Emerson lectured in Amherst proper. The first time, on March 21, 1855, Emily probably missed him. She was en route home from Washington D.C. where her father was serving a term as congressman. But a review appeared in the *Springfield Republican*, its breezy style indicating that Dickinson's dear

---

76 Jean McClure Mudge, "Emily Dickinson and 'Sister' Sue'," *Prairie Schooner* 52: 1 (Spring 1978): 90-107. See also Jean McClure Mudge, *Emily Dickinson and the Image of Home* (Amherst, Mass.: University of Massachusetts Press, 1975), 137.
77 Leyda, 1: 167-69.
78 Habegger, 220.
79 ED to Mrs. T. W. Higginson, Christmas 1876, *EDL* 2: 569.

friend, the paper's editor Samuel Bowles, was its probable author, and also because its subject matter was Emerson's style, not what he said: "It makes an ordinary head ache to listen well to Ralph Waldo Emerson . . . . There is no more spare language on his ideas, than there is flesh on his bones corporeal. A word less on the one, or an atom less on the other, and there would be a fatal catastrophe. His lecture last night . . .was a chain of brilliant ideas strung as thickly as Wethersfield onions when packed for export . . . ."[80]

Less than five months later, on the college's commencement day, August 8, 1855, Emerson was again in town. The guest of students rather than the administration, he was not featured for the major morning address.[81] Rather, he spoke that afternoon on one of his favorite themes, "A Plea for the Scholar."[82] Emily—at twenty-four still regularly attending church and enjoying parties as well as visiting friends—would have had high incentive to go.[83] Afterward, she may even have served refreshments to Emerson at her father's annual commencement tea. Emily and her younger sister Lavinia (Vinnie) often shared hostess duties in place of their invalid mother.[84] But as the students' honoree rather than the administration's, perhaps Emerson was not invited, and no record remains to confirm she was even there.[85]

The *Express* summarized Emerson's remarks: "[He] wished scholars to become a CLASS; to take high and sacred ground, aloof from the traffickers

---

80   Leyda, 1: 331.
81   The Rev. F. D. Huntington of Harvard University gave the commencement address. Leyda 1: 334. The *Hampshire and Franklin Express* titled Emerson's address, "Plea for the Scholar," which he had given the year before at Williams College. "An Address to the Social Union of Amherst College, 8 August 1855," *The Later Lectures of Ralph Waldo Emerson, 1843-1871*, 2 vols, eds. Ronald A. Bosco and Joel Myerson (Athens, GA: University of Georgia Press, 2001), 349. Hereafter *LL*.
82   Emerson reported that certain "learned professors" heard him, noting that they misread his remarks as supporting "the old Christian immortality . . . . " *Journals of Ralph Waldo Emerson with Annotations*, eds. Edward W. Emerson and Waldo E. Forbes, 1849-1855 (Boston, Mass.: Houghton Mifflin, 1912), 8: 576; *Catalogue of the Officers and Students of Amherst College, for the Academical Year 1854-5*, http://clio.fivecolleges.edu/amherst/catalogs/1854/index.shtml
83   Mudge, *Image of Home*, 71.
84   Edward Dickinson, treasurer of the College since 1835, did his best to keep alive the town-gown camaraderie that Emerson noted over thirty years before. In August 1855, Dickinson hosted his annual commencement tea for the last time at the family's Pleasant Street home; thereafter, it would be held at the Homestead on Main Street, Emily's birthplace, to which they returned that November. Ibid., 76, 243 No. 3.
85   Between March and October 1855, a gap exists in Dickinson's remaining letters. *EDL* 2: 318-20; see also, "Summary of Corrected Dates of Letters," Appendix 5, Habegger, 644.

and politicians. The mission of the scholar was to shed the light by which, and to direct the way in which, others should work . . . [He] was too comprehensive and metaphysical to be at all times easily understood . . . It was a series of subtle minded, comprehensive, epigrammatic, detached thoughts."[86] Such was the immediate local reaction. But Dickinson would have been electrified by his words: "Thought! It is the thread on which the system of nature and the Heaven of heavens are strung . . . the Mind itself, all mixed and muddy as it is in us, is ever prophesying a grander future." And his final congratulations to those accepting "the white lot of the scholar," whose work was "the noblest offices of the human being," would have challenged her to the core.[87]

Ever since his "American Scholar" address (1837), Emerson had regularly pressed others to become, like him, "Man Thinking," an independent "scholar"—or writer—in America. The poet, the most lauded of all "generalizers," epitomized this role, he had argued in 1837. In 1855, he repeated the point, exaggerating, "'Tis wonderful, 'tis almost scandalous, this extraordinary favoritism shown to poets."[88] In the next five years, Dickinson's dedication to writing poetry made her Emerson's model scholar. She would be "Woman Thinking." But beyond gender, being a true scholar-poet required, justified, and could only be surely practiced, as Emerson emphasized, in solitude. Her preference for solitude, even seclusion, leaned on yet more of his advice.

Emily's pencil marked this passage on a down-turned page in Emerson's address "Literary Ethics" (1838), republished in his *Miscellanies* (1860): "Let him [the poet] know that the world is his, but he must possess it by putting himself into harmony with the constitution of things. He must be a solitary, laborious, modest, and charitable soul." The following unmarked paragraph contained a key question and answer: "And why must the student be solitary and silent? That he may become acquainted with his thoughts." On another up-turned page of "Literary Ethics," Emerson gave the solo scholar a saving goal: "Truth shall be policy enough for him."[89]

Two years later, on December 16, 1857, just a week past Dickinson's twenty-seventh birthday, students once again invited Emerson to lecture in Amherst. This time he chose to speak on "The Beautiful in Rural Life," a

---

86 Leyda 1: 334. See also *LL* 1: 350-66.
87 *LL* 1: 361, 366.
88 Ibid., 357.
89 Mudge, *Image of Home*, 138-39.

simple but heartfelt topic, no doubt designed to allay the cool bafflement his "Plea for the Scholar" had produced. It was also only a fourth as long.[90] Anticipation had been high. The series' first lecture, on "Lost Arts" by Wendell Phillips, had drawn a crowd of a hundred and fifty. The *Express* touted Emerson as "the prince of lecturers" and added that he was a not-to-be-missed bargain at twelve and half cents (the same cost as his 1849 lecture in Northampton). Yet, as that paper afterward reported, the lecture ". . . greatly disappointed all who listened. It was in the English language instead of the Emersonese in which he usually clothes his thoughts, and the thoughts themselves were such as any plain common-sense person could understand and appreciate."[91] Whether high or lowbrow, Emerson's attempts to woo Amherst could win only a handful of the adventurous and cultured. Invariably, they were the young intellectual elite.

Of these, Sue, Emily, and Austin—now Sue's husband—led such a list. Their expectations had been quickened by recently reading Emerson's poem "Brahma," re-titled from "Song of the Soul," in the November issue of the *Atlantic Monthly*. Its perceived difficulty, along with the controversy and even satire it spawned, made Emerson all the more enticing. Sue and Austin were bursting with pride to be Emerson's hosts at the Evergreens, their handsome new house in the Italian villa style next to the Homestead. From Emily's bedroom window, she could easily see the Evergreens across a small lot. Recalling the occasion thirty-five years later, Sue was still dazzled by Emerson's effect, ". . . When I found he was to eat and sleep beneath our roof, there was a suggestion of meeting a God face to face, or one of the Patriarchs of Hebrew setting . . . or, as Aunt Emily says, 'As if he had come from where dreams are born.'" [92]

But Sue misquoted Emily's exact words. She had actually written, "It must have been as if he had come from where dreams are born!"[93] Her conditional "*It must have been* . . ." suggests that she was not there. Idolizing him, it would seem, made him inapproachable. If so, then Dickinson

---

90   Cf. Emerson's 1855 and 1857 speeches in *LL* 1: 350-66; 2: 37-40.

91   Leyda 1: 351.

92   Sue must have shared her opinion of "Brahma" with Emily in 1857: "It seemed subtle to the thoughtful, absurd to the dull and uncultured, and soon became the butt of newspaper jokes and caricatures, and a frequent topic in general society . . . . I ventured to question the "Rosetta Stone" [RWE] after the lecture, as we sat about the fire—for he was our guest at the time—and he smiled in his grave, wise way, when I spoke of it as a sort of Sphinx, and replied, 'Oh there is nothing to understand! How can they make so much fuss over it!'" (Susan Dickinson, "Annals of the Evergreens," 1892).

93   ED to Susan Huntington Dickinson, probably 1857, *EDL* 1: prose fragment 10, 913.

had deeper reasons for keeping apart on such occasions. In two separate, undated notes she wrote, ". . . a climate of Escape is natural to Fondness . . ." and "Consummation is the hurry of fools . . . , but Expectation the Elixir of the Gods—."[94] Exposure would have been premature. A distant awe was more lasting and safe.

Nevertheless, in 1858, shortly after her close encounter with Emerson, Dickinson began to compile her best poems, continuing to do so for the next seven years.

5.8 Emily Dickinson at 29? and unknown friend, 1859?

---

94   Emily Dickinson undated aphorisms, *EDL* 3: prose fragments 58 and 69, 921-22.

In 1861, she accelerated this process, editing earlier draft poems and producing a quantity of new ones. She copied those she thought her best on quality stationery, and sewed them into 40 packets of about 800 poems. The rest she gathered into 10 loose sets. The whole lot numbered 1,116, or over sixty per cent of what became her total body of 1,789 poems.[95] For posterity, Dickinson was in effect announcing, as did the first line of a packet poem, "This is my letter to the World" (1862), while also proving herself to be the artist she defined in another, "This Was a Poet" (c. 1862).[96]

In this last poem, Dickinson states her aesthetic hopes, distilling Emerson's advice in "The Poet." Her marked lines in his essay highlighted what became hallmarks of her work. Emerson had written, "Why covet a knowledge of new facts? Day and night, house and garden, a few books, a few actions serve us as well as would all trades and all spectacles. We are far from having exhausted the significance of the few symbols we use. We can come to use them yet with a terrible simplicity." Dickinson's wavering pencil line extended down the margin to include the following three sentences: "It does not need that a poem should be long. Every word was once a poem. Every new relation is a new word."[97] Reading this advice when she first experimented with poetry, then again as her full powers swelled, Dickinson hardly needed more instruction.

In April 1861, Thomas Wentworth Higginson, Emerson's younger friend and admirer, invited "young contributors" to submit poetry to the *Atlantic Monthly*. Exactly a year later, in mid-April 1862, at her peak productivity, Dickinson responded, sending Higginson a few sample poems. (Emerson, a founder of the *Atlantic*, would have seen any poems published there.) However, Higginson soon advised Emily, as she put it, to "delay 'to publish.'" Undismayed, Dickinson fired off a rather rapid series of letters. She asked him to be her "'friend'" and "Preceptor." By July, she set the terms of their relationship by signing herself "Your Scholar." Then, as she moved past apprenticeship in the second half of the 1860s, she sent Higginson hints of her progress. Out of habit, she might still sign her letters "Your Scholar," but she was now also "E. Dickinson," or just

---

95   *P* 1: xviii-xix; Sewall, 2: 537-38; *The Poems of Emily Dickinson: Variorum Edition*, 3 vols., ed. R. W. Franklin (Cambridge, Mass.: The Belknap Press of Harvard University Press, 1998), 1: 639. Hereafter *Fr*.

96   "This is my letter to the World," *P* I 441, 340; *Fr* 1: 519; "This Was a Poet—," *P* I 448, 346-47; *Fr* 1: 446.

97   R. W. Emerson, "The Poet," *Essays: Second Series* (Boston: 1862), 23.

"Dickinson"—a genderless self-elevation to a new assurance, even beyond Emerson's "scholar."[98]

For a full week, October 17-25, 1865, Emerson was again in Amherst to lecture on American Life in a six-part series at the Baptist church.[99] Emily may have been in Cambridge, repeating a second round of eye treatments begun the year before.[100] But apart from these few and necessary trips, she had been at home in Amherst steadily moving toward a sure affirmation in 1869, re-enforced by Emerson's support of solitude, that "I do not cross my Father's ground to any House or town."[101] Soon afterward, when Thomas Wentworth Higginson invited her to hear Emerson speak to a small gathering in Boston, she did not accept.[102]

In the 1870s, Emerson's three final lectures at the college—"Greatness of the Scholar" and "Character" in 1872, then "Superlative or Mental Temperance" in 1879—would not have drawn Dickinson.[103] She was familiar with the first two, and perhaps Emerson's decline in these years was becoming known. Besides, just the year before, she had had proof that her work (only seven poems had been published) at least approached his. In 1878, her poem "Success is counted sweetest / By those who ne'er succeed" (written in 1859, sent to Higginson in 1862, and submitted by a friend, Helen Hunt Jackson) appeared in a collection of anonymous poems, *A Masque of Poets*. Titled "Success" by the book's editors, it was widely attributed to Emerson. (He had privately lectured on the subject, once publicly in Amherst in October 1865, but six years after Dickinson had written her poem.) The *New York Times* judged it "eminently successful."[104] With the knowledge of the Emerson attribution, Emily also learned from Sue that she recognized her lines. The news made her turn "so white" that Sue regretted telling her.[105] But Dickinson's instant reaction could well

---

98   ED to T.W. Higginson, *L* 2: 404, 409, 412, 415, 460.

99   Leyda 2: 102; Emerson's six lectures and two speeches in the area were Oct. 17: "Social Aims in America;" Oct. 18: "American Life;" Oct. 19: "Resources;" Oct. 20: "Table Talk;" Oct. 21: "Books, Poetry, and Criticism;" Oct. 22, Sunday: "Immortality," Free Congregational Association and "Natural Religion," both at Florence, near Northampton; Oct. 23: "Success;" Oct. 24: probably "American Life" in Amherst. Von Frank, 409-10.

100 Sewall 2: Chronology, xxii; *L* 2: 441-44.

101 *EDL* 2: 460.

102 Ibid., 462.

103 *JMN* 16: 277; on February 28, 1879, Emerson spoke at College Hall to a poor audience. Leyda 2: 309-10.

104 *P* 1: 67, 53; also xxx-xxxi; *Fr* 112; Leyda 2: 302-03.

105 Habegger, 559.

have been shock upon having reached a pinnacle previously unknown even to herself.

Despite her deep and longstanding debt to Emerson, in the end Dickinson took a solo route. Though their subjects, searching styles, and forms (hymnody, definition, and aphorism) might be similar, Emerson was more controlled and less anguished than Dickinson. He habitually disguised his "woman's heart" as well as his inner life against a pressing, judgmental public, while she, unpublished, could write powerfully uninhibited statements of fragility, fear, and occasional fierce triumph. Also, Emerson, the public lecturer, saw himself primarily strengthening others, while Dickinson did not. For her, signs of suffering were a badge of integrity: "I like a look of Agony,/ Because I know it's true —"[106] Today, Dickinson's poems in comparison to Emerson's—larger in number but shorter in length, arrestingly spare yet deeply penetrating—are, on the whole, widely judged to be the better art.

Once Dickinson had become a poet both of and beyond Emerson's image, she would pay direct homage to him for the rest of her life. In 1875, when Concord and Amherst both celebrated centennials (Concord, the Revolution; Amherst, its incorporation), Dickinson obliquely equated the two towns and, by extension, Emerson and herself. (He was nationally famous as the "Sage of Concord," and she, locally known as the "myth of Amherst," soon called herself simply "Amherst.")[107] To her Norcross cousins in Concord, Emily wrote, "I have only a buttercup to offer for the Centennial, as an 'embattled farmer' has but little time." Since her cousins by now attended the same First Church in Concord as did Emerson, Dickinson's identifying with the "embattled farmers" of his "Concord Hymn" (1836), an often-repeated phrase that year, would have been instantly recognized by them. She felt engaged in a similar, even revolutionary fight. No matter that her bullets were buttercups and that she patrolled more "limited meadows."[108] She sensed that her "shots" of poetry—"My Life had stood—a Loaded Gun" (1863)[109] —like those of the Minute Men, would also one day be heard "round the world."

---

106 "I Like a look of Agony," *P* 1 241, 174: *Fr* 339.

107 Mudge, *Image of Home*, 198, 271, Nos. 6, 7, 8. This sort of title came easily to Dickinson; she had long named favorite friends with their home cities: Bowles was her "Springfield;" Wadsworth, "Philadelphia;" Otis P. Lord would become "Salem."

108 *EDL* 2: 539.

109 *P* 2: 754, 575; *Fr* 764.

Three days after Emerson's death on April 27, 1882, Dickinson wrote a dear friend: "Today is April's last—it has been an April of meaning to me . . . My Philadelphia [Charles Wadsworth] has passed from Earth [on April 1] and the Ralph Waldo Emerson—whose name my Father's Law Student taught me, has touched the secret Spring. Which Earth are we in?"[110] Dickinson's return to her own "Spring" on May 15, 1886, left that puzzle for her family, and posterity, to ponder.

William James (1842-1910)

In 1904, long-time Harvard professor William James, when asked about Emerson's legacy, at first responded that only a few current Harvard students knew anything about him. But he added, "It is utterly impossible to trace Emerson's influence, at Harvard, or anywhere else. Such things run underground."[111] In contrast, James himself, his novelist brother Henry, and their close circle of friends knew Emerson so well that they often quoted him in letters without any attribution needed. William's wide correspondence, lectures, and publications in America and abroad made him a direct conduit of Emerson's ideas and style to thousands more.

Only weeks after his birth in January 1842, William entered Emerson's orbit. That March, his father Henry James, Sr., fascinated by the same Emerson lecture series that had drawn Whitman, brought him to his house near Washington Place in New York City to admire and give blessings to baby William.[112] (Emerson, grieving little Waldo's recent death, must have viewed the infant with heavy heart.) Like Emerson, James Sr. was a renegade from his father's faith, in his case, Presbyterianism. For a lifetime, the two were separately dedicated to pursuing religious questions and culture with a capital "C." But in contrast to Emerson's independence from any organized movement, James adapted his thinking to Swedenborgian spirituality and Fourierist social thought.[113]

Not surprisingly, James Sr. was ambivalent about Emerson's ideas. At one point, he described his friend's idealism as the work of a "sort of police-spy" on nature for merely pedantic reasons, and at another, criticized his

---

110   *EDL* 3: 727.
111   William James (WJ) to John Madison Fletcher, April 1, 1904, in *The Correspondence of William James*, eds. Ignas K. Skrupskelis and Elizabeth M. Berkeley (Charlottesville, VA: University Press of Virginia, 2002), 10: 391. Hereafter *CWJ*.
112   Gay Wilson Allen, *William James, A Biography* (New York: Viking Press, 1967), 13.
113   Leon Edel, *Henry James: A Life* (New York: Harper & Row, 1985), 8-10.

experimentalism as "a man without a handle."[114] But like Lowell and Whitman, James was wholly won by Emerson's character, his sheer being. When Emerson lectured in New York City in the next two decades, James invariably hosted him. The two became even closer when the James family moved to New England in the 1860s. Then in the late 1860s and early 1870s, James Sr. read his "Emerson" paper to a few small audiences that, as William noted, outlined his father's "irritation" as well as his "enchantment" with Emerson. Emerson's psychological marriage of male and female traits were one of his great assets, James Sr. argued, but his lack of accounting for the "fierce warfare of good and evil" disturbed him.[115]

Yet Emerson cast his spell, and James described himself as his friend's "loving bondman." Together the Emerson-James angle on existence—soulful, aesthetic, impressionistic, subjective, and open, yet with a strong moral sense to which was added James's criticism, seemingly even stronger than Emerson's own—was passed on to William, his next child Henry, and his last-born, daughter Alice. (Two middle sons, Garth and Wilky, were not intellectuals.) To produce offspring with Emerson's depth, it helped that James Sr. had inherited wealth from his father William, a real estate entrepreneur in upper New York State. The son spared no expense in educating his brood in New York City; Newport, Rhode Island; Cambridge; Concord; and abroad in England, Switzerland, France, and Germany. As infants, then again at the cusp of their teen years, William and Henry began what was essentially an ongoing "Grand Tour" of Europe lasting into adulthood. Adjusting to these myriad environments required observation, comparison, and above all, language. Even before the family moved first to Boston in 1864, and two years later to Cambridge, William, Henry, and Alice started lifetime friendships with Emerson's children. (At Lawrence Scientific School in Cambridge in 1861, William took a class in comparative anatomy with Emerson's son, Edward Waldo.)[116] With such a cosmopolitan start, it is not surprising that the brothers—William, the young artist-scientist who matured into a pioneering psychologist and philosopher, and Henry, a psychological novelist who at first was even

---

114   Henry James, Sr. to William James, March 18, 1868, *CWJ* 4: 267-68; see William's reaction to his father's comments on Emerson in WJ to Henry James, April 5, 1867, *CWJ* 1: 45. Edel, *Henry James: A Life*, 10.

115   Henry James, Sr., "Emerson," *Atlantic Monthly* 94 (1904), 743.

116   Daniel W. Bjork, *William James: The Center of His Vision* (New York: Columbia University Press, 1988), 41.

more famous than his brother—grew to embody the most sophisticated American thinking in the half-century after the Civil War.[117]

When William James spoke on the centennial celebration of Emerson's birth in Concord on May 25, 1903, he attested that Emerson had been one of his primary "hearteners and sustainers" since youth, who had urged him and others "to be incorruptibly true to their own private conscience." That was true, too, of young James's good friend, Oliver Wendell Holmes, Jr. Holmes's parents had given him five volumes of Emerson's works on his seventeenth birthday in 1858. Soon a freshman at Harvard, Holmes wrote a highly enthusiastic essay about Emerson for the *Harvard Magazine*. When the two met by chance on the street a month later, Holmes told him, "If I ever do anything, I shall owe a great deal of it to you." Much later in life, Holmes simply stated that Emerson "set me on fire."[118] While Holmes was first devouring Emerson, William James was studying in Switzerland and Germany, then painting in Newport in 1860-1861, and not arriving in Cambridge to study science until 1861. But he already knew Emerson personally, and had long before read the same works in his father's library that were enthralling Holmes. Also, James's father was not, like Holmes Sr., a northern racist,[119] and was therefore closer to Emerson, who, by the Civil War, had long been an abolitionist leader.

As William slowly decided on a profession—trying painting, science, and his father's wishes—he also suffered recurring ill health and thus had time to read widely. Early, he began a habit of easily quoting Emerson in his letters: bits of his essays and poems, the latter evidently known by heart.[120] When he was twenty, he made regular visits to "R.W." and his

---

117　Gerald E. Myers, introduction to *CWJ*, 11 vols. (Charlottesville, VA: University Press of Virginia, 1992), 1: xix-xxxi; xliv-v. See also, Gerald E. Myers, "Chronology of the Life of William James," in his *William James: His Life and Thought* (New Haven, CT: Yale University Press, 1986), xvii-xviii.

118　Louis Menand, *The Metaphysical Club: A Story of Ideas in America* (New York: Farrar, Strouse, and Giroux, 2001), 23-25.

119　Ibid., 22.

120　WJ to Thomas Wren Ward, January 7, 1868, *CWJ* 4: 246. WJ to Catherine E. Havens, March 18, 1877, ibid., 556-57. WJ to HJ, July 4, 1898, almost exactly quotes last line of E's poem, "Good-Bye": "I wish I might see the wonder of Lamb House myself—But what profits the pomp of emperors; when man in the bush may meet with God?" Ibid., 3: 38. WJ to Carl Stumpf, May 26, 1893, ibid., 7: 425, 427. WJ to Theodore Flournoy, August 13, 1895, ibid., 8: 71, 73. WJ to Katharine O. Rodgers, August 5, 1899, ibid., 9: 17-18; see also 593; WJ to WJ, Jr., May 14, 1900, advises reading Emerson's essays on self-reliance, spiritual laws, the Over-Soul, etc., ibid., 597-98. WJ to Pauline Goldmark, August 2, 1902, ibid., 10: 97. WJ to Sarah W. Whitman, June 12, 1904, ibid., 10: 413. WJ to Pauline Goldmark, September 12, 1907, ibid., 11: 443-44.

family in Concord.[121] And in 1867, he went off to Berlin with a letter of introduction from Emerson to his devoted friend Hermann Grimm, noted for his hospitality to Americans.[122] William returned to study at Harvard Medical School and received his M.D. in 1869, at the same time as Emerson, recently welcomed back to the college after thirty years, was preparing his lecture series of 1870-1871 on "Natural History of the Intellect."

5.9 William James at 27, 1869.

121 WJ to Alice James, June 15, 1862, ibid., 4: 74. WJ to Ralph Waldo Emerson, April 6, 1867, ibid., 156-57; WJ to his mother Alice G. James, June 12, 1867, ibid., 178; WJ to Edmund Tweedy, December 18, 1867, writes of Emerson's works having "gone right to [Hermann] Grimm's heart" (ibid., 241).
122 WJ to R. W. Emerson, April 6, 1867, ibid., 4: 156-57.

In 1870, when depression led James to think of suicide, he credited the French philosopher Charles Renouvier for jolting him into recovery by leading him to affirm his own power of choice: "My first act of free will shall be to believe in free will."[123] Beneath that restorative idea lay a deep mine of Emersonian suggestions toward confident independence: make your own world (*Nature*) ; be "Man Thinking" ("American Scholar" address) ; listen to that inner "iron-string" ("Self-Reliance"); and look forward to perpetual change, constant transition, and enlarging perspectives ("Circles"). This closeness to Emerson continued. When fire damaged Emerson's Concord house in 1872, William was concerned and knew that his older friend had gone abroad. (Brother Henry met him at the Louvre and the Vatican.) On Emerson's return, William dined with him in Boston and Concord, noting his decline.[124]

By 1876, Emerson was seventy-three and retired at home, while James at thirty-four had become an assistant professor in the pioneering field of physiology at Harvard. He taught a fluid mixture of physiology, psychology, and philosophy that followed Emerson's focus on the mind in 1870-1871, combined with his own scientific, ethical, and philosophical pursuits.[125] A decade later, William wrote to congratulate brother Henry on his review of James Elliot Cabot's biography of Emerson (1887), noting Ellen and Edward Emerson's appreciation, especially Edward's emotional reaction to Henry's warm ending.[126] With these longstanding and complex family ties, it is little wonder that James built on Emerson's ideas for his personal values and public thoughts.

In the 1880s, James's earlier attraction to philosophy—to spiritual and abstract matters—reengaged him while he also stayed true to the scientific, concrete, and testable. In his last thirteen years, he began to produce the rich work that made him internationally famous. *The Will to Believe, and*

---

123 Myers, *James*, 46.

124 WJ to Alice James, 27 July 1872, *CWJ* 4: 427, 428n; WJ to Alice James, December 11, 1873, ibid., 468; WJ to Robertson James, June 24, 1874: WJ speaks of Emerson's "almost absolute oblivion of proper names, & his increasingly groping way of talk." Ibid., 494; also WJ to RJ, September 20, 1874, WJ writes of "old mr. Emerson more gaunt & lop sided than ever" (ibid., 501). Edel, *Henry James*, 135-36, 151.

125 Myers, "Chronology of the Life of William James," *James*, xvii-xviii; Myers, *CWJ* 1: xxxiv.

126 WJ to Henry James, February 6, 1887, *CWJ* 2: 80-81. HJ's review of Cabot's *A Memoir of Ralph Waldo Emerson* was published in *Macmillan's Magazine* 57 (Dec 1887), 86-98, http://catalog.hathitrust.org/Record/000389431. In 1869, Emerson also showed his interest in the James' brothers by his pleasure in reading Henry's letters from Italy. WJ to HJ, December 5, 1869, *CWJ* 1: 128.

Other Essays in Popular Philosophy appeared in 1897, followed by *The Varieties of Religious Experience* in 1902. Pervading these books were the same concerns voiced by Emerson and James Sr., but with William's own slant and conclusions. Then, in 1903, to prepare for Emerson's centennial celebration at Concord, James re-read all of Emerson's works.

5.10 William James at 61, 1903.

The overview exhilarated him, and Emerson's example gave him a career lesson. He wrote Henry:

> The reading of the divine Emerson, volume after volume, has done me a lot of good, and, strange to say has thrown a strong practical light on my own path. The incorruptible way in which he followed his own vocation, of seeing such truths as the Universal Soul vouchsafed to him from day to day and month to month, and reporting them in the right literary form, and thereafter kept his limits absolutely, refusing to be entangled with irrelevancies however urging and tempting, knowing both his strength and its limits, and clinging unchangeably to the rural environment which he once for all found to be most propitious, seems to me a moral lesson to all men who had genius, however small, to foster . . . Emerson is exquisite![127]

William's heart weakened in 1898. Aware that his time was limited, he would now follow Emerson's example and dedicate himself to "the one

---

127 WJ to HJ, May 3, 1903, *CWJ* 3: 234. Henry called both Emerson and Hawthorne "exquisite geniuses" and "exquisite provincials." Apparently, he was greatly moved by Emerson's supposed innocence—his father's angle on Emerson—that Henry Jr. equated with provinciality. See Edel, *Henry James, A Life*, 121.

remaining thing . . . to report in one book, at least, such impression as my own intellect has received from the Universe." He observed that Henry, too, had "been leading an Emersonian life,"[128] living in the English countryside, at Lamb House in Rye, since 1897. On May 24, the day before the Emerson memorial, Henry answered William: "It affects me much even at this distance . . . —this overt dedication of dear old E. to his immortality."[129] Just after the event, William described it as a "sweet & memorable" occasion, an "aesthetic harmony" bringing back New England's "Golden Age" with its combination of "simplicity & rusticity" with "great thoughts & great names." Having devoured Emerson straight through, he now felt "his real greatness as I never did before." But after hearing "so much" from the other speakers, James also noted, ". . . There are only a few things that *can* be said of him, he was so squarely & simply himself as to impress every one in the same manner." James found down-home, Emerson-like words to praise him: "He's really a critter to be thankful for."[130]

Still, James Sr.'s reservation about Emerson's optimism had cast its shadow. Writing a friend only weeks after the Concord ceremony, young James criticized Emerson for his "'once-born'ness," his "extraordinary healthy-mindedness" that made him fail to comprehend "the morbid side of life."[131] For James, Emerson belonged to the first of two main religious types—the "healthy-minded" and "sick-minded"—that he had named in *Varieties of Religious Experience* just the year before. He and his father, both long-term sufferers of physical and psychological complaints, were the latter type.[132] But the younger James differed from his father as well as Emerson. Though he shared their quest for truth, ethics, and belief, he rejected their monist sense of a single agency at the heart of reality. He argued for a universal pluralism. Nevertheless, William's recent immersion in all of Emerson boosted his confidence. It was high time that he produce his own "magnum opus," "a general treatise" on a "pluralistic and radically empirical philosophy . . . ."[133] James, like Emerson, now increasingly

128 WJ to HJ, May 3, 1903, *CWJ* 3: 234.
129 HJ to WJ, May 24, 1903, *CWJ* 3: 240.
130 WJ to Frances R. Morse, May 26, 1903, *CWJ* 10: 251-52; WJ to WJ, Jr., May 29, 1903, ibid., 252-53.
131 WJ to H.W. Rankin, June 10, 1903, *CWJ* 10: 266-67.
132 Allen, *William James*, 166-67, 432-33; Bjork, *William James*, 97-98.
133 WJ to ?, February ?, 1903, *CWJ* 10: 208.

preferred reaching the public by lecturing and publishing rather than teaching,[134] and lost no time in moving forward.

In 1907, four years after the Emerson centennial, he published *Pragmatism*, and two years later, both *A Pluralistic Universe* and *The Meaning of Truth*. The latter tried to clarify *Pragmatism*, especially for critics who dismissed his test for truth as mere workability. In fact, James's pragmatism was not a theory of truth at all. Stimulated by both religious inquiry— exploring ultimate reality while accepting its elusiveness—and the desire to be scientific, James proposed a *method* of selecting one's beliefs from contending hypotheses: choosing between consequences. Admittedly, the process was subjective—even passionate—but the results were pragmatic (useful). As he wrote, "True ideas are those that we can *assimilate, validate, corroborate and verify. False ideas are those that we can not.*"[135] This was James's complex scientific, psychological, even emotional test for his longstanding desire for a satisfying faith. After all, his *Will to Believe* had preceded his first description of pragmatism (in a lecture of 1898) by only a year. And as a close friend noted about him, "You perceive that philosophy is vain, because mysticism and not reason is the final word."[136]

Emerson's concerns—a devotion to nature, the transcendent and mystic, self-reliance, ever-expanding horizons, even a limited personal god—and his perspective and style remained James's gold standard throughout his creative later years. They led him to unfavorably compare George Santayana to Emerson in 1905, when Santayana's *Life of Reason* appeared. James assessed his colleague's book as "a paragon of Emersonianism," but also found it "profoundly alienating" in its "'preciousness' and superciliousness." He asserted, "The same things in Emerson's mouth would sound entirely different. E. receptive, expansive, as if handling life through a wide funnel with a great indraught, S. as if through a pin point orifice that emits his cooling spray outward . . . like a nose-disinfectant from an 'atomizer.'"[137] Early the next year, at Stanford, James asked his wife to bring with her from Cambridge Emerson's *Miscellanies* and both sets of his

---

134 Robert Dawidoff, *CWJ* 3: xxvii-xxviii.

135 As quoted in Myers, *James*, 298.

136 Benjamin P. Blood to WJ, August 28, 1907, *CWJ* 11: 433.

137 WJ to Dickinson S. Miller, November 10, 1905, *CWJ* 11: 111-12. Santayana, having received a similar letter from James, countered that he was a Latin to whom only politics are serious, and that Emerson apparently did not care about humanity's insane, disastrous acts in the name of religion. He also felt that James had missed his (Santayana's) allusion to a lost perfectionism in "some idealized reality." George Santayana to WJ, December 6, 1905, ibid., 578.

Essays for a speech on war and arbitration that he was preparing.[138] He also stayed in close touch with the Emerson family, attending Ellen's funeral in January 1909.[139]

Later that year, James answering a query, assessed Emerson the intellectual with the same ambivalence as his father. Though he felt that Emerson lacked "metaphysic *argument*," his "transcendentalist and platonic phrases *named* beautifully for him that *side* of the universe which for his soul . . . was all-important." And if Emerson might undercut his own thinking in following pages, James did not fault this "literary inconsistency." He could state his largely ideal "monistic formulas" dogmatically, but he did not "*suppress the facts they ignored*," James noted, "so no harm was done." For example, James found the ending of Emerson's essay "History," with its "platonic formulas" "simply *weak* . . . but there are readers whom they inspire," he acknowledged, "so let them pass!"[140] James ignored Emerson's metamorphosis from a young Romantic idealist to a more mature thinker, whose remaining idealism was frequently informed by harsh realities, private and public.[141] James's pluralism may also have led him to miss Emerson's "Worship" (1850), where he had defined mind as "finer matter" and observed divinity pervading every atom. Had James noted this shift, he might have seen that Emerson could have agreed with *Pragmatism*'s facts-first, results-oriented, ethical thinking.

James might have misread Emerson, but his ethical and emotional ties with his father's old friend had been and always remained tight. All his life, he agreed with Emerson's note in the "American Scholar" that character always trumps intellect. After eleven years of increasing heart trouble, ten months before he died in August 1910, James noted to a friend, ". . . the mere fact of being still part of this real world—the wonderful apparition, as Emerson calls it, has a zest which neutralizes a good many things. I never admired nature more than I did this summer. The great thing is to live *in* the passing day, and not look farther!"[142]

---

138 WJ to Alice G. James, January 30, 1906, ibid., 581.
139 WJ to Alexander R. James (son), January 17, 1909, *CWJ* 12: 149-50.
140 WJ to William C. Brownell, September 2, 1909, ibid., 314-15. Brownell's article, "Emerson," appeared in *Scribner's Magazine* 46 (November 1909), 608-24.
141 Barbara Packer points to the essential political and social context of the 1850s in which Emerson wrote his lectures, later collected in *The Conduct of Life* (1860). Historical Introduction, "The Conduct of Life," *CW* 6: xv-lxvii.
142 WJ to Henry P. Bowditch, November 9, 1909, ibid., 360.

Frank Lloyd Wright (1867-1959)

A dramatic example of Emerson's influence on the arts is the work of architect Frank Lloyd Wright. Wright's family, then his first employer Louis Sullivan, and finally Lewis Mumford, the public intellectual, architectural critic, and friend of Wright, all championed Emerson. For Wright, so constantly guided by Emersonian principles throughout his life, the result was a startlingly new, indigenous modern architecture, at once American and international in scope. Yet in his *Autobiography* (1943), Wright omitted naming Emerson when listing those he had "long ago consulted and occasionally remembered."[143] Wright's high confidence, pride, and tendency to shave the truth made it difficult for him to credit anyone with guiding his genius.[144]

Emerson's message came to Wright early. His father, an Amherst graduate, sometime Baptist minister, and musician, taught his children to play a piano made by the Emerson Company (no relation). As a child, Frank's younger sister was awestruck that Emerson, the man whom she thought made this instrument, also wrote books. She reported that parents, aunts, and uncles often began their sentences, "As Mr. Emerson says . . . ."[145] Emerson's words gave Wright a rudder to face a life filled with considerable turmoil.

While Wright, like Emerson, grew up with fresh, post-war expectations (for Emerson, the Revolution; for Wright, the Civil War), Reconstruction in the 1870s was subverting emancipation in the South. In the North, tensions divided an old agrarianism and abolitionism and a variety of Calvinists, Lutherans, and Unitarians. Among these last were latter-day Transcendentalists, including Wright's family in Richland Center, Wisconsin.[146] This stirring mixture of social, religious, and philosophical matters gave birth to Progressive reform ideas and to the feisty, change-oriented, democratic atmosphere of Wright's childhood.

In 1876, when Frank was nine, his art-loving mother Anna Lloyd-Jones came home from the Philadelphia Centennial Exposition, with its focus on

---

143 Frank Lloyd Wright, "Index," *An Autobiography* (New York: Duell, Sloan, and Pearce, 1943), 561.

144 He boasted not to have read Sullivan, since working side by side with him, his ideas had been "an open book", ibid.

145 Maginel Wright Barney, *The Valley of the God-Almighty Joneses* (New York: Appleton-Century, 1965), 59-60.

146 Finis Farr, *Frank Lloyd Wright* (New York: Charles Scribner's Sons, 1961), 15.

Britain's Aesthetic Movement, bringing materials to continue stimulating her son's interest in architecture. The movement's periodicals and books were already in the house. Earlier, Boston art critic James Jackson Jarves' *The Art-Idea* (1864) had nurtured a philosophical basis for America's Aesthetic Movement by combining Emerson's ideas with those of John Ruskin, Britain's premier art critic and social reformer. Together, these sources linked created beauty, democratic education, and moral uplift. By the 1890s, this hybrid British-American Aesthetic Movement was moving in two directions that both influenced Wright: the Arts and Crafts Movement and Art Nouveau.[147]

Before Frank was in his teens, his father's spirited but failed ministries led the family to Rhode Island and Massachusetts where Anna immersed herself in Transcendentalist thought, especially Emerson.[148] Frank also read widely, from sleazy adventure stories to leading architectural books by Ruskin and Viollet-le Duc, as well as Plutarch, Shakespeare, Goethe, Carlyle, and a host of others.[149] Simultaneously, during the summers from age eleven, he endured numbingly hard work on his uncle's farm, but that experience gave him unforgettable memories of nature.

At eighteen, Frank witnessed his father's forced departure from the house by Anna and her family. Two years later, in 1887, after leaving high school without graduating and taking two semesters of civil engineering at the University of Wisconsin, Wright headed for Chicago. Its disastrous fire of 1871 had led to a building boom that was producing the "Chicago School" of experimental, urban, and largely commercial design. Within a year, Wright placed himself with the company of Adler and Sullivan, one of Chicago's most successful firms. Sullivan quickly recognized him as a gifted draftsman. Wright's mother came to live with him in the suburb of Oak Park, where she gave a course on Emerson to a women's group.[150] With this continuing link, Wright readily made the

---

147 Harvard art historian Charles Eliot Norton, friend to Emerson, Ruskin and Carlyle, also devotedly advocated art as a key instrument in building a democratic culture. He worked to coalesce America's technology with aesthetics. Kevin Nute, *Frank Lloyd Wright and Japan* (New York: Van Nostrand Reinhold, 1993), 10-11.

148 Ibid., 24; Farr, 7-8; Wright, *Autobiography*, 17; F. L. Wright, *Frank Lloyd Wright: Collected Writings*, ed. Bruce Brooks Pfeiffer (New York: Rizzoli, 1992), 113-14. Hereafter, *Wright CW*.

149 Ada Louise Huxtable, *Frank Lloyd Wright* (New York: Lipper/Viking, 2004), 37-38.

150 A founder of the Nineteenth Century Woman's Club, Anna Wright gave "classes in Emerson and Browning and papers on . . . the naturalist John Burroughs." Meryle Secrest, *Frank Lloyd Wright* (New York: Knopf, 1992), 225.

Emersonian-like motto of his mother's Welsh family, "Truth against the world," his own.[151]

But Wright's truth strayed from Emerson's. The frugal Emerson always dressed in simple black. Wright, often a dandy in dress, was capable of carrying self-reliance to excess: he fudged the facts of age and education, carried on several romantic intrigues leading to three marriages, and regularly failed to pay bills.[152] Yet while ignoring Emerson's moral expectations, Wright's adoption of his inspiration from nature and his romantic spirit produced buildings of great natural integrity, despite occasional—or some said, more than occasional—leaky roofs.

In Louis Sullivan, Wright found an artistic soul mate and mentor, interested in philosophy, music, and art in general. Besides Emerson and Ruskin, Sullivan was also influenced by a wide range of Romantic and Gothic Revival figures such as the American sculptor Horatio Greenough and the English artist-writer A.C. Pugin, a leading student of medieval architecture. Emerson, who had met Greenough in Rome in 1833, noted that Greenough's 1843 paper on architecture had predated Ruskin's thoughts on architecture's "*morality*" (Emerson's emphasis). In responding to a letter from Greenough, Emerson referred to his theory of proper structure: "[It is] a scientific arrangement of spaces and forms to function and to site; an emphasis of features proportioned to their *gradated* importance in function: color and ornament to be decided and arranged and varied by strictly organic laws . . . ."[153] From sources such as these, Sullivan developed an architecture built on the centrality of nature: form should follow function and a building's decoration should emerge organically, flower- or vine-like, from its basic design. To these, he added the Progressive values of individualism and democracy.[154] This collation of thoughts poured into his designs for the radically new skyscraper and high-rise, sure symbols of the optimism and ambition that built them.

---

151 Ibid., 46.
152 Huxtable, xv-xvi.
153 Farr, 79-80.
154 Mark Gelernter, *A History of American Architecture: Buildings in Their Cultural and Technological Context* (Hanover, NH: University Press of New England, 1999), 212-14.

Four years later, Wright, helped by family connections to establish a clientele, opened his own Chicago office. Sullivan had fired him for taking time from the firm's domestic commissions to work on what Wright himself called his "bootleg" houses.[155] But now in the period 1893-1910, he independently launched a series of suburban dwelling designs that, despite variations, exhibited his so-called "prairie style": low horizontal outlines; a naked exposure of natural and manufactured materials (brick, reinforced concrete, or glass); informal and free-flowing interior spaces around a central fireplace; and when possible, a marriage of building to site.[156] Wright seemed to be fulfilling Emerson's hope for a coming genius, not yet on the scene while he was alive, who would be connected to the "sea-wide, sky-skirted prairie." That prairie epitomized America's virgin land and was a vital part of Wright's beloved native Wisconsin landscape. Emerson had written, "I know not why in real architecture the hunger of the eye for length of line is so rarely gratified."[157]

As with his aesthetic ideas, Wright's style also hardly emerged *sui generis*. He avidly studied a variety of modernist artistic and scientific models. Beyond Chicago's urban engineering experiments were the international Arts and Crafts movement, technological schools in England and the Continent, the "shingle style" of American architects from the East and Mid-West, and Japan's architecture and art.[158] Such inventive bricolage—puttering with many designs to combine with his own solutions—defined his genius. But what truly enabled Wright to unify miscellaneous sources was his commitment to Emerson's call in *Nature*: to make a moral, beautiful new world.

Midway through Wright's life, Emerson's influence was renewed through the critic and Emerson devotee Lewis Mumford. In 1953, Mumford both praised and blamed Wright's work in two *New Yorker* articles. The occasion was an exhibition, *Sixty Years of Living Architecture*, on the site of Wright's future Guggenheim Museum (finished in 1958). Mumford first heralded Wright as "the most original architect the United States

---

155   Huxtable, 70.
156   *Frank Lloyd Wright & Lewis Mumford: Thirty Years of Correspondence*, eds. Bruce B. Pfeiffer and Robert Wojtowic (New York: Princeton Architectural Press, 2001), 5.
157   Farr, 79.
158   Huxtable, 76-77.

has produced, and—what is even more important— . . . the most creative architectural geniuses of all time . . . the Fujiyama of American architecture . . . a volcanic genius that may at any moment erupt with a new plan or a hitherto unimagined design for a familiar sort of building."[159]

5.11 Frank Lloyd Wright at 59, c. 1 March 1926.

By the mid-twentieth century, Mumford had become a major cultural critic who leaned on Emersonian insights in becoming proficient in art, architecture, literature, theater, sociology, and politics. Already, twenty-five years before, he had commented on Wright, internationally known for his plans and perspective drawings in the Wasmuth Portfolio (1910) and for his long-term project in Tokyo, the Imperial Hotel (1913-1922). Then, Mumford had called him the successor to H.H. Richardson and Louis Sullivan, found in him a counterforce to Europe's mere mechanism (Le Corbusier), and celebrated his unity of function and style with landscape. For Mumford, Wright was as poetic as Carl Sandburg and Sherwood

---

159 *Wright and Mumford Correspondence,* 27.

Anderson in expressing mid-American values. After a second similar article by Mumford, Wright complained that he did not understand him. Afterward, they began an alternately convivial and contentious relationship.[160]

Mumford had problems with Wright's refusal to support World War II and other matters that led to an estrangement in 1941. That distancing lasted a decade, but on Wright's initiative, their relationship was restored. By 1953, with leftover tensions in play, Mumford's article about the Guggenheim exhibition was more critical of Wright. He complained of Wright's "America First streak," his disdain for European architecture, and his inability to learn from others different from himself. Nevertheless, Mumford applauded Wright's total humanism: ". . . his lifework has expressed the full gamut of *human* scale, from mathematics to poetry, from pure form to pure feeling, from the regional to the planetary, from the personal to the cosmic. In an age intimidated by its successes and depressed by a series of disasters, he awakens, by his still confident example, a sense of the fullest *human* possibilities."[161]

This critical but celebratory review magnifies the differing reflections on Emerson's iconoclasm that had encouraged the Mumford-Wright conflicts. Mumford on Wright was an Emerson-like voice speaking critically—with appreciation and rebuke. Wright thought himself Emerson's arch-advocate and practitioner. Yet the human, ethical, and organic architectural principles that both men championed against an increasingly materialistic, mechanized society were also completely Emersonian. In 1929, in one of his earliest letters to Mumford, Wright explained the enclosed draft of his latest article for the *Architectural Record*. He had defended his core values from anticipated criticism and commented, ". . . how silly and ungrateful to brand as weakness the radiation of character from my work. Just in proportion to this force, the artist will find his work outlet for his proper character, says Emerson. But no 'mannerist' could have made my varied group of buildings? I cannot hope, nor should I want to emancipate myself from my age and my country. And this quality in my work will have a higher charm, a greater value than any individual-quality could have." His next two paragraphs continued in this Emersonian vein: "The New in art is always formed out of the Old—if it is truly valid as New." And "Art does

160 Ibid., 6, 8, 9, 10-11, 21, 22-23.
161 Ibid., 38-39.

exhilarate and its intoxicating aim is truly no less than the creation of man as a perfect 'flower of Nature.' What an excursion!"[162]

In 1951, Wright and Mumford exchanged comments about Mumford's latest book, *The Conduct of Life*, a work twenty-one years in the making. As he explained to Wright, Mumford had taken the same title as Emerson's 1860 collection of essays "in order to emphasize the underlying affiliation, despite all differences in personality and philosophy, which you, dear FLW, were first to recognize." Wright replied, "I've missed you Lewis. Your's [sic] is an Emersonian mind but on your own terms. What a man he was and how we need such-now! I've read your little book [*Man the Interpreter*] and, what? A man you are. I shall never cease to be aware of the fact that I owe to you primal appreciation and support when it took real courage for you to render it. That I count as one of the real honors that have 'fallen into my lap.'"[163] Two years later, after Mumford's critical review of the new U.N. building appeared, Wright quickly wrote him: "Vive the *New Yorker*! What other magazine would have dared? But the court-jester always spoke what other courtiers never dared utter. Emerson would put his hand on your shoulder and say 'my son?'" The question mark, as habitual for Wright as his underlinings, often means "is that not so?"[164]

This spiritual sonship with Emerson is a constant thread in Wright's life, from easily recalled Emerson references in early speeches to his later books. In 1896, three years into his independent practice, Wright spoke on "Architect, Architecture, and the Client." Besides invoking Tolstoy, Hugo, and Whistler on art, Wright quoted Emerson's simple maxim, "Art is life." Four years later in another speech, Wright again interlaced Emerson's thoughts with his own, ". . . we worship at the shrine of Nature and go to her for inspiration . . . ." "We walk in the cool, calm shade of the trees, and they say to us as they said to Emerson long ago, 'Why so hot my little man?' And we wonder why, indeed, so hot!" In his book on urban planning, *The Disappearing City* (1932), Wright includes Emerson among America's fathers, who initiated a democracy "more just and therefore [allowing] more freedom for the individual than any existing before in all the world . . . ."[165]

---

162 Probably "Surface and Mass—Again!" *Architectural Record* 66 (July 1919), 92-94. Ibid., 61.

163 Ibid., 195-96.

164 Ibid., 233.

165 *Wright CW* 2: 28, 43; 3: 75.

Emerson's concept of the organic in nature and art became Wright's central working principal. In *Architecture and Modern Life* (1939) he claimed, "[Architecture] is the organic pattern of all things. [The organic] remains the hidden mystery of creation until the architect has grasped and revealed it." Combining the two, Wright saw organic architecture fed by life, then returning to shape everyday existence and its routine rhythms toward new efficiencies and freedoms. Houses so built would not only guide human patterns of activity, sparing their time, but would stimulate "their sense of form in space, in color, in mass, and in action." As their "very texture of living" was improved, people would become better human beings. Wright's range of concern also matched Emerson's in serving the full scope of human needs, from contemplation to defecation. He asked: "Shall the child pause at the window for the view before he climbs fifteen steps to his play room?" And he lifted the lowly outhouse, now inside, to new respect: ". . . to those who believe with the modern poet that all significant experience may be the subject of art, even the building of a privy may involve architectural values."[166] Today's focus on bathroom design and appointments echoes Wright's insistence that organic architecture should serve both body and soul.

In 1958, Wright's tributes to Emerson reached a climax in his appendix to *The Living City*. He saw America leaving the city for the country to be in touch with nature once again, a process made practical by the car. More importantly, he argued that such a movement would literally "ground" people. When "every man, woman, and child may be born to put his feet on his own acres," and when his house arose organically from that setting, "then democracy will have been realized."[167] This appendix included excerpts from Emerson's essay "Farming" from *Society and Solitude* (1870), his words ringing true to Wright from his boyhood experiences on the farm. Emerson celebrated the farmer's primary creative role and farming itself as practical and poetic, but above all, as holy work. Despite Wright's complaints about laboring on his uncle's land, he now read Emerson's encomiums about farming and the farmer (a "continuous benefactor") as analogous to architecture and his own work. Emerson wrote, "[The farmer] . . . makes the land so far lovely and desirable, makes a fortune which he cannot carry away with him, but which is useful to his country long afterwards." For Emerson, this farmer (become architect for Wright)

---

166 Ibid., 3: 217-18.
167 Ibid., 5: 251.

was nothing less than someone whom the greatest poets "would appreciate as being really a piece of the old Nature, comparable to sun and moon, rainbow and flood; because he is, as all natural persons are, representatives of Nature as much as these."[168]

Frank Lloyd Wright died in April 1859 at the age of ninety-one. The funeral service was in Madison, Wisconsin, at the Unitarian church where Wright was a member. It began with Psalm 121, "I will lift up mine eyes unto the hills." Afterward, an excerpt from Emerson's "Self-Reliance" was read: "Whoso would be a man must be a nonconformist. He who would gather immortal palms must not be hindered by the name of goodness, but must explore if it be goodness. Nothing is at last sacred but the integrity of your own mind."[169] Wright may not always have followed Emerson's precepts of strict personal morality and high self-discipline. But as an architect, his effort to make his own way and to plumb artistic integrity consistently testified to Emerson's constant mentoring.

Countless Others

More than a century ago, William James noted that Emerson's influence, impossible to trace, had gone "underground." Today, except for some lasting aphorisms, Emerson's matter and method may seem buried. But beneath public awareness, they still exist as aquifers of unconscious values, social norms and habits of mind. More visibly and self-consciously, scores of Americans in literature, philosophy, political theory, social reform, and the arts have emerged from the Emerson font: Robert Frost, John Dewey, W. E. B. Du Bois, Martin Luther King, Charles Ives, Aaron Copeland, Fitz Hugh Lane and the Luminist School in Emerson's own time, and Georgia O'Keeffe in ours, to name a few. The endless stream extends to a widely diverse lot—from his namesake Ralph Waldo Ellison to Allen Ginsberg, from Toni Morrison to Barack Obama. For Americans, Emerson is a given at birth, but someone who needs to be brought to one's full consciousness. For immigrants, he is a promise. For everyone, in a world that so evidently needs transforming, his simple recognition that "We change whether we like it or not" should be reassuring.

---

168 Ibid., 341-43. Just the year before, Wright had published *A Testament*, a reprise of his life and thoughts. He headed one section of the book, "POET—"Unacknowledged legislator of the world" with no attribution to the original Shelley quote. But he credited Emerson, Thoreau, and Whitman with his self-image as a poet-architect, the world's first, he claimed. *A Testament* (New York: Horizon Press, 1957), 58-59.
169 Secrest, 13.

EMERSON
IN THE WEST AND EAST

6.1 Europe in Emerson and Emerson in Europe

Beniamino Soressi

A subtle chain of countless rings
The next unto the farthest brings;
The eye reads omens where it goes,
And speaks all languages the rose;
And, striving to be man, the worm
Mounts through all the spires of form.

Emerson, "Nature," 1836

Emerson's phrase, "a subtle chain of countless rings," metaphorically suits this subject: the mutual influence of the West on Emerson and of Emerson on the West. These "rings" of influence indeed make up "a subtle chain," seemingly impossible to track, especially when generated by a variety of secondary sources. Nevertheless, its larger links may be identified, first with a brief overview of Emerson's debt to the West, then with a longer look at his effect upon well-known writers and political thinkers in South and Central America, England, and the Continent. In his fifties, Emerson noted, ". . . we go to Europe to be Americanized."[1] The Old World, he had long realized, would be reflected in any definition of the New.

---

1   *The Collected Works of Ralph Waldo Emerson*, eds. Robert E. Spiller, et al. (Cambridge, Mass.: The Belknap Press of Harvard University Press, 1971-2013), 6: 78. Hereafter *CW*.

http://dx.doi.org/10.11647/OBP.0065.08

Central to all these mutual influences was a call to change in thought and in social reform by both idea and example. Unfortunately in Germany, Nietzsche misused central Emersonian ideas, which Hitler and the Nazis then further perverted. In Italy, the poet-politician D'Annunzio and Mussolini were closer to Emerson's texts per se, yet similarly corrupted his original intent. Fortunately, in other countries, especially France and England, he had more accurate adherents—from Baudelaire to Camus, George Eliot to Kipling. Through such widely read writers, Emerson energized the West's general impulse toward adopting more democratic values.

A convenient starting place for a brief overview of Emerson's indebtedness to the West is his choice of six figures from European culture in his book *Representative Men* (1850).

6.1 Plato, copy Silanion portrait, c. 370 B.C.E.

6.2 Emanuel Swedenborg, before 1818.

6.3 Michel de Montaigne, [n.d.].

6.4 William Shakespeare at 46, 1610.

He first featured Plato, the 5th-4th century B.C. Greek philosopher and classical advocate of idealism, who postulated a pristine unseen realm of ideas as a model for their imperfect reflection in this rough real world. He also wished to celebrate Plato's tolerance of unsystematic thinking, his own mental habit. Emerson thus revealed an unstated pattern in his selections: These great men exhibited interests and abilities that he either shared already or that he admired and adopted as his own.

This was true of his second subject Swedenborg (1688-1772), the Swedish scientist, religious philosopher, and mystic who appealed to Emerson for his theories of correspondence and for distinctively uniting science with mysticism, another one of Emerson's goals (see Chapter 4). The French essayist Montaigne (1533-1592), Emerson's third figure, complemented Swedenborg with his radical, frank, but balanced skepticism, halfway between idealism and empiricism, a position that by 1844, Emerson had also announced as his own. For his fourth subject, Emerson chose Shakespeare (1564-1616), a close reader of Montaigne, as the poet-dramatist par excellence for his penetrating eye and idiosyncratic creativity. Napoleon (1769-1821), the Corsican commoner who had become a great soldier-statesman, although cynical and egotistic, earned Emerson's praise for his absolute and practical self-confidence. Finally, Goethe (1749-1832), the poet, dramatist, novelist, and scientist, epitomized the universally talented, all-encompassing writer.

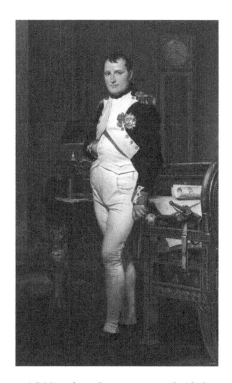

6.5 Napolean Bonaparte at 43, 1812.

6.6 Johann Wolfgang von Goethe at 79, 1828.

Of these six, by time and personal connection, Emerson was closest to Napoleon, champion of European political revolution, and to Goethe, generator of the Continent's Transcendentalism, the Romantics' revolt against the Enlightenment's strict rationalism. In 1826, he had met Napoleon's nephew, Achille Murat, in Charleston, South Carolina. Two years before, Emerson's brother William had privately seen Goethe at his house in Weimar.[2]

Besides Plato, other classic Greek and Roman authors familiar to him from school and college helped to shape Emerson's early thinking. Heraclitus' sense of nature as an ever-flowing and changing river fed Emerson's view of a world of constant process and potential paradox. But equally influential was Parmenides' view of reality as a static, hard material sphere, eternally filling all space (the One). Such a notion supported Emerson's idea of an immutable unity at nature's core. He was intrigued, too, by the later neo-Platonists Plotinus and Proclus, who refined and synthesized these two images. Plotinus advanced an early theory of signs as well as the idea that Parmenides' One, emanating into ordinary things, reflected its perfection there. Proclus united old and new ideal views of the cosmos with pagan theological imagery. On a more immediate note, the Stoics Seneca and Marcus Aurelius complemented the Bible in instructing Emerson on how to deal with hardship. And Plutarch, model enough as a moral essayist, also taught Emerson to see history through the lens of biography.

Among later authors, in his essay "The Poet," Emerson praised Dante whose *La vita nuova* (*The New Life*, 1295) showed him "dar[ing] to write his autobiography in colossal cipher, or into universality."[3] It seemed to him "the Bible of Love . . . as if written before literature, whilst truth yet existed . . . ."[4]

Boehme's *Aurora Consurgens* (*Dawn, The Dayspring*, 1612) impressed Emerson with the possibility of achieving a natural and radically individual spiritual philosophy without any formal education. And on his aesthetic side, he admired Michelangelo's fearless, bold translations of inner torment into immediate brushworks and Promethean chisel strokes. As a model for

2   P. S. Field, *Ralph Waldo Emerson* (Lanham, MD: Rowman & Littlefield, 2003), 61.

3   *CW* 3: 21.

4   *The Journals and Miscellaneous Notebooks of Ralph Waldo Emerson*, 16 vols., eds. William H. Gilman, et al. (Cambridge, Mass.: Harvard University Press, 1960-1982), 8: 430. Hereafter *JMN*.

his own ambitions, Emerson applauded Francis Bacon's tireless search for power through knowledge. In contrast, Hume's radical empiricism and his anti-causation theory chafed against Emerson's life-long belief in "soul," with its free will, and in causation as a natural law. For a time, he found some comfort in the Scottish School of Common Sense adopted by Unitarianism, but rejected its pure rationality as he moved toward a Transcendentalism of the heart. Electrified by the grandly beautiful cosmologies of the scientists Herschel and Humboldt, Emerson played them against Milton's universal drama of humanity's fall.

6.7 Dante Alighieri, after 1841.

Emerson's sensitivities naturally drew him to the Old World's Romantics: from the young German writer Novalis, for exalting the synergies of poetry and philosophy, to Hegel, for his extreme idealism and belief in the generative force of *Geist*, or spirit. Schleiermacher's individualistic interpretations naturally appealed to him. So, too, did J. G. Herder's anthropocentrism and his view of man as an animal able to compensate for a loss of instinct by acquiring art and technology. In his essays "Thoughts on Modern Literature" and "Europe and European Books," Emerson found that Wordsworth's "wisdom of humanity" and his "just moral perception"[5] spoke to the essential, as did the English poet's sense of the "elemental" correspondences between nature, mind, life, and immortality. On a practical note, the iron determinism of the Belgian Adolphe Quételet's social statistics appealed to Emerson, as did the quirky wealth of W. S. Landor's *Imaginary Conversations*. More significantly, as seen in Chapter 1, he was early on attracted to Coleridge's literary criticism and poetry as well as to his fragments of 1834 and 1836. Altogether, these works enhanced Emerson's understanding of familiar classical figures, and, for the first time, introduced him to Spinoza and more contemporary German Romantic philosophers, especially Kant, Fichte, and Schelling. Complementing these thinkers, the startlingly fresh power of the French women novelists Mme. de Staël and George Sand showed Emerson a distinctive female perspective on manners and the art of conversation.

From this rich European legacy, Emerson built his own approach to pursuing the truth and transformed the whole into his "new thinking." For the most part, he had a positive, receptive view of Europe's immense cultural and economic heritage. But early and often, as in "Friendship," he came to warn against the tyranny of antique ideas, the Old World's actual or virtually "dead persons,"[6] and its corrupting luxuries.[7] One of the first steps in Emerson's revolution was to try to end America's depressing nostalgia for England and Europe, a national "tape-worm," he came to call it in "Culture," eating away one's mind.[8] By proclaiming the authority and trustworthiness of each individual, as guided by a universal Over-Soul, he hoped that the passion for developing one's potential "genius" would spread first in families and communities, then to the whole country. For Western intellectuals, this new faith in the infinite capacity of the single soul marked Emerson's most visible, radical difference from past thinking. Previously unrecognized as Emerson followers, certain Hispanic writers in the New World deserve first mention.

---

5   *CW* 10: 113, 247.
6   R. W. Emerson, 12 March 1833, journal entry, *Emerson in His Journals*, ed. Joel Porte (Cambridge, Mass.: Harvard University Press, 1982), 99; *CW* 2: 126.
7   "The Fortune of the Republic," *Emerson's Antislavery Writings*, eds. Len Gougeon and Joel Myerson (New Haven, CT: Yale University Press), 139, 140-41.
8   *CW* 6: 77.

Emerson in Latin America

Jorge Luis Borges (1899-1986), the Argentine poet, critic, and short-story writer, notably represents those Americans outside the United States who clearly caught Emerson's infectious message.

6.8 Jorge Luis Borges at 77, 1976.

Borges' devotion to Emerson, both thoroughgoing and lifelong, led him to state, "Yo tengo el culto de Emerson" ("I've made a cult of Emerson").[9] In his short story, "La otra muerte" ("The Other Death," 1949), Borges openly preferred Emerson, the "great poet,"[10] to Poe,[11] and even ranked Emerson's poetry above his essays.[12] Elsewhere Borges celebrated Emerson's verse as "spontaneously original," unique but never deliberately transgressing accepted poetic convention.[13] (In contrast, Whitman "*tries too hard*.")[14] For Borges, Emerson's "tranquil felicity" made him "the

9   A. Barnechea, *Peregrinos de la lengua* (Madrid: Alfaguara, 1997), 39.
10   J. L. Borges, W. Barnstone, *Borges at Eighty: Conversations* (Bloomington, IN: Indiana University Press, 1982), 38.
11   "The Other Death" (1949), in *The Aleph* (New York: Penguin, 1949), 58.
12   This preference was despite his admiration of "The Poet," knowledge of little-known essays, and having translated *Representative Men, De los héroes. Hombres representativos* (Buenos Aires: Jackson, 1949).
13   J. L. Borges and O. Ferrari, *En diálogo* (Mexico [sic]: Siglo XXI, 2005), 141-42, 213.
14   S. Rodman, J. L. Borges, *Tongues of Fallen Angels* (New York: New Directions, 1974), 14.

most elevated intellectual poet," one who produced "very interesting ideas."[15] Nor did Emerson's famous aloofness diminish Borges' empathy, noting, "If a poet writes in a reserved way, he is expressing himself."[16] Emerson's poems were for Borges "engraved" or "sculpted," yet not so much visual and spatial as musical and temporal, "renewing the past each time he remembered it."[17] In his poem, "Emerson," Borges echoed Emerson's vision in "Days" of a coming better humanity ("Quisiera ser otro hombre"). Of all the poems, Borges favored "History," "The Past," (which he translated), and in particular "Brahma." This last he thought very "clean" in delineating identity, quoting the line: "When me they fly, I am the wings."[18]

Emerson's ideas took root in many themes that Borges later explored: the pervasiveness of illusions and dreams; the varieties of time-perception, identity and otherness; the identification of "I" and the Eye; and the interconnections between the micro- and macro-worlds. He found especially appealing Emerson's notion in "Nominalist and Realist" that all works are inspired by, and emanate from, one impersonal writer.[19] In 1967, Borges stated: "I think that Emerson is a finer writer and a finer thinker than Nietzsche."[20] At a time when Europe's literary and philosophical circles were attempting a "Nietzsche Renaissance," to retrieve him from his ignominious association with the Nazis (of which more below), Borges' statement was audaciously bold.

Until his last days, Borges held Emerson in the highest regard. Blind and losing his memory, he wrote, "Elogio de la sombra" ("In Praise of Darkness," 1969), a poem recalling Emerson's "Illusions." In it, he lists greatly cherished things he knows he will forget; among them, Emerson is the single literary name. In the winter of 1962, Borges had visited Emerson's house, an experience reflected in both the line in "Elogio," "*Emerson and the snow and many things*," and in another work, "Poema de la Cantidad" ("Poem of Quantity," 1970): "solitary and lost lights / which Emerson

15   J. L. Borges and O. Ferrari, *En diálogo*, 136.
16   Ibid., 141.
17   Ibid., 213.
18   J. L. Borges, *Other Inquisitions*, trans. by R. L. C. Simms (Austin, TX: University of Texas Press, 1964), 69.
19   Ibid., 10.
20   Recorded and quoted by R. J. Christ, *The Narrow Act* (New York: Lumen Books, 1995), 45-46.

would have admired so many nights / from the snows and the rigors of Concord."

Well before Borges, José Martí (1853-1895), Cuba's late-nineteenth-century poet, journalist, and revolutionary, had taken Emerson's model of the active reformer more to heart than the Argentinian.

6.9 José Martí at 41, 1894.

At eighteen, during Cuba's first attempt to throw off Spanish rule in the Ten Years' War, Martí was imprisoned for six months for denouncing a pro-Spanish high school classmate. Afterward, he studied in Spain, then left for Mexico, and, for a time, taught in Guatemala. Moving to New York City, he reported on the U.S. for a wide readership in Hispanic America. Fascinated by America's model, he excitedly introduced his audiences to Emerson, whose *Nature* and *Representative Men* were his favorite works. In 1882, just three weeks after his hero's death, Martí wrote a radiant hagiographic essay, "Emerson," in which each of his encomiums competes with the next, together creating a myth— eventually widespread–of an Emerson "who found himself alive, and shook from his shoulders and his eyes all the mantles and blindfolds that the past casts over men." "His mind was priestly; his tenderness, angelic; his wrath, sacred. When he saw enslaved men, and thought of them, he spoke as if, at the foot of a new biblical mountain, the Tablets of the Law were once again being smashed. His anger was Mosaic." Martí's unrelieved praise exceeds any evaluation of Emerson, then or since. [21]

In additional appreciation, he translated Emerson's poem "Good-Bye, Proud World." Two of Martí's own poems include Emerson in their titles: "Cada uno a su oficio. Fábula nueva del filósofo norteamericano Emerson" ("Each to His Own Work," 1889), and an undated long poem, simply titled, "Emerson." The latter focused on a mood of "Panic": "Nobody hinders his will / And lands and waters / Are atoms of his brilliant body / Which obey his invincible will." A similar exuberance fed Martí's continuing protest against Spanish rule in Cuba. In 1892, he started the Cuban Revolutionary Party, and three years later, returning to the island to help lead its second struggle for independence, was almost immediately killed in battle. Nevertheless, Martí became an "Apostle of Independence" in his country. Eventually, though Emerson was decidedly not a socialist, his work came to inspire Fidel Castro through Martí's example.[22]

Emerson in England and Scotland

In his lifetime, Emerson made three trips to England and Europe. On his first trip (1832-1833), he was only twenty-nine and unknown, yet succeeded in meeting four leading writers. Coleridge, Wordsworth, and Landor represented an older, already distinguished generation.

---

21   José Martí, *Obras Completas* (La Habana: Editorial Nacional de Cuba, 1964), 13: 18-23, 30.

22   Ibid., 17: 154, 324-27. "José Martí," http://www.loc.gov/rr/hispanic/1898/marti.html; https://en.wikipedia.org/wiki/Jos%C3%A9_Mart%C3%AD; http://www.biography.com/people/jos%C3%A9-mart%C3%AD-20703847

6.10 William Wordsworth at 69.

But the rising Scottish historian and social critic, Thomas Carlyle (1795-1881), was only eight years Emerson's senior. Carlyle's friend John Stuart Mill had warned him in advance, "From one or two conversations I have had with [Emerson] I do not think him a very hopeful subject."[23] But Carlyle and his wife Jane gave Emerson a warm welcome. Jane remembered the visitor who "in the Desert [of rural Scotland], descended on us, out of the clouds as it were, and made one day there look like enchantment for us, and left me weeping that it was only *one* day."[24] In turn, Emerson liked Carlyle's frank simplicity. Their ensuing letters for a time document an intensely appreciative exchange. Each served the other as literary critic, agent, and press officer in their respective countries. Later, they would maintain their ties but differ over social issues, especially slavery in America.

23   J. S. Mill, August 2, 1833, in *The Earlier Letters of John Stuart Mill 1812-1848* (Toronto and London: Routledge & Kegan Paul, 1963), 171.

24   Jane W. Carlyle to Emerson, November 7, 1838, *The Correspondence of Thomas Carlyle and Ralph Waldo Emerson* (Boston, Mass.: Houghton Mifflin, 1883) 1: 192. Hereafter, *CCE*.

Most importantly, Carlyle uniquely strengthened Emerson's sense of his own powers. *Nature*, the Scot said, gave him "true satisfaction." He correctly noted it as "the Foundation and Ground-plan" of Emerson's work.[25] Of "The American Scholar" (1837), he said, "I could have *wept* to read that speech; the clear high melody of it went tingling through my heart." Carlyle, a clergyman's son like Emerson, blessed his friend's debut: "May God grant you strength; for you have a *fearful* work to do! Fearful I call it; and yet it is great, and the greatest."[26] In the same breath, he demanded that his friend practice patient self-reliance: "Do not hasten to write; you cannot be too slow about it. Give no ear to any man's praise or censure."[27]

6.11 Thomas Carlyle in his 60s, c. 1860s.

Carlyle sent Emerson's lectures and books to friends in England and Europe, and forwarded their reactions back to Emerson in Concord. As early as 1838, he wrote of the favorable opinion of Harriet Martineau, the English feminist and social observer. She had met Emerson during her two-year

25   T. Carlyle to Emerson, Feb. 13, 1837, *CCE* 1: 112.
26   T. Carlyle to Emerson, Dec. 8, 1837, *CCE* 1: 142.
27   Ibid.

tour of America in 1834-1836. In her *Retrospect of Western Travel* (1838), she was one of the first foreigners to publicize Emerson's representativeness as an American as well as his special gifts: "There is a remarkable man in the United States, without knowing whom it is not too much to say that the United States cannot be fully known . . . . [He] is yet in the prime of life. Great things are expected from him, and great things, it seems, he cannot but do . . . . He is a thinker without being solitary, abstracted, and unfitted for the time. He is a scholar without being narrow, bookish, and prone to occupy himself only with other men's thoughts." Martineau went further, praising Emerson for neglecting "no political duty," for being "ready at every call to action."[28] At this early date, such a description of Emerson's activist side by a foreigner was clearly both remarkable and prescient. Perhaps exaggerated, it nonetheless came six years before his 1844 Concord abolitionist speech showed his true colors to family and friends.

Before Emerson's lectures appeared as essays and his reputation grew, Carlyle's personal advice vitally encouraged him. His Scottish friend judged him to be producing "a *sort* of speech which is itself *action*, an artistic sort." He had glimpsed Emerson's gift to create words that breathed. Wishing him to sharpen this talent, he exhorted, "You *tell* us with piercing emphasis that man's soul is great; *show* us a great soul of a man, in some work symbolic of such: this is the seal of such a message, and you will feel by and by that you are called to this. I long to see some concrete Thing, some Event, Man's Life, American Forest, or piece of Creation, which this Emerson loves and wonders at, well *Emersonized*, depictured by Emerson, filled with the life of Emerson, and cast forth from him then to live by itself."[29] Carlyle was virtually defining Emerson's true vocation and also, like Martineau, predicting his entry into social reform.

When Emerson's *Essays I* appeared in 1841, Carlyle welcomed them as the only true, alive sensibility that responded intelligently to his own. Emerson's was "a voice of the heart of Nature" that, although too imperfect to express the infinite, was itself "an Infinitude."[30] Carlyle positively described his friend's ethereal words as "light–rays darting upwards in the East," the promises of a "new era." Nevertheless, shortly after *The Dial*

---

28   H. Martineau, *Retrospect of Western Travel* (London: Saunders & Otley, 1838), 203-04. Martineau's *Retrospect* and her *Society in America* (1837) have been compared to Tocqueville's *Democracy in America* (1835, 1840).
29   T. Carlyle to Emerson, February 8, 1839, *CCE* 1: 217.
30   T. Carlyle to Emerson, May 8, 1841, *CCE* 1: 352.

appeared that same year, Carlyle found it "shrill, incorporeal, spirit-like."[31] Despite his own lapses from the concrete, this historian-philosopher always disliked whatever in Emerson he found excessively abstract, and rightly assessed his influence on *The Dial*, even though at that moment, Margaret Fuller was its editor.

By his second trip to England and Europe in 1847-1848, Emerson had become a literary star, internationally known as the author of *Nature*, *Essays I* and *II* (1841, 1844) , the founder-editor of *The Dial* (1842-1844), and, in short, the champion of avant-garde American culture. But his "Divinity School Address" (1838), in challenging the need for any clergy to interpret spiritual experience, had spawned fierce theological controversies at home and abroad, leading opponents to call him a corruptor of youth. Also, Emerson's "Man the Reformer" (1841) had circulated underground in Britain as a little classic of radicalism before his arrival at Liverpool in November 1847. At Mechanics' Institutes, he addressed huge crowds of aspiring young workers and professionals in industrial cities such as Liverpool and Manchester as well as smaller elite audiences in London. Leading figures, from politicians and aristocrats (Lord Lovelace, Lady Byron, and the man of letters Monckton Milnes) to writers (Thackeray, De Quincey, Leigh Hunt, and Matthew Arnold), all took note of him. In contrast, Emerson was in fundamental disagreement now with Carlyle over a range of economic, political, and social issues. Emerson was dismayed to find his old friend an "epicure in diet" and a "*sansculotte*-aristocrat," a "magnificent genius" lost in dogmatism and aimlessness. The two further disagreed about Carlyle's current hero, Cromwell.[32] However, their friendship would continue in an intermittent correspondence all their lives.

When George Eliot (1819-1880) first met Emerson in June 1848, she was already familiar with his essays. A month later, she extravagantly described him as "the first *man* I have ever seen."[33] Twelve years later "with venerating gratitude," she recalled his "mild face, which I daresay is smiling on some one as beneficently as it one day did on me years and years ago."[34] At the same moment, Eliot was appreciating the "fresh beauty and meaning" of "Man the Reformer," which she had turned to for her "spiritual good." Despite

---

31   T. Carlyle to John Sterling, December 18, 1841, *The New England Transcendentalists and the Dial*, ed. J. Myerson (Rutherford, NJ: Fairleigh Dickinson University Press, 1980), 73.

32   *JMN* 11: 172.

33   Eliot to S. Hennell, July 1848, in *The George Eliot Letters*, ed. Gordon S. Haight (New Haven, CT: Yale University Press, 1954), 1: 270. Hereafter *GEL*.

34   Eliot to S. Hennell, August 27, 1860, *GEL* 3: 337.

this appreciation, Eliot rarely noted any indebtedness to Emerson in her own works, except in *Romola* (1863). In her chapter "The Blind Scholar and his Daughter," Emerson's declaration of intellectual independence ("The American Scholar") transfigures her character's emancipation.[35] However, Eliot's interest in reading his works continued all her life. His *Society and Solitude* (1870) gave her "enough gospel to serve one for a year."[36] And on New Year's Day 1877, anticipating her own death which came three years later, Eliot recalled Emerson's stirring poem "Days."[37]

On this second trip to England, Emerson's awareness of the Continent's revolutionary unrest was heightened by his concern for Margaret Fuller, in Italy for the *New-York Tribune* to report on that country's fight for unification. In this context, he re-encountered Wordsworth. Fourteen years before, as he recounted in *English Traits*, his general admiration for Wordsworth's "great simplicity" had been qualified by surprise at finding certain "hard limits to his thought," assessing him at that time as "one who paid for his rare elevation by general tameness and conformity."[38] Now on this second visit, he and Harriet Martineau happened to awaken the seventy-eight-year-old Wordsworth from a nap. After silently pulling himself together, the poet gave way to a spate of bitterness about the French and then the Scots, intoning that Scotsmen were incapable of writing English. That included Carlyle, he said, "who is a pest to the English tongue."[39] Emerson could not know that Wordsworth had long thought the same of him. Seven years before, he had sardonically written a friend, "Our two present Philosophers [Emerson and Carlyle], who have taken a language which they suppose to be English for their vehicle, are verily 'Par nobile fratrum' ["a noble pair of brothers"], and it is a pity that the weakness of our age has not left them exclusively to the appropriate reward, mutual admiration. Where is the thing that now passes for philosophy at Boston to stop?"[40] Although Emerson had always qualified his appreciation of Wordsworth, after his death in 1850, he remarked in *English Traits*, "His adherence to

35 See E. Fontana, "George Eliot's *Romola* and Emerson's 'The American Scholar,'" *ELN*, 32, 1995.
36 Eliot to Oscar Browning, May 8, 1870, *GEL* 5: 93.
37 *GEL* 6: 327.
38 *CW* 5: 12.
39 Ibid., 166.
40 Wordsworth to H. Reed, August 16, 1841, *The Letters of William and Dorothy Wordsworth* (Oxford: Clarendon Press, 1988), 7: 230-31.

his poetic creed rested on real inspirations. The Ode on Immortality is the high-water-mark which the intellect has reached in this age."[41]

In 1850, Carlyle praised *Representative Men*, ignoring the difference between Emerson's essentially democratic, self-affirming uses of great men and his own hierarchical treatment of parallel figures in *Heroes, Hero-Worship, and the Heroic in History* (1841). But he disagreed with Emerson about Plato, whom he disliked. He also regretted that his friend had ended each of his profiles with criticism. Six years later, Carlyle's enthusiasm for Emerson's *English Traits* was less qualified. By 1860, he especially liked *The Conduct of Life*, and ten years later, *Society and Solitude* as well. Yet he criticized a continuing optimism in Emerson, ignoring his friend's exploration of nature's predictably unsentimental ways in "Fate."[42] During Emerson's third trip to Europe in 1872-1873—for the most part, an old man's enjoyment of his celebrity—he twice saw Carlyle for a final time, their dwindling contact soon to end in old age and infirmity.

An American friend and admirer of Emerson, Charles Eliot Norton (1827-1908), co-editor of the *North American Review* and art professor at Harvard, was also a long-time resident in England and on the Continent. Eventually, he edited the Emerson-Carlyle correspondence. Paralleling Carlyle's trans-Atlantic role in enhancing Emerson's reputation in the West, Norton also promoted Emerson in letters and gifts of his books to friends. Norton's contacts included the Rossetti brothers—the poet-painter Dante Gabriel and the editor William—as well as the editor-critic Leslie Stephen. In America in 1863, Stephen met Norton and, probably through him, Emerson. Almost forty years later, Stephen published a comprehensive short exposition of Emerson's writings.[43] Not surprisingly then, Stephen's daughter Virginia Woolf (1882-1941) came to applaud Emerson's "firm and glittering" analogies. In her novel about women in modern times, *Night and Day* (1919), the suffragette Mary muses, "I must reflect with Emerson that it's being and not doing that matters."[44] But earlier, Woolf had largely dismissed Emerson as a mere "schoolmaster."[45] Her surface attention contrasts with the lesser novelist Dorothy Richardson, whose Miriam in

41   *CW* 5: 168.
42   T. Carlyle to Emerson, April 6, 1870, *CCE* 2: 324.
43   Leslie Stephen, "Emerson," *Studies of a Biographer* (London: Duckworth & Co., 1902), 3.
44   V. Woolf, *Night and Day* (1919), ed. J. Briggs (London and New York: Penguin, 1992), 38.
45   V. Woolf, "Emerson's Journals" (1910), *The Essays of Virginia Woolf: 1904-1912*, ed. A. McNeillie (London: Hogarth Press, 1986), 1: 339.

Pilgrimage (13 vols., 1915-1938) either quotes or mentions Emerson more than any other writer.[46]

The Irish author Oscar Wilde (1854-1900), wit and celebrated aesthete, was strongly attracted to Emerson, principally at first for his ideas on art and for his whimsy. Later, he adopted some of his more substantial ideas. Wilde's early focus on only a part of Emerson's legacy produced a rather ambiguous effect. On the one hand, believing Emerson to be a "fine thinker"[47] and, with Whitman, one of America's two best poets,[48] he heavily borrowed phrases, even whole sentences from Emerson. In the United States in 1882 to give a lecture series popularizing aestheticism, Wilde echoed Emerson's views on the unity of beauty and utility.

6.12 Oscar Wilde at 28, c. 1882.

46 D. Richardson, *Pilgrimage* (London: Dent, Cresset Press, 1938), 3: 41, 128; 4: 545. On Emersonian sources in *Pilgrimage* and in Richardson's letters, see G. H. Thompson, *Notes on Pilgrimage: Dorothy Richardson Annotated* (Greensboro, NC: ELT Press, 1999), 97, 140, 144, 250.
47 O. Wilde, "The Soul of Man under Socialism," *The Soul of Man. De Profundis. The Ballad of Reading Gaol*, ed. Isobel Murray (Oxford: Oxford University Press, 1999), 13.
48 For Wilde's judgment on Emerson as a poet, see his interview, January 16, 1882, cited in R. Ellmann, *Oscar Wilde* (New York: Vintage Books, 1988), 167.

But on the other hand, in the same series he called the symbolism of Transcendentalism escapist and "Asiatic."[49] In this series, too, he quoted from "Man the Reformer," then without attribution stole several sentences of Emerson's (with variants) with which he concludes his "Domestic Life." As Wilde's tour ended, he at least recognized the "Attic genius" of "New England's Plato," perhaps because Emerson had died only weeks before. Then in "L'Envoi," an introductory essay of the same year, Wilde recalled Emerson's comment in "Nominalist and Realist": "I am always insincere, knowing that there are other moods,"[50] revealing that at this stage he was principally drawn to Emerson the droll "master of moods" rather than the model authentic man.[51]

In his critical dialogue *The Decay of Lying* (1889), Wilde continued to emphasize the puckish Emerson. But in assigning him the role of artist as absolute liar "for art's sake," Wilde ignored the moral limits Emerson gave to imaginative creation. In another dialogue, *The Critic as Artist* (1890), Wilde culls Emerson's essays "Compensation" and "The Over-Soul" for his characters' exchanges on the human psyche. Wilde's Ernest announces, ". . . Men are wiser than they know" and "We are wiser than we know." And his Gilbert wryly says he lives "in terror of not being misunderstood," paraphrasing "Self-Reliance" ("Is it so bad, then, to be misunderstood? . . . To be great is to be misunderstood."). Elsewhere in this dialogue, Wilde quoted or referred to "Self-Reliance" at least three more times.

Again, this time bridging the individual and politics in *The Soul of Man Under Socialism* (1891), Wilde leaned heavily on Emerson. Drawing on "Self-Reliance," "The Poet," and also on his "Considerations by the Way," Wilde quotes and paraphrases Emerson's treatment of a slew of subjects: conformity, freedom, imitation, autonomy, misunderstanding, individualism, tradition, property, mobs, philanthropy, and man as ·symbol.[52] Wilde's single novel *The Picture of Dorian Gray* (1891), the story of a

---

49   O. Wilde, "Art and the Handicraftsman," June 2, 1882, *Essays and Lectures* (Charleston, SC: BiblioBazaar, LLC, 2007), 103-14.

50   O. Wilde and Rennell Rodd, *Rose Leaf and Apple Leaf* (Philadelphia, PA: J. M. Stoddart & Co., 1882), 18.

51   In 1885, Wilde wrote to A. P. T. Elder, editor of a fledgling American literary journal: "I see no limit to the future in art of a country which has already given us Emerson, that master of moods . . . ." *The Complete Letters of Oscar Wilde*, ed. Merlin Holland (New York: Fourth Estate, 2003), 249.

52   O. Wilde, *The Soul of Man Under Socialism* (article, *Fortnightly Review* XLIX: 290, February 1891, 292-319; book, 1904). See O. Wilde, *Soul of Man* (1999), 11-13: 114, 197-98, 200-02, 204-06, 209-10, 212-16.

handsome young degenerate, follows this same Emerson-indebted pattern. His Lord Henry condenses, paraphrases and typically exaggerates ideas from "Self-Reliance" and "Success," as in "People are afraid of themselves, nowadays. They have forgotten the highest of all duties, the duty that one owes to oneself."[53]

After his imprisonment in 1895, Wilde, perhaps seeking to justify his life choices, selected Emerson's essays as prime reading matter, now gravitating to his more serious thoughts. Wilde's posthumous published letter *De Profundis* (1905) comments on a central passage from "Success": "'Nothing is more rare in any man,' says Emerson, 'than an act of his own.' It is quite true. Most people are other people. Their thoughts are someone else's opinion, their life a mimicry, their passions a quotation."[54] Wilde could adopt this much, but not the full load of Emerson's thought.

Emerson was also widely read among British philosophers, such as A. N. Whitehead and the novelist-lecturer John Cowper Powys (1872-1863). Powys's *One Hundred Best Books* (1916) cites an edition of Emerson's major writings and praises his "clear, chaste, remote and distinguished wisdom . . . with its shrewd preacher's wit and country-bred humor." He also noted a vital link in the chain of Emerson's influence in Europe: "Nietzsche found him a sane and noble influence principally on the ground of his serene detachment from the phenomena of sin and disease and death." Powys was one of the first to call attention to the now well-known Emerson-Nietzsche connection. That relationship, generally overlooked by mainstream criticism, especially in Europe, had already excelled any other in scope and rich ramification in the West.[55]

Emerson in German-Speaking Europe

The indebtedness of the German philosopher Friedrich Nietzsche (1844-1900) to Emerson has long been known, but for the most part only in specialist circles.[56] Furthermore, like José Martí in Cuba, Nietzsche superbly illustrates the literal revolutionary effect of Emerson's ideas in his native country and throughout Europe. But Nietzsche's frequent celebration,

---

53   O. Wilde, *Oscar Wilde: The Major Works* (Oxford and New York: Oxford University Press, 2000), 61.

54   O. Wilde, *Soul of Man* (1999), 114.

55   J. C. Powys, *One Hundred Books* (New York: G. A. Shaw, 1916), 26.

56   See, for example, studies by Hubbard, Stack, Cavell, Kateb, Lopez, Conant, Mikics, Bloom, Zavatta, and others.

especially on the Continent, has more than eclipsed his malignant role in departing from Emerson's core intent. In fact, his misinterpretations of Emerson, taken up and further falsified by the Nazis, fed Germany's political ambitions and contributed to the catastrophes of World War II.

6.13 Friedrich Nietzsche at about 31, c. 1875.

In 1862, the seventeen-year-old Nietzsche's delight with a new translation of *The Conduct of Life* led him to buy Emerson's *Essays I* and *II*.[57] Later, he acquired other works, including a second copy of *The Conduct of Life* and translations by Herman Grimm. From the start, Nietzsche copiously underlined and made exclamatory notes of praise in the margins of these works: "Ja!," "Gut!," "Sehr Gut!," "Das ist recht!," "Das ist wahr!" Directly or indirectly, Nietzsche referred to Emerson over a hundred times in his

---

57   *Die Führung des Lebens,* trans. E. S. von Mühlberg (Leipzig: Steinacker, 1862); *Versuche* (I and II series), trans. G. Fabricius (Hannover: Meyer, 1858).

books and manuscripts, and regularly in his notes and letters. He rarely traveled without his Emerson.[58]

Arguably, Emerson was Nietzsche's first as well as his last intellectual mentor. The American had already magnetized him a year before he began studying Plato and three years before he took up Schopenhauer. Then for over twenty-five years, Emerson remained a vital touchstone as Nietzsche wrote *Unzeitgemäße Betrachtungen* (*Untimely Considerations*, 1873-1876); rejected Schopenhauer in 1876-1877; and composed *Also Sprach Zarathustra* (*Thus Spoke Zarathustra*, 1885). Nietzsche's *Götzen-Dämmerung* (*The Twilight of the Idols*, 1888) further praised Emerson. A draft of *Ecce Homo* (also 1888) contains one of Nietzsche's most heartfelt confessions of Emerson's influence, and an original interpretation of him as a radical skeptic. So great was Nietzsche's debt that, evidently to disguise the importance of Emerson as a constant source, he censored this mention of him.[59]

Yet Nietzsche often departed from Emerson's original meaning. His treatment of fate and freedom heads the list of misinterpretations. The year he first devoured Emerson (1862), Nietzsche published essays of his own on his hero's subjects—fate, freedom, and history—topics that Heidegger later described as Nietzsche's "essential center."[60] In a near-paraphrase of Emerson's "Fate," Nietzsche urged the simultaneous embrace of, and resistance to, circumstance. But he went further, proposing a cultural revolution that far exceeded anything Emerson had envisioned: the subversion of the entire Christian tradition. The teen-age Nietzsche claimed that Christianity had inculcated a system of moral "slavery" and human degradation by preaching original sin and guilt, the superiority of soul to body, and an afterlife beyond this existence. By the 1880s, Nietzsche was adding to Christianity other traditions he thought equally injurious, whether religious or not: Buddhism, Platonic idealism, Socialism, and Democracy. For him, their valuation of equality and an ethic aligned with

---

58   G. J. Stack, *Nietzsche and Emerson: An Elective Affinity* (Athens, OH: Ohio University Press, 1992), 34.

59   In a chapter draft, "Why I Am So Wise," Nietzsche, *On the Genealogy of Morals. Ecce Homo*, eds. W. Kaufmann, et al. (New York: Vintage Books, 1989), 25.

60   G. J. Stack, "Nietzsche's Earliest Essays: Translation of and Commentary on Fate and History and Freedom of Will and Fate," in *Philosophy Today*, 37 (1993), 153-69. On the connection with Heidegger's *Nietzsche* (San Francisco: HarperSanFrancisco, 1991), 1: 134; see translators' notes, D. F. Krell and Stanley Cavell, *Philosophical Passages* (Oxford: Wiley-Blackwell, 1995), 40.

the poor, weak, and diseased promoted false goals and a debilitating herd mentality.[61]

In contrast, Emerson's criticism of Congregational and Unitarian forms of Christianity in early nineteenth-century New England had focused on removing the powers of clergy and dogma which he felt separated the single believer from God. Emerson's Jesus of Nazareth was an admirable man, even a model human being, but was neither wholly, nor even partially, "God's son." Such a role falsely elevated him above the rest of humanity. As for Platonism, Buddhism, and other philosophies or faiths, Emerson explored them with deep curiosity, looking for spiritual enlightenment. Too individualistic to support socialism, he nevertheless firmly and with vigor championed both equality and democracy. Their effects could disappoint, but they were infinitely preferable to a hermetic hierarchy or monarchy. Emerson would have considered Nietzsche's *Der Antichrist* (*The Antichrist*, 1888), opposing both Christian thought and democracy, a travesty of his concept of self-reliance, which he always linked to a larger ethical norm.

Nietzsche had made his departure from this central Emersonian idea clear in *Thus Spoke Zarathustra* (1885). In large part inspired by Emerson's "Character,"[62] Zarathustra embodied Nietzsche's famous concept of an "Ubermensch," "Man above men," or a so-called super-man. In Emerson's "Power," his *"plus* man"[63] had rejected conformity not to be independent for its own sake but to act authentically, drawing energy and motivation from a higher moral spirit. Since the 1830s, Emerson had developed this concept of the extraordinary man from his "Man Thinking" ("The American Scholar" and "The Poet") as well as from his select group profiled in *Representative Men*. Again, he rooted humanity's "plus" state in an intimacy with creation's overarching ethical order. In contrast, Nietzsche's *Ubermensch* epitomized not only a *surplus* of humanity and life, but also was *above* any moral, religious, or even cosmic law.

Similarly, in his posthumous work, *Der Wille zur Macht* (*The Will to Power*, 1901), Nietzsche continued to reverse Emerson on this subject. Once again, Emerson's sense of life as "a search after power" arose from a belief that legitimate authority comes only to a soul in harmony with the heart of nature: universal moral law. His "Divinity School Address" (1838) early

---

61   See, for example, Nietzsche, *Beyond Good and Evil*, Preface, aphorism 56; *The Antichrist*; *The Will to Power*, especially sections 751-53.
62   M. Montinari, *Reading Nietzsche* (Urbana, IL: University of Illinois Press, 2003), 71-72.
63   *CW* 6: 31.

announced a personal and profoundly meditative quest, both endless and experimental, aiming for, but always short of, eternal truth. No such idealism framed Nietzsche's *Will to Power*. For him, philosophers never innocently and disinterestedly explore for truth's sake. Their actual goal is all-encompassing power, from worldly influence and infinite fame to physical, political, and technological control.[64] Nietzsche's natural will to power not only inverted Emerson's understanding of the soul in tune with cosmic force. But in addition, his attitude, an apparent realism laced with cynicism, added an amoral touch. In effect, Nietzsche questioned the very sincerity of his hero's idealistic pursuit of truth.

In "Considerations by the Way," Emerson theorized on the "good of evil" as impetus: "Good is a good doctor, but Bad is sometimes a better.[65] Nietzsche explored this basic idea in *Beyond Good and Evil* (1886). Then, only two years later in *The Antichrist*, he developed a rough and rigid antithesis to Emerson's views, turning upside down the Christian concept of the ethical. Instead of empathizing with the weak, ill, enslaved, obedient, peaceful, ignored, or poor, he championed the healthy, rich, and powerful in all of history's traditional hierarchies—political, military and social.

Nietzsche's ultimate sense of time and focus also radically differed from Emerson's with implications for his concept of free will. Emerson argued for engagement in this present existence, emphatically stating, "There is no other world. God is one and omnipresent; here or nowhere is the whole fact."[66] But Nietzsche's *The Gay Science* (1882) introduced the concept of "the Eternal Return," which conceived of the world as endlessly repeating itself in every detail.[67] This ultimately closed arc implied a static, wholly determined universe. Such a vision was quite the opposite of Emerson's early and continuing sense of the world's change, movement, and expansion, and humanity's parallel action within it. In "Circles" (1841), he had written, "Our life is an apprenticeship to the truth, that around every circle another

---

64   For both writers on power, see Emerson, *CW* 6: 30-32; and Nietzsche's *Writings from the Late Notebooks* (Cambridge and New York: Cambridge University Press, 2003), especially 15, 50, 73, 134.

65   *CW* 6: 134-35, 137-39.

66   "The Sovereignty of Ethics" (1878), *The Complete Works of Ralph Waldo Emerson*, ed. E. W. Emerson (Boston, Mass.: Houghton Mifflin, 1903-1904), 10: 199. Hereafter *W*. See also Emerson's "Circles," "Illusions," "Works and Days," and the first part of "Poetry and Imagination." Cf. Nietzsche's representative views, "Afterworldsmen," *Thus spoke Zarathustra* (London and New York: Penguin, 1961), 58-60.

67   Friedrich Nietzsche, *The Gay Science*, trans. W. Kaufmann (New York: Vintage, 1974), 273.

can be drawn; that there is no end in nature, but every end is a beginning
. . . ."[68] Writing "Fate" in the 1850s, he was more explicit in championing
free will: "To hazard the contradiction,—freedom is necessary." In short,
it was determined. He went on, "a part of Fate is the freedom of man . . .
Intellect annuls Fate. So far as a man thinks, he is free." This fundamental
paradox arose from Emerson's lifelong existential experience of "choosing
and acting."[69]

As his *Beyond Good and Evil* (1886) reveals, Nietzsche's politics also
radically distanced him from Emerson. The two differed on such major
issues as progressive democratic goals, abolition, feminist ideals, peace,
and war. Contrary to his posthumous reputation, Nietzsche was not a Nazi,
nor was he a fascist, nationalist, socialist, pan-German enthusiast, or racial
purist. He hated anti-Semites and mass movements. But in his later super-
reactionary opinions, he eclipsed Emerson's sense of empowering "each
and all." Nietzsche came to advocate a pro-slavery, autocratic new order,
his "warmongering" attitude pushing him to invoke a "new terrorism."[70]
More famously, he gave a new framework to his earlier transformation of
Emerson's "representative men" into lawless "Ubermenschen," ripe for the
Nazis' misuse. Emerson had noted one "good of evil": "Wars, fires, plagues,
break up immovable routine, clear the ground of rotten races and dens of
distemper, and open a fair field to new men." Nietzsche went much further,
proposing a true theory of active eugenics "in order to shape the man of the
future through breeding and . . . the annihilation of millions of failures."[71]

In brief, the later Nietzsche had quite corrupted Emerson's leading ideas.
In turn, the Nazis, heralding Nietzsche as a prophet, either perpetuated
earlier untruths about him or invented new ones. Thus, any alleged claims of
a link between the real Emerson and the National Socialists, past or present,
are quite false. Nietzsche's association with the Nazis began with his sister
Elisabeth, wife of a fervent anti-Semite, who imposed her own bias upon
her brother's posthumous book *Will to Power*, censoring Nietzsche when he
spoke *against* anti-Semites.[72] Then in 1918, just after Germany's humiliating

---

68   *CW* 2: 179.

69   *CW* 6: 12-13. See also E. W. Emerson's *CW of RWE* 6: 24.

70   In a draft for *The Genealogy of Morals* (1887) in *Sämtliche Werke: kritische Studienausgabe in
      15 Bänden* (Berlin and New York: De Gruyter, 1974), 7: 3, 220-21. Hereafter *SW*.

71   *CW* 6: 135; Nietzsche, *The Will to Power* (New York: Vintage, 1968), 506.

72   See M. Ferraris, "Storia della volontà di potenza," in Nietzsche, *La volontà di potenza*
      (Milano: Bompiani, 1994), 615. See Colli and Montinari's notes to *SW*. Georges Bataille
      had shown similar manipulations by Nietzsche's cousin R. Oehler in "Nietzsche et les
      fascistes," *Acéphale*, January 21, 1937, 3-11.

defeat in World War I, a successful German book mythologized Nietzsche as a pivotal Germanic-Nordic-Greek myth-creator for the German people.[73] The next year, a booklet interpreted him as "Prophet" of an extreme, dictatorial form of "Socialism."[74] But not until the mid-1920s did a full "Nazification" of Nietzsche take place, when certain German writers applied his "master morality" and presumed anti-Semitism to a proto-Nazi racial interpretation of the "Jewish question."[75] Also in the pre-Nazi years, the chief editor of Nietzsche's works, Alfred Baeumler (who became a Nazi in 1933), assumed Nietzsche to be anti-Jewish and celebrated him as both a philosopher and a political scientist. Others profiled him as godfather of a new German nation and "wisdom," based on a life-enhancing amoral law.[76]

Meanwhile, Elisabeth Nietzsche had started a correspondence with Mussolini in 1923, which led to their meeting in the early 1930s. In 1932, she also became a friend of Hitler's.[77] In the next two years, Hitler visited the Nietzsche-Archive in Weimar at least three times, paid tribute to Elisabeth with private gifts, and was photographed looking at Nietzsche's bust.[78] Nietzsche's cousin Richard Oehler reproduced one such picture in his 1935 book, where he combined quotations from Nietzsche and *Mein Kampf* (1925-1926).[79] In the later 1930s, most Nazis were either ignorant of, or deliberately overlooked, Nietzsche's deep indebtedness to the democratic Emerson. Martin Heidegger, then a member of the Nazi party and an Anglophobe, censored a German scholar's study of the Nietzsche-Emerson connection.[80]

73 Ernst Bertram, *Nietzsche. Versuch einer Mythologie* (Berlin: Bondi, 1918).

74 H. Bund, *Nietzsche als Prophet des Sozialismus* (Breslau: Trewendt & Granier, 1919).

75 F. Haiser, *Die Judenfrage vom Standpunkt der Herrenmoral: Rechtsvölkische und linksvölkische Weltanschauung* (Leipzig: Weicher, 1926); A. Schickedanz, *Das Judentum, eine Gegenrasse* (Leipzig: Weicher, 1927).

76 For example, see A. Baeumler, *Nietzsche, der Philosoph und Politiker* (Leipzig: Reclam, 1931); F. Mess, *Nietzsche: Der Gesetzgeber* (Leipzig: F. Meiner, 1930).

77 M. Ferraris, "Storia," in *La volontà di potenza*, 648.

78 C. Diethe, *Nietzsche's Sister and The Will to Power* (Urbana, IL: University of Illinois Press, 2003), 151-52.

79 R. Oehler, *Nietzsche und deutsche Zukunft* [*Nietzsche and the Future of Germany*] (Leipzig: Armanen, 1935).

80 In Nazi Germany in the 1930s, E. Baumgarten was the principal student of the Emerson-Nietzsche relationship, *Der Pragmatismus. R. W. Emerson, W. James, J. Dewey* (Frankfurt: Klostermann, 1938), 81-96; and secondarily, J. Simon, *Ralph Waldo Emerson in Deutschland* (1851-1932) (Berlin: Junker und Dünnhaupt, 1937) and H. Hildebrand, *Die Amerikanische Stellung zur Geschichte und zu Europa in Emersons Gedankensystem* (Bonn: Verlag Hanstein, 1936). For Heidegger's censorship, see M. Lopez in "Emerson and Nietzsche: An Introduction", *ESQ*, 43 (1997), 1-35.

On Mussolini's sixtieth birthday in 1943, Hitler gave him a complete edition of Nietzsche's works, an act that symbolized the culmination of Nietzsche's legacy to the Nazi-Fascist movements.[81]

The deep, continuous tie between Emerson and Nietzsche serves as a master key for Emerson's entrance into the viscera of twentieth-century European culture. Students of Nietzsche's would inevitably be introduced to Emerson. In turn, their writings referred to both. For example, Belgian Nobel Prize-winner Maurice Maeterlinck, a key figure in the French symbolist movement, wrote a far-reaching essay "Emerson" (1897) that emphasized the everyday presence of a world of transcendental, spiritual mystery and beauty. In Austria, novelist Robert Musil (1880-1942) read Maeterlinck's essay and quickly noted the Emerson-Nietzsche relationship. Musil soon dedicated himself to what he termed "essayism," or Emerson's constant experimentation. He was also drawn to his exaltation of individual action and his aversion to both philosophical systems and the slavish adulation of history.

Throughout his career, Musil quoted, paraphrased, or integrated Emerson into his writing.[82] As a young engineering student at the turn of the century, he read a German edition of the *Essays*,[83] to which he returned in 1905 and again in the 1920s. The radical dynamism of "Circles," as applied to both morals and politics, was a particular favorite. Sometime between 1899 and 1904 in an undated journal entry, Musil celebrated *The Conduct of Life* as a model of "an advanced culture."[84] Eleven more times, his journals refer to Emerson at moments when he was recording seeds for his novels, *Die Verwirrungen des Zöglings Törleß* (*The Perturbations of Young Torless*, 1906) and his masterwork, *Der Mann ohne Eigenschaften* (*The Man Without Qualities*, 1930, 1933, 1943, incomplete). Many of his journal entries draw on "The Poet," particularly on Emerson's idea that man is "only *half* himself, *the other half is his expression*" and on the daily need to express one's own "painful secret," or inmost truth.[85]

---

81   G. Zachariae, *Mussolini si confessa* (Milano: Garzanti, 1948), 25.

82   G. Howes has extensively shown Emerson's influence in his "Robert Musil and the Legacy of Ralph Waldo Emerson" (Ph.D. dissertation, University of Michigan, 1985). See also H. Hickman's studies of 1980 and 1984 on the young Musil.

83   *Essays: Erste Folge* (Leipzig: Diederichs, 1902). It included "Self-Reliance," "The Over-Soul," "Circles," "Compensation," "Heroism," "History," "The Poet," and Emerson's early lecture on "Literary Ethics."

84   R. Musil, *Diaries: 1899-1941* (New York: Basic Books, 1999), 23.

85   *Notebook* II, 25.VII; *CW* 3: 6.

In *The Man Without Qualities*, Musil took Emerson's experimentalism, a theme pervading his novel, and made it a "sense of possibility." From the beginning, his main character Anders (later Ulrich) is characterized by his enthusiasm for "the new, the technical, the Emersonian."[86] Emerson's "Circles" had stated: "Men walk as prophecies of the next age . . . I am only an experimenter. Do not set the least value on what I do, or the least discredit on what I do not, as if I pretended to settle any thing as true or false." After Emerson, Musil has Anders/Ulrich say: "Men walk in the world as prophecy of the future, and all their deeds are tests and experiments, for every deed can be surpassed by the next." Musil/Anders/Ulrich goes on to quote Emerson without attribution: "The virtues of society are vices of the saint." In the same breath, as if to finally credit him, his hero names Emerson as "a Man whom I love." Significant traces of Emerson extend into the novel's other characters: Clarisse, Leinsdorf, Arnheim, and Lindner. In reading Emerson along with Maeterlinck, Novalis, and Nietzsche, Musil thought, "We experience the most powerful movement of the mind."[87] In these authors, he found a vital, immediate relationship to the world, where contemplation and action are one.

Maeterlinck's "Emerson" of 1897 immediately inspired Rainer Maria Rilke (1875-1926), the twentieth-century bohemian Austrian poet.[88] That winter, he read Emerson's *Essays*,[89] and twice quoted them in his *Florenzer Tagebuch* (*Florentine Diary*, 1898). Like Musil, he was drawn to "Circles": "I simply experiment, an endless seeker, with no Past at my back."[90] Rilke echoes this thought in his essay "Notizien zur Melodie der Dinge" ("Notes on the Melody of Things", 1898): "We are right at the start, do you see. As though before everything. With a thousand and one dreams behind

---

86   R. Musil, *Tagebücher*, ed. A. Frisé (Reinbek bei Hamburg: Rowohlt, 1976), 2: 1099, cited in Howes (1985), 221.

87   R. Musil, "Geist und Erfahrung,"*Das neue Merkur* (1921), 3: 12.

88   J. Simon, *RWE in Deutschland* (1937), first vaguely recognized Emerson's influence; Ernst Zinn solidified the connection in his edition of Rilke, *Sämtliche Werke* (Frankfurt: Insel-Verlag, 1955-1966), as did Jan Wojcik, in "Emerson and Rilke: A Significant Influence?" *Modern Language Notes* 91 (1976), 565-74 and Marilyn Vogler Urion, "Emerson's Presence in Rilke's Imagery: Shadows of Early Influence," *Monatshefte für Deutschen Unterricht, Deutsche Sprache und Literatur* (1993), 85: 153-69. *Das neue Merkur* (1921), 3: 12.

89   Dähnert's edition (Leipzig: Reclam, 1897) included: "Circles," "Compensation," "Spiritual Laws," "Love," "The Over-Soul," "Art," "The Poet," "Character," and "Nature" (1844).

90   *CW* 2: 188.

us and no act."[91] Other images from "Circles" as well as "The Poet" and "The Over-Soul" were evident in this essay, including Pentecostal figures of "cloven flames and fiery men who speak holy words," of doors opening, mountain peaks and men as trees. Notable, too, is the figure of the poet-speaker whose work implants his perceptions in everyone. Emerson's "The Poet" refers to the men "of more delicate ear" than most of us who, hearing nature's "primal warblings," write, however imperfectly, "the songs of nations."[92] Rilke writes: ". . . a broad melody always wakes behind you, woven out of a thousand voices, where there is room for your own solo only here and there. To know when you need to join in: that is the secret of your solitude: just as the art of true interactions with others is to let yourself fall away from high words into a single common melody."[93]

This essay was part of a veritable flood of creativity that poured from Rilke in 1898.[94] In that year, his major essay "On Art" and another prose text, "Intérieurs," heavily drew from Emerson, the latter even mimicking his style.[95] In 1899, Rilke published a collection of poems in an Emerson/Whitman-like mode, *For My Joy* (*Mir Zur Feier*). Metamorphosis was its major theme, with at least four poems probably inspired by Emerson. The same year his *Book of Hours*, vol. 1, also appeared, its title alluding to Emerson's "Genius of the Hour" (from "Art") that "dwells in the hour that now is" (from "Over-Soul"). The book also repeats other favorite Emerson themes such as the creative glance of the poet and existence as a state of perpetual becoming. Rilke's *Book of Images*, a collection of poems written between 1898 and 1901, includes other themes that echo Emerson: the creative power of imagination, memory's selectivity, and fully living in the moment.

Emerson in French-speaking Europe

Adam Mickiewicz (1798-1855), a central figure in Polish literature, was also a multilingual poet claimed by several nations, especially France.

---

91   R. M. Rilke, "Notes on the Melody of Things," in his *The Inner Sky: Poems, Notes, Dreams*, trans. D. Searls (Boston, Mass.: David R. Godine, 2009).

92   *CW* 3: 6.

93   R. M. Rilke, *Notes*, section XVI.

94   For example, see J. Ryan, *The Vanishing Subject* (Chicago, IL: University of Chicago Press, 1991), 53. On Emerson's possible influences on Rilke's most mature works, see J. Ryan's discussion of the 1918 poem "To Music," *Rilke, Modernism and Poetic Tradition* (Cambridge and New York: Cambridge University Press, 1999), 161-62.

95   R. M. Rilke, *Intérieurs*, section XIII, *Werke* (Darmstadt: Wiss. Buchges, 1996), 4: 98-99.

6.14 Adam Mickiewicz at 44, 1842.

Among Romantics, he became ranked with Byron and Goethe. Mickiewicz and his colleague at the Collège de France, historian Edgar Quinet (1803-1875), shared a common passion for Emerson, beginning with *Nature* (1836), which they read in 1838. Only six years later, Quinet added Emerson's name to his list of the greatest modern philosophers after Vico, Condorcet, Herder, and Hegel. In the period 1843-1845, Mickiewicz and Quinet quoted and copied several passages from Emerson in both their journals and course lectures. For Mickiewicz, Emerson was "the American Socrates," similar to, but "more profound" than, the French spiritual and social philosopher Pierre Leroux. He also likened Emerson's sensitivity to that of Polish and Slavonic people, attuned to the "continual influence of the invisible world on the visible world." In Paris in 1847, Margaret Fuller used a gift of Emerson's *Poems* (1846) to win an introduction to the handsome, vibrant, and inspiring Pole, who shared her enthusiasm for women's rights.[96]

Through his teaching and translations, Mickiewicz contributed to the diffusion of Emerson's essays in France. In his courses, he quoted the first lines of "Man the Reformer" and ideas that probably derived from Emerson's "Farming." With "History," he translated these essays for "La Tribune des Peuples," his newly founded internationalist leftist magazine. Ideas from Emerson's "Self-Reliance" " and "Spiritual Laws" have been

---

96   A. Mickiewicz, *Les slaves* (Paris: Comptoir des imprimeurs réunis, 1849), 216-17, 456-57. Megan Marshall, *Margaret Fuller: A New American Life* (Boston, Mass.: Houghton Mifflin Harcourt, 2013), 286-87.

identified in seven of Mickiewicz's "Apothegms in Verses."[97] Besides his students, he introduced Emerson to the French historian Jules Michelet. Yet Mickiewicz regretted Emerson's apparent isolation from his time, nation, and land,[98] revealing an ignorance of the American's far-reaching readership and lecture audiences as well as his active antislavery and pro-women's rights work.

Of other leading French authors who enhanced Emerson's reputation in Europe, the poet Charles Baudelaire (1821-1867) made a strong contribution.[99]

6.15 Charles Baudelaire at 41, c. 1862.

---

97   See M. Z. Markiewicz, "Mickiewicz vulgarisateur d'Emerson," *Revue de littérature comparée* (1955), 29.

98   A. Mickiewicz, *Les slaves*, 457.

99   E. Montégut, a friend of Baudelaire, also wrote on Emerson; see "Un penseur et un poète américain," *Revue des deux mondes*, August 1, 1847. On the Emerson-Baudelaire relationship, see Dudley M. Marchi's "Baudelaire's America—Contrary Affinities," *Yearbook of Comparative and General Literature* 47 (2000), 37-52.

The two may have brushed shoulders, but did not meet in Paris in 1848, when the radical Baudelaire and the curious Emerson attended two separate revolutionary rallies. Although Baudelaire's American idol, Edgar Allan Poe (d. 1840) had not favored Emerson (and vice versa), Baudelaire was attracted to him via a French translation.[100] In addition, he knew at least parts of *Representative Men*, evident from his vitriolic attack on Voltaire in *Mon coeur mis à nu* (*My Heart Laid Bare*, 1864). Baudelaire suggested Emerson should have written an essay about the eighteenth century *philosophe* entitled *"the Anti-Poet, the King of Gawkers, the Prince of Superficials, the Anti-Artist, the preacher of janitresses."*[101] Baudelaire's purchase of *English Traits*[102] and an edition of *The Conduct of Life* in English showed his attraction to Emerson's most intense confrontations with urban, industrial culture. The latter book, especially, was a guide to an empowering ethics for modern life, a project for which Poe was no model.

The Conduct of Life is also widely present in Baudelaire's diary-like works, beginning in their first pages: *My Heart Laid Bare* (1864) and *Fusées* (*Rockets*, 1867). In *Rockets*, he either quotes or paraphrases from "Power" and other essays, taking up Emerson's ideas on concentration, the value of constant ambitions, and the virtue of repeated practice. In these writings, Baudelaire, the *bohémien* par excellence, repents his wasteful ways, seeks empowerment (with uncertain results) through self-reliance, and promises himself to refrain from any dissipation. A whole section of Baudelaire's journals on *Hygiène* (*Hygiene*, 1867) includes a long series of quotes, in English this time, from *The Conduct of Life*.

On the theme of concentration, Baudelaire often repeated a sentence from Emerson's "Considerations by the Way" in his book on Delacroix (1863): "The hero is he who is immovably centered." And he praised Emerson as "the overseas moralist" who, "though passing for leader of the boring Bostonian school, has nonetheless a certain acumen à la Seneca, proper to sharpen meditation." The wisdom Emerson applies, he wrote, "to the conduct of life and to the domain of affairs can equally be applied to the domain of poetry and art."[103] Baudelaire's attraction to Emerson, particularly his idea of the supremacy of the solitary artist, may have

---

100 See Montégut's preface, *Essais de philosophie américaine* (Paris: Charpentier, 1850).
101 C. Baudelaire, *My Heart Laid Bare* (New York: Vanguard, 1951), 186 (my translation).
102 C. Pichois, J.-P. Avice, *Dictionnaire Baudelaire* (Tusson, Charente: Du Lérot, 2002), 65.
103 C. Baudelaire, *Eugene Delacroix: His Life and Work* (New York: Lear Publishers, 1947), 44 (text re-translation mine).

helped him shift from advocating a confrontational socialism to an ethic of radical authenticity.[104]

In contrast to Baudelaire, the philosopher and writer Henri Bergson (1859-1941) was almost bilingual in English and French and thus could read Emerson in the original.

6.16 Henri Bergson at 68, 1927.

In 1917, he declared that he "loved Emerson," undoubtedly a result of his admiration for William James, Emerson's younger friend and close reader, as seen in Chapter 5.[105] Bergson's earliest references to Emerson in 1906-1907 borrow ideas from the beginning of his "Character" that focus on the gap between character and action.[106] He cites Emerson's examples of the English statesman William Pitt and George Washington as unusual men, whose characters alone distinguished them. Although Bergson rarely referred to Emerson—only three times in thirty years—the span of his references testifies to a lasting regard. Like Dickinson and Nietzsche, he may also have resisted compromising his own originality by too frequent

---

104 D. M. Marchi, has suggested this kind of shift, as possibly stimulated by reading Emerson. Marchi, *Baudelaire's America*, 52.

105 H. Bergson, "Speech, France-America Society on March 12, 1917," *Mélanges*, ed. André Robinet (Paris: Presses Universitaires de France, 1972), 1244.

106 Idem, "The Theories of Free Will" (Lecture series given at the Collège de France in 1906-1907), *Mélanges*, 718.

reference. Bergson echoes Emerson in his similar interest in the nature of time, organic vital force, intuition, and the comic. His final notice was in 1936, when he once again spoke of William James, this time to say his work reminded him of Emerson.[107] There, Bergson slightly misquoted Emerson's "Character," in defining it as "a reserve of force which acts solely by its presence." (Interestingly, James recognized Bergson's indebtedness to Emerson when he re-read Emerson and thought of Bergson.)[108]

Marcel Proust (1871-1922) knew Emerson early, probably from high school, and also favored writers who were Emerson followers: Bergson, Baudelaire, Thoreau, Carlyle, and George Eliot. Proust's diary and correspondence of his early twenties contain frequent references to Emerson.

6.17 Marcel Proust at 21.

107 H. Bergson to Prof. J. Chevalier, February 1836, in Bergson 1972, 1543.
108 E. H. Cady and L. J. Budd state that James, in his copy of the "Nominalist and Realist," "wrote 'Bergson,' by the sentence: 'It is the secret of the world that all things subsist and do not die, but only retire a little from sight.'" *On Emerson* (Durham, NC: Duke University Press, 1988), 53.

Then in 1895, the year before his first novel appeared, he claimed to have read Emerson's *Essais* "drunkenly."[109] The same year, he encountered a French edition of *Representative Men*. And in the next, Proust's *Les plaisirs et les jours (Pleasures and Days*, 1896) used four selections from Emerson as chapter headings. In *Pastiches et mélanges (Mixtures*, 1919), he refers to Emerson at least six times.[110] From this early and continuous interest, it is not surprising that Emerson ideas appear in vital parts of Proust's best-known work, the autobiographical novel *À la recherche du temps perdu (In Search of Lost Time*, 1913-1927). In the third volume of this novel, *Le côté de Guermantes (The Way of Guermantes*, 1920-1921), the narrator Marcel describes a conversation that "had been entirely about Emerson, Ibsen and Tolstoy."[111]

More recently, Albert Camus (1913-1960), the Franco-Algerian philosopher and novelist, emerged as yet another admirer of Emerson and a keen reader of his *Journals*.

6.18 Albert Camus at 44, 1957.

---

109 M. Proust letter of 1895, *Lettres à Reynaldo Hahn* (Paris: Gallimard, 1956), 34.
110 Partly translated in *Against Sainte-Beuve and Other Essays*, trans. J. Sturrock (London, New York: Penguin Books, 1988) and in *The Lemoine Affair*, trans. Charlotte Mandell (Brooklyn, NY: Melville House, 2008).
111 M. Proust, *The Guermantes Way*, trans. C. K. Scott-Moncrieff, et al. (New York: Modern Library, 2003), 377.

In his own journals of 1951-1952, Camus so frequently quotes Emerson that he identifies them with a mere "E," as with "The only immortal is the one for whom all things are immortal."[112] In other places, only a sentence separates an Emerson "wall-gate/door" quotation from Camus' Emerson-sounding notes: "The time of criticism and polemics is over—Creation . . . *Totally* eliminating criticism and polemics—From now on, the single and constant affirmation . . . The worst of fortunes is a bad temperament."[113] Elsewhere, Camus records three more Emerson thoughts. One on radical authenticity is certainly from his journal: "What remains but to acquiesce in the faith that not lying, nor being angry, we shall at last acquire the voice and language of a man."[114]

In his last four years, Camus evidently felt particular affinities with Emerson. His exemplary short story, "Jonas, or the Artist at Work" (1957), reflects Emersonian themes—from self-reliance to the individual's conflicting needs for solitude and for society. The same year, Camus twice refers to Emerson in his lecture, "L'artiste et son temps" ("The Artist and His Time"), given four days after his acceptance speech for the Nobel Prize. Early in his remarks, he paraphrases the American: "Man's obedience to his own genius, Emerson said magnificently, is faith *par excellence*."[115] Ending inspirationally, he directly quotes Emerson on a major point: "Every wall is a door." (Camus substitutes "door" for Emerson's "gate.")[116] For Emerson, life's adversities (walls) are potential openings to new possibilities. After the unprecedented horrors of World War II, Camus was re-conceiving the role of the artist, urging writers to leave their escapist, fictional creations and confront the "wall" facing them—the hard facts of radical evil. Emerson's figure assured Camus that there was indeed a way out, but he stressed,

112 Albert Camus, *Notebooks 1951-1959* (Chicago, IL: Ivan R. Dee, 2008), 28. The Emerson quotation is from "Worship" (1860), but Camus may have found it in Emerson's *Journals* of 1846, *JMN* 9: 452.

113 Camus, *Notebooks*, 22. Emerson's journal entry of 27 February 1870, may have been the source for the dangers of criticism and on the necessity of affirmation, while ones of 7 October 1863: "An impassive temperament is a great fortune," and "Temperament is fortune" (*JMN* 10: 40) might have been the sources for Camus's last sentence.

114 Camus, *Notebooks*, 26; *JMN* 8: 79. The source of the first and third sentences is unclear.

115 Camus, *Discours de Suède* (Paris: Gallimard, 1958), 30. The Emerson quotation, present in Camus' journals of 1951-1952, appears to have been either a mistranslation or an inaccurate quotation from memory, probably deriving from Emerson's comment "obedience to a man's genius is the *particular* of Faith: by and by, I shall come to the *universal* of Faith." *JMN* 9: 62.

116 Emerson refers to hope as based on the infinity of the world, saying that "every wall is a gate." *JMN* 9: 137.

only through the wall itself. Camus may now be added to those who have attempted to rescue Emerson from an army of critics who, early and late, have erroneously dismissed him as a cosmic optimist, ignoring the reality of evil and thus failing to effectively protest against it.

Emerson in Italy

The proto-Nazi and Nazi transformation of Nietzsche's Ubermensch to support the concept of a "master race," a full reversal of Emerson's "plus" man, was largely done in ignorance of the Emerson-Nietzsche relationship. This was not the case in Italy. The poet and politician Gabriele D'Annunzio (1863-1938), the "godfather" of Italian fascism, made the connection between the two, no doubt when reading both in the same period.[117]

6.19 Gabriele D'Annunzio, early 20th century.

---

117 D'Annunzio's first documented reference to Nietzsche appears in *Il Mattino*, September 25, 1892.

That may help explain his elitist interpretation of Emerson. As early as 1893, D'Annunzio clearly linked his futuristic ideas to the American, writing, "The artists of the future . . . will be the representative men, to use Emerson's phrase: they will be, like Leonardo, the exemplar interpreters and messengers of their times."[118] Two years later, the idea had taken firm hold: D'Annunzio stressed the poet's elevated role of prophet, seeing artists alone as "representative men . . . in modern societies . . . ." To Emerson's quest for the "great and constant fact of Life," he attached a Messianic note, "[We] wait for a Man of Life,"[119] adding that "the new Renaissance" would be "the restoration of the worship of Man."[120] In 1899, D'Annunzio repeated Emerson's expectation of poets to be "liberating gods," saying, "The people are thirsty for poetry, they wait for the poet, the great dramatic poet, as a liberator. The future belongs to the poets."[121]

D'Annunzio's early library was auctioned in 1910. But his later collection, with Emerson's works frequently underlined, documents how thoroughly the American influenced his ambitions and even, to some degree, his sensitivity. In a French translation of Emerson's "The Tragic," D'Annunzio read, "He has seen but half the universe who never has been shown the House of Pain," then exclaimed, "Lien commun! [A common bond!]."[122] The comment is arresting. Only a few Emerson followers perceived his tragic sense. D'Annunzio also marked Oliver Wendell Holmes, Sr.'s biography of Emerson where it noted his unique "seraphic voice and countenance."[123] (By name and style, D'Annunzio and his biographers referred to him as an "archangel.") More ominously, he also marked several passages in "Self-Reliance." One, "I cannot sell my liberty and my power, to save their sensibility [that of friends],"[124] would have strengthened D'Annunzio's devil-may-care flamboyance. In the same year, 1912, D'Annunzio appeared

---

118 D'Annunzio, "Una tendenza,"*Il Mattino*, January 30-31, 1893, *Interviste a D'Annunzio* (Lanciano: Carabba, 2002), 53.

119 Ibid., cf., Emerson, *CW* 3: 12.

120 Interview, January 1895, in D'Annunzio "Una tendenza," 55. D'Annunzio's knowledge of *Representative Men* clearly predated his 1904 copy, in which he highlighted many passages.

121 *CW* 3: 17, 18. Interview with F. Pastonchi, *La Stampa*, October 1, 1899, in D'Annunzio "Una tendenza," 18.

122 Emerson, *Les forces eternelles et autres essais*, trans. K. Johnston, with preface by B. Perry (Paris: Mercure de France, 1912), 147. This edition includes "Perpetual Forces," "The Method of Nature," "Circles," "The Tragic," "Friendship," "Woman" (D'Annunzio's library, Vittoriale).

123 Ibid., 18, marked by d'Annunzio with a strong left line.

124 Ibid., 19, marked by d'Annunzio with left and right lines.

to have translated this idea into his "*me ne frego*" ("I don't care"), expressing a callous, "so-what" attitude disregarding all others and any challenge. The slogan became a famous Fascist cry,[125] and illustrates how fully D'Annunzio, like Nietzsche, departed from Emerson's true intent.

D'Annunzio's heavily-marked Emerson passages detail many more instances of ideas that inspired his radical corruptions. Above all, he grafted onto Emerson's ideal of the poet-prophet the notion of the poet-*duce*, the poet as political leader. Without any exterior check, D'Annunzio would embody the artist-as-politician in a blend of narcissistic aestheticism, super-masculinity, bullying rhetoric, and amoral behaviour, all within an excessive lifestyle. Such a leader was at total odds with Emerson's goals for the poet-in-society and in high contrast to his simple manner and style. Later, D'Annunzio's readings of Nietzsche's work further skewed his interpretations of Emerson. In the end, he betrayed even his own ideal of the poet-*duce*, living a sequestered life of private consumption at his paradise-retreat, the Vittoriale, adored by fans and financially supported by continuous aid from Mussolini.[126]

Benito Mussolini (1883-1945) was undoubtedly happy to keep D'Annunzio, a celebrated World War I hero, literary star, and muted rival, out of public notice. The two had been close for years, from fighting together in Fiume in 1919 to Mussolini's March on Rome in 1922, and often corresponded.

Given this contact, D'Annunzio might well have first introduced Emerson to Mussolini, although the destruction or sale of Mussolini's personal libraries has obscured the scope and dating of this influence. But Mussolini's long essay about Nietzsche, *La filosofia della forza* (*The Philosophy of Power*, 1908),[127] would have made him exceedingly curious about the German's principal source. Thus his claims in 1925 and 1931 that Emerson was among his favorite authors should be taken seriously, not as mere political or diplomatic boasting.[128] In 1925, he countered an argument that American civilization is "dominated exclusively by mechanical

---

125 *Gabriele D'Annunzio*, ed. J. de Blasi (Florence: Sansoni, 1939), 200.

126 A. Bonadeo, *D'Annunzio and the Great War* (Madison, WI: Fairleigh Dickinson University Press, 1995), 146.

127 B. Mussolini, "La filosofia della forza," *Il pensiero romagnolo*, November 29, December 6, 13 (2008).

128 As Denis Mack Smith suggested in his *Mussolini* (New York: Knopf, 1982), 132. On the Emerson-Mussolini relationship see Giorgio Mariani, "Read with Mussolini", eds. G. Mariani, et al., 123-31.

or materialistic factors and by the thirst for financial gain," by pointing not only to William James but to Emerson himself.[129] Six years later, in support of his "deep sympathy to the people of the great Republic" and its contributions to "modern progress," Mussolini adduced a list of writers: "Longfellow, Whitman, Emerson." He remarked outright, "Personally, I am a great admirer of Emerson and James."[130]

6.20 Benito Mussolini at 40
presides over Fascists' first anniversary celebration.

Associates of Mussolini also bore witness to his knowledge of Emerson. The *Duce's* personal doctor reported: ". . . very often we happened to entertain ourselves at length on Hegel, Schopenhauer, Kant, Emerson and other philosophers."[131] Much closer to Mussolini was his intellectual soul mate, lover, and first biographer Margherita Sarfatti, a journalist familiar with Emerson. In her *Life of Benito Mussolini* (1925), she quoted Emerson,

129 B. Mussolini, "United Press" interview, December 21, 1925, 123.
130 B. Mussolini, Radio message of January 20, 1931, 123-24.
131 G. Zachariae, *Mussolini si confessa* (Milano: Garzanti, 1948), 42.

implying a parallel with her subject: "The reward of a duty performed lies in the acquisition of strength to perform a duty that is more difficult."[132]

Mussolini's interest in Emerson's ideal of the heroic "great man," or a superior "representative man," as a unifying guide for the whole nation paralleled D'Anunnzio's. But he went further. Mussolini's leader would shed D'Annunzio's poetic and mystical aestheticism to be more stoic and Roman, an even stronger strong man. At a moment when Italy was weakened by war and an ineffectual king, and even before elevating himself from prime minister to dictator in 1925, Mussolini had famously said, "Liberty is a rotten carcass."[133] Ruthlessly absorbing all political power unto himself, he was, like Nietzsche, openly attacking democracy. After 1925, Mussolini quickly eviscerated most of Italy's democratic institutions, built a vast military force, began territorial expansion, and ended by allying himself with an even more potent "Nietzschean" *Ubermensch*, Hitler. D'Annunzio and Mussolini's selective sampling of Emerson missed his widest context and deepest presence, his "Over Soul." Emerson's aphorism, "Moral qualities rule the world, but at short distances, the senses are despotic," definitively distances him from these two Italians.

Simultaneously, however, a handful of non-Fascist Party Italian writers were accurately reading and interpreting Emerson. The novelist Federigo Tozzi (1883-1920) extolled *Nature*, and the professor of pedagogy Giuseppe Lombardo Radice (1879-1939) celebrated his educational philosophy in a long essay, *Emerson: profeta dell'educazione nuova* (*Emerson: Prophet of the New Education*, 1926). Despite this interest, the Fascists' use of Emerson led to his general disrepute in post-World War II Italy. For a time, that sentiment grew into an anti-Emerson tradition.[134] Then in the late 1950s, Agostino Lombardo, the founder of American Studies in Italy, exalted him as one who illustrated "America becoming conscious of itself," his endorsement temporarily resuscitating Emerson's reputation. But influenced by F. O. Mathiessen's *American Renaissance* (1941), a work that faulted Emerson for failing to be as realistic as his contemporaries, Lombardo finally found the

---

132 Margherita G. Sarfatti, foreword by Benito Mussolini, *The Life of Benito Mussolini* (Whitefish, MT: Kessinger Publishing, 2004), 88. The quotation's possible source might be "Immortality" (Italian translation, 1931): "Don't waste life in doubts and fears; spend yourself on the work before you, well assured that the right performance of this hour's duties will be the best preparation for the hours or ages that follow it." E. W. Emerson's *CW of RWE* 8: 328.

133 Jean McClure Mudge, *The Poet and the Dictator: Lauro de Bosis Resists Fascism in Italy and America* (Greenwood, CT: Praeger, 2002), 2, 58-60.

134 In G. Mariani, "The (Mis)Fortune of Emerson in Italy," *Anglistica* 6: 1 (2002), 103-31.

American "too much a philosopher to be a poet, and too much a poet to be a philosopher."[135] Twentieth-century novelists Elio Vittorini and Cesare Pavese were similarly cautious or downright critical.[136]

In the twenty-first century, Italy has shifted toward a more positive view of Emerson with only a touch of its earlier ambivalence. Several translations of Emerson's works have appeared. And in the fall of 2003, a large International Bicentennial Conference was held, an event honoring Emerson that was unprecedented in Europe.[137] Yet that same year, a leading philosopher, Gianni Vattimo, called for a re-examination of Emerson as a "forerunner of Nietzsche,"[138] reawakening the negative cast the German had made of his American idol. And in 2008, a newspaper review of an Italian translation of *The Conduct of Life*—, "Emerson. The Secret Master of Nietzsche," spoke of both his importance and neglect, while pairing him once again with Nietzsche.[139] In the same year, however, novelist Paola Capriolo's review of the same book called it a true classic, "with sparkling humor and vibrant poetic brightness."[140] In 2008, too, Mario A. Rigoni, a leading critic of the poet Leopardi, noted affinities between the Italian and Emerson.[141] Recently as well, the contemporary poet and Emerson scholar Roberto Mussapi has celebrated his essays as "pregnant and vital as voice itself, written in a fluvial prose, all embracing and illuminating."[142]

Emerson in Russia

Emerson's arch-individualistic and anti-communitarian views, as well as his ideas on capitalism and property, did not bode well for his future reception in either Revolutionary or Cold War Russia. But decades before, during Emerson's last trip to Europe in 1872-1873, he had met Ivan Turgenev (1818-1883) in Paris. Turgenev had earlier alluded to Emerson in his novel *Ottsi i Dyeti* (*Fathers and Sons*, 1862), deriding him by association with the women's movement via a fictional, faux-intellectual Russian woman and the real-life novelist George Sand. The greater Russian novelist Leo

---

135 Ibid., 110.

136 Caterina Ricciardi, "Ralph Waldo Emerson and Elio Vittorini," *Emerson at 2000*, 113-21.

137 Ibid.

138 *La Stampa*, 25 May 2003, 19.

139 *Libero*, 2 July 2008, 29.

140 *Corriere della Sera*, 9 September 2008, 43.

141 A. Rigoni, *Corriere della Sera*, 14 January 2008, 35.

142 *Avvenire*, 29 June 2008, 18.

Tolstoy (1828-1910) more fully commented on Emerson in his diaries, more positively than Turgenev on the whole and over many more years.

6.21 Leo Tolstoy at 59, 1887.

At age thirty, Tolstoy began with qualified praise of Emerson for his essays on Goethe and Shakespeare.[143] By his late fifties, after remarking that Emerson "is good" (possibly referring to "Experience"), Tolstoy told himself, "Read Emerson. Profound, bold, but often capricious and confused."[144] Finally, in his late sixties, he exultantly found that "Self-Reliance" was "marvelous."[145] In 1900, his publishing house, Posrednik (*The Intermediary*) printed an abridged version of the essay, followed two years later by a version of "The

---

143   L. Tolstoy, 24 March 1858, *Tolstoy's Diaries* (New York: Charles Scribner's Sons, 1985), 2: 49. Hereafter, *TD*. He read Herman Grimm's German translation of Emerson (1857).

144   L. Tolstoy, 12, 13 May 1884, *TD* 2: 214.

145   L. Tolstoy, 22 May 1894, in ibid.

Over-Soul," followed by several others.[146] Tolstoy's wife and other family members also read Emerson.[147]

In Tolstoy's essay "Message to the American People" (1901), he encouraged U.S. readers to rediscover their writers of the 1850s. He listed "Garrison, Parker, Emerson, Ballou, and Thoreau, not as the greatest, but as those who, I think, specially influenced me." In his preface to Polenz's *Büttnerbauer* (1895), he had already included "Emerson, Thoreau, Lowell, Whittier" in "the great galaxy" of American literature. And his two collections of classic wisdom, *The Cycle of Reading* (1906) and *Path of Life* (begun in 1910), included many Emerson excerpts.[148] Quotations in the latter work were largely from "Self-Reliance." But he also singled out a paragraph from the little-known essay, "Works and Days" (1870), affirming the idea that "each day is the best day," each hour "a critical, decisive hour." Of Emerson themes, Tolstoy commented on immortality, the importance of living "outside" time, and prioritizing the depth of one's life above its duration. In yet another diary entry, Tolstoy revealed Emerson's weight with him: "Read: Emerson was told that the world would soon end. He replied: 'Well, I think I can get along without it.' Very important."[149]

Toward the East

Rudyard Kipling (1865-1936), yet another follower of Emerson who became a Nobel laureate in literature (1907), began reading Emerson's poems when he was eight. Around 1880, the fifteen-year-old Kipling listed Emerson as his second choice after Whittier (another Emerson aficionado) on a school poll of students' favorite poets. Four years later, Kipling wrote a poetic parody, "Kopra-Brahm,"[150] dedicated to Emerson. An antic mix of ethereal and common material subjects, the poem's first two lines are: "Cosmic force and Cawnpore leather / Hold my walking-boots together." ("Cawnpore leather" deliberately mauled the pronunciation of an Indian hide from the city of Kanpur.) Kipling's poem draws heavily on images

---

146 See K. W. Cameron, *Emerson and Thoreau in Europe: The Transcendental Influence* (Hartford: Transcendental Books, 1999), 118.

147 S. A. Tolstaya, *The Diaries of Sofia Tolstaya* (London: Cape, 1985), 441.

148 L. Tolstoy, *Path of Life*, trans. Maureen Cote (Huntington, NY: Nova Science Publishers, 2002), 15, 81, 87, 92, 148, 151-52, 170, 205, 208, 233, 255, 260, 262, 273, 306.

149 L. Tolstoy, January 3, 1890, in *TD* 1: 275. Several sources report this anecdote of unclear origin.

150 R. Kipling, *The Writings in Prose and Verse: Early Verse* (New York: Charles Scribner's Sons, 1900), 90.

and characters from Emerson, notably "Brahma, to which the title alludes, but also to one of Emerson's "Fragments on the poet and the poetic gift," where he whimsically boasted, "[The poet] could condense cerulean ether / Into the very best sole-leather."[151] A native Englishman born in Bombay and educated in Britain, Kipling returned to live in India for several years. Then for four years (1892-1896), he was in Vermont, where he met Emerson's friend, Charles Eliot Norton. Norton corresponded with young Kipling and admired his poetry. He also gave him books, including his own edition of the Emerson-Carlyle correspondence (1894), reinforcing Kipling's strong boyhood memories of Emerson.

6.22 J. Rudyard Kipling at about 34, c. 1899.

Apparently Kipling was also drawn to Emerson's essays—even to obscure ones.[152] As Emerson had done, Kipling also introduced his prose with

---

151 *W* 9: 332.

152 R. Kipling [mostly 1889], *Letters of Travel* (Garden City, NY: Doubleday, Page, 1920), 13. Kipling quotes Emerson in "Success" on Euripides' comment about Zeus whom he says "hates busy-bodies and those who do too much."

poems, or quoted Emerson directly. Quotations from "Give All to Love" prefaced Kipling's "The Children of the Zodiac" (1891), and others from "Brahma" for *The Day's Work* (1898). When Kipling left India for Japan in 1889, he introduced his impressions of the new country via quotes, with a slight final variant, from Emerson's "Woodnotes, II."[153] Kipling's poem "The Inventor," in *The Muse among the Motors* (1904), is dedicated to Emerson, emulating his style and themes, but with a more regular rhythm. It presents a Benjamin Franklin-like figure who reflects Emerson's Promethean desires: his fascination with power, the overcoming of space and time, and a hope for the renewal of man. In a late memoir, *Something of Myself* (1937), Kipling retained his earlier allegiance to Emerson, quoting a little known fragment from his *May-Day and Other Pieces* (1867).[154]

Emerson's pervasive presence in Kipling appears in his famous "If" (1895), which once competed with Poe's "Raven" as the West's best-known poem. While composing it, Kipling was in close contact with Norton and also re-reading Emerson. "If" concentrates and popularizes both Emerson's ideas and spirit: "trust yourself," "don't look too good, nor talk too wise," "start again at your beginnings," "talk with crowds and keep your virtue, / Or walk with kings—nor lose the common touch," "Yours is the Earth and everything that's in it / And—which is more—you'll be a Man, my son!"[155]

From the stanza that heads this chapter, Emerson's phrase—"a subtle chain of countless rings"—concisely sets the stage for humanity's progressive evolution. Insight makes it possible: "The eye reads omens where it goes, / And speaks all languages the rose . . . ." The meanings gained collectively define the "rose," what may be known about creation and ourselves. Such knowledge is universal since it "speaks all languages." Emerson's climactic ending, "And, striving to be man, the worm / Mounts through all the spires of form," alludes to just the sort of unified effort that he, his Western educators, and followers all symbolize: the human mind, perpetually advancing from its lowliest origins, spirals upward to new heights of consciousness.

---

153 R. Kipling, *From Sea to Sea* (Whitefish, MT: Kessinger Publishing, 2004), 291.
154 R. Kipling, *Something of Myself* (Cambridge and New York: Cambridge University Press, 1990), 78.
155 Kipling first published "If" in *Rewards and Fairies* (London: Macmillan & Co., 1910), 181-82.

6.2 Asia in Emerson and Emerson in Asia

Alan Hodder

Please tell Maganlalbhai [Gandhi's nephew] that I would advise him to read Emerson's essays. They can be had for nine pence in Durban. There is a cheap reprint out. Those essays are worth studying. He should read them, mark the important passages and then finally copy them out in a notebook. The essays to my mind contain the teaching of Indian wisdom in a Western garb.

Mahatma Gandhi, letter to his son, 25 March 1907

Asia in Emerson

While Emerson has often been viewed as the most American of writers — formulator of such a reputedly distinctive American ideal as self-reliance — it is important to recognize that he was at the same time an unprecedentedly cosmopolitan thinker, drawing on a far-flung range of sources, Eastern as well as Western. Our first public intellectual, he was at the same time our first global intellectual, and as his fame spread throughout the middle and final decades of the nineteenth century, his writings in English and in translation often found an appreciative, at times even an ardent, readership, in various non-Western lands as well. Indeed, numbered among his most admiring readers were several who went on to play momentous roles in the modern religious, literary, or political history of their respective nations, most notably India and Japan. Among Indians, these included

http://dx.doi.org/10.11647/OBP.0065.09

Hindu religious reformer and missionary, Swami Vivekananda; Indian poet and Nobel laureate, Rabindranath Tagore; and even Mohandas ("Mahatma") Gandhi himself, chief architect of Indian independence. As colonial subjects themselves, such Indian leaders participated centrally in the tense, politically fraught, ongoing cultural and political exchange between Europe and its Asian colonial possessions. No less significant for modern East-West religious and cultural exchange was D. T. Suzuki, the great ambassador of Zen in the West, whose work also contributed significantly to modern Japanese self-definition *vis-à-vis* the West.

The most conspicuous expression of Emerson's international outlook was perhaps his precocious and, in retrospect, quite prescient interest in the classical religious and literary traditions of China, Persia and, most especially, Hindu India. For many centuries, the rich heritage of Asian civilizations had been effectively closed to the European West as a result of the vigorous expansion of Islam in the seventh century, the dominion of the Islamic Caliphates from the seventh through the twelfth centuries, and the rise of the Ottoman Empire in the fifteenth century. But with Vasco da Gama's circumnavigation of the Cape of Good Hope in 1498, and the subsequent opening of the Indian and East Asian spice trade, barriers to intercultural exchange between Asia and Europe were once again lifted, inaugurating a period of cultural renewal in Europe that the French scholar, Edgar Quinet, referred to as the "Oriental Renaissance." For many European scholars and artists of the Romantic period, news of the long forgotten and, to many, unsuspected cultural richness of India and China came as an intellectual windfall. To such Romantic thinkers, India in particular came to be viewed as the cradle of Western civilization, despite what they considered the decadence of many contemporary Hindu customs.[156]

For the sake of convenience, we might date the beginning of this renaissance to the founding in 1784 of the Asiatic Society of Bengal, a scholarly association composed initially of some thirty British civil servants working in Calcutta under the auspices of the East India Trading Company. The Society's grand ambition was to discover everything that could be known about the human and natural history of the vast Indian subcontinent and to propagate that knowledge for a wider English and European readership. Within a few years, a torrent of translations, monographs, and articles on a

156 See Raymond Schwab, *The Oriental Renaissance: Europe's Discovery of India and the East, 1680-1880,* trans. Gene Patterson-Black and Victor Reinking (New York: Columbia University Press, 1984).

wide range of subjects issued from the Society's press totally transforming European knowledge of several Asian civilizations, past and present. While the various authors of these studies were often accomplished amateur scholars in their own right, they all worked in one capacity or another for the East India Company and later, the British Raj. Among the chief contributors to the Society's work were Sir William Jones (1746-1794), an accomplished philologist, and the Society's founder and second president, who arrived in Calcutta in 1783 to join the Supreme Court in Bengal; Charles Wilkins (1749-1836), a printer for the East India Company and first European to learn Sanskrit, who produced the first English translation of the Bhagavad Gītā; Henry Thomas Colebrooke (1765-1837), an accountant turned magistrate, who wrote widely on classical Hindu religion and culture; Brian Houghton Hodgson (1800-1894), a British civil servant residing in Nepal, who put together an invaluable collection of Sanskrit manuscripts bearing on the origins and development of Buddhism; and Horace H. Wilson (1786-1860), another magistrate, who went on to become one of the most accomplished Sanskritists of his generation. But for the work of this gifted cadre of British scholar-magistrates, Emerson's knowledge of Asian traditions would have been all but impossible.

For such lately independent partisans of American liberty as Emerson and his Transcendentalist friends, the British discovery of the traditions of India and beyond was not without a certain pointed political irony since it was underwritten and occasioned by the same British colonial apparatus that Americans had only just recently thrown off after a long and costly war of independence. Generally speaking, nineteenth-century European and American knowledge of Asian traditions and cultures often arose as an instrument or byproduct of the continued political and economic expansion of Britain and other European colonial powers in various spheres of South and East Asia. For British magistrates working in India, one principal early motive for the acquisition of Sanskrit and the translation of selected Hindu texts was to facilitate political jurisdiction over the Indian population. Jones's own scholarly program serves as a notable case in point. One of the first Sanskrit texts he chose to translate was the ancient Hindu legal code, the Manu-smṛti or "Laws of Manu"—a choice dictated as much by legal and political considerations as by his own scholarly interest. His groundbreaking translation, which he entitled *The Institutes of Hindu Law* (1794), proved to be one of the first books that Emerson—and after him,

Thoreau—consulted in his first tentative efforts to acquire a knowledge of Indian traditions.

Although Emerson was arguably the first American to embrace Asian religious and philosophical traditions as an important complement and corrective to biblical traditions, his interest in Asian civilizations was not wholly unprecedented in earlier American colonial history. Puritan patriarch Cotton Mather had corresponded with Danish missionaries in Madras as far back as the 1720's, and later in the century, Benjamin Franklin conceived an active interest in Confucianism that later led to a learned exchange with Sir William Jones, with whom he had worked in Paris in the run-up to the American Revolution. In 1794, Joseph Priestly, a transplanted English Unitarian, produced the first serious study of Asian religions in America, and somewhat later, Hannah Adams included an account of Asian religions in her own comparative survey of world religions. Yet, for all these earlier intercultural transactions, no one did more to prepare the ground for later American interest in Asian cultures, particularly Asian religious cultures, than Emerson and his Concord neighbors, most notably Henry David Thoreau and Amos Bronson Alcott.[157]

In light of his appreciative reception of Asian religious and literary traditions later in life, Emerson's first reactions to what he could glean about the cultures of India and the Far East do not seem in retrospect especially promising. Since the start of American maritime contacts with India and China in the mid-1780s, Emerson's hometown of Boston had become a clearing-house for information about the far-off cultures of South and East Asia. Fantastic stories of Indian juggernauts, widow burning, and ascetics draped on hooks passed over India Wharf and the Boston waterfront together with the muslins, spices, and teas of the East India trade. Sensationalistic travel accounts appearing in the magazines and newspapers of the day found a ready readership. Since as early as 1803, Emerson's father, William Emerson, himself published several articles on India and the Far East in the *Monthly Anthology and Boston Review*, a journal which he edited till his death in 1811. Of course, much of the information provided in these sources proved to be anecdotal and often quite bigoted,

---

157 For full-length studies of early American interest in Asian religions, see Carl T. Jackson, *The Oriental Religions and American Literature: Nineteenth-Century Explorations* (Westport, CT: Greenwood Press, 1981); and Arthur Versluis, *American Transcendentalism and Asian Religions* (New York and Oxford: Oxford University Press, 1993).

reflecting the blend of fascination and repugnance often characterizing the popular imagination in the still provincial and strait-laced town of Boston.[158]

It is no surprise then that as a young man, Emerson never fully escaped the sense of religious chauvinism and moral superiority characteristic of his time and place. On the one hand, he unthinkingly absorbed the platitudes of the Romantic era, conceiving Asia, and particularly India, as the land of mysticism and the cradle of civilization. "'All tends to the mysterious East,'" he piously affirmed in one of the earliest entries of the journal he called his "Wide World."[159] By the same token, he was quick to mock the "immense goddery" of the Hindu pantheon. In a letter to his Aunt Mary Moody Emerson in 1822, he even dismissed European orientalist scholarship as "learning's El Dorado."[160] In preparation for his senior class poem for the Harvard College Exhibition of 1821, he pored through various available journals and books, reading everything about India that he could get his hands on, but the poem that resulted, "Indian Superstition," simply reflected the biases of his time and place. There he depicted India as an ancient, once proud civilization that in more recent times had fallen into unfortunate confusion and superstition. If anything, his attitude to Chinese civilization at this time in his life was even more censorious: "In the grave and never-ending series of sandaled Emperors whose lives were all alike, and whose deaths were all alike, and who ruled over myriads of animals hardly more distinguishable from each other, in the eye of an European, than so many sheeps' faces—there is not one interesting event, no bold revolutions, no changeful variety of manners & character. Rulers & ruled, age and age, present the same doleful monotony, and are as flat and uninteresting as their own porcelain-pictures."[161]

Blunting the harshness of this reception somewhat, however, were several subsequent influences. While plainly put off by the theology and/

---

158 For the following treatment of Emerson's Asian readings, see also my previous article: "Asia," in *Ralph Waldo Emerson in Context*, ed. Wesley T. Mott (New York: Cambridge University Press, 2014), 40-48.

159 Ralph Waldo Emerson, *Journals and Miscellaneous Notebooks of Ralph Waldo Emerson*, 16 vols, eds. William H. Gilman, et al. (Cambridge, Mass.: Harvard University Press, 1960-1982), 1: 12. Hereafter *JMN*.

160 *JMN* 2: 86; Ralph Waldo Emerson, *The Letters of Ralph Waldo Emerson*, 10 vols, eds. Ralph L. Rusk and Eleanor Tilton (New York: Columbia University Press, 1939-1994), 1: 116-17. Hereafter *L*. See also Alan D. Hodder, "Emerson, Rammohan Roy, and the Unitarians," in J. Myerson (ed.), *Studies in the American Renaissance* (Charlottesville, VA: University of Virginia Press, 1988), 133-34.

161 *JMN* 1: 83.

or ritualism of Indian and Chinese traditions, Emerson apparently found some of the belletristic literature quite charming. Of particular appeal was the so-called Oriental tale—of which the Arabian Nights and Samuel Johnson's "Rasselas" provided noteworthy instances. Another example, Robert Southey's "The Curse of Kehama," Emerson perused carefully in preparation for his senior-class poem. Perhaps more important in turning the tide of his early prejudice was the Indian reformer, Rammohan Roy, later hailed as the father of modern India, whose life and career Emerson found profiled in the pages of the *Christian Register* in 1820-1821.

6.23 Rammohan Roy at 50, 1822.

A highly educated brahmin from Bengal, Roy had dedicated his life to reforming contemporary Hindu social and religious customs in accordance with what he conceived to be classical Vedic and Upanishadic ideals. Like other members of the Unitarian community, Emerson was so taken with this socially enlightened man of the East that by the middle of the next decade, he placed Roy on a short list of the world's greatest and most self-reliant individuals, each of whom, "annihilates all distinction of circumstances."[162]

When over the course of the next few years, Emerson's interests in Asian thought expanded to include other primary and secondary sources, he also found much to appreciate in India's philosophical contributions. In the early 1830s, he copied out a passage from the Mahābhārata, the great national epic of India, which was contained in Gérando's history of comparative philosophy, noting that Idealism was "a primeval theory."[163] Soon thereafter, he read a précis of the Bhagavad Gita, arguably the pivotal text of the Hindu Renaissance, which was contained in French scholar Victor Cousin's survey of the philosophical traditions of the world.

6.24 Victor Cousin, late 50s–early 60s, c.1850s.

162 *JMN* 4: 283.
163 *JMN* 3: 362.

In a letter to the celebrated Indologist Friedrich Max Müller in 1873, Emerson traced the beginnings of his mature interest in Hindu thought to this first encounter with the Gita in Cousin's sketch.[164] Interestingly, Emerson's earliest investigations of the philosophical traditions of India roughly coincided with the vocational crisis that led in 1832 to his formal resignation from his pastorate at Boston's Second Church, signaling a new sense of intellectual freedom and the development of his own eclectic religious and philosophical vision.

Despite these few isolated instances, throughout the tumultuous period of the late 1820s and early 30s when, in rapid succession, Emerson experienced the death of his first wife, resigned his ministry, and set off on a precarious new career as a lecturer and essayist, his journal was relatively silent about his interests in Asian religious literature. What references that do occur, however, make it clear that he was now conceiving these Eastern sources in a new light, having all but completely cast off the pejorative views of his student days. One particularly noteworthy instance of this occurs in his discussion of the universal religious sentiment and critique of institutional Christianity in the address that he delivered to the graduating class of Harvard's Divinity School in 1837: "The sentences of the oldest time, which ejaculate this piety, are still fresh and fragrant. This thought dwelled always deepest in the minds of men in the devout and contemplative East; not alone in Palestine, where it reached its purest expression, but in Egypt, in Persia, in India, in China. Europe has always owed to oriental genius, its divine impulses. What these holy bards said, all sane men found agreeable and true."[165]

Over the course of the next several years, Emerson also acquainted himself with such non-Western sources as the Zendavesta, Zoroaster, Sir William Jones's translation of the Laws of Manu, H. H. Wilson's translation of the *Meghadūta*, selected articles on Asian traditions from the *Edinburgh Review*, various translations of the Confucian classics, "The Arabian Nights" and anthologies containing works by the Sufi poets Saadi and Hafez, and Charles Wilkins's translation of the *Hitopadeśa*. By this point, his growing exposure to religious writings of the East encouraged him to look beyond the scriptural canons of Christians and Jews to a more global scriptural anthology or world bible, an impulse he shared with several

---

164 *L* 1: 322-23; 6: 245-46.

165 *The Collected Works of Ralph Waldo Emerson*, 10 vols, eds. Robert E. Spiller, et al. (Cambridge, Mass.: Harvard University Press, 1971-2013), 1: 80. Hereafter *CW*.

of his Transcendentalist friends, including Henry Thoreau and Bronson Alcott. This conception led in 1842 to the publication of the "Ethnical Scriptures" column in the Transcendentalist literary magazine, *The Dial*. Having recently taken over editorship of the journal from Margaret Fuller, Emerson introduced this new column, with Thoreau's assistance, to highlight excerpts of recent translations of a range of non-Western texts that they had profited from in their readings.[166]

Emerson also made important use of the teachings of Confucius and other Chinese sages of the Confucian school as these had been rendered in recent English translations of the Neo-Confucian canon of the Four Books.[167] Together with Thoreau, he included excerpts from Joshua Marshman's translation of the sayings of Confucius for the April 1843 issue of *The Dial*, and both writers periodically drew upon their knowledge of Confucian teachings in their subsequent writings as well.[168]

1843.]   *Ethnical Scriptures.*   493

ETHNICAL SCRIPTURES.

SAYINGS OF CONFUCIUS.

Chee says, if in the morning I hear about the right way, and in the evening die, I can be happy.

A man's life is properly connected with virtue. The life of the evil man is preserved by mere good fortune.

Coarse rice for food, water to drink, and the bended arm for a pillow — happiness may be enjoyed even in these. Without virtue, riches and honor seem to me like a passing cloud.

A wise and good man was Hooi. A piece of bamboo

6.25 "Ethnical Scriptures, Sayings of Confucius," *The Dial*, 1843.

---

166 Cf. *The Dial: A Magazine for Literature, Philosophy, and Religion* (New York: Russell & Russell, 1961), 3: 82.

167 For an instructive analysis of the parallels between Emersonian and Neo-Confucian thought, see Yoshio Takanashi, *Emerson and Neo-Confucianism: Crossing Paths over the Pacific* (New York: Macmillan, 2014).

168 *The Dial*, 3: 493-94.

For Emerson, Confucius came to serve as paragon of the moral law, particularly as it governed society and social relations.

6.26 Confucius, 551-479 BCE.

According to Confucius, social welfare and harmony must always be rooted in individual character, in the essential human virtues of humaneness and benevolence. In the Confucian emphasis on individual social responsibility, Emerson found a salutary counterbalance to Transcendentalist tendencies to solitude. Confucius thus typified for Emerson the virtues of charity, moderation, gentility, and a humane worldliness. In his speech to a visiting delegation of Chinese officials in Boston in 1868, he extolled Confucius and Confucian teachings as the hallmark of China's contributions to world civilization:

> Confucius has not yet gathered all his fame. When Socrates heard that the oracle declared that he was the wisest of men, he said, it must mean that other men held that they were wise, but that he knew that he knew nothing. Confucius had already affirmed this of himself: and what we call the Golden Rule of Jesus, Confucius had uttered in the same terms five hundred years

before. His morals, though addressed to a state of society unlike ours, we read with profit to-day. His rare perception appears in his Golden Mean, his doctrine of Reciprocity, his unerring insight,—putting always the blame of our misfortunes on ourselves . . . .[169]

Emerson's study of Islamic literature and culture was more selective but no less consequential. While he sampled various travel accounts and classical texts, including George Sales' English version of the Qur'ān, he showed no particular regard for Islamic theology as such. Instead he focused almost exclusively on the poetry of Persian Sufism, particularly the poetry of Saadi and Hafiz.

6.27 Saadi Shirazi in a rose garden, c. 1645.

169 *The Complete Works of Ralph Waldo Emerson*, Centenary Edition, 12 vols., ed. Edward Waldo Emerson (Boston, Mass.: Houghton Mifflin, 1903-1904), 11: 472-73. HereafterW.

6.28 Title page, *Hafiz of Shiraz, Selections from his Poems,* 1875.

6.29 Frontispiece to *Hafiz of Shiraz.*

Although familiar with some of the conventions of Arabic and Persian literature since his school days, especially as it was manifested in the Oriental tales noted earlier, he conceived a great fondness for Sufi poetry when he read Joseph von Hammer's German translations in 1841. Subsequently, he looked to Persian poetry as an inspiration for his own verse, even to the point of adopting the cryptic name of "Seyd" (a kind of anagram of the name of the Sufi poet Saadi) as his designation of the ideal poet. Although the Puritan in Emerson shied away from the sensuality of Sufi poetry, he admired its richness of imagery and expansiveness of expression. Above all perhaps, he found in the ecstatic, aphoristic, and somewhat disjointed character of this verse a model and sanction for his own preferred mode of literary performance, both in poetry and prose.[170]

The beginning of Emerson's most sustained engagement with Asian religious philosophy, however, may be dated to the summer of 1845, when he received a copy of Charles Wilkins's complete English translation of the *Bhagavad Gita*.

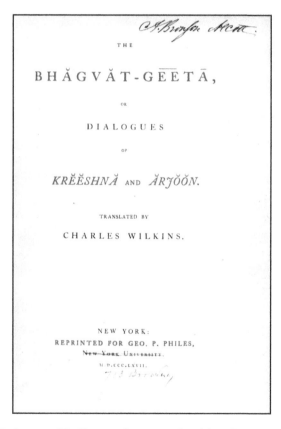

6.30 Title page, *The Bhagvat-Geeta*, translated by Charles Wilkins.

---

170 See Arthur Christy, *The Orient in American Transcendentalism: A Study of Emerson, Thoreau, and Alcott* (New York: Octagon Books, 1978), 137-54.

The fact that he mischaracterized this text at the time as "the much renowned book of Buddhism" probably says more about the elementary state of Asian studies in the U.S. in the 1840s than it does about Emerson's study to that point.[171] But reading it in full at this midpoint of his career instigated a wave of appreciation for Hindu religious and philosophical teachings that would carry him to the end of his life. Three years after the *Gita*'s arrival in Concord, he and his Transcendentalist friends were still reveling in the inspirations of modern Hinduism's favorite sacred text: "I owed,—my friend and I,—owed a magnificent day to the Bhagavat Geeta. It was the first of books; it was as if an empire spake to us, nothing small or unworthy but large, serene, consistent, the voice of an old intelligence which in another age & climate had pondered & thus disposed of the same questions which exercise us."[172]

By this point, having also examined H. H. Wilson's translation of the Vishnu Purāṇa and, somewhat later, Röer's translation of selected Upanishads, Emerson began to form a more rounded conception of Hindu religious philosophy. His essay on Plato, included in *Representative Men* (1850), reflects this recent immersion in these classical Hindu texts and quite a considerable assimilation of their teachings. What chiefly impressed him about this material theologically were their characterizations of divine reality in impersonal and monistic terms: "In all nations, there are minds which incline to dwell in the conception of the fundamental Unity. The raptures of prayer and ecstasy of devotion lose all beings in one Being. This tendency finds its highest expression in the religious writings of the East, and chiefly in the Indian scriptures, in the Vedas, the Bhagavat Geeta, and the Vishnu Purāṇa. Those writings contain little else than this idea, and they rise to pure and sublime strains in celebrating it."[173] In point of fact, both the Gita and the Vishnu Purāṇa also contain strong theistic elements, but consistent with his critique of Christian theism in his address to Harvard's Divinity School, it was their characterizations of reality as impersonal and absolute that he found especially compelling.

Emerson's essay on Plato also exhibits the influence of an intellectual orientation typical of European orientalists generally, most notably in his inclination to essentialize "Eastern" thought in general terms and then to juxtapose it in abstract terms with the civilizations of "the West." Here

---

171   *L* 3: 290.
172   *JMN* 10: 360.
173   *W* 4: 28.

perhaps is the most conspicuous instance of this tendency: "The country of unity, of immoveable institutions, the seat of a philosophy delighting in abstractions, of men faithful in doctrine and in practice to the idea of a deaf, unimplorable, immense Fate, is Asia; and it realizes this faith in the social institution of caste. On the other side, the genius of Europe is active and creative: it resists caste by culture: its philosophy was a discipline: it is a land of arts, inventions, trade, freedom. If the East loved infinity, the West delighted in boundaries." [174] The sort of dichotomizing of East versus West exemplified by this passage provides yet another instance of the kind of invidious Western cultural projection that Edward Said famously dubbed "orientalism," though here appearing on American soil. As Said showed, this way of thinking consistently operated in the service of Europe's larger colonial ambitions on Middle Eastern and, by extension, American, Asian, and African territories.[175] Of course, as Americans still recovering from Britain's recent colonial project in North America, Transcendentalists like Emerson occupied a more ambiguous political position than European orientalists did, but his language and general way of thinking about "the East" is nonetheless clearly indebted to standard orientalist tropes. To be sure, Emerson's particular motive for conceptualizing the relationship between East and West in this general way was partly rhetorical—to illustrate his pet doctrine of polarity, with East and West defining the two poles to which Plato was assigned the role of mediator—but he never entirely abandoned this schematic and stereotypical way of thinking about Asian cultures even in his more studious moments.

To judge from the numerous entries Emerson made in his journals from the mid-forties on, in which he copied long passages from his Indian readings and reflected on their significance, he explored this area of literature assiduously during the last few decades of his life. References to Hindu images or ideas in particular surface repeatedly in both his late prose and poetry. The lectures and essays appearing in the late-life collections *Representative Men*, *The Conduct of Life* —, and *Society and Solitude* frequently advance or illustrate an argument with reference to exotic ideas from the Hindu classics in which he was immersing himself. For example, his doctrines of "compensation" and "fate" often found illustration in the Indian doctrine of action or *karma*; he compared "illusion" to the Hindu goddess "Yoganidra" and the doctrine of māyā; and, as several commentators have

---

174   W 4: 30.
175   Edward Said, *Orientalism* (New York: Random House, 1979).

pointed out, even the quintessentially Emersonian doctrines of the "self" and the "over-soul" found a vivid expression in the Vedantin notions of ātman and brahman respectively.[176] Although such Indian doctrines often performed a mainly illustrative role, Emerson turned to them repeatedly as if to highlight and dramatize the universal value of his ideas.

Two particularly remarkable instances of this Hindu appropriation occur in the poetry of this period. "Hamatreya" (1847), a poem drawing explicitly upon a passage from the Vishnu Purāṇa, offers a scornful critique of Yankee acquisitiveness in the face of the evanescence of human life and the inevitability of death. More noteworthy is Emerson's famous poem, "Brahma," produced some ten years later, which he based on a verse from the Kaṭha Upaniṣad. Here Emerson presents a vision of the immortality of the soul thoroughly indebted in both its conception and terminology to the classical philosophy of the Upanishads. Although some early readers dismissed the poem as incomprehensible, Emerson refused to change a line, adhering closely to the form and message encountered in his reading. Despite such instances of explicit indebtedness, Emerson never adopted as whole cloth what he read of Hindu or other Asian religions; on the contrary, he always utilized this material selectively as vehicles by which to extend and dramatize his own ceaseless expression. What he admired most about the Hindu books, he wrote in 1849, was their scope and largeness of treatment: they offered "excellent gymnastic for the mind."[177]

Emerson in Asia

Just as Emerson had extolled the virtues of Asian civilization to his American and European readers, it was not long before Asian readers returned the favor by proclaiming the value of Emerson's writings among their own countrymen and women. Such readers felt a special enthusiasm and even kinship for Emerson's essays, and found much to admire, not least his seemingly familiar visions of the self and the over-soul, his promotion of self-reliance and the God within, and his inspired paeans to nature. But as in the case of Emerson's discovery of the East, the East's discovery of Emerson was largely contingent upon larger movements of world history, in particular nineteenth and early twentieth-century colonial politics, and the opening up of various Asian cultures to the political, commercial, and

---

176 CW 6: 313. Cf. Christy, *Orient in American Transcendentalism*, 73-113.
177 *JMN* 11: 137.

cultural interests of the West. With the consolidation of British political power in India in the late-eighteenth century and growing European dominion throughout the Asian world generally, Emerson's writings began to circulate through the newly established channels of colonial conquest and power. For some readers in Eastern lands, Emerson's essays came as refreshment from an unsought source; for others, as inspiration and support in their own struggles for personal and national self-determination. But of various scattered Asian responses to Emerson's writings in the late nineteenth and early twentieth centuries, the quickest and most concerted came from English-speaking readers in India and Japan.

Knowledge of Emerson's writings among nineteenth-century Western-educated Hindus owed itself initially to the educational sponsorship of the Brahmo Samaj ("The Society of God"), a religious society founded in 1828 by the Bengali social reformer, Rammohan Roy, which was closely associated with English and American Unitarians residing in India. Raised in the colonial and cosmopolitan setting of early nineteenth-century Calcutta, Roy made it his mission in life to purify the Hinduism of his day of its inveterate concern with image worship, caste restrictions, and the repression of women, particularly such notorious practices as child marriage and the immolation of widows on their husbands' funeral pyres. In its place, Roy advocated a more tolerant, socially responsible, and monotheistic Hinduism, informed by Christian morality, as well as by the philosophical and contemplative vision of the ancient Vedic traditions, particularly the Upanishads. Roy found particular support for his reform program among members of the English Unitarian community of Bengal, whose vision of a universal faith coincided very closely with his own. Throughout the subsequent decades of the nineteenth century, under a succession of talented and charismatic leaders, the Brahmo Samaj expanded its work of religious and social reform, drawing to itself, like a magnet, a whole host of young, idealistic, Western-educated Hindus who saw in the universalizing vision of the Samaj the promise of a more progressive, independent, and cosmopolitan India.[178]

In 1855, Charles H. A. Dall, a Unitarian missionary from Boston, arrived in Bengal to establish an American Unitarian presence on the subcontinent and to help strengthen relations between the already-existing English Unitarian community and the Brahmo Samaj. Keen to ensure that

---

178 Cf. Spencer Lavan, *Unitarians in India: A Study in Encounter and Response* (Boston, Mass.: Skinner House, 1977); David Kopf, *The Brahmo Samaj and the Shaping of the Modern Indian Mind* (Princeton, NJ: Princeton University Press, 1979).

the religious and theological contributions of the American Unitarian movement did not go unnoticed, Dall circulated copies of the complete works of William Ellery Channing, Emerson, and Theodore Parker among his Brahmo friends and students. Though Emerson had long since broken off formal relations with Boston's mainstream Unitarian establishment, he knew Dall personally and even conferred with him upon Dall's return to Boston in 1866 about Dall's experiences in India.[179] From this time forward, young members of the Brahmo Samaj began to absorb Emerson's essays, together with the more obligatory fare of the British educational system.

One decided early beneficiary of Emerson's writings was Protap Chandra Majumdar, a third-generation leader of the Brahmo Samaj, who rose to prominence in the Brahmo movement under the tutelage of its charismatic mid-century leader, Keshab Chandra Sen. Having been introduced to liberal Christianity by Charles Dall, Majumdar adopted a form of Christian humanism and scientific theism more devoutly pro-Christian than even that espoused by other Brahmo leaders, a fact that quickly endeared him to several important Unitarian leaders in England and the United States. Before his death in 1905, Majumdar made three trips to the West at the invitation of his Unitarian friends. In the first of these, commencing in 1883, Majumdar even made his way to Concord in hopes of paying his respects to Emerson personally, but unluckily, Emerson had passed away only a few months before. On his return to Calcutta the next year, Majumdar was asked to compose a tribute to the lately deceased Emerson on the topic, "Emerson As Seen From India," that would be read at the 1884 session of the Concord School of Philosophy. Majumdar readily agreed and responded with as fervent a tribute as his sponsors could possibly have hoped for. Noting the suggestive parallels between Emerson's writings and Vedic nature worship, and between Emerson's "Over-Soul" and the teachings of the Upanishads, Majumdar extolled Emerson as the very embodiment of "the wisdom and spirituality of the Brahmans."[180] Several years later, in a lecture entitled "The World's Religious Debt to Asia," which he delivered at the Parliament of World Religions in 1893, Majumdar publicly made this

---

179 JMN 16: 37.
180 Protap Chunder Mozoomdar, "Emerson as Seen from India," in *The Genius and Character of Emerson: Lectures in the Concord School of Philosophy*, ed. F. B. Sanborn (1885). Reprinted in *The Genius and Character of Emerson: Lectures in the Concord School of Philosophy*, ed. F. B. Sanborn (Port Washington, NY: Kennikat Press, 1971), 365-71.

connection once again, crediting Emerson's "Over-Soul" as the inner link between the human and divine.[181]

Appearing at the Parliament also was the young Hindu scholar-teacher, Swami Vivekananda, monastic leader of the newly emergent Ramakrishna order, who would soon seize the limelight from his senior colleague and many of the other Asian delegates as well.

6.31 Swami Vivekananda at 30, September, 1893, Chicago.

Born Narendranath Datta, Vivekananda was a highly gifted, Western-educated Bengali who had participated in the activities of the Brahmo Samaj as a young man, embraced its liberal Unitarian values, and strongly supported its agenda of political and social reform. The turning point in

181 Richard Hughes Seager, ed., *The Dawn of Religious Pluralism: Voices from the World's Parliament of Religions, 1893* (La Salle, IL: Open Court Press, 1993), 444.

his life came, however, in his meeting in 1881 with the revered Hindu saint Ramakrishna, whose teachings and example inspired in him, and many other like-minded young Brahmos, a renewed appreciation for the spiritual power of their native faith. Vivekananda's presentation in Chicago in 1893 created something of a sensation—few of the delegates attending the conference could muster the kind of eloquence and erudition that he did—and his fame quickly spread, leading to lecture dates and tours throughout the United States.[182] In the winter of 1900, Vivekananda was back in the United States and among his various engagements was a lecture series on Sanskrit literature to the local Shakespeare Society in Pasadena, California. Commenting on the Hindu classic, the *Bhagavad Gita*, Vivekananda took the opportunity to point out to his audience its critical importance for Emerson and, furthermore, the importance of Emerson for all subsequent American history: "I would advise those of you who have not read that book to read it. If you only knew how much it has influenced your own country even! If you want to know the sources of Emerson's inspiration, it is this book, the Gita . . . and that little book is responsible for the Concord Movement. All the broad movements in America, in one way or another, are indebted to the Concord party."[183] Such grandiose assertions notwithstanding, Emerson's principal distinction, as far as Vivekananda was concerned, was that he effectively served as a conduit for the timeless wisdom of the Vedas and Upanishads.

This early appropriation of Emerson by Western-oriented Indian teachers effectively set the terms for Emerson's subsequent reception among Hindus, both by members of the Brahmo Samaj and among English-speaking Indian readers more generally. For Indian nationalists, including Vivekananda, Emerson was important first because of the political and spiritual value they saw in his insistence on self-reliance, and second, because they conceived Emerson's teachings on self-reliance as having, at least in part, an Indian, even a Vedic provenance, by virtue of his own readings of classical Indian texts. This sort of response is evident even in the case of Rabindranath Tagore, the celebrated Bengali poet and Nobel laureate.

---

182 Ibid., 421-32.
183 Swami Vivekananda, *Complete Works of Swami Vivekananda* (Calcutta: Advaita Ashrama, 1978), 4: 95.

6.32 Rabindranath Tagore in his sixties, before 1930.

In an interview on one of his several trips to the United States, Tagore, remarked: "I love your Emerson. In his work one finds much that is of India. In truth he made the teachings of our spiritual leaders and philosophers a part of his life."[184] Like Vivekananda, his Bengali countryman and contemporary, Tagore was an outspoken advocate of Indian independence and a warm admirer of Mahatma Gandhi, even though he opposed certain key features in Gandhi's program of reform. In a less explicitly political context, the same pattern may be observed in the writings of the Hindu monk and missionary, Paramahansa Yogananda, who founded the Self-Realization Fellowship in Los Angeles in 1925. By this point in time the habit of invoking Emerson's authority to illustrate and validate Hindu religious

184 Bailey Millard, "Rabindranath Tagore Discovers America," *The Bookman* 44 (November 1916): 247-48. See also R. K. Gupta, *The Great Encounter: A Study of Indo-American Literary and Cultural Relations* (Maryland: Riverdale Company, 1987), 131-37.

philosophy had become a matter of common practice among Western-educated Indian leaders and reformers. The famous account Yogananda wrote about his spiritual life, *Autobiography of a Yogi* (1946), was heavily footnoted with references to Emerson's essays as if to confer acceptability in an American context.[185]

From a political standpoint, the most noteworthy example of Indian indebtedness to Emersonian thought, however, was perhaps Gandhi himself, India's greatest modern statesman and principal architect of Indian independence. It appears that Gandhi had become acquainted with Emerson's essays as early as 1907, when he cited Emerson in an essay on personal morality. Two years later, while serving a sentence in the Pretoria jail in South Africa, he was reading Emerson again, along with Ruskin, Carlyle, Tolstoy, and the Upanishads. In a letter to his son Manilal, dated March 25 of that year, Gandhi enthusiastically recommended Emerson's essays, along with the work of Tolstoy: "Please tell Maganlalbhai that I would advise him to read Emerson's essays. They can be had for nine pence in Durban. There is a cheap reprint out. Those essays are worth studying. He should read them, mark the important passages and then finally copy them out in a notebook. The essays to my mind contain the teaching of Indian wisdom in a Western garb."[186] Over the course of the next several decades, through a period of tumultuous social and political change in India and abroad, Gandhi periodically affirmed the importance of Emerson's ideas. He was especially enamored of Emerson's memorable dictum from "": "A foolish consistency is the hobgoblin of little minds, adored by little statesman and philosophers and divines."[187] In a speech delivered in 1928, for example, Gandhi defended Tolstoy's "seeming contradictions" by invoking Emerson's choice aphorism and did so several times thereafter, when defending himself against charges that his own personal and political life was sometimes betrayed by inconsistencies.[188]

While references to Emerson do not bulk large in Gandhi's writings—at least relative to such primary intellectual and spiritual resources as the *Bhagavad Gita*, Tolstoy, the Sermon on the Mount, and the Upanishads—they are nevertheless suggestive in view of the apparent close affinities

---

185 Paramahansa Yogananda, *Autobiography of a Yogi* (Los Angeles, CA: Self-Realization Fellowship, 1946). See notes to pp. 27, 40, 44, 63, 69, 270.

186 Mohandas Gandhi, *The Collected Works of Mahatma Gandhi* (New Delhi: Government Publications Division, 1979), 9: 208-09, 241.

187 *W* 1: 33.

188 Gandhi, *Collected Works*, 42: 469; 67: 284.

between Emerson's self-reliance and Gandhi's program of *Swaraj* ("self-rule"). In general terms, *Swaraj* was the principal term Gandhi used to signify his overall political program to achieve Indian self-rule and independence from Britain at the earliest possible moment. The primary sense of *Swaraj* was thus clearly political, where it was often simply synonymous with home-rule, but it also had important economic, social, cultural, and educational applications as well. One of the main thrusts of *Swaraj* from an economic standpoint was the Khadi movement by means of which Gandhi hoped to recover Indian economic self-sufficiency through the boycott of British textiles and the resuscitation of India's homegrown manufacture of cotton cloth. But while the primary application of *Swaraj* was broadly political, social, and economic, he always conceived of it as simply the outer expression of individual moral and spiritual self-culture. He related *Swaraj* to the more abstract term *satyagraha* ("truth-seizing"), which he himself coined, and to *ahimsa* ("nonviolence") and *swadeshi* ("self-reliance"). Indeed, he consistently insisted that the success of the independence movement depended on the cultivation of individual self-rule, self-sufficiency, and self-reliance. In his *Young India* column of 1920, for example, he asserted that "Government over self is the truest *Swaraj*, it is synonymous with *moksha* or salvation, and I have seen nothing to alter the view that doctors, lawyers, and railways are no help, and are often a hindrance, to the one thing worth striving after."[189]

Gandhi discovered the link between the outer and inner dimensions of *Swaraj* in his reading of the *Bhagavad Gita*, a text that he valued highly along with other Indian nationalist leaders and of course Emerson himself. Ironically, Gandhi first encountered the *Gita* as a student in London on the recommendation of two young Theosophist friends in the form of Edwin Arnold's English translation. "The book struck me as one of priceless worth," he wrote in his autobiography many years later. "The impression has ever since been growing on me with the result that I regard it today as the book *par excellence* for the knowledge of Truth."[190] Setting aside the actual literal and historical setting of the poem, Gandhi sought the heart of the *Gita*'s teaching in the doctrine of

---

189 Mohandas Gandhi, *Young India*, December 8, 1920. For a helpful analysis of the relation of self-reliance to other aspects of Gandhi's thought, see Raghavan Iyer, "Introduction," in *The Moral and Political Writings of Mahatma Gandhi*, ed. Raghavan Iyer (Oxford: Clarendon Press, 1973), 9.

190 Mohandas K. Gandhi, *Gandhi: An Autobiography: The Story of My Experiments with Truth* (Boston, Mass.: Beacon Press, 1993), 67.

disinterested or selfless action (*karma-yoga*) as represented in the second chapter. In context, the character of this teaching was clearly religious and moral, and Gandhi recognized it as such. The point of disinterested or selfless action for Gandhi was the liberation of the self, and the point of liberation of the self was the realization of God. This was the heart of Gandhi's ethics, and the basis of his approach to social and political reform. Emerson was not the source of this crucial feature of Gandhi's religious and political thought, but he clearly provided an important touchstone, as we see in the reference to the essay "Self-Reliance" above. And to Gandhi, as to other Indian readers before him, Emerson's example was all the more appealing because it seemed to him so congruent with traditional Indian views of the self and the immanence of the divine— "the teaching of Indian wisdom in a Western garb."

On July 1, 1942, six months after the United States entered World War II, Gandhi drafted a letter to Franklin Delano Roosevelt apprising him of his views regarding India's support for and participation in the ongoing war. Writing by this point as the acknowledged head of the Indian National Congress and leader of the independence movement, Gandhi began his letter to the American President in warmly personal terms, mentioning his many American friends and correspondents, and the scores of Indians then receiving higher education in the U. S. He then adds the apparently innocuous remark: "I have profited greatly by the writings of Thoreau and Emerson." Pleasantries aside, Gandhi then proceeds to make clear that his own support for the Allied cause, like that of the Indian National Congress as a whole, would be necessarily contingent on the full realization of Indian independence, adding the pointed observation: "I venture to think that the Allied declaration that the Allies are fighting to make the world safe for freedom of the individual and for democracy sounds hollow so long as India, and for that matter, Africa are exploited by Great Britain and America has the Negro problem in her own home." To Roosevelt, the logic of Gandhi's political position could hardly find a more compelling articulation. The seemingly casual juxtaposition of Emerson and Thoreau, two icons of American freedom, with India's actual subjugation to British imperial rule highlighted the political duplicity in the Allied expectation of Indian support.[191]

---

191 Gandhi, *Collected Works*, 76: 264-65.

6.33 Mahatma Gandhi in his early 60s, c. late 1930s.

6.34 Jawarlal Nehru at 53 with Gandhi at 73, 1942.

Even Jawaharlal Nehru, Gandhi's successor as president of India, though less concerned with any supposed affinities between Emersonian and Indian thought, nevertheless found in Emerson's essays support for burgeoning Hindu self-reliance and national self-determination.[192] While Nehru obviously read Emerson in more overtly political terms than did some of his predecessors, none of these Indian responses can be entirely separated from the larger colonial and postcolonial situation, if only because this was what brought Emerson to India in the first place. To read Emerson as a Western exponent of ancient Vedic wisdom served not only to inspire these modern Indian readers in terms they could appreciate, but also to bolster their claims for independence and a pivotal position in world civilization.[193]

---

192 Lawrence Buell, *Emerson* (Cambridge, Mass.: Harvard University Press, 2003), 195.

193 For a fuller analysis of the Indian reception of Emerson and Emerson's reception of India, see my previous article, "'The Best of Brahmins': India Reading Emerson Reading India," *Nineteenth-Century Prose* 30 (Spring/Fall 2003): 337-68.

Hardly less significant from a cultural standpoint was the response of Japanese readers and scholars to Emerson's writings, especially during the Meiji (1868-1912) and Taisho (1912-1926) eras of modern Japanese political history. The first significant encounter apparently took place in Boston on July 30, 1872 when an assemblage of local merchants and dignitaries, including Emerson himself, hosted a delegation of fifty Japanese officials at the Revere House. Although Emerson was still reeling from the devastating impact of an accidental fire that nearly burned down the family home in Concord a few days before, he responded to the invitation to speak with characteristic aplomb. In his brief remarks to the assembled guests, he candidly acknowledged what he described as his "extreme ignorance of Japan," before going on to summarize previous Western contacts with the Far East, up to the arrival of Commodore Matthew Perry off the coast of Japan in 1852, and highlighting Japan's distinctive contributions to world culture. "I remember," he noted, "that in my college days our professor in Greek used to tell us always in his records of history, 'all tends to the mysterious East,' and so slow was this progress that only now the threads are gathered up of relation between the farthest East and the farthest West."[194]

Sponsoring the Japanese embassy's momentous visit to the United States in 1872 was the new, outward-looking Meiji government in Tokyo, which had come to power only a few years before. The restoration of the Meiji emperor had quickly resulted in the abandonment of the old feudal system and, eventually, Japan's emergence as a modern industrial state. While beholden to the West for recent advances in science and technology, Japanese rulers also saw the need to retain and foster certain indigenous spiritual traditions, in particular, the naturalistic traditions of Shinto, which became, in effect, Japan's state religion, and Neo-Confucianism, which had combined classical Confucian ethics with a more contemplative and transcendentalist metaphysics. Japan thus found itself on the cusp of change, and for a number of influential scholars and teachers, Emerson was seen to support both the new selective respect for things Western and the ancient indigenous wisdom traditions of China and Japan.[195] Like the Hindu teachers cited above, some Japanese scholars saw features of their

---

194 The full text of Emerson's remarks was reprinted verbatim in the Boston newspaper, *The Commonwealth*, on August 10, 1872.

195 See Yoshio Takanashi, "Emerson, Japan, and Neo-Confucianism," *ESQ* 48 (1st and 2nd Quarters 2002): 41-45.

own most valued traditions reflected back to them in the writings of this man of the modern west.

One of the first personal expressions of Emerson's impact on Japan comes to us from an eyewitness—the young Japanese baron, Naibu Kanda, who had been sent to Amherst College for his education.

6.35 Naibu Kanda, c. 21, 1879.

On March 19, 1879, Kanda recorded in his journal his reactions to a talk on "mental temperance" that Emerson had given earlier that evening to a rapt gathering of Amherst College students. "We sat there for one hour charmed by every sentence which he uttered," Kanda wrote, "and when he ended I could not but feel that I had received an impetus toward a life of greater simplicity and truthfulness." For Kanda the magic of Emerson's words never entirely wore off. Returning to Japan in 1879, the young baron soon began what became a life-long career as an English instructor at Tokyo University, from which position he dispensed Emerson's essays and communicated his enthusiasm to a willing generation of Japanese readers.[196]

By the next decade, Emerson's writings had also caught the attention of a select group of Japanese scholars and writers, including Tokutomi Soho, a popular social commentator and advocate of modernization, who included quotations from Emerson's writings in the literary magazine *Komumin no tomo* ("The People's Friend"). In 1888, Nakamura Masanao produced a Japanese translation of Emerson's essay "Compensation," which was followed two years later, by Sato Shigeki's translation of the essay, "Civilization." By the 1890's, Emerson's writings began to exert a strong influence on Japanese literary culture more widely, and before long, quotations from Emerson found their way into Japanese newspapers, magazines, and even common usage as well. One of the chief sponsors of this enthusiastic reception of Emerson in Japan was the Romantic writer Kitamura Tokoku, who in 1894 produced a Japanese biography of Emerson, *Emerson*, the first such treatment of any American author.

Kitamura also contributed numerous short essays on Emerson to the journal *Bungakukai* ("Literary World"), which had become the mouthpiece of a small group of self-avowed "romantic" writers, including Kunikida Doppo and Tokutomi Roka, who looked to Kitamura as their leader and shared in his admiration of Emerson. The high tide of Japanese interest in Emerson came, however, during the Taisho period. In 1917, Hirata Tokuboku and Togawa Shukotsu brought out a translation of Emerson's complete works in eight volumes, thus laying a firm foundation for the further propagation and popularization of Emerson's writings in Japan throughout the next few decades. Although popular interest in Emerson tapered off in the years leading up to the Second World War, Emerson studies enjoyed a brief revival immediately following the war when Emerson was viewed as a principal philosopher of American democracy.[197]

---

196 Bunsho Jugaku, *A Bibliography of Ralph Waldo Emerson in Japan from 1878 to 1935* (Kyoto: The Sunward Press, 1947), xi-xiii.

197 Takanashi, "Emerson, Japan, and Neo-Confucianism," 41-43. See also Takanashi, *Emerson and Neo-Confucianism.* We also wish to thank our colleague Hideo Kawasumi

For readers in Japan, Emerson's writings expressed and resonated with their love of the natural world, their admiration for simplicity in art and life, and their reverence for a metaphysical dimension of reality—be it the great emptiness or the over-soul—that infused and transcended the material world.[198]

Among early Japanese interpreters, however, perhaps the most noteworthy for Western readers—and consequential from an inter-religious, inter-cultural, and political standpoint—was D. T. Suzuki, the pre-eminent exponent of Zen Buddhism in the West for much of the twentieth century and, for many early students, its principal interpreter.

6.36 D.T. Suzuki at 90, 1960.

of Seikei University for information on Emerson's reception in Japan.
198 Yukio Irie, "Why the Japanese People Find a Kinship with Emerson and Thoreau," *ESQ* 27 (2nd Quarter 1962): 13-16.

It was Suzuki's representation of Zen, after all, that galvanized the interest of the first Anglo-American students of Zen Buddhism—from such Beat writers as Jack Kerouac and Allen Ginsberg, to the philosopher Alan Watts—and through them, of later more committed practitioners, as well. In retrospect, Suzuki's remarkable success in making Zen not only palatable but compelling to many Americans owed itself in considerable part to his success in presenting Zen in recognizably Western forms of discourse and understanding. By the same token, Zen as Suzuki conceived of it superseded all other forms of spirituality—East as well as West. The effect was to confer on Japan a position of religious, cultural, and philosophical superiority.

Suzuki arrived in the United States for the first time in 1897 to assist Paul Carus, editor of the journal *Open Court*, in interpreting and translating various Asian religious and philosophical classics for Western readers. Suzuki's apprenticeship with Carus effectively inaugurated a dialogue and collaboration with Western students of Asian, and especially Buddhist, culture that would continue until his death in 1966. Beginning in the decade of the 1930s, Suzuki turned his attention increasingly to the propagation of Zen among Western readers. Several books published during this period dealt extensively with the nature of Zen and its relationship to the Japanese character. Perhaps the most influential of these, *Zen and Japanese Culture* (1959), was first presented in a series of lectures that Suzuki presented in the West in 1938 during the run-up to the Second World War. Here he described Zen as a form of pure unmediated experience, beyond all subject-object dichotomies and conceptual distinctions, which was the foundation and essence of all religious experience. In Suzuki's understanding, Zen was not only the essence of other forms of Buddhism, but also of all religions and philosophies generally. By the same token, he was quick to conceive of it as uniquely characteristic of Japanese spirituality and the Japanese national character. For Suzuki, Japan was the natural home of Zen and only among the Japanese had it assumed its highest forms of expression.[199]

Crucial to the formation of Suzuki's conception of Zen as a universal form of religious experience was his reading of several Western philosophers, not least Emerson himself. In *Zen and Japanese Culture*, Suzuki pauses at one point to note the "deep impressions made upon me while reading Emerson

---

199 For the now classic critique of the interplay between Zen and Japanese nationalism in Suzuki's work, see Robert Scharf, "The Zen of Japanese Nationalism," *History of Religions* 33: 1 (August 1993): 1-43.

in my college days." Yet, like the Indian readers discussed previously, he conceived of Emerson less as an original, distinctively Western source in his own right than as a Western reflection of essentially Asian insights. Citing a reference to Buddhism in one of Emerson's letters, Suzuki notes: "Emerson's allusion to 'sky void idealism' is interesting. Apparently he means the Buddhist theory of śūnyatā ("emptiness" or "void"). Although it is doubtful how deeply he entered into the spirit of this theory, which is the basic principle of the Buddhist thought and from which Zen starts on its mystic appreciation of Nature, it is really wonderful to see the American mind, as represented by the exponents of Transcendentalism, even trying to probe into the abysmal darkness of the Oriental fantasy." Indeed, reading Emerson for the first time, he goes on to note, was like "making acquaintance with myself." Yet, while Emerson's efforts were clearly laudable, they were still, in his view, rather elementary: "The American Transcendentalist's attitude toward Nature has no doubt a real mystical note, but the Zen masters go far beyond it and are really incomprehensible."[200]

As had Vivekananda before him, not only did Suzuki construe Emerson as a Western exponent of essentially Asian—in this case Japanese—wisdom, he also conceived of Transcendentalism as a sort of wellspring of subsequent American culture: "Let us note here, in passing, how Oriental thoughts and feelings filtered into the American mind in the nineteenth century. The Transcendentalist movement begun by the poets and philosophers of Concord is still continuing all over America. While the commercial and industrial expansion of America in the Far East and all the world over is a significant event of the twentieth century, we must acknowledge at the same time that the Orient is contributing its quota to the intellectual wealth of the West—American as well as European."[201] Here in this pointed juxtaposition of American commercial wealth with Japanese intellectual wealth, we witness yet another instance of the ideological and political uses to which Emerson was put in the colonial and postcolonial eras. Emerson provided Suzuki with a pretext to push back against the mounting political and cultural influence of the West by virtue of Emerson's own estimable but imperfect efforts to incorporate the spiritual wisdom of the East—and even to assert the cultural and religious superiority of Japan in the years leading up to World War II.

---

200 Daisetz T. Suzuki, *Zen and Japanese Culture* (Princeton, NJ: Princeton University Press, 1959), 343-44.
201 Suzuki, *Zen and Japanese Culture*, 344.

What we are left with then is another vivid instance of the complex cultural exchange at work in so many of these early East-West encounters. Like his Indian contemporaries and predecessors, Suzuki essentially viewed Emerson as an expression of Asian thought by virtue of Emerson's sometime reliance on Asian traditions as an expression of his own thought. None of these Asian readers apparently conceived of Emerson or his writings in primarily a political sense. It was his literary, philosophical, or religious contributions that struck them most of all. Yet how these exchanges took place, whether from West to East or East to West, and what they came to signify, were strongly determined by underlying political realities. Asian intellectuals and political leaders from Vivekananda to Suzuki immediately recognized the potential of Emerson's writings to aid in the realization of their own visions of self-determination and social justice, and wasted no time in enlisting his help.

Emerson: A Chronology
1803-1882

Year	Private Life	Professional Work	U.S. Events	World Events & Inventions
1801-1809			President Thomas Jefferson's term.	1801, Toussaint L'Ouverture, black hero of Haiti's revolt against France, becomes its first governor and helps forward Emerson's times, an "Age of Revolution."
1803	Born 25 May, Boston, 2nd son of 5 surviving children.		Louisiana Purchase for $15 million doubles U.S. land area.	
1804			Louis & Clark explore Louisiana Purchase.	Napoleon's Civil Code completed.
1806			Webster compiles first American Dictionary.	British gain control of Cape Colony, South Africa.

http://dx.doi.org/10.11647/OBP.0065.12

Year	Private Life	Professional Work	U.S. Events	World Events & Inventions
1807			U.S. ignores slave trade prohibition for high cotton profits.	UK ends slave trade, serfdom abolished in Prussia. Fulton's steamboat.
1809-1817			President James Madison's term.	
1811	Father dies; his sister, Mary Moody Emerson (MME), helps educate family.			Simón Bolívar declares Venezuela independent of Spain.
1812-1817	Attends Boys' Latin School, begins writing poetry, in Concord during part of war.		1812-1814, war with England.	Brothers Grimm *Fairy Tales*, Jane Austin, *Pride and Prejudice*. Cylinder printing press.
1814	Writes rebus letter to brother William.		White House burned, Creeks defeated in South.	First practical steam locomotive.
1815	Corresponds with MME.		U.S. society begins transformation by market economy.	Napoleon defeated, European monarchies return.
1817-1825			President James Monroe's term.	
1817-1821	At Harvard College, freshman orderly to president, witnesses theological rifts in Congregationalism.		First Seminole War.	
1818	Works in Commons to pay college fees, supports sophomore rebellion.			British gain virtual rule over India.

Year	Private Life	Professional Work	U.S. Events	World Events & Inventions
1819	Impressed by young professors of elocution and of Germany's "higher criticism."		Sermon "Unitarian Christianity" by W. E. Channing, Financial Panic, Florida Purchase, whaling industry starts in Pacific.	*Savannah* first steamship to cross Atlantic. Stethoscope.
1820	At 16, begins journal, berates self for being "idle, vagrant, stupid & hollow." Essay "The Character of Socrates," wins 2nd place, Bowdoin prize.		The Missouri Compromise, first Christian missionaries in Hawaii.	In 1820s, U.S. manufacturers produce interchangeable parts, and in same period, Latin American revolts lead to strongmen rule (caudillos) rather than republics, Romanticism at height in Europe. Galvanometer.
1821	"Dissertation on the Present State of Ethical Philosophy" wins 2nd place, Bowdoin Prize, ranked 30th of 59 in class, gives class poem.			Peru declares independence from Spain. Faraday's electric motor/ generator.
1822	Teaches school, in journal: "Let those who would pluck the lot of Immortality from Fate's Urn, look well to the future prospects of America."	Publishes essay, "The Religion of the Middle Ages," in *The Christian Disciple*, a Unitarian review.	American abolitionists found Monrovia, Liberia's future capital.	Brazil separates from Portugal.

Year	Private Life	Professional Work	U.S. Events	World Events & Inventions
1823	Walks to Western Massachusetts, in journal: "The true epochs of history should be those successive triumphs . . . such as the Reformation, the Revival of letters, the progressive Abolition of the Slave-trade."		Monroe Doctrine strengthens U.S. independence by declaring the American continents closed to European colonization and affirming U.S. lack of interest in Europe's quarrels.	
1824	Decides on the ministry as a vocation largely based on his oratorical gifts.		Henry Clay's American System, Marshall decision strengthens interstate commerce.	Mexico becomes a republic. Electromagnet.
1825-1829			President John Quincy Adams' term.	
1825	Enters Harvard Divinity School, but eye complaints interrupt studies, resumes school-teaching.		American Unitarian Association formed, Erie Canal opens.	1825-1830: Indonesians revolt vs. Dutch rule. First English passenger railway, friction match.
1826	Licensed to preach, but ill health leads to trip to Charleston SC, supported by Uncle Samuel Ripley.			First photographic image produced in France, Ohm's Law measures electrical resistance.
1827	Arrives St. Augustine, FL, reports on a slave auction, makes friends with Achille Murat, Napoleon's nephew, meets Ellen Louisa Tucker in NH.	48 sermons.		Uruguay becomes independent state.

Year	Private Life	Professional Work	U.S. Events	World Events & Inventions
1828	Engaged to Ellen, brother Edward has nervous breakdown.	109 sermons.	Workingman's Party forms in Philadelphia, NYC and Boston, Cherokees cede homelands to U.S. in Alabama.	First steam railroad in the U.S.
1829-1837			President Andrew Jackson's term	
1829	Marries Ellen Tucker, in journal: "We live among eggs, embryos, & seminal principles & the wisest is the most prophetic eye."	At Second Church, Boston: junior, then senior pastor; chaplain to MA state senate, 209 sermons.	James Marsh's American edition of Coleridge's *Aids to Reflection.*	Greece wins independence from Turks. Typewriter, practical locomotive.
1830	In journal: "'Alii disputent, ego mirabor' [Let others wrangle, I will wonder], said Augustin. It shall be my speech to the Calvinist & the Unitarian."	100 sermons.	Indian Removal Act, first wagon trains cross Rockies to California.	French invade Algeria vs. the Ottomans. First U.S. locomotive.
1831	Ellen (19) dies of TB (Feb), walks daily from Boston to her grave in Roxbury.	Boston School Committee, "Lord's Supper" sermon to his congregation.	Nat Turner's Rebellion, National Lyceum Association, Garrison's "Liberator."	Mazzini founds Young Italy. Electromagnetic induction.
1832	Opens Ellen's coffin, months later resigns pastorate, sails for Europe (Dec. 25) for 9 months.	68 sermons.	Tocqueville in U.S. (Boston, NY, Philadelphia), Jackson's Nullification Proclamation, Bank Bill veto.	Goethe dies First electric carriage, Braille developed in France.

Year	Private Life	Professional Work	U.S. Events	World Events & Inventions
1833	Travels from Malta to Continent and UK, returns to Boston (Oct).	Meets leading English writers, including Carlyle, begins "The Uses of Natural History" series, preaches most Sundays.		Factory Act in Britain limits work day for all ages. Calculating machine (mechanical computer) improves on Pascal's seventeenth century adding/subtracting device.
1834	Moves to Concord, brother Edward dies (Oct), inherits first half of Ellen's estate, begins writing Carlyle.	"Natural History" lectures continue, 78 sermons.	Middlesex County, Mass., Anti-Slavery Society begins.	UK slavery ends in West Indies. First mechanical reaper.
1835	Buys house ("Bush"), marries Lydia Jackson of Plymouth, Mass.	Gives Concord's 200th anniversary address, "Lives of Great Men" & "English Literature" series, 71 sermons, 26 lectures.	*New York Herald and* Roger's *Herald of Freedom* begin, Tocqueville's *Democracy in America* I is published, Second Seminole War.	Ottomans regain control in Tripoli & Benghazi, North Africa. Photographic paper.
1836	Meets Margaret Fuller, brother Charles dies (May), son Waldo born (Oct), reads *Institutes of Hindu Law.*	Transcendental Club formed, *Nature* published, "Philosophy of History" series, 73 sermons, 27 lectures.	Texas wins Mexican War after defeat at the Alamo.	Colt revolver, Prussian "needle gun" introduces breech-loading.
1837-1841			President Martin Van Buren's term.	

Year	Private Life	Professional Work	U.S. Events	World Events & Inventions
1837	Meets Thoreau, inherits second half of Ellen's estate, Grimké sisters in Concord.	"Concord Hymn," poem; "American Scholar" Address, "Human Culture" series, briefly speaks vs. slavery, 73 sermons, 29 lectures.	Concord Female Anti-Slavery Society formed, First American Women's Anti-Slavery Convention, Financial Panic.	DC motor, magnetic telescope, S.F.B. Morse's telegraph.
1838	Emerson and Thoreau agree: self-reform first, then society's; Mary M. Brooks leads Concord women & town vs. slavery.	Protests Cherokee removal from GA, "Divinity School Address," "Human Life" series, 13 sermons, 44 lectures.	Cherokees forced out of GA, Second American Women's Anti-Slavery Convention: A. Grimke & L. Mott are notable leaders.	French begin to read Emerson. Stereoscope.
1839	Daughter Ellen born (Feb).	3 sermons, ends preaching; 44 lectures; "The Present Age" series.	Abolitionists divide in New England.	1839: Opium War begins between Britain and China. Vulcanized rubber, Daguerreotype.
1840	Attends reformers' Chardon Street Convention, Boston, declines to join Brook Farm.	*The Dial* begins with Fuller as editor, 31 lectures.	F. Douglass's first speech in Concord, Boston Vigilance Committee (multiracial), Tocqueville's *Democracy in America* II is published.	First World Anti-Slavery Convention, London.
1841-1845			Presidents Harrison and Tyler's terms.	

Year	Private Life	Professional Work	U.S. Events	World Events & Inventions
1841	Thoreau temporarily moves into "Bush," daughter Edith born (Nov), reads Persian poets (Saadi, Hafiz) & more Eastern literature.	*Essays I* published, "The Times" series, "Man the Reformer" in UK press, 11 lectures.	Brook Farm community (ongoing for 6 years), Fruitland—Alcott's utopian experiment— (lasts 7 months).	Carlyle: Emerson is "a voice of the heart of Nature."
1842	Son Waldo dies (Jan), funds Alcott trip to England, in NYC meets Henry James, Sr. & Horace Greeley.	Becomes editor of *The Dial* and in it prints "Ethnical Scriptures," 19 lectures.	Treaty establishes U.S.-Canada border, Wm Phillips delivers "Slavery" speech at Concord Lyceum.	Opium War ends: Britain forces China to open more ports, cede Hong Kong.
1843	Sends Thoreau to NYC, Daniel Webster at "Bush," promotes Phillips' speeches on slavery.	Translates Dante's *Vita Nuova*, speaks in Boston series on reform with Thoreau, "New England" lecture series, 26 lectures *The Dial* focus: Confucian sayings.	Phillips twice more speaks on slavery at Concord Lyceum.	Mercerized textiles (stimulus to more cotton production).
1844	Son Edward born (July), buys 41 acres near Walden Pond, decries Samuel Hoar's eviction from Charleston SC, opposes Texas Annex. and Mexican War, reads *Bhagavad Gita*.	*Essays II* published, Concord address on anniversary of slavery's end in the West Indies, last issue of *The Dial*, 30 lectures.	Railroad comes to Concord, New England Anti-Slavery Convention: disunion of the U.S.; F. Douglass favors disunion in Concord address.	Dominican Republic becomes independent of Haiti.
1845-1849			President James K. Polk's term.	

Year	Private Life	Professional Work	U.S. Events	World Events & Inventions
1845	Permits Thoreau to build cabin on his Walden Pond land, continues to promote Phillips, refuses to lecture in New Bedford lyceum over blacks' segregated seating, reads classical Hindu texts.	"Representative Men" lecture series, 14 lectures.	Phillips in Concord opposes Texas statehood and slavery, Texas (& CA) annexed by U.S.	Irish Potato Famine, 1 million emigrate. Rotary printing press, double tube tires.
1846	Calls Thoreau's night in jail to protest the Mexican War, "one step to suicide;" does not sign Concord's disunion petition.	*Poems* published, speaks at Thoreau's cabin on second anniversary of end of West Indian slavery, 55 lectures.	Defeat of Wilmot Proviso ends hope of prohibiting slavery in any territory previously owned by Mexico, Bear Republic established in California; in Boston, a fugitive slave led to safety.	War with Mexico, 1846-1847. Sewing machine, coal-gas 4 cycle engine.
1847-1848	Lectures in UK (Oct-July), disagrees with Carlyle, Thoreau at "Bush" with Lydian, children.	Lectures to UK workers and elite. In Paris, meets de Tocqueville. 1847, 55 lectures 1848, 53 lectures (abroad, 40; U.S., 13).	1847-1848 Mormons in Utah 1848, Seneca Falls Convention, Free Soil Party (lasts 6 years).	1847, Liberia established as home for freed American slaves, Istanbul slave market abolished, Revolutions in Europe, 1848; Second French Republic; Karl Marx, *The Communist Manifesto.* Arc light.
1849-1853			Presidents Taylor and Fillmore's terms.	

Year	Private Life	Professional Work	U.S. Events	World Events & Inventions
1849	Prepares lectures, begins smoking cigars, Frederika Bremer at "Bush," on Hindu texts: "excellent gymnastics for the mind."	"Mind and Matters" series, 54 lectures, *Nature*; *Addresses and Lectures* published, speaks on third anniversary of end of West Indian slavery.	California Gold Rush, Thoreau's "Civil Disobedience," Harriet Tubman escapes slavery, leads 300 to freedom on Underground RR.	Missionary-explorer David Livingstone reaches Africa's interior, Lake Ngami; construction begins on Suez Canal. Hydraulic turbine, safety pin.
1850	Mourns Fuller's death in shipwreck off Fire Island.	*Representative Men*, "Conduct of Life" lectures begin; first western tour Ohio; from 1850 to last work, refers to Hindu texts, 48 lectures.	Webster's March 7th speech in Congress, Compromise of 1850 includes Fugitive Slave Act, Boston Vigilance Committee accelerates activities, Melville's *Moby Dick*.	1850s South American Republics end slavery, apogee of Romantic music, 1850-1864: Taiping Rebellion, Chinese immigrate to U.S.
1851	Excoriates Webster's "betrayal" of North, supports Thoreau & family's aid to escaped slaves via Concord's Underground RR.	Speaks vs. Fugitive Slave Act 9 times, 34 lectures.	Boston: escaped slave Thomas Sims returned to SC, Charles Sumner elected MA Senator, U.S. Underground RR grows.	First industrial fair, London. Electric locomotive, icemaking machine, ophthalmoscope.
1852	Praises Stowe's novel, *Uncle Tom's Cabin*.	Edits *Memoirs of Margaret Fuller Ossoli*, 69 lectures in N.E., Canada, Middle Atlantic states, delegate to woman's rights convention, Worcester, Mass.	Harriet Beecher Stowe's *Uncle Tom's Cabin* sells 10,000 copies in U.S. in first week; 300,000 in the U.S. and 1.5 million in the UK in first year, revolutionizes attitudes toward slavery.	Napoleon III crowned Emperor of France. Airship, elevator and its brake, Singer's sewing machine, gyroscope.
1853-1857			President Franklin Pierce's term.	

Year	Private Life	Professional Work	U.S. Events	World Events & Inventions
1853	Mother dies (Nov); in journal, quotes Elizabeth Hoar: ". . . Bloomer dress is very good & reconcilable to men's taste, if only it be not offensively sudden; so a woman may speak, & vote, & legislate, & drive coach, if only it comes by degrees."	44 lectures extend to Mid-West for first time; in IL, Lincoln hears him.	Gadsden Purchase: Mexican land for RR to Pacific becomes part of New Mexico Territory.	Commodore Mathew Perry sails into Japan's Edo bay, forcing trade with U.S.; India has RR and telegraph lines. Glider, potato chip.
1854	In journal: ". . . the races . . . must be used temporarily . . . by the Linnaean classification . . . not as true and ultimate." Thoreau in *Walden*: "Plainly Boston does not wish liberty, & can only be tricked into a rescue of a slave."	60 widely given lectures, speaks vs. Fugitive Slave Law in NYC.	Kansas-Nebraska Act, Boston: fugitive slave Anthony Burns returned to VA, Boston conventions: Free Soil Society and New England Anti-Slavery Society.	1854-1856 Crimean War, Russia defeated by UK, France.
1855	Praises *Leaves of Grass*, helps found Concord Academy and Saturday Club.	Anti-slavery addresses in Boston, New York, Philadelphia; "Woman" speech at Woman's Rights Convention, Boston; 59 lectures.	Whitman's *Leaves of Grass* published.	India begins to read Emerson. Bessemer furnace.
1856	In journal: "If I knew only Thoreau, I should think cooperation of good men impossible."	*English Traits*, speaks for Kansas Relief, 66 lectures from N.E. to Mid-West.	Civil War in Kansas, John Brown's Massacre, Sumner beaten on Senate floor for Kansas speech.	1856-1860 Second Opium War between Britain and China. Steel converter.

Year	Private Life	Professional Work	U.S. Events	World Events & Inventions
1857-1861			President James Buchanan's term.	
1857	Entertains John Brown with Thoreau at "Bush," donates to Harriet Tubman in Concord.	Praises Brown's speech in Concord, "Brahma," poem, 48 lectures.	Dred Scott Decision, *Harper's Weekly*, Financial Panic.	Mutiny in India vs. UK, Africa slave trade ends in Ottoman Empire.
1858	Declares self "absolute" abolitionist, camps in Adirondacks.	36 lectures.	Lincoln's "House Divided" speech, Lincoln/Douglas Debates.	Tolstoy praises Emerson on Goethe and Shakespeare. Steelmaking furnace, Mason jar.
1859	Agitated re Brown, journal entries lapse, begins transcribing MME's "Almanack," brother Bulkley dies (May).	Quotes friend: Brown's gallows will be as "sacred as the cross," 44 lectures.	John Brown raid and capture at Harper's Ferry.	Darwin's *Origin of Species*. Spectroscope, storage battery, escalator.
1860	fails to persuade Whitman to minimize sex in *Leaves of Grass*.	*The Conduct of Life*, 54 lectures in NE, NY, Mid-West, Toronto.	Lincoln elected, SC secedes, U.S. Pony Express, U.S. slaves at c. 4 million, nearly 60% more than in 1820.	Italian unification begins, Japanese cross Pacific in Western-style ship. Vacuum cleaner, linoleum, repeating rifle.
1861-1865			President Abraham Lincoln's term.	
1861	In journal: "only as our existence is shared, not as it is self-hood . . . is [it] divine."	Pro-Union crowd hoots him off stage; at Anti-Slavery Soc. in Charleston, Mass.: "sometimes gunpowder smells good." 30 lectures.	Lincoln's first Inaugural, Confederate Constitution, Civil War begins at Fort Sumter, Lincoln asks for volunteers.	Russian serfs emancipated, Pasteur popularizes germ theory of disease. Machine gun.

Year	Private Life	Professional Work	U.S. Events	World Events & Inventions
1862	Quotes dying Thoreau: "I wish so to live . . . that . . . I may dream of no heaven but that which lies about me." Thoreau dies (May), gives funeral oration.	Delivers "American Civilization" at Smithsonian, meets Lincoln in White House, address printed in *Atlantic Monthly*, 29 lectures.	Civil War on sea/ land, Homestead Act, Pacific Railroad Act.	1862-1867 French puppet empire in Mexico, Nietzsche reads & copies Emerson verbatim, Bismarck appointed Prussian Prime Minister.
1863	In journal: "I am a bard least of bards." MME dies (Oct).	"Boston Hymn," poem, celebrates Emancipation, reviews cadets at West Point, 31 lectures.	Lincoln's Emancipation Proclamation, Gettysburg Address.	Player piano.
1864	In journal: "If we escape bravely from the present war, America will be the controlling power."	Gives "American Life" and "Fortune of the Republic," elected to new American Academy of Arts & Sciences, 17 lectures.	Cheyenne Massacre, Atlanta Campaign.	Baudelaire echoes Emerson. Experimental automobile.
1865-1869			Presidents Lincoln and Johnson's term.	
1865	Eulogy for Lincoln, "the true representative of this continent."	Writes preface to Saadi's *Gulistan*, 77 lectures from NE to Mid-West.	Civil war ends, Lincoln shot. 13th Amendment ends slavery in U.S.	Young Ottoman Society founded. RR sleeping car, pneumatic tool.
1866	Reads poem "Terminus" to son Edward.	Receives LLD, Harvard University, 43 lectures.	Transatlantic Cable, Freedman's Bureau Act, Civil Rights Act.	American University founded in Beirut, diamonds discovered in South Africa. Dynamite.

Year	Private Life	Professional Work	U.S. Events	World Events & Inventions
1867	In journal: ". . . a cleavage is occurring in the hitherto firm granite of the past, and a new era is nearly arrived."	*May-Day and Other Pieces published*, delivers Harvard PBK Address, elected Harvard Overseer, Free Religious Assoc. and Radical Club, 80 lectures.	Johnson vetoes 1st Reconstruction Act and Reconstruction Acts 2-4, Alaska bought from Russia.	Dominion of Canada declared, Austria-Hungary monarchy established. Typewriter.
1868	In journal: ". . . the delight in another's superiority, is as M.M.E. Says, 'My best gift from God.' . . . the moral nature is . . . higher than the intellectual"; brother William dies (Sept).	Meets Emma Lazarus, NYC; speaks to Chinese officials, Boston; extols Confucius; 25 lectures.	Ku-Klux-Klan. 14th Amendment. Louisa May Alcott's *Little Women.*	Meiji (Enlightened) Restoration in Japan. Air brake.
1869-1877			President Ulysses S. Grant's term.	
1869	In journal: ". . . the charm of [studying religion] is in finding the agreements & identities in all the religions of men."	Elected VP, NE Women's Suffrage Association, profiles MME ("Amita") for NE Women's Club, 37 lectures.	Transcontinental RR, reduces Native American buffalo herds by half.	Suez Canal opens, Mohandas Gandhi born. Oleomargarine.
1870	Wishes Julia Ward Howe ("Battle Hymn") of NYC were Massachusetts born: "We have no such poetess in New England."	"National History of the Intellect," Harvard philosophy course; preface, *Plutarch's Morals; Society and Solitude,* 27 lectures.	15th Amendment, Enforcement Acts re 14th, 15th Amendments.	Franco-Prussian War, German Empire, 1870-1900 11 million Europeans immigrate to U.S., transatlantic slave trade ends. Celluloid, stock ticker.

Year	Private Life	Professional Work	U.S. Events	World Events & Inventions
1871	Aborts Harvard course for trip to CA by RR, meets John Muir, Bret Harte visits him in Concord.	39 lectures from Chicago to DC.	Apache War begins, Ku-Klux-Klan Act, Chicago Fire.	Japanese Mission to study Western ideas. Compressed air rock drill.
1872	Memory lapses increase after fire to "Bush," trip to Europe, Egypt, sees Henry James in Paris.	Speaks at Howard Institute (later University), addresses Japanese in Boston, is feted in Europe, 20 lectures.	Liberal Republican Party.	Japan claims Ryuku Islands. Gasoline engine.
1873	Returns home (May), more conscious of memory loss.	begins new term as Harvard Overseer	Financial Panic.	Car coupler, blue jeans.
1874	Excludes himself, Whitman & Poe in new poetry collection.	*Parnassus*, anthology of his favorite poems.	Independent Greenback Party formed.	Barbed wire.
1875	Ends journal entries.	Reads Minutemen Memorial in Concord, centennial of Revolution, *Letters and Social Aims*.	Civil Rights Act.	Magazine gun.
1876	Hosts Emma Lazarus; on Virginians: "They are very brave people down there, and say just what they think."	*Selected Poems*, lectures at the University of Virginia to indifferent audience.	Sioux War ends, Mark Twain's *Tom Sawyer*.	Carpet sweeper, Bell's telephone, refrigerator.
1877-1882			President Rutherford B. Hayes' term.	

Year	Private Life	Professional Work	U.S. Events	World Events & Inventions
1877	Increasingly withdrawn, unable to converse at length.		Southern sentiment vs. blacks rises, North loses interest in Reconstruction.	Queen Victoria becomes Empress of India. Microphone, phonograph.
1878	On himself: "a lecturer who has no idea what he's lecturing about, and an audience who don't know what he can mean."	Reads "Education" at Concord Lyceum.	Reconstruction ends.	Edison's electric light, cream separator, disc cultivator, cystoscope.
1879	"Strange that the kind Heavens should keep us on earth after they have destroyed our connection with things!"	Lectures at Amherst College, speaks on memory at Concord School of Philosophy (CSP).	Japanese student at Amherst College takes Emerson's work to Tokyo University.	Second Afghan War: Britain controls Afghanistan. Cash register, incandescent light bulb, Ivory soap.
1880	Family asks James E. Cabot to be literary executor/biographer.	Speaks on aristocracy at CSP, reads 1867 lecture at Concord Lyceum.	James Garfield elected president.	Kipling at 15 lists Emerson his 2nd favorite poet. Photophone.
1881	Whitman on Emerson at home, "A good color in his face . . . and the old clear-peering aspect quite the same."	Reads paper on Carlyle at Massachusetts Historical Society.	Clara Barton founds American Red Cross.	Carbon filament.
1882	27 April, dies of pneumonia at home, buried Sleepy Hollow Cemetery, Concord.	Late March, attends Longfellow's funeral but cannot remember his name.	Oscar Wilde tours US, often quotes Emerson.	Cuban José Martí writes "Emerson" in Spanish. Electric fan, electric flatiron, Christmas lights.

Selected Bibliography

Primary Sources

The Collected Works of Ralph Waldo Emerson, 10 vols. Edited by Robert E. Spiller, et al. Cambridge, Mass.: Harvard University Press, 1971-2013.

The Complete Works of Ralph Waldo Emerson, Centenary Edition, 12 vols. Edited by Edward Waldo Emerson. Boston, Mass.: Houghton Mifflin, 1903-1904.

The Early Lectures of Ralph Waldo Emerson. Edited by Stephen E. Whicher, et al. Cambridge, Mass.: The Belknap Press, 1959-1972.

The Journals and Miscellaneous Notebooks of Ralph Waldo Emerson, 16 vols. Edited by William H. Gilman, et al. Cambridge, Mass.: Harvard University Press, 1960-1982.

The Later Lectures of Ralph Waldo Emerson, 1843-1871, 2 vols. Edited by Ronald A. Bosco and Joel Myerson. Athens, GA: University of Georgia Press, 2001.

The Letters of Ralph Waldo Emerson, 10 vols. Edited by Ralph Rusk and Eleanor Tilton. New York: Columbia University Press, 1939-1994.

Ralph Waldo Emerson: Collected Poems and Translations. Edited by Harold Bloom and Paul Kane. New York: The Library of America, 1994.

Books

Adams, John Quincy. *The Diary of John Quincy Adams, 1794-1845*. Edited by Allan Nevins. New York: Charles Scribner's Sons, 1951.

Ahlstrom, Sydney. *A Religious History of the American People*. New Haven, CT: Yale University Press, 1972.

Alcott, Bronson. *The Journals of Bronson Alcott*. Edited by Odell Shepard. Boston, Mass.: Little, Brown, 1938.

Allen, Gay Wilson. *William James, A Biography*. New York: Viking Press, 1967.

—. *Waldo Emerson*. New York: Viking Press, 1981.

Barish, Evelyn. *Emerson: The Roots of Prophecy*. Princeton, NJ: Princeton University Press, 1989.

Bernhard, Virginia and Elizabeth Fox-Genevese, eds. *The Birth of American Feminism: The Seneca Falls Women's Convention*. St. James, N.Y.: Brandywine Press, 1995.

Bjork, Daniel W. *William James: The Center of His Vision*. New York: Columbia University Press, 1988, http://psycnet.apa.org/books/10061/ and http://dx.doi.org/10.1037/10061-000

Borges, J. L. and W. Barnstone. *Other Inquisitions*. Translated by R. L. C. Simms. Austin, TX: University of Texas Press, 1964.

— *Borges at Eighty: Conversations*. Bloomington, IN: Indiana University Press, 1982.

—. and O. Ferrari. *En diálogo*. Mexico [sic]: Siglo XXI, 2005.

Bosco, Ronald A. and Joel Myerson. *Emerson in His Own Time*. Iowa City, IA: University of Iowa Press, 2003.

— eds. *Emerson Bicentennial Essays*. Boston, Mass.: Massachusetts Historical Society and the University Press of Virginia, 2006.

Brown, Lee Rust. *The Emerson Museum: Practical Romanticism and the Pursuit of the Whole*. Cambridge, Mass.: Harvard University Press, 1997.

Buell, Lawrence. *Emerson*. Cambridge, Mass.: Harvard University Press, 2003.

Cabot, James Elliot. *A Memoir of Ralph Waldo Emerson*. Cambridge, Mass.: Riverside Press, 1887, http://catalog.hathitrust.org/Record/000389431

Cameron, Kenneth. *Transcendental Climate*. Hartford, CT: Transcendental Books, 1963.

Camus, Alfred. *Notebooks 1951-1959*. Chicago, IL: Ivan R. Dee, 2008.

Capper, Charles. *Margaret Fuller: An American Romantic Life, The Private Years, Vol. I*. New York: Oxford University Press, 1992.

Capps, Jack L. *Emily Dickinson's Reading, 1836-1886*. Cambridge, Mass.: Harvard University Press, 1966.

Christy, Arthur. *The Orient in American Transcendentalism: A Study of Emerson, Thoreau, and Alcott*. New York: Octagon Books, 1978.

Cole, Phyllis. *Mary Moody Emerson and the Origins of Transcendentalism*. New York: Oxford University Press, 1998.

Collison, Gary. *Shadrach Minkins: From Fugitive Slave to Citizen*. Cambridge, Mass.: Harvard University Press, 1997.

The Correspondence of Emerson and Carlyle. Edited by Joseph Slater. New York: Columbia University Press, 1964.

The Correspondence of William James, 11 vols. Edited by Gerald E. Myers. Charlottesville, VA: University Press of Virginia, 1992.

The Correspondence of William James. Edited by Ignas K. Skrupskelis and Elizabeth M. Berkeley. Charlottesville, VA: University Press of Virginia, 2002.

Conway, Moncure Daniel. *Emerson at Home and Abroad*. Boston, Mass.: James Osgood, 1882.

Crain, Caleb. *American Sympathy: Men, Friendship, and Literature in the New Nation*. New Haven, CT: Yale University Press, 2001.

Crane, Gregg D. *Race, Citizenship, and Law in American Literature*. New York: Cambridge University Press, 2002.

Dahlstrand, Frederick C. *Amos Bronson Alcott: An Intellectual Biography*. London: Associated University Presses, 1982.

Dickinson, Emily. *The Letters of Emily Dickinson*, 3 vols. Edited by Thomas H. Johnson and Theodora Ward. Cambridge, Mass.: The Belknap Press of Harvard University Press, 1958.

— *The Poems of Emily Dickinson*, 3 vols. Edited by Thomas H. Johnson. Cambridge, Mass., 1963.

— *The Poems of Emily Dickinson: Variorum Edition*, 3 vols. Edited by R. W. Franklin. Cambridge, Mass.: The Belknap Press of Harvard University Press, 1998.

Donald, David Herbert. *Lincoln*. New York: Simon & Schuster, 1995.

— *Charles Sumner*. New York: De Capo Press, 1996.

Edel, Leon. *Henry James: A Life*. New York: Harper & Row, 1985.

Eliot, George. *The George Eliot Letters*. Edited by Gordon S. Haight. New Haven, CT: Yale University Press, 1954.

Emerson, Benjamin Kendall. *The Ipswich Emersons*. Boston, Mass.: D. Clapp, 1900.

Emerson, Edward Waldo. *Emerson in Concord: A Memoir*. Boston, Mass.: Houghton Mifflin, 1888.

Emerson, Ellen Tucker. *Emerson in His Journals*. Edited by Joel Porte. Cambridge, Mass.: Harvard University Press, 1982.

— *The Letters of Ellen Tucker Emerson*, 2 vols. Edited by Edith E. W. Gregg. Kent, OH: Kent State University Press, 1982.

— *The Life of Lidian Jackson Emerson*. Edited by Delores B. Carpenter. East Lansing, MI: Michigan State University Press, 1992.

Emerson, Lidian Jackson. *The Selected Letters of Lidian Jackson Emerson*. Edited by Delores Bird Carpenter. Columbia, MO: University of Missouri Press, 1987.

Emerson, Mary Moody. *Selected Letters of Mary Moody Emerson*. Edited by Nancy Craig Simmons. Athens, GA: University of Georgia Press, 1993.

Emerson, Ralph Waldo. *Emerson's Antislavery Writings*. Edited by Len Gougeon and Joel Myerson. New Haven, CT: Yale University Press, 1995.

— *Emerson's Prose and Poetry*. Edited by Joel Porte and Saundra Morris. New York: W. W. Norton & Co., 2001.

Farr, Finis. *Frank Lloyd Wright.* New York: Charles Scribner's Sons, 1961.

Field, P. S. *Ralph Waldo Emerson.* Lanham, MD: Rowman & Littlefield, 2003.

Frederickson, George M. *The Inner Civil War: Northern Intellectuals and the Crisis of the Union.* Urbana, IL: University of Illinois Press, 1993.

Fuller, Margaret. *The Portable Margaret Fuller.* Edited by Mary Kelley. New York: Penguin Books, 1994.

Horace H. Furness, ed. *Records of a Lifelong Friendship: Ralph Waldo Emerson and William Henry Furness.* Boston, Mass.: Houghton Mifflin, 1910.

Garvey, T. Gregory, ed. *The Emerson Dilemma: Essays on Emerson and Social Reform.* Athens, GA: University of Georgia Press, 2001.

— *Creating the Culture of Reform in Antebellum America.* Athens, GA: University of Georgia Press, 2006.

Gandhi, Mohandas K. *The Moral and Political Writings of Mahatma Gandhi.* Edited by Raghavan Iyer. Oxford: Clarendon Press, 1973.

— *The Collected Works of Mahatma Gandhi,* vols. 9, 42, 67, 76. New Delhi: Government Publications Division, 1979.

— *Gandhi: An Autobiography: The Story of My Experiments with Truth.* Boston, Mass.: Beacon Press, 1993.

Gougeon, Len. *Virtue's Hero: Emerson, Anti-Slavery, and Reform.* Athens, GA: University of Georgia Press, 1990.

— *Emerson & Eros: The Making of a Cultural Hero.* Albany, NY: State University of New York Press, 2007.

Goodwin, Doris Kearns. *Team of Rivals: The Political Genius of Abraham Lincoln.* New York: Simon & Schuster, 2005.

Greenham, David. *Emerson's Transatlantic Romanticism.* New York: Palgrave Macmillan, 2012. http://dx.doi.org/10.1057/9781137265203

Guarneri, Carl J. *The Utopian Alternative: Fourierism in Nineteenth-Century America.* Ithaca: Cornell University Press, 1994.

Gupta, R. K. *The Great Encounter: A Study of Indo-American Literary and Cultural Relations.* Riverdale, MD: Riverdale Company, 1987.

Habegger, Alfred. *My Wars Are Laid Away: The Life of Emily Dickinson.* New York: Random House, 2001.

Harding, Walter. *The Days of Henry Thoreau: A Biography.* New York: Alfred A. Knopf, 1970.

Haskins, David Greene. *Ralph Waldo Emerson: His Maternal Ancestors.* Boston, Mass.: Cupples, Upham & Co., 1887.

Herndon, William H. *The Hidden Lincoln.* Edited by Emanuel Hertz. New York: The Viking Press, 1938.

— *Herndon's Life of Lincoln*. New York: Da Capo Press, 1983.

Hodder, Alan D. *Emerson's Rhetoric of Revelation*. University Park, PA: Pennsylvania State University Press, 1989.

Holmes, Oliver Wendell. *Ralph Waldo Emerson*. Boston: Houghton Mifflin, 1885.

Howe, Daniel Walker. *The Unitarian Conscience: Harvard Moral Philosophy, 1805-1861* (1970); reprint. Middletown, CT: Wesleyan University Press, 1988.

Hudspeth, Robert N. *"My Heart is a Large Kingdom": Selected Letters of Margaret Fuller*. Ithaca: Cornell University Press, 2001.

Hutchison, William R. *The Transcendentalist Ministers: Church Reform in the New England Renaissance*. New Haven, CT: Yale University Press, 1959.

Huxtable, Ada Louise. *Frank Lloyd Wright*. New York: Lipper/Viking, 2004.

Kaplan, Justin. *Walt Whitman: A Life*. New York: Simon & Schuster, 1980.

Keane, Patrick J. *Emerson, Romanticism, and Intuitive Reason: The Transatlantic "Light of All Our Day."* Columbia, MO: University of Missouri Press, 2005.

Kennedy, Lawrence W. *Planning the City Upon a Hill: Boston Since 1630*. Amherst, Mass.: University of Massachusetts Press, 1992.

Kipling, Rudyard. *The Writings in Prose and Verse: Early Verse*. New York: Charles Scribner's Sons, 1900.

— *Something of Myself*. Cambridge: Cambridge University Press, 1990.

Leyda, Jay. *The Years and Hours of Emily Dickinson*, 2 vols. New Haven, CT: Yale University Press, 1960.

Lincoln, Abraham. *This Fiery Trial: The Speeches and Writings of Abraham Lincoln*. Edited by William E. Gienapp. New York: Oxford University Press, 2002.

Lothstein, Arthur S. and Michael Brodrick, eds. *New Morning: Emerson in the Twenty-first Century*. Albany, NY: State University of New York Press, 2008.

Loving, Jerome. *Walt Whitman: The Song of Himself*. Berkeley, CA: The University of California Press, 1999.

McAleer, John. *Waldo Emerson: Days of Encounter*. Boston, Mass.: Little, Brown & Co., 1984.

McPherson, James M. *Battle Cry of Freedom: The Civil War Era*. New York: Ballantine Books, 1988.

— *Abraham Lincoln and the Second American Revolution*. New York: Oxford University Press, 1990.

— *This Mighty Scourge: Perspectives on the Civil War*. New York: Oxford University Press, 2007.

McFeely, William S. *Frederick Douglass*. New York: W. W. Norton & Co., 1991.

Mariani, Giorgio, et al., eds. *Emerson at 200: Proceedings of the International Bicentennial Conference*. Rome: Aracne, 2004.

Marshall, Megan. *Margaret Fuller: A New American Life*. Boston, Mass.: Houghton Mifflin Harcourt, 2013.

Martí, Jose. *Obras Completas*. La Habana: Editorial Nacional de Cuba, 1964.

Menand, Louis. *The Metaphysical Club: A Story of Ideas in America*. New York: Farrar, Straus, and Giroux, 2001.

Miers, Earl Schenck, ed. *Lincoln Day by Day: A Chronology, 1809-1865,* 3 vols. Washington, D.C.: Lincoln Sesquicentennial Commission, 1960.

Miller, Frederick DeWolfe. *Christopher Pearse Cranch and his Caricatures of New England Transcendentalism*. Cambridge, Mass.: Harvard University Press, 1951.

Miller, Perry, ed. *The Transcendentalists: An Anthology*. Cambridge, Mass.: Harvard University Press, 1950.

— ed. *The American Transcendentalists: Their Prose and Poetry*. New York: Doubleday Anchor Books, 1957.

Montinari, M. *Reading Nietzsche*. Urbana, IL: University of Illinois Press, 2003.

Mott, Wesley T. *"The Strains of Eloquence": Emerson and His Sermons*. University Park, PA: Pennsylvania State University Press, 1989.

— and Robert E. Burkeholder, eds. *Emersonian Circles: Essays in Honor of Joel Myerson*. Rochester: University of Rochester Press, 1997.

— ed. *Ralph Waldo Emerson in Context*. New York: Cambridge University Press, 2014. http://dx.doi.org/10.1017/cbo9781139235594

Mudge, Jean McClure. *Emily Dickinson and the Image of Home*. Amherst, Mass.: University of Massachusetts Press, 1975.

— *The Poet and the Dictator: Lauro de Bosis Resists Fascism in Italy and America*. Greenwood, CT: Praeger, 2002.

Myerson, Joel. *The New England Transcendentalists and the Dial: A History of the Magazine and Its Contributors*. Rutherford, N.J.: Fairleigh Dickinson University Press, 1980.

National Geographic Concise History of the World, an Illustrated Time Line. Edited by Neil Kagan. Washington, D.C.: National Geographic Society, 2006.

Nicoloff, Philip L. *Emerson on Race and History: An Examination of English Traits*. New York: Columbia University Press, 1961.

Nietzsche, Friedrich. *The Will to Power*. New York: Vintage, 1968.

— *Writings from the Late Notebooks*. Cambridge: Cambridge University Press, 2003.

Nute, Kevin. *Frank Lloyd Wright and Japan*. New York: Van Nostrand Reinhold, 1993.

Oates, Stephen B. *With Malice Toward None: A Life of Abraham Lincoln*. New York: Harper Perennial, 1977.

The Oxford Handbook of Transcendentalism. Edited by Joel Myerson, et al. Oxford: Oxford University Press, 2010.

Packer, Barbara L. *Emerson's Fall: A New Interpretation of the Major Essays.* New York: Continuum Books, 1982.

— *The Transcendentalists.* Athens, GA: University of Georgia Press, 2007.

Painter, Nell Irvin. *The History of White People.* New York: W.W. Norton & Co., 2010.

Paul, Sherman. *Emerson's Angle of Vision: Man and Nature in American Experience.* Cambridge, Mass.: Harvard University Press, 1952.

Perry, Bliss. *Emerson Today.* Princeton, NJ: Princeton University Press, 1931.

Petrulionis, Sandra H. *To Set This World Right: The Anti-Slavery Movement in Thoreau's Concord.* Ithaca, NY: Cornell University Press, 2006.

Pommer, Henry F. *Emerson's First Marriage.* Carbondale, IL: Southern Illinois University Press, 1967.

Porte, Joel. *Representative Man: Ralph Waldo Emerson in His Time.* New York: Oxford University Press, 1979.

Ratner-Rosenhagen, Jennifer. *American Nietzsche: A History of an Icon and His Ideas.* Chicago: University of Chicago Press, 2012.

Remini, Robert V. *Andrew Jackson: The Course of American Freedom, 1822-1832: Volume 2.* New York: Harper & Row, 1982.

Reynolds, Larry J. *European Revolutions and the American Literary Renaissance.* New Haven, CT: Yale University Press, 1988.

Richardson, Robert D., Jr. *Emerson: The Mind on Fire.* Berkeley, CA: University of California Press, 1995.

Roberson, Susan L. *Emerson in His Sermons: A Man-Made Self.* Columbia, MO: University of Missouri Press, 1995.

Robinson, David M. *Apostle of Culture: Emerson as Preacher and Lecturer.* Philadelphia, PA: University of Pennsylvania Press, 1982.

— *The Unitarians and the Universalists.* Westport, CT: Greenwood Press, 1985.

— *Emerson and the Conduct of Life: Pragmatism and Ethical Purpose in the Later Work.* Cambridge and New York: Cambridge University Press, 1993.

Rosenwald, Lawrence. *Emerson and the Art of the Diary.* New York: Oxford University Press, 1988.

Rusk, Ralph L. *The Life of Ralph Waldo Emerson.* New York: Charles Scribner's Sons, 1949.

Sacks, Kenneth S. *Understanding Emerson.* Princeton, NJ: Princeton University Press, 2003.

Sanborn, Franklin B. ed. *The Genius and Character of Emerson: Lectures at the Concord School of Philosophy.* Boston: James R Osgood & Co., 1885.

— *Transcendental and Literary New England.* Edited by Kenneth W. Cameron. Hartford: Transcendental Books, 1975.

Sarfatti, Margherita. *The Life of Benito Mussolini. Translated by Dux*. Whitefish, MT: Kessinger Publishing, 2004.

Seager, Richard Hughes, ed. *The Dawn of Religious Pluralism: Voices from the World's Parliament of Religions, 1893*. La Salle, IL: Open Court Press, 1993.

Sealts, Jr., Merton M. *Emerson on the Scholar*. Columbia, MO: University of Missouri Press, 1992.

— and Alfred R. Ferguson. *Emerson's* Nature: *Origin, Growth, Meaning*, 2nd edition, enlarged. Carbondale, IL: Southern Illinois University Press, 1979.

Secrest, Meryle. *Frank Lloyd Wright*. New York: Knopf, 1992.

Sewall, Richard. *Life of Emily Dickinson*, 2 vols. New York: Farrar, Straus, and Giroux, 1974.

Simpson, Lewis P. *Mind and the American Civil War: A Meditation on Lost Causes*. Baton Rouge, LA: Louisiana State University Press, 1989.

Smith, Harmon. *My Friend, My Friend: The Story of Thoreau's Relationship with Emerson*. Amherst, Mass.: University of Massachusetts Press, 1999.

Stack, G. J. *Nietzsche and Emerson: An Elective Affinity*. Athens, OH: Ohio University Press, 1992.

Stauffer, John and Zoe Trodd, eds. *Meteor of War: The John Brown Story*. New York: Brandywine Press, 2004.

Suzuki, Daisetz T. *Zen and Japanese Culture*. Princeton, NJ: Princeton University Press, 1959.

Tharaud, Barry, ed. *Emerson for the Twenty-First Century: Global Perspectives on an American Icon*. Newark, Del.: University of Delaware Press, 2010.

Thayer, James B. *A Western Journey with Mr. Emerson*. Facsimile reprint by Kennikat Press, Port Washington, NY, 1970.

Thomas, Benjamin P. *Lincoln, 1847-1853: Being the Day-by-Day Activities of Abraham Lincoln from January 1, 1847 to December 31, 1853*. Springfield, IL: The Abraham Lincoln Association, 1936.

Thomas, John L. *The Liberator: William Lloyd Garrison, A Biography*. Boston: Little, Brown & Co., 1963.

Thoreau, Henry David. *The Heart of Thoreau's Journals*. Edited by Odell Shepard. New York: Dover, 1961.

Tolstoy, Leon. *Tolstoy's Diaries*. New York: Charles Scribner's Sons, 1985.

— *Path of Life*. Translated by Maureen Cote. Huntington, NY: Nova Science Publishers, 2002.

Transcendentalism: A Reader. Edited by Joel Myerson. Oxford: Oxford University Press, 2000.

Traubel, Horace. *Intimate with Walt: Selections from Whitman's Conversations with Horace Traubel, 1888-1892*. Edited by Gary Schmidgall. Iowa City, IA: University of Iowa Press, 2001.

Van Cromphout, Gustaaf. *Emerson's Modernity and the Example of Goethe*. Columbia, MO: University of Missouri Press, 1990.

Van Leer, David. *Emerson's Epistemology: The Argument of the Essays*. Cambridge, Mass.: Cambridge University Press, 1986.

Von Frank, Albert J. *An Emerson Chronology*. New York: G.K. Hall & Co., 1994.

— *The Trials of Anthony Burns: Freedom and Slavery in Emerson's Boston*. Cambridge, Mass.: Harvard University Press, 1998.

Von Mehren, Joan. *Minerva and the Muse*. University of Massachusetts Press, 1994.

Walls, Laura Dassow. *Emerson's Life in Science: The Culture of Truth*. Ithaca, NY: Cornell University Press, 2003.

West, Cornel. *Democracy Matters*. New York: Penguin, 2004.

Whicher, Stephen E. *Freedom and Fate: An Inner Life of Ralph Waldo Emerson*. Philadelphia, PA: University of Pennsylvania Press, 1953.

White, Jr. Ronald C. *The Eloquent President*. New York: Random House Trade Paperback, 2005.

Wilde, Oscar. *The Soul of Man. De Profundis. The Ballad of Reading Gaol*. Edited by Isobel Murray. Oxford: Oxford University Press, 1999.

— *Oscar Wilde: The Major Works*. Oxford: Oxford University Press, 2000.

Wills, Garry. *Lincoln at Gettysburg: The Words That Remade America*. New York: Simon & Schuster, 1992.

— *"Negro President": Jefferson and the Slave Power*. Boston, Mass.: Houghton Mifflin, 2003.

Wilson, Eric. *Emerson's Sublime Science*. New York: St. Martin's Press, 1999.

Wright, Conrad. *The Liberal Christians: Essays on American Unitarian History*. Boston, Mass.: Beacon Press, 1970.

Wright, Conrad E., ed. *American Unitarianism, 1805-1861*. Boston: Massachusetts Historical Society and Northeastern University Press, 1989.

Wright, Frank Lloyd. *An Autobiography*. New York: Duell, Sloan, and Pearce, 1943.

— *A Testament*. New York: Horizon Press, 1957.

— *Frank Lloyd Wright: Collected Writings*. Edited by Bruce Brooks Pfeiffer. New York: Rizzoli, 1992.

— *Frank Lloyd Wright & Lewis Mumford: Thirty Years of Correspondence*. Edited by Bruce Brooks Pfeiffer and Robert Wojtowic. New York: Princeton Architectural Press, 2001.

Zwarg, Christina. *Feminist Conversations: Fuller, Emerson, and the Play of Reading*. Ithaca, NY: Cornell University Press, 1995.

Articles

Cameron, Kenneth Walter. "Young Emerson's Orientalism at Harvard." In *Indian Superstition*, by Ralph Waldo Emerson, edited by Kenneth Walter Cameron, 13-48. Hanover, N.H: Friends of the Dartmouth Library, 1954.

Capper, Charles. "'A Little Beyond': The Problem of the Transcendentalist Movement in American History," *Journal of American History* 85 (September 1998): 502-39. http://dx.doi.org/10.2307/2567749

Cole, Phyllis. "Woman Questions: Emerson, Fuller, and New England Reform." In *Transient and Permanent: The Transcendentalist Movement and its Contexts*, edited by Charles Capper and Conrad Edick Wright, 408-46. Boston: Massachusetts Historical Society and Northeastern University Press, 1999.

Collison, Gary. "Emerson and Antislavery." In *Historical Guide to Ralph Waldo Emerson*, edited by Joel Myerson, 179-209. New York and Oxford: Oxford University Press, 2000.

Conlin, Michael F. "The Smithsonian Abolition Lecture Controversy," *Civil War History* 46: 4 (2000): 301-23. http://dx.doi.org/10.1353/cwh.2000.0002

Cromwell, Adelaide M. "The Black Presence in the West End of Boston, 1800-1864: A Demographic Map." In *Courage and Conscience: Black & White Abolitionists in Boston*, 155-67. Bloomington, IN: Indiana University Press, 1993.

Dant, Elizabeth A. "Composing the World: Emerson and the Cabinet of Natural History," *Nineteenth-Century Literature* 44 (June 1989): 18-44.

Finseth, Ian. "Evolution, Cosmopolitanism, and Emerson's Antislavery Politics." *American Literature* 77: 4 (2005): 729-60. http://dx.doi.org/10.1215/00029831-77-4-729

Gougeon, Len. "Emerson and the Woman Question: The Evolution of His Thought," *The New England Quarterly* 71 (March-December 1998): 570-92.

Haskins, David Greene. "Ralph Haskins." In *Memorial Biographies of the New England Historic Genealogical Society*, 467-70. Boston: NEHGS, 1880.

Hodder, Alan D. "'The Best of Brahmins': India Reading Emerson Reading India," *Nineteenth-Century Prose* 30 (Spring/Fall 2003): 337-68.

Howe, Daniel Walker. "The Cambridge Platonists of Old England and the Cambridge Platonists of New England." In *American Unitarianism, 1805-1861*, edited by Conrad E. Wright, 87-110. Boston, Mass.: Massachusetts Historical Society and Northeastern University Press, 1989.

Irie, Yukio. "Why the Japanese People Find a Kinship with Emerson and Thoreau," *Emerson Society Quarterly* 27 (2nd Quarter 1962): 13-16.

Johnson, Linck C. "Reforming the Reformers: Emerson, Thoreau, and the Sunday Lectures at Amory Hall, Boston," *ESQ: A Journal of the American Renaissance* 37 (4th Quarter 1991): 235-89.

— "'Liberty is Never Cheap': Emerson, 'The Fugitive Slave Law,' and the Antislavery Lecture Series at the Broadway Tabernacle," *New England Quarterly* 76 (December 2003): 550-92.

Marchi, Dudley M. "Baudelaire's America – Contrary Affinities," *Yearbook of Comparative and General Literature* 47 (2000): 37-52.

Mudge, Jean McClure, "Emily Dickinson and 'Sister Sue,'" *Prairie Schooner* 52: 1 (Spring 1978): 90-107.

Myerson, Joel. "A Calendar of Transcendental Club Meetings," *American Literature* 44 (May 1972): 197-207.

Orth, Ralph H. "Emerson's Visit to the Tomb of His First Wife," *Emerson Society Papers* 11 (Spring 2000): 3.

Perry, Bliss. "Emerson's Most Famous Speech." In *The Praise of Folly and Other Papers*, 81-112. Boston: Houghton Mifflin, 1923.

Reed, Sampson. "Observations on the Growth of the Mind." In *Sampson Reed: Primary Source Material for Emerson Studies*, compiled by George F. Dole, 17-49. New York: Swedenborg Foundation, 1992.

Robinson, David M. "Emerson's Natural Theology and the Paris Naturalists: Toward a 'Theory of Animated Nature,'" *Journal of the History of Ideas* 41 (1980): 69-88.

— "Poetry, Personality, and the Divinity School Address," *Harvard Theological Review* 82 (1989): 185-200.

— "'For Largest Liberty': Emerson, Natural Religion, and the Antislavery Crisis," *Religion & Literature* 41: 1 (March 2009): 3.

Scharf, Robert. "The Zen of Japanese Nationalism," *History of Religions* 33: 1 (August 1993): 1-43.

Stack, George J. "Nietzsche's Earliest Essays: Translation of and Commentary on Fate and History and Freedom of Will and Fate," *Philosophy Today* 37 (1993): 153-69.

Takanashi, Yoshio. "Emerson, Japan, and Neo-Confucianism," *Emerson Society Quarterly* 48 (1st and 2nd Quarters 2002): 41-45.

Von Frank, Albert J. "Emerson's Boyhood and Collegiate Verse: Unpublished and New Texts Edited from Manuscript." In *Studies in the American Renaissance*, edited by Joel Myerson, 1-56. Boston, Mass.: Twayne, 1983.

Wright, Conrad. "'Soul is Good, but Body is Good Too,'" *Journal of Unitarian and Universalist History* 37 (2013-2014): 1-20.

List of Illustrations

Index

This book need not end here...

At Open Book Publishers, we are changing the nature of the traditional academic book. The title you have just read will not be left on a library shelf, but will be accessed online by hundreds of readers each month across the globe. We make all our books free to read online so that students, researchers and members of the public who can't afford a printed edition can still have access to the same ideas as you.

Our digital publishing model also allows us to produce online supplementary material, including extra chapters, reviews, links and other digital resources. Find *Mr. Emerson's Revolution* on our website to access its online extras. Please check this page regularly for ongoing updates, and join the conversation by leaving your own comments:

http://www.openbookpublishers.com/isbn/9781783740970

If you enjoyed this book, and feel that research like this should be available to all readers, regardless of their income, please think about donating to us. Our company is run entirely by academics, and our publishing decisions are based on intellectual merit and public value rather than on commercial viability. We do not operate for profit and all donations, as with all other revenue we generate, will be used to finance new Open Access publications.

For further information about what we do, how to donate to OBP, additional digital material related to our titles or to order our books, please visit our website: http://www.openbookpublishers.com

Lightning Source UK Ltd.
Milton Keynes UK
UKOW07f1400220416

272608UK00013B/13/P